ARCHITECTS
OF AN
AMERICAN
LANDSCAPE

ARCHITECTS OF AN AMERICAN LANDSCAPE

Henry Hobson Richardson,
Frederick Law Olmsted, and
the Reimagining of America's
Public and Private Spaces

HUGH HOWARD

Grove Press
New York

Published simultaneously in Canada
Printed in the United States of America

First Grove Atlantic hardcover edition: January 2022
First Grove Atlantic paperback edition: January 2023

Library of Congress Cataloging-in-Publication data is available for this title.

ISBN 978-0-8021-6231-1
eISBN 978-0-8021-5924-3

Grove Press
an imprint of Grove Atlantic
154 West 14th Street
New York, NY 10011

Distributed by Publishers Group West

groveatlantic.com

23 24 25 26 27   10 9 8 7 6 5 4 3 2 1

To the all-girl band,
Betsy, Slim, Biff, and, unexpectedly, Alice

I cannot express, or make those who did not know him even dimly understand, how much Richardson was in one's life, how much help and comfort he gave one in its work. . . . He was the greatest comfort and the most potent stimulus that has ever come into my artistic life.

——FREDERICK LAW OLMSTED

Contents

FAREWELL, FRIEND

Consult the genius of the place in all.

—ALEXANDER POPE

High in the Rocky Mountains, a long, black steam locomotive chugged up the steady grade, coal smoke billowing from its stack. A tumble-down array of workers' shanties came into view as the train neared the highest point, elevation 8,242 feet, on the nation's first transcontinental rail line.

For much of the preceding twenty years, Sherman Station, Wyoming, named for Union general William Tecumseh Sherman, had been a busy place, with a roundhouse and train sheds, two hotels, a pair of saloons, a general store, a post office, and even a schoolhouse. But what the railroad brought it could also take away. With the Union Pacific Railroad no longer making scheduled stops at Sherman Station, the population of the settlement between Cheyenne and Laramie had dwindled to fewer than a hundred people.

To the surprise of the passengers on this particular blustery January day in 1887, the brakeman brought the train to a halt in a cloud of hissing steam. A few moments later, a precisely dressed gentleman made his way down the steep steps of a Pullman car.

The man walked with an uneven gait, the result of a carriage accident more than twenty-five years before, his game left leg more painful than usual since he had been tossed about like a sack of potatoes in a train collision a week earlier. The other passengers watched from their seats as sixty-five-year-old Frederick Law Olmsted, a man widely known as America's first and finest park maker, headed for the top of a nearby hill. His fame and reputation were such that, in 1872, Republicans dissatisfied with their party's nominee, Horace Greeley, had convened to discuss an alternative "conscience ticket," and Olmsted's name had been bandied about as the choice for vice president.

At Olmsted's request, the train had paused so he could complete a small errand on behalf of Charles Francis Adams Jr., president of the Union Pacific Railroad and a friend of many years standing.

To the other riders, one thing was evident at a glance: Sherman Station was well on its way to oblivion. Its hotels closed and the railyard quiet, Sherman would soon enough become a ghost town. But as they watched, the stranger made his way across the windswept high prairie toward the town's one remaining attraction, which stood barely a hundred yards from the track bed. Built of immense blocks of rough-hewn local granite, the rugged and plain pyramid might

The Ames Monument atop its eminence with some later visitors, ca. 1930.
By then the rail line had been relocated several miles south and Sherman had
simply vanished. The Saint-Gaudens bas-relief is of Congressman Oakes Ames.

have been an antediluvian survivor, fixed in place since the distant past. But it was almost new, constructed just four years before.

Officially, this piece of pure geometry celebrated the completion of the transcontinental railroad, an achievement that, in the eyes of many, was "the greatest triumph of modern civilization, of all civilization, indeed."[1] But the monument was a reminder of a larger story too, one of an extraordinary national transformation. Since Olmsted's birth in 1822, a largely coastal nation with just one state west of the Mississippi River had banished the frontier, and the Union, reunited and recovering from the ravages of the Civil War, now consisted of thirty-eight contiguous states that extended to the Pacific. The United States was an increasingly urban country where agriculture was giving way to a booming manufacturing economy, and the railroad had played an outsize role in driving those changes.

On reaching the monument's base, Olmsted examined it, his gaze rising and falling as he took the measure of the sixty-foot-tall stack of stone. But none of those observing him were privy to the swirl of memories and emotions that surfaced in his mind.[2] He could not help but think of the author of this monument, his great friend and longtime collaborator, the architect Henry Hobson Richardson.

In his eccentric autobiography, *The Education of Henry Adams*, Charles Adams's younger brother observed that the advent of the railroad meant "the old universe was thrown into the ash-heap and a new one created."[3] The Adams brothers, together with Olmsted and Richardson, had watched their world change over the course of the nineteenth century.

In 1826, when Olmsted was just four years old, a self-educated engineer named Gridley Bryant attached three miles of wooden rails to stone sleepers, connecting his quarry in Quincy, Massachusetts, to a wharf on the Neponset River. Enormous blocks of hewn stone were then brought by horse-drawn railcars to barges for delivery to Charlestown's Bunker Hill, where another, earlier monument was under construction. The Granite Railway demonstrated to Bryant's American contemporaries that a railroad with a solid track bed could deliver freight faster than canal barges and haul much larger loads than horse carts traveling on rutted and muddy turnpikes. Three years later, the Baltimore and Ohio Railroad made clear the advantage of a powerful steam engine.

In 1842, the year Olmsted turned twenty, tracks belonging to the Western Railroad joined New England with points west, and a decade after that a new rail line spanned the Alleghenies, linking Maryland's salt waters to the Ohio River. By the time Henry Adams and Henry Hobson Richardson graduated from Harvard College in the late 1850s, Gridley Bryant's three-mile experiment had become a matrix of thirty thousand miles of iron rails. That total had more than tripled by the time Olmsted visited the Wyoming monument.

As Henry Adams noted, the railroad, together with the steamship and the telegraph, set astonishing changes in motion. The natural cycle of the day gave way to the mechanical. The coming and going of trains occurred with such regularity, observed Henry David Thoreau, that even farmers in the field "set their clocks by it, and thus one well conducted institution regulate[d] a whole country."[4]

Technology replaced geography as the chief determinant of whether a city prospered, with the railroad superseding waterways as the primary conveyor of goods. With the advent of steam power, the global rate of economic growth, which had rarely reached 1 percent per year for centuries, jumped to roughly 4 percent.

People's appreciation of time changed. When President Thomas Jefferson dispatched Meriwether Lewis and William Clark westward at the turn of the century, their Corps of Discovery needed eighteen months to reach the Pacific Coast. In stark contrast, as the century neared its end, a rail passenger could travel from the Atlantic to the Pacific in roughly eighty hours.* People ceased thinking of long-distance travel in terms of months and years, and instead made their calculations in hours and minutes. The weeks once required for transatlantic sea travel became days.

The meanings of "near" and "far" shifted. In the eighteenth century, a tiny minority of citizens traveled more than a few miles

---

* In 1879, an excursion train carrying the president of the Pennsylvania Railroad had transited the 3,322 miles from New York to San Francisco in eighty-three hours. Herman Barnum Poor, "The Pacific Railroad," *North America Review* 128 (June 1879), p. 671.

from their birthplaces. In the nineteenth, a new mobility meant average people traveled farther, more frequently, and affordably.

When Olmsted was a child, no one in the United States lived more than two miles from undeveloped land. Towns had been small enough that open space—churchyards, the town square or common, even farmland—was within easy walking distance. Nature was near. But that, too, shifted and Olmsted, as much as any other man, had helped his fellow Americans adapt to these nearly unfathomable changes.

As Olmsted grew to adulthood, places for recreation and healthful exercise disappeared before his eyes. He saw how unregulated development and increasing population density impoverished people, robbing them of physical health and spirit. Inspired to become a park maker, he imagined rural scenes, health-giving escapes possessed of the life force to sustain city dwellers in the face of the hyperactivity of the metropolis. By 1887, his vision of fine parks, combined with his superior skills at hiring, buying, and managing, had propelled a brilliant career, as he breathed fresh air into one American city after another. He shared with the poet William Wordsworth a belief that pastoral scenery possessed a moral influence that acted upon humankind for its benefit. Olmsted repeatedly made the argument that "the enjoyment of scenery employs the mind without fatigue and yet exercises it; tranquilizes it and yet enlivens it; and thus, through the influence of the mind over the body, gives the effect of refreshing rest and reinvigoration."[5]

Olmsted's hundreds of commissions had grown to include city parks, residential developments, private estates, campuses for hospitals and universities, the grounds of the U.S. Capitol, city squares, and wilderness reservations. In all of them, he sought to assure access to the natural world for the common man, woman, and child.

Olmsted addressed challenges that went well beyond increasingly bustling cities. The rails were a powerful centrifugal force that contributed to the spread of population far beyond the farms, market towns, and port cities of his New England boyhood. Watching from the window of his Pullman car, he had seen in the preceding days that the once vast open prairie—the "Great American Desert," as one journalist had called the Great Plains—had "disappeared at the snort of the iron horse."[6] The Homestead Act of 1862 had invited settlers into the great spaces, and on this trip twenty-five years later, Olmsted saw expanses of newly cultivated fields and substantial and prosperous new towns. Bison had been replaced by sheep and cattle, prairie grass by corn and wheat.

The rails brought a great leap in prosperity too, making some Americans wealthy beyond their dreams, underwriting what Mark Twain would call the Gilded Age. Among those who accumulated great railroad fortunes was a family named Ames. Hailing from North Easton, Massachusetts, several Ames men had been great patrons of Olmsted and Richardson, and that connection had led directly to this mountaintop pause at the granite pyramid, officially called the Ames Monument.

Forty feet above Olmsted's head on opposite sides of the pyramid were two nine-foot bas-relief busts, the work of the eminent sculptor Augustus Saint-Gaudens. A likeness of Oakes Ames looked east, while that of his brother, Oliver Ames Jr., looked west. The former had been summoned by Abraham Lincoln to the White House on January 20, 1865. The sixteenth president, convinced a transcontinental line was an essential national and military objective, asked the Massachusetts congressman to oversee its construction. Despite Lincoln's assassination a few months later, Oakes and his brother, Oliver, then president of the Union Pacific Railroad, put their political, economic, and industrial clout to work, and by 1869, a continuous run of rails linked the East and West Coasts.

Olmsted called the blustery hilltop "a most tempestuous place."[7] With only the whistling wind for company, he took in the Colorado Rockies, the Medicine Bow range, and the Black Hills. The unspoiled panorama may have reminded him of his efforts to conserve other natural wonders like Yosemite and Niagara Falls or of his work as an urban park maker in Manhattan, Brooklyn, Buffalo, Washington, Detroit, and Louisville. But as he soon acknowledged in a letter to a mutual friend, Olmsted sensed most of all the accompanying presence of Henry Hobson Richardson, the man who had designed the monument in 1879 but who did not—could not—join him in Sherman. Their occasional partnership and two-decade friendship had ended abruptly with Richardson's death eight months before.

In life, Henry Hobson Richardson desired nothing less than to earn a place at the very top of his profession. By age forty-six he had attained it. In an 1885 survey of seventy-five prominent architects, his peers chose no fewer than five Richardson buildings as among the ten best in the United States. According to the building industry's principal publication, *American Architect and Building News*, Richardson's Trinity Church in Boston, consecrated eight years earlier, stood at number one, with 84 percent of the first-place votes.[8] An enormous man who weighed some 350 pounds, Richardson had gained an equally gargantuan reputation in just twenty years of practice.

Richardson opened his first office in New York a few months after the Civil War ended, vowing to create what he called a "bold, rich, living architecture . . . to which posterity may point with pride."[9] For many years, American architecture had been a rudderless ship, adrift with each of its ports of call unmistakably Old World. For much of the first half of the nineteenth century, American builders, inspired by Greek temples, constructed columned mansions for the well-to-do and plain farmhouses with gable fronts. Writ large or small, all were recognizable descendants of the Parthenon, with symmetrical façades topped by triangular pediments, echoing the shape of the great temple on the Acropolis. By the 1850s, the iconic villa form—the so-called Italianate style with its brackets and cupolas—proved wildly popular in the countryside and on the streets of growing towns.

In a postwar building boom, new styles emerged that incorporated picturesque and colorful English, German, and French elements, as well as variations on the Gothic, with steep gables decorated with "gingerbread." But each of these fashions amounted to trickle-down types, their sources rooted in antiquity, the Italian Renaissance, or medieval times. Everything on the American streetscape was derivative of forms from across the Atlantic.

Richardson was the man with the training and imagination to create distinctly American architecture. In increasingly congested cities, the churches got bigger, the municipal buildings bulkier. Large-scale downtown stores were needed. Happy to oblige clients looking for new answers, Richardson did so in unique ways.

His designs reflected an openness and a taste for simplicity. He disdained the gingerbread and other ornamentation increasingly favored by his Victorian peers, whose work, observed a leading member of the next generation of architects, Ralph Adams Cram, was "vulgar, self-satisfied and pretentious." According to Cram, "Richardson burst upon an astonished world as a sort of savior from on high, as indeed a Moses to lead us out of the wilderness."[10]

In 1881, Olmsted had followed Richardson and settled permanently in the Boston suburb of Brookline, where both established homes and offices. Olmsted watched as Richardson left large architectural footprints behind wherever he went. Harvard gained a home for its law school, Austin Hall, in a style people called Richardson Romanesque, and a brick classroom building, Sever Hall, that has never ceased to exact sighs of admiration from architects everywhere. His courthouse in Pittsburgh and his churches were widely imitated.

Along with two of his early apprentices, Stanford White and Charles Follen McKim, who would later depart his office to found McKim, Mead, and White, the most admired architectural firm of the next generation, Richardson originated a manner of cladding gracious country houses with a skin of wood shingles that inspired a new manner, later dubbed the Shingle style, that suited settings as varied as the New England coast and the Midwest prairie. Inside those same houses, he pioneered another striking innovation. In an era when people expected their homes to be rectangular boxes divided into a series of smaller boxes, he devised floor plans that consisted less of rooms than of spaces that flowed into one another. Such "open plans" were soon coming off the drawing boards of other architects.

Among his diverse municipal, religious, and residential works, the Ames Monument held a unique place. It was an unmistakable link in the architectural chain that led to Richardson's late manner of building. He had been temporarily bedridden—and not for the first time—when the commission for the Ames Monument came to him, which meant he could not indulge his habit of walking the site of a proposed structure. To get the lay of the land, he relied instead upon sepia-toned photographs of stone formations near Sherman. In these works of nature, shaped over millennia, he found an inspiring natural architecture, and he responded with a monument "in a style calculated to last for centuries."[11] His design was as much a symbol as a building, a steep, stepped pyramid that rose six stories, a man-made abstract form of immense stones that itself resembled a mountain.

As he worked at its design, he had confided in Olmsted, showing him early sketches; as a result, Olmsted referred to it as "our monument."[12] Indeed, the stonework was reminiscent of Olmsted and Richardson's earlier experiments in building bridges in Boston parks and their joint design for a Massachusetts estate called Stonehurst. The monument was a distant relation of the Gate Lodge, a unique Richardson structure built for Frederick Ames, son of Oliver Jr., a building destined to become a permanent fixture in American architectural texts.

With Richardson's death, Olmsted lost an irreplaceable and irrepressible confidant. Out of fondness for the man and respect for his work, Olmsted chose to become a self-appointed caretaker of Richardson's reputation. At his behest, a book was now in the works, and in 1888, *Henry Hobson Richardson and His Works* would be the first biography ever published of an American architect.

But Olmsted tended to Richardson's legacy in other ways too. He had a particular task to perform standing in the high meadow within sight of the Continental Divide. Reports had it that the pyramid "was being spoiled by pebbles blown against it," and the Union Pacific Railroad, the monument's underwriter, having paid the $64,000 construction cost, had an interest in its survival. So Olmsted dutifully looked, examining the monument's granite surface and checking its condition. He quickly decided that the granite looked as it should. "I have no doubt that at times the monument is under a hot fire of little missiles," he would report, "but they only improve it, I think."[13] With his official task completed, he limped back down the hill.

After Olmsted regained his seat, the train resumed its eastbound journey, the sparse high country again speeding past. In a matter of hours, this leg of his trip from Salt Lake City, where he had consulted on a proposed Union Pacific hotel project, would end in Chicago. There, too, even after his death, Richardson's ingenious problem-solving was changing the built landscape. Two of Richardson's commissions were under construction in that city, future landmarks of American architecture. Neither the new wholesale store for Mr. Marshall Field nor the house on "Millionaire's Row" for John Glessner would look anything like the buildings around it.

As the train rattled on, another passenger engaged Olmsted in conversation. The man expressed surprise to learn that what they had seen was a monument. "[He] told me," Olmsted reported, "that he had several times passed it before and it had caught his eye from a distance but until he saw me looking at it he had supposed it to be a natural object." The observation aligned with Olmsted's own opinion. "I never saw a monument so well befitting its situation," he wrote to Richardson's biographer, "or a situation so well befitting the special character of a particular monument."[14]

Olmsted was pleased by the passenger's words, but his brief interlude atop the barren mountain was, in the end, neither about the pyramid's condition nor the changes wrought by the railroad that the Ames Monument symbolized. Rather, the moment had principally been personal. The short trek up the hill had permitted him a last encounter with his friend's genius, a chance to witness how their imaginations once melded.

Standing alone in the cold and whistling wind beneath the towering western sky, the grieving Olmsted sensed the absent Richardson. He found his eyes "half drowned" as he shed tears of mourning.[15]

Today people tend to nod knowingly when they hear the name Frederick Law Olmsted. He has been the subject of popular biographies, and his legacy is remembered and honored in many cities.

In contrast, the mention of Henry Hobson Richardson leaves most people uncertain. Almost no one seems to recall that the two lived as neighbors in both New York and Massachusetts, or that they worked as regular collaborators for twenty years, each often functioning as the other's creative alter ego. Together they left an indelible imprint on buildings and parks, both public and private.

As members of the intellectual vanguard, they witnessed the nation's artistic emergence during the post–Civil War years. With the writings of Mark Twain, Henry James, and William Cullen Bryant, men they knew personally, the American voice changed. Richardson and Olmsted were present at the creation of new intellectual and academic disciplines, including horticulture, in which their neighbor Charles Sprague Sargent played an essential role, and "scientific history," a fact-based approach to the past advanced by the work of Richardson's dear friend Henry Adams. Olmsted helped establish forestry as a professional practice at his great, late-in-life project, G. W. Vanderbilt's North Carolina estate, Biltmore. Both Richardson and Olmsted were engaged in advancing the treatment of mental illness at a psychiatric hospital (an "insane asylum" in the day's parlance) they designed together in Buffalo, New York.

They joined forces with American artists such as Frederic Edwin Church, whose canvases captured sublime landscapes; John Singer Sargent, who painted Olmsted's portrait; and Augustus Saint-Gaudens, who, after working on Richardson's Trinity Church, emerged as a world-class sculptor. They adopted the work of photographers like Carleton Watkins, using images of never-before-seen clarity and detail to advance their projects. The dramatis personae of Olmsted's and Richardson's lives included such illustrious artists and designers as John La Farge and Louis Comfort Tiffany, as well as presidents, governors, and other powerful politicians with whom they dined and collaborated.

Some of the places they created honored the life of the mind, as reflected in that new notion, the public library, and in numerous college buildings and campuses. They helped shape America's suburban railscape. Richardson designed bridges for rustic-seeming roadways in Olmsted's parks. At their psychiatric hospital, town halls, rail stations, and estates for the wealthy, they left their joint imprint. Above all else, Olmsted and Richardson heard a higher calling, building large, dreaming larger, and always in a uniquely American vein.

No one had a bigger impact on the development of the American landscape than Frederick Law Olmsted (1822–1903), who founded the discipline of landscape architecture and laid the early groundwork for American environmentalism. Henry Hobson Richardson (1838–1886), meanwhile, was the man universally recognized as the most influential architect of the era.

The two men never established a professional partnership; their bond was akin to a brotherhood. In most ways they were unalike. Somber and serious, man-of-the-mind Olmsted usually seemed preoccupied with big thoughts. Richardson had a way of bursting into a room in a manner that everyone noticed, always passionate and in the moment, full of laughter, unafraid of tears. But together they evolved a fresh vision, one that more often than not employed rude stonework to meld their constructions to existing terrain.

Together they addressed the demands of an increasingly urban culture while catering to both democratic values and the American compulsion for pragmatic answers. As the nation came into its own, these two men of genius employed the gifts of nature and their innate passion for beauty to redefine the country's rapidly changing landscape.

⌒

Chapter One

AN IMPRACTICAL MAN
FINDS HIS VOCATION

I had no more thought of being a landscape
architect than of being a Cardinal.

—FREDERICK LAW OLMSTED

Crossroads present themselves over the course of a long life. In the case of Frederick Law Olmsted, a man with firm opinions about such things—for one, he strongly disliked right-angle intersections—the most essential turn in his life took him entirely by surprise.

On August 8, 1857, at age thirty-five and best known as a writer, he attempted to concentrate on his literary labors. For the preceding two weeks, a small inn at the mouth of New Haven Harbor had been his refuge from the heat and din of his Manhattan flat. He worked at a pile of proof sheets, the text for the closing articles in a series running that summer in the *New York Daily Tribune* titled "The Southerners at Home."

For several years, Olmsted had made his living as a travel writer. Earlier newspaper pieces bearing the byline "Yeoman" had been the basis of *A Journey in the Seaboard Slave States* and *A Journey through Texas*, two books chronicling his wide-ranging travels in the American South. His latest writings recounted his further observations on riding a horse named Belshazzar, accompanied only by his dog, Judy, from Louisiana to Richmond, Virginia. In the *Tribune* articles, he reported on whom he met and what he saw.

As the Sunday afternoon wore on, he made slow progress, in part because he wrestled with an almost overwhelming range of worries, both near and far. The subject of his writing posed one dilemma.

He had undertaken his first southern expedition in October 1852 with an admitted ignorance of American slavery. He had read Harriet Beecher Stowe's novel *Uncle Tom's Cabin*, the year's runaway success, which, in a matter of months, had sold an almost unimaginable two hundred thousand copies. But he had no firsthand knowledge of enslavement, having grown up in New England, where the practice, though legal in the eighteenth century, had been abolished before his birth.

His travels to the South had been a revelation. He arrived in the slave states thinking abolition impractical, believing like many in the North that sudden emancipation would be no kindness for uneducated people unused to thinking or acting for themselves. On seeing the reality of slavery firsthand, however, he recognized the absurdity of the assumption that slave life was not so different from the lot of rural laborers, seaman on merchant ships, or the inhabitants of city slums. After witnessing whippings and other cruelties, he understood slavery was an unmitigated and growing evil, one that deprived the enslaved of their humanity and brought out the very worst in their owners.

Olmsted's first letters home, published in the recently established *New-York Daily Times*, had had an impact on the national conversation. Some in the South thought him ill qualified to write about slavery, and one Savannah paper described him as an interloper, "sent among us to spy out the nakedness of the land" for "evil" motives.[1] But in the North, his widely read pieces contributed to a rapid rise in the circulation of the *Times*. When collected in book form, his writings became must-reads for abolitionists, even as many in the South grumbled about the ill light he cast upon slaveholding culture. Across the Atlantic, men as varied as Charles Darwin, Karl Marx, and John Stuart Mill expressed admiration for Olmsted's reporting.

Sitting in his Connecticut room, his writing and editing were made more difficult by another worry. As he wrote to a friend, "My eyes have failed lately."[2] Since his teens he had been subject to recurring eye problems. As the proof pages blurred, he found reading and writing difficult. He had tried to compensate for lost time by working late into the night, but that compounded his difficulties by leaving him sleepless.

Then there was the matter of his finances. His writing success had led him to invest in a publishing firm, but a letter he received two days earlier from his partner at Dix and Curtis had added to Olmsted's accumulating tensions. On Friday, he had absorbed the succinct message, which, though not entirely unexpected given recent setbacks, hit hard. "We failed today," wrote George William Curtis: the firm of Dix and Curtis had gone bankrupt.[3] That meant the loss of his substantial investment of $5,500, which he had borrowed from his father. He would also have to find another publisher to release his new columns in book form, and a hoped-for new career as an editor, begun with such optimism barely two years earlier, now survived only as a shared obligation to repay the company's debts.

Yet of all the concerns that distracted him, what weighed heaviest was the health of his younger brother, John Hull Olmsted. An ocean separated them, with John spending the summer in Geneva, Switzerland, with his wife, Mary, and their three young children, the youngest born just weeks before. Everyone hoped the Alpine air might be curative, but Fred had his doubts. As he told a friend after his brother's departure for Europe, "I much fear I shall never see him again."[4]

His worry was warranted. John's weight plummeted toward a hundred pounds, and his paroxysms of bloody coughing were becoming more frequent. A physician by training, John himself knew how sick he was and that his consumption wasn't getting any better. As for Fred, he faced the painful thought that he might lose his brother, a loss that would open a great chasm in his life. Since childhood, the two brothers, separated by just three years, had shared friends, passions, and travels. John was, as their father said, "almost your only friend."[5]

At age thirty-five, Fred Olmsted was a journeyman, a man of multiple trades but truly expert at none. In a pattern that dated to childhood, he tended in own his words to "run wild," his attention quick to drift.[6] Soon after taking on a fresh challenge, he would abandon it for a newer enthusiasm.

He had come from fixed roots. His family had been prominent in Hartford, Connecticut, since its founding in 1636, an Olmsted an original proprietor of the town. By the time Fred was born, on April 26, 1822, more than six thousand people inhabited the little city that was Connecticut's capital. He grew up within sight of Charles Bulfinch's imposing State House, with its great columned portico, but Hartford remained a rural place, where most householders tended gardens on lots large enough for barns and room to tether the family cow. It was a community with a dozen churches, fourteen taverns and hotels, and twenty dry-goods stores. One of those stories was operated by John Olmsted, Fred's father.

John would be an important presence in his son's life for a half century, but the early death of Fred's mother left the boy, as he expressed it, with "a tradition of memory rather than the faintest recollection of her." John remarried, but young Fred's pious and distant stepmother was soon occupied with raising Olmsted's half siblings. In his later recollections, he revealed that her chief influence on him was, significantly, "her strong love of nature."[7]

Olmsted learned to read, write, and do his sums at a series of dame schools, taught by local women in their homes. His attendance at the last of them ended abruptly when the teacher, Miss Rockwell, burned to death after her clothes caught fire, a not-uncommon occurrence in the age of full-length skirts and hearth cooking. At age seven, Fred began a peripatetic educational journey away from home, boarding with a series of ministers, each charged with his religious and scholastic education. His time at the final school, in Newington, Connecticut, would be the longest, as he stayed almost five years. By then, the task had become college preparation, since John Olmsted expected his son to attend Yale College.

Despite his sustained separations from his family, the limited time Fred spent with his father during childhood shaped his perception of the world in ways his education did not. As a small boy, he rode with his father, seated on a pillow resting on the front of the father's saddle. After Fred graduated to riding his own horse, he wandered independently. By age twelve he knew "most of the charming roads of the Connecticut Valley."[8]

During summer vacations, John took sons Fred and John and their younger brothers and sisters on journeys deep into New England and New York State. In those days, before the railroads offered a speedier alternative, they traveled hundreds of miles in a wagon pulled by two horses or rode in stagecoaches and canal boats. The pace was slow, but the family ventured as far afield as the Maine coast, the Hudson Valley, Quebec, and most memorably of all, Niagara Falls.

As he remembered these bucolic interludes, Fred gained less a particular understanding for specific places than an "impression of the enjoyment my father and mother constantly found in scenery." Their appreciation seemed more spiritual than scientific or intellectual. "Both being of silent habits," his father and stepmother did not speak of their feelings or perceptions. Even so, John Olmsted in particular exerted an "unpremeditated and insensible influence" on his son's regard for what Fred reverently came to refer to as "the scenic." Nature would always exercise a decisive power over him.

With the suddenness of a lightning strike, a case of poison sumac altered the trajectory of Fred's life in his fifteenth year. Though the country boy should have known better, he seemed to have leapt headfirst into a copse of the small, leafy trees. The plant's resins produced a severe rash that covered his face, and he returned home from school with his features badly swollen by sumac blisters. Barely able to open his eyes, he thought he was going blind.

The problem persisted for months. His father took him to New York to consult an oculist, who recommended sea bathing. But another of Dr. Wallace's recommendations would have a larger impact: "Advised to give up college on account of eyes," John Olmsted noted in his diary.[9] The doctor said reading and study might permanently jeopardize the boy's eyesight. With that pronouncement, the plan for Fred to sit for Yale's entrance examinations fell away. On recalling his education late in life, he wrote that "while my mates were fitting for college I was allowed to indulge my strong natural propensity of roaming afield and day-dreaming under a tree."[10]

As the boy's eyes recovered, John Olmsted found Fred a place under the tutelage of a surveyor in Andover, Massachusetts. For eighteen months, he learned of metes and bounds and the basic skills of the trade, though he found the "play-practice" of laying out imaginary towns more to his liking.[11] His brief apprenticeship also permitted Fred to indulge his habit of exploring the countryside, both in Massachusetts and back in central Connecticut, when the surveying work took the team to Collinsville, just west of Hartford. The accident of his eye infection proved providential, enabling a blossoming of Olmsted's wanderer temperament, his insatiable curiosity, and his affinity for nature. He exhibited a restlessness that would be a lifelong trait, and several decades later, he would look back on his adolescence and remark: "I was nominally the pupil of a topographical engineer but really for the most part given over to a decently restrained vagabond life, generally pursued under the guise of an angler, a fowler or dabbler on the shallowest shores of the deep sea of the natural sciences."[12] By chance, an inclination to the natural world became a preoccupation for the boy as he became a man.

In the fall of 1840, his father got him an indoor job, and eighteen-year-old Fred went to work for a silk importer based in Lower Manhattan. Working as a clerk, he ferried across the harbor each morning from a rooming house in Brooklyn; competent but bored, he left after a year and half. Next, he went to sea aboard a merchant ship. Serving as a seaman, he traveled to China and back, but life on the *Ronaldson* suited him even less than clerking in a store had. John Olmsted did not recognize the jaundiced and rail-thin son who hailed him on a New York pier after twelve months at sea.

Fred recuperated at home from the poor nourishment and illnesses of his sea travels. He flirted both with religious faith and with a series of young women, among them Elizabeth Baldwin, the daughter of Connecticut's governor, but he neither married nor formally joined a church. During a semester spent auditing classes at Yale, where his brother John had enrolled, he made a number of enduring friends. When no urge to gain a degree overcame him, he decided his next venture would be on dry land.

After a few months at work on an uncle's farm, where he found the physical labor and routine appealed to him, he apprenticed for the 1846 growing season on an upstate New York farm. Ninety percent of Americans still lived in rural areas, but the traditional mode of subsistence agriculture was slowly becoming more business-like. Competition from Midwestern farmers, now able to ship grains and livestock east via canal and rail, pressured farmers in the Northeast to specialize, to produce more perishable foods, like fruits, vegetables, and dairy products, and to market them locally. New publications like the *Cultivator* disseminated scientific advances in drainage and fertilizers.

That summer Olmsted made the acquaintance of the founder of another new magazine, the *Horticulturalist and Journal of Rural Art and Rural Taste*. The son of a nurseryman from Newburgh, New York, Andrew Jackson Downing was also the author of several books and a man whose writings influenced the public taste in gardens, landscape, and architecture. Borrowing liberally from British writers, Downing wished to awaken in the minds of his "readers and countrymen more lively perceptions of the BEAUTIFUL, in every thing that relates to our houses and grounds." His book *Treatise on the Theory and Practice of Landscape Gardening*, published in 1841, had been the first to examine the American home in the context of its grounds, providing readers practical guidance and encouraging them to plan their properties in a way that produced "picturesque" landscapes. He offered advice on laying out plantings. He favored porches and verandas, and in his next book, *Cottage Residences* (1842), he included house plans. In short, Downing gave his readers permission to think about home, both house and landscape, not as mere shelter but as "the habitation of man in a cultivated and refined state of society."[13]

Delighted to meet the nation's leading authority on both horticulture and domestic architecture, Olmsted managed to leave something of an impression. He and Downing would remain in contact, with Olmsted soon contributing articles to the *Horticulturist*. He had decided to join those pursuing the profession people called "scientific farming." He liked the stimulation of the hands-on labor, the brains-on learning, and the challenges of reading the marketplace.

His work on other people's farms had also given him new confidence. "I've considerable faith that I shall make a good farmer," he told a friend, and once again aided by his father, he set out to establish himself on his own farm on the Connecticut coast.[14] He spent 1847 at Sachem's Head, overlooking Long Island Sound, but realizing more land was needed to turn a profit, his father underwrote the

purchase of a property on Staten Island, New York, where Fred
planted fruit trees, particularly pears. The popularity of Downing's
books had created a market among fashionable householders for
trees to beautify their properties, and in 1849, the Olmsted farm became primarily a nursery business. He took on a half dozen hired
men and a foreman. One of his go-to references was Downing's *Fruits
and Fruit Trees of America.*

On the south side of Staten Island, Fred was surrounded by gentlemen farmers, among them William Henry Vanderbilt, eldest son
of "the Commodore," Cornelius Vanderbilt, the nation's richest man.
Another neighbor was the prominent book publisher George Palmer
Putnam, and nearby lived William Cullen Bryant, poet and editor of
the *New York Post.* After the seclusion of Sachem's Head, Olmsted welcomed the society on Staten Island. "I was a good farmer and a good
neighbor," he would recall years later. He was also accumulating influential friends.

*Olmsted, age twenty-eight, a
man still seeking his vocation.*

Yet his nearly exclusive devotion
to farming did not last beyond the
decade, and as Olmsted himself
described it, he "managed to
make several long and numerous short journeys, generally
paying [his] expenses by writing on rural topics for newspapers."[15] His urge to travel took
him to England in 1850, thereafter repeatedly to the American
South, and then to Europe in
1856. The journeys dovetailed with
his new urge to be a writer, sparked by
his first published piece in the pages
of the *Horticulturist.*

Rising from his chair late in the afternoon of August 8, 1857, Olmsted turned from his editing task. He expected to find refreshment

in the seaside inn's dining room, but to his delight he saw a familiar face at one of the tables.

Although Charles Elliott made his living as an iron merchant, his passions lay elsewhere. The author of several books, including one called *Cottages and Cottage Life*, he, too, had been a protégé of Downing's. His unexpected presence at the inn on Morris Cove promised a welcome and diverting conversation on common ground, and Olmsted took a seat. The two diners soon zeroed in on a matter in which they both had an interest. A major park was about to be created on Manhattan Island, and the very notion of such a thing signaled a fundamental change.

On completing their transatlantic crossing in the seventeenth century, European settlers like *Mayflower* pilgrim William Bradford had stepped ashore to face untamed beasts and seemingly wild men in what Bradford called "a hideous and desolate wilderness."[16] The arrivals set about clearing land for their homesteads and farms, seeking to banish the wild. Over two centuries, these new Americans had succeeded, but now that very success had begun to seem, at least to some, like a growing social and spiritual liability.

In the eyes of Ralph Waldo Emerson, the most influential of the Transcendentalists, nature's loveliness was a gift from God, and its disappearance impoverishing. The Transcendentalists believed intuition and imagination permitted them to see spiritual truths, and an increasingly dense network of cities and towns meant fewer and fewer people were regularly exposed to the vitality and the nourishing sense of the infinite that Nature offered.

Over the previous fifty years, the landscape of Manhattan Island in particular had changed. In addition to the natural geological advantage of its fine harbor, such transportation advances as the steamboat and the state's Erie Canal, dug between 1817 and 1825, made the city a world-class center of commerce. The city's population neared three-quarters of a million people, more than ten times what it had been in 1800, with the early arrivals, mostly Dutch and Anglo peoples, now joined by a flood of German and Irish immigrants.

New York and the nation as a whole enjoyed a wave of prosperity. New inventions enabled improvements in productivity and communication. Cyrus McCormack's mechanical reaper, patented in 1834, meant an acre of grain could be harvested in an hour. In the same decade, the advent of Samuel F. B. Morse's single-wire telegraph made possible near-instant communication over great distances. The modern sewing machine came into use in the 1840s in a design perfected by Elias Howe and Isaac Merritt Singer, transforming the cottage craft of tailoring into an industry.

Economic growth meant Manhattan's cityscape powered constantly northward. In the early years, when the town was called New Amsterdam, the seventeenth-century Dutch inhabitants had constructed a walled fortification to protect their village at the island's southern tip, giving rise to the name Wall Street. But the settlement continued to expand, reaching today's Fourteenth Street by the turn of the nineteenth century. In the hopes of introducing a logic to what had been willy-nilly development, the New York State Legislature adopted the Commissioners' Plan of 1811, a gridiron scheme that imposed a rectangular matrix of streets and avenues. With this template in place, farms, forests, and open country disappeared even more rapidly, and virtually all traces of native vegetation were gradually being erased, replaced block by block with freshly graded streets. By the 1850s, the streetscapes south of Thirty-Eighth Street had been built up, while freestanding houses dotted many blocks farther north.

One result of this urbanization was a paucity of places where New York's citizens could experience the natural landscape that Emerson, Downing, and others cherished. A dozen-odd green spaces survived in the most developed sections, but most were small squares, typically ornamental gardens and gathering spaces. Some, like Gramercy Park, were private and excluded all but surrounding property owners. The closest thing to a park in the vicinity was Green-Wood Cemetery, established in nearby Brooklyn in 1838. Though the site was a rural cemetery by design, the thousands who flocked there demonstrated the collective appetite for fresh air and solitude. Over time, however, more and more mausoleums and tombstones diminished the pleasure-ground aspect of its 438 acres. Other cities had similar spaces, such as Mount Auburn Cemetery outside Boston, established in 1831, but at the time of Olmsted's and Elliott's accidental encounter, not a single naturalized municipal park existed in an American city.

While royal grounds and hunting preserves in European capitals had been converted to public use, no such reserves existed in the United States. The idea of a people's park for Manhattan gained real momentum only when William Cullen Bryant broached it in an editorial published in 1844.[17] Olmsted's neighbor on Staten Island and America's best-known Romantic poet, Bryant was editor of the powerful *Evening Post*. As a man who perceived a holiness in "woody wilderness" and who called primeval forests "God's first temples," Bryant proposed taking action to create "a range of parks and public gardens . . . to remain perpetually for the refreshment and recreation of the citizens."[18] People had paid attention, and in 1848, Downing had added his voice to Bryant's. He argued for a "New York Park" in a series of public letters and even drafted a preliminary plan. Public support continued to grow, reaching a key flexion point when the New York State Legislature passed the Central Park Act in 1853.

The city then began to purchase land north of Fifty-Ninth Street between Fifth and Eighth Avenues for the purpose of creating a public park. In keeping with sparse uptown habitation, relatively few New Yorkers would be displaced, since the rugged terrain with its rocky elevations and steep declines hadn't lent itself to extensive development. But there were a few enclaves. The best established was Seneca Village, an area just east of Eighth Avenue in the vicinity of West Eighty-Fifth Street. First settled in 1825, Seneca Village had become home to about 225 people, the majority of whom were African American, together with a few German and Irish immigrant families. Many of these settlers owned their land, which under New York's strict voting laws entitled the Black men to vote. But a press campaign dismissed all the residential districts that lay within the bounds of the proposed park as shantytowns, and given the low status accorded to people with dark skin in a deeply racist era, the residents' objections were quickly dismissed. All of the once-vibrant community of Seneca Village, which by 1855 boasted some fifty houses, trade shops, two doctors' offices, and even a cemetery, was taken by eminent domain. Its structures were demolished, along with those in Harsenville, the Piggery district, and the other habitations within the park's limits.

The entire land acquisition process required several years, with title to 7,250 building lots purchased from 561 owners, in return for compensation of some $5 million. In April 1857, the legislature passed another act, this one creating the eleven-man Board of Commissioners of the Central Park, and Elliott had been among the first appointees. The board would administer the laying out and draining of the new park grounds and the employment of gardeners, engineers, surveyors, clerks, and laborers as necessary.

The initial big thinking of Bryant and Downing had given way to the debating of the details. At their table at the inn, Elliott described to Olmsted how in-fighting made every decision difficult. Many politicians, Democrat and Republican alike, saw the patronage and perquisites associated with such a large project as a means of consolidating power and influence. Elliott, trying to carry out his old mentor Downing's vision of a project to serve the common good, felt caught in the crossfire.

"Sitting next to me at the tea-table," Olmsted remembered, "Elliott told me . . . of the history of the Commission."[19] Olmsted quickly warmed to the subject of this park, having long since become a partisan for parks in general.

Seven years earlier, Fred Olmsted had stumbled upon his future. Bored with his genteel farming venture on Staten Island, he and his brother John had sailed for England. Their object was a wide-ranging tour of the Old World. They landed at the port of Liverpool in May 1850 and ferried across the River Mersey a few days later.

When they stepped ashore in the suburb of Birkenhead, the brothers saw something entirely new to them. Birkenhead was to Liverpool as Brooklyn was to Manhattan. However, Birkenhead, a sleepy a village of a dozen houses until the steamship boom the preceding generation, had emerged as a planned city almost overnight, its streets and squares extending logically away from the shipyards in the harbor.

At the insistence of a baker who befriended them, the brothers left their knapsacks in the man's shop and embarked on a walking tour of the city's "New Park." To the Americans, Birkenhead's park was a revelation. "Five minutes of admiration," Fred noted, "and a few more spent in studying the manner in which art had been employed to obtain from nature so much beauty, and I was ready to admit that in democratic America there was nothing to be thought of as comparable with this People's Garden."[20]

The designer, Joseph Paxton, had begun with flat agricultural fields. Earth and stone excavated to create a pond had been deposited elsewhere on the park's 120 acres. With the fill regraded and carefully planted under Paxton's far-seeing eye, a rolling landscape had emerged, featuring a mix of meadows, rock gardens, sports grounds, and shady glens that, observed from winding paths, conveyed a sense of privacy to visitors sauntering through. The views seemed ever-changing. There were no straight roads, the luxuriant plantings set off the lawns, and islands in the man-made ponds prevented the viewer from taking in the expanse of water all at once. The head gardener at Chatsworth, home to the Dukes of Devonshire and among the finest landscape gardens in England, Paxton had created a fine city park with public funds. Birkenhead existed not for the enjoyment of rich and titled aristocrats but for people of all classes. Parliament had, for the first time, set aside land for use as a municipal public space.

Olmsted instantly embraced both the idea and its execution. Birkenhead was far from the last pleasure ground Olmsted examined on the journey, which he recorded in his first book, *Walks and Talks of an American Farmer in England,* published in 1852 and dedicated to Andrew Jackson Downing. Enraptured by what he saw, Olmsted wrote admiringly of the public and private landscapes he had seen across England and in a brief detour to the continent at stops in Paris and Germany. "What artist [is] so noble . . . as he who, with far reaching conception of beauty and designing power, sketches the outline, writes the colors, and directs the shadows of a picture so great that Nature shall be employed upon it for generations, before the work he has arranged for her shall realize his intentions."[21]

Until that Sunday afternoon meal spent overlooking the Connecticut shore a few years later, Olmsted had been little more than a witness to feats of park making, a writer who liked what he saw but played no role in shaping landscapes beyond his own agricultural acreage. But the two men's conversation—and the course of Olmsted's life—began to shift when Elliot explained that the commissioners "at their next meeting . . . intended to elect a superintendent."

"Must he be a politician?" Olmsted inquired.

Elliott shook his head. "The park [is to] be managed independently of politics."

Olmsted agreed that a well- and equitably run people's park could do inestimable good, and Elliott, pleased at his friend's enthusiasm and evident passion, mused aloud that he wished Olmsted were a fellow commissioner. Then, in his next breath, Elliot gave voice to a fresh idea.

"Why not take the superintendency yourself?" he asked.

The possibility of such a job had never crossed Olmsted's mind, but he did not demur. Unexpected as it was—and yet so logical, even inevitable—the idea appealed to him.

"I'm not sure I wouldn't if it were offered me," he allowed.

Elliott quickly explained that if Olmsted wanted the job, he would have to go New York, file an application, and—Elliot warned him—he would have to fight through the hurly-burly of city politics.

As Olmsted told the story two decades later, he decided in that instant to take the evening boat back to New York. He would think hard on the matter, he told himself, and confided as much in Elliott. "I'll do it," he said, "if no serious objection occurs to me before morning."[22] None did.

After his impromptu meeting with Charles Elliott, Olmsted duly submitted his application. The matter was out of his hands when, on September 11, 1857, the eleven-man board met a few blocks south of city hall to decide upon which candidate to hire. Anxious and impatient, Olmsted occupied himself that day by writing to his ailing brother, who had recently moved to Nice, on France's Mediterranean coast. He began the letter with the matter foremost in his mind.

"I have moved to town," he told John Hull Olmsted, "& done nothing else since I last wrote but canvass for the Superintendent's office."[23]

Deciding he wanted the job was one thing; getting it was another. His challenge had been to marshal the argument that he was the man best equipped to fill the post of superintendent of the Central Park, despite a working history that suggested no particular professional continuity. In his letter of application, he summed up his qualifications in brief. "For ten years I have practically engaged in the direction and superintendence of agricultural laborers and gardeners in the vicinity of New York," he wrote, "and my observations on this subject have been extensively published." He added that in recent travels he had visited "most of the large parks of Europe."[24] Taken together, as he saw it, his labor as a farmer and nurseryman and his writing and traveling qualified him to become a park maker. He left out the fact that he had never supervised more than eight farmhands—the park crew would number in the thousands—or that, for most of the last five years, his travels had been in pursuit of other matters.

He had found New York friends to back his claims. He accompanied his application with a letter of introduction from Charles Elliott. The nation's most famous writer, Washington Irving, had obliged with an endorsement, as had Alexander Hamilton's son, James, a force in New York politics, and Peter Cooper, an inventor, investor, and one of New York's richest men. Newspaperman Horace Greeley, book publishers Henry Holt and Charles Scribner, and *Post* editor William Cullen Bryant signed on too. All told, nearly two hundred prominent men lent their names to Olmsted's application. Botanist Asa Gray made perhaps the most cogent argument. "I know Mr. Olmsted well," Gray wrote from Cambridge, "and I do not know another person so well fitted for [the position] in all respects, both on practical and scientific grounds."[25]

Olmsted wrote to his brother from a friend's law office, which happened to be located in the same building as the committee room where the board met to weigh the fate of the applicants. His competition included a builder, a surveyor, a chemistry teacher, and John Woodhouse Audubon, the painter son of naturalist John James Audubon.

For Olmsted, who desired this job as much as anything he had ever sought, the hours-long wait seemed an eternity, and he wrote to his brother in fits and stops between bouts of anxious pacing.

When word of the decision finally reached him, he added a postscript to the letter. The news was excellent: "After a very long session, and much debate, I am elected." The committee had offered him the job at an unimpressive annual salary of $1,500.

Olmsted had lost his mother before he knew her and been robbed of a Yale education. Yet his boyhood circumstances also fostered an appreciation for the natural world, for its verities and injustices, which endowed him with a unique moral compass. He would soon demonstrate that he was surprisingly well equipped to effect a change in the way Americans regarded—and more especially in how they inhabited—their cities.

In September 1857, as he remembered much later, "I was unexpectedly invited to take a modest public duty," an event that "led to making Landscape Architecture my calling in life."[26] He was handed the dream job he hadn't known he wanted, a public duty that would prove to be anything but modest. He would make America's first major city park and the essential prototype for all others.

Chapter Two

CHILDHOOD DAYS
IN LOUISIANA

His childhood seems to have been of the happiest, and the memory
of his companions shows him to us in a most attractive light.

——M. G. VAN RENSSELAER

"Master Henry H. Richardson," wrote the principal at Classical Academy in New Orleans, "is a boy of much more than ordinary mental capacity." He read his Virgil and Caesar in Latin, George Blackman reported, and possessed a smattering of Greek. At age fifteen he spoke French with "tolerable facility" and had a solid working knowledge of history and geography. Best of all, the student, who wanted to be an engineer, excelled in "Mathematical Studies," noted Blackman, "in which department I consider him the most promising pupil I have ever had under my care."[1] These words of endorsement were written in the spring of 1854, at the same time that Frederick Olmsted, Richardson's elder by sixteen years, was in the midst of one of his journalistic journeys to the South.

Blackman's recommendation was intended to help young Henry Hobson Richardson gain admission to the United States Military Academy. Founded as the nation's first engineering college a half century before, West Point remained one of the few and by far the most respected school of engineering and science in the country. Its graduates laid out more than military fortifications, since for decades virtually every American civil engineer had been West Point–trained. The school's graduates planned roads, rail lines, townscapes, waterfronts, and uncounted other internal improvements required by the rapidly expanding nation.

Richardson's candidacy was buttressed by other qualifications. At age ten, his passion for drawing had persuaded his father to place him under the tutelage of a man reputed to be the best drawing teacher in New Orleans. His bloodlines were of the best sort in an era when people believed them to be as important in young men and women as in the breeding of cows and horses. His great-grandfather, Joseph Priestley, was widely remembered as both a churchman and a natural philosopher (that is, a scientist). Priestley had been the first to identify oxygen, which he called "dephlogisticated air," a discovery of immense scientific significance for the element's role in plant and animal metabolism, and of practical use since it also led to Priestley's invention of soda water.

The addressee of Headmaster Blackman's letter, Secretary of War Jefferson Davis, himself a graduate of West Point, was encouraged to look with favor upon the application. The boy's auspices were excellent in most every way, arriving as they did with a request from the Honorable Judah P. Benjamin, one of Louisiana's senators, asking that young Mr. Richardson be "duly registered on the list of applicants."

That summer, however, brought double-barreled bad news for Richardson. First his father, a hardware merchant, died unexpectedly on a business trip to Philadelphia. Then a letter arrived from the military academy, informing him of its decision regarding his future. West Point had determined that Richardson's pronounced stutter "rendered him unfit" for service as an army officer.[2]

Richardson, "an eager, active, affectionate, generous, and merry boy," apparently took the rejection in stride, his spirits undiminished.[3] In the fullness of time, had he been admitted, Richardson might well have followed the path taken by Davis and Benjamin, along with more than 250 West Point graduates, including Robert E. Lee and Stonewall Jackson. A half dozen years later, they would collectively shift their allegiance from the U.S. government to join the rebellious South with Davis and Benjamin serving, respectively, as president and secretary of state of the Confederate States of America. By then Richardson, who had long since grown accustomed to what would be a lifelong halt in his speech, had pointed his life in another direction.

In autumn 1854, Richardson enrolled at his hometown college, the recently established University of Louisiana.* He would spend a few more months in New Orleans, a city that itself offered a remarkable case history for any civil engineer.

Natural forces had begun New Orleans's creation story. The Mississippi River had deposited mud and silt along a long, slow curve of a crescent-shaped riverbank roughly a hundred miles upstream from the river's mouth. In pre-Columbian days, Native Americans had chosen this natural levee as a convenient portage to nearby waterways and lakes, before the French, in 1718, established the first permanent settlement at the site. They named it La Nouvelle Orléans, in honor of France's ruler, Phillipe II, Duc d'Orléans.

Given its location a few feet below sea level, the village flooded regularly. Levees had to be raised and drainage canals dug, work done by enslaved people to a plan devised by a changing cast of French engineers. One of them, Adrien de Pauger, laid out a checkerboard of streets built around a central square and church, protected by the earthworks that lined the river. This was a proud, European-style neighborhood that, by the time Richardson, age nine, enrolled at Mr. Blackman's school, would be interchangeably known as the Old Quarter (Vieux Carré) or the French Quarter.

New Orleans had become an American Venice over the intervening decades, its geography—and the free labor of the enslaved—enabling extravagant growth. The city's strategic location at the gateway to the Mississippi, one of the world's great arteries of trade, meant that the protective levees were always crowded with boats and ships at anchor. Barges and flatboats brought to the great port anything and everything made or grown upstream, the produce and products of a vast territory that extended from the Appalachians to

---

* Founded as the Medical College of Louisiana in 1834—the busy quays of the port of New Orleans provided easy entry for deadly diseases like malaria, yellow fever, and smallpox—it had become a public university in 1847. Later, in 1884, in honor of donor Paul Tulane, the school would be renamed Tulane University.

the Rockies and even Canada. Their wharves lined with warehouses, the merchants of the town grew rich, dispatching their wares to the East Coast and beyond on ships that, by Richardson's day, were increasingly powered by steam. Since acquisition of the Louisiana Territory by the United States in 1803, New Orleans's population had doubled almost every decade, with the count of its citizens rising fifteenfold. According to the 1850 census, there were 116,000 New Orleanians, making it the nation's fifth-largest city, trailing only New York, Baltimore, Boston, and Philadelphia.

On September 29, 1838, Catherine Caroline Priestley Richardson had given birth to son Henry Hobson at Priestley Plantation outside New Orleans. Her well-established family—the Priestleys had settled in the territory before the Louisiana Purchase—had made its money in sugarcane. Though a later arrival from Bermuda, her husband and the baby's father, Henry Dickenson Richardson, had also profited from slavery-based agriculture, having worked as a cotton broker at T. S. Hobson & Company before joining another of his wife's family's businesses, Priestley and Bein Hardware Company.

As he matured, Catherine and Henry Richardson's eldest child studied with a fencing instructor. He indulged a passion for music, becoming proficient on the flute. The younger Henry took pride in his appearance—according to his brother, "he had better clothes and more of them than any one man needed."[4] The Richardsons lived in town, though they spent summer months and winter vacations at Priestley Plantation, some sixty miles upriver in Saint James Parish, where Henry became a capable horseman.

Many architects have vivid visual memories, and Henry revealed his mnemonic gift early. Taught the game of chess by his father, he reveled in taking on several opponents simultaneously—and doing so blindfolded. The byways of his childhood offered him much to take in. The French Quarter had an architectural style that one British architect admired for "the motley & picturesque effect of the stuccoed French buildings."[5] The characteristic second-floor balconies entered Richardson's mental inventory of architectural details and would reemerge much later.

After Louisiana had become the Union's twenty-third state in 1812, bold new institutional buildings started to appear. By then

American architectural tastes had veered from the vernacular to the historical, with ancient Rome providing models for public monuments in Washington, D.C., in Thomas Jefferson's Virginia, and in the Boston of architect Charles Bulfinch. Richardson knew Federal-era buildings in New Orleans—his family even occupied one—but he also witnessed the flowering of the next neoclassical phase, the Greek Revival. The streets he walked were, year by year, lined with more and more grand, pedimented and porticoed mansions, particularly in the American quarter where the Richardsons resided.

During summers spent at Priestley Plantation, when the risks of yellow fever were high in the city, Richardson, together with his mother and three younger siblings, visited grand plantation homes. There he saw sheltering roofs that overhung tall porches and galleries, providing protection from the hot sun and frequent heavy rains of Louisiana's subtropical climate. An element borrowed from Caribbean houses in English West Indian colonies, the expansive roofs also gained purchase in Richardson's memory; they would be antecedents of the sheltering roofs characteristic of Richardson's rail stations a quarter century later. They also resembled the "Jamaican planter's house," as some called it, that the mature Richardson would rent in suburban Boston, complete with its tall wraparound porch supported by two-story piers.

The young man also observed a mix of utilitarian buildings that dotted the low-lying sugar country, including cane mills, cabins for the enslaved, barns, and sugarhouses with tall chimneys. Richardson much later would devise purpose-specific buildings for his clients, both corporate and private, that echoed in many particulars what he had seen on the terra firma of southern Louisiana. Just as Olmsted's embrace of the natural world was formed by his childhood circumstances, what Richardson saw of the built environment in prosperous New Orleans would always inhabit his imagination.

Richardson's years in New Orleans came to a close with his departure in 1855 for the North. As he turned seventeen, he had a new out-of-town target, this one prestigious Harvard College. He would spend a few months with a private tutor improving his Greek, then a prerequisite for enrollment at the Cambridge, Massachusetts, college. Richardson was no particular rarity among the applicants, since many boys from wealthy mercantile families in the South came north. To judge from their diaries and correspondence, the attitude among undergraduates, regardless of their place of origin, seemed to be that the rising national divisions over slavery would be left to their fathers.

Catherine and Henry had raised a tall and handsome son, the youth's thick dark hair complementing his hazel eyes. "Vivacious and sympathetic in manner, forcible and amusing in conversation, clever, ardent, and impressionable," he was "generous to a fault."[6] Henry Hobson Richardson would never return to New Orleans.

While Olmsted was investing almost every waking hour creating New York's Central Park, Richardson pursued his studies at Harvard; he had enrolled in February 1856 as a member of the graduating class of 1859. Near the dusty crossroads that was Harvard Square, "Fez" Richardson, as his college friends called him, enjoyed "days of carelessness and plenty." In the recollection of one upperclassman, "the seriousness of life had laid hold upon him less even than it does upon most college men."[7]

He did take drawing lessons in Boston, but Richardson, away from home for the first time, behaved as if he thought that having fun should be his primary undergraduate occupation. Religious services were mandatory at Harvard, but Fez cut chapel forty times in a single term.[8] He joined the Hasty Pudding Club, devoted to theatrics. At the Pierian Sodality he played his flute in the group's musicales. He accepted an invitation to join the Porcellian, Harvard's most exclusive social club. His company was in demand and, in his frequent appearances in the diary of Benjamin Crowninshield, an undergraduate friend, Richardson mixed "Jamaica Rum Punch," played whist in his rooms and billiards in Boston, and gained a reputation as "a jolly good fellow" for his "generous hospitality."[9] He was the sort of young man his peers liked to be with, already exhibiting a charismatic mix of enthusiasm and curiosity that would win him the friendship of many clients—and their commissions.

Even in faraway Louisiana, his family sensed his distraction. Richardson's mother was a widow no more, having remarried an old friend of the family's, John D. Bein, who had lost his spouse in a cholera epidemic within months of Henry Dickenson Richardson's death. Worried about his stepson on behalf of his new wife, Bein wrote directly to the president of Harvard in the spring of 1857. The boy, he confided, "has been much too lavish with the money that has been remitted him." Just as worrisome, he had not written to his mother in three months. Bein requested that President James Walker, at his "first opportunity," give Henry "a good lecture."[10]

Regardless of stern words from his elders, however, Richardson failed to achieve high academic standing at Harvard. Even in mathematics, a singular strength in his earlier education, his name did not appear in the upper rankings.

Whatever his lack of scholarly diligence, Richardson made up for it in Cambridge with his genuine gift for friendship. In contrast to northern boys he was, in the words of one fellow student, "[a] slender companionable Southern lad, full of creole life and animation."[11] People were drawn to this amusing young man who, unembarrassed at his stammer, loved food, drink, and, perhaps above all, good talk. If occasionally he was carried away by his enthusiasm, he was someone people happily forgave, "[who] could make friends of his worst enemy in five minutes."[12]

One member of his circle, Henry Adams, great-grandson and grandson of the second and sixth U.S. presidents, became a lifelong confidant. Adams shared Richardson's lackadaisical attitude to college, as well as "the habit of drinking." In Adams's ironic view of his Cambridge years, Harvard "taught little, and that little ill, but it left the mind open, free from bias, ignorant of facts, but docile [and] . . . ready to receive knowledge."[13] To Adams, Fez's absence of academic discipline hardly amounted to a notable failure. He chose instead to see another value in the Harvard experience. "A student [like] Richardson," Adams later observed, "who came from far away New Orleans, and had his career before him to chase rather than to guide, might make valuable friendships at college."[14]

Indeed he did. The goodwill of more than a dozen other Harvard friends would lead to many important commissions, some for churches and public buildings, others for country and city houses.

Women played a role in Richardson's education too, and as early as his sophomore year, his friends noted he was less likely to indulge his taste in alcohol when under "feminine influence."[15] He was a handsome man. At age twenty, as seen in a sepia-toned photograph taken for his Harvard yearbook, his features were defined by high cheekbones and the fine line of his firm but graceful chin. But one woman in particular occupied his attentions by the end of his junior year. Classmate David Hayden had introduced him to his younger sister, Julia. Their engagement was announced in February of Richardson's senior year.

A confident-looking Richardson as a college senior, engaged to be married and a man with a profession freshly in mind.

In his last months at college, he not only committed himself to Julia but turned his gaze directly on architecture. He never said why, and neither his friends nor family could explain what led him to think of the architectural profession.[16] But his time in Cambridge and Boston had exposed him to buildings different from those he had known in New Orleans. The new library at Harvard, Gore Hall, was the most impressive edifice he had seen in the Gothic Revival style.* The picturesque building seemed to direct the observer's eye to the heavens, with its pointed arches and carved pinnacles extending upward from its eaves, and inside it resembled a cathedral with a central nave. A very different building, Boylston Hall, was constructed on campus during Richardson's Cambridge years. It used rough-textured granite, as did Boston's historic Charles Street Jail, in a neighborhood Richardson knew well. Much later, he retrieved design ideas from these buildings as he planned libraries and even a Pennsylvania jail. The styles of the earlier buildings would seem passé by then, but he would apply recollected details in his own original way. Quarry-faced stone in particular would become a hallmark of his work.

---

* Gore Hall was later demolished, and Widener Library built on its site.

Architecture was a relatively new career option in the late 1850s. Less than fifty years before, there had been no architects in the United States, just a motley mix of jumped-up masons and joiners often called "undertakers" (because they *undertook* to construct a building), along with a few gentleman amateurs like George Washington and Thomas Jefferson who made sketches for their builders to follow. In the intervening decades, some experienced men had drifted in from England and France, and a few young Americans opened practices. There were other signs that a profession was emerging. In 1857, a handful of men banded together to form a professional organization, the American Institute of Architects. A few small architectural partnerships began operating in the biggest cities.

Apparently, Richardson's careerist turn pleased John Bein, who welcomed the news of his stepson's newfound architectural aspiration. "I . . . have been thinking seariously regarding your future prospects," he wrote in May 1859. "A good Architect, if he is industrious, Cannot but Succeed."[17] In the same letter, he went so far as to propose a plan. "I have thought that Six or Nine Months in London & Paris . . . will do you more good than three times the time spent in N.O. . . . You can live in either London or Paris at a very Moderate expense [and] . . . I know your aim will be to study & get to the top of the ladder."

Bein's notion suited Richardson, and after collecting his Harvard diploma, he sailed for Europe on July 20, 1859. His marriage to Julia would have to wait while he went in search of an architectural education.

Chapter Three

INVENTING THE CENTRAL PARK

A great object of all that is done in a park, of all the art of a park, is to
influence the mind of men through their imagination.

——FREDERICK LAW OLMSTED

On his first day, the new park superintendent wore the wrong
clothes. Dressed as a gentleman, Olmsted arrived for what he
thought was a ceremonial call on the man in charge, head engineer
Egbert L. Viele. Instead, Olmsted's new boss dispatched him on a
guided tour of the raw acreage that would be the Central Park.

Trailing a park worker named Hawkin, Olmsted saw work gangs
burning brush on the warm fall day and immediately regretted he
had not left his fashionable jacket behind. He soon wished for cruder
footwear too, like the heavy boots his roughly dressed guide wore,
into which the man had tucked his trouser legs. After they waded
knee-deep into a low-lying patch of mud, Hawkin watched with
amusement as Olmsted used the trunk of a nearby tree to scrape the
odorous muck off his legs. "Suppose you are used to this sort of business?" Hawkin inquired. Though Hawkin's face remained expres-
sionless, Olmsted "felt very deeply that he was laughing in his sleeve."[1]

The tour took hours, as the September afternoon grew hot and
muggy. The park site was intimidatingly large, a half mile across and
extending more than two miles northward from Fifty-Ninth Street.
Few significant structures still stood within the boundaries. These included the Arsenal, just off Fifth Avenue, a fortresslike structure formerly used to store munitions that now housed park offices, and the
vacated Sisters of Charity Mount Saint Vincent Convent, well uptown

near 103rd Street. Mostly, though, the two men plodded through the remains of "pig-sties, slaughter-houses, and bone-boiling works," a sickening stench in the air. The overall impression Olmsted got was of rocks and swamps; in his words, it was "a very nasty place." No wonder, then, with few trees, no inherently beautiful features, and "scarcely an acre of level, or slope unbroken by ledges," as Olmsted wrote to Asa Gray, that it had not been subject to real estate development.[2]

As the superintendent of the park, Olmsted had been hired to carry out the improvements delineated by Viele, which consisted largely of draining wetlands and removing squatters' shacks and fences. Viele's topographical survey would guide this process, but many people were displeased that much of the proposed park would be little improved. Among those who made their voices heard was Calvert Vaux (rhymes with *Fox*), the late Mr. Downing's partner. He thought Viele's superficial approach—officially called the "Plan for the Improvement of The Central Park"—amounted to a serious disservice to Downing's memory.

Vaux pointed out the plan's inadequacies to anyone who would listen. Among those who did was Olmsted's friend Commissioner Elliott, who arranged for Vaux to speak to the board. An Englishman, Vaux had trained as an architect in London, but at age twenty-five, captivated by Downing's vision and attracted by the possibilities of America, he abandoned his struggling business in England just hours' after making Downing's acquaintance to join him in the United States. Within three months, Downing had made him a partner. Now thirty-two and a noted architect and author in his own right, Vaux had a forceful voice, and he helped convince the park commissioners to conduct a public competition for a fully developed design. Printed handbills announced cash prizes for the four best park plans, with the overall winner to be awarded $2,000.

Vaux made no secret of his desire to submit an entry, and, as an admirer of Olmsted's book about his English peregrinations, *Walks and Talks*, he asked the new superintendent if he wished to collaborate. They had met six years earlier at Downing's nursery in Newburgh, New York, and Vaux recognized how useful Olmsted's day-to-day, firsthand knowledge of the actual topography of the park would be. Olmsted initially refused, out of concern for his boss's feelings, but when asked, Viele professed complete indifference. Needing money, Olmsted set to work with Vaux, whose architectural and drafting skills would clearly be invaluable.

The contest rules for the park design competition required all entrants to work to the same template for the rectangular Central Park, which would extend from Fifth to Eighth Avenues east to west and 59th to 106th Streets south to north.* Enclosed within this designated parkland was the Receiving Reservoir, part of an aqueduct system that brought fresh water to Manhattan from the Croton River north of the city. Despite having spent $5 million acquiring the land, the construction budget was set at about $1.5 million, a sum that— to no one's surprise—would prove insufficient.† The proposals were to allow for the creation of four or more east–west crossings for traffic, along with a parade ground, an exhibition hall, a fountain, three playgrounds, and a winter skating area.

From the start, the Vaux-Olmsted collaboration clicked. Some evenings, despite the shorter winter days, they walked the empty expanse of the park after Olmsted's workday ended. They were two small silhouettes in the moonlight—Olmsted stood five feet six, Vaux under five feet—carrying on private conversations that ranged from convivial to argumentative. The two men liked each other and found their thinking tended to come together as they regarded the barren plat and pictured its transformation.[3]

Although Vaux had trained as an architect, he and Olmsted agreed that the guiding principle had to be "Nature first and 2nd and 3rd—Architecture after a while."[4] When not on-site, they spent long nights and Sundays at Vaux's Eighteenth Street home, considering the park with the complementary eyes of designer and farmer.

Olmsted found the work unexpectedly familiar. As a beginning farmer a decade before, he had instinctively looked at his Staten Island farm as a landscape designer would. He had planted trees that had nothing to do with his nursery business, including elms, cedars, lindens, beeches, and walnuts, along with a hedge of Osage orange, sim-

* The original northern boundary would be extended, in 1863, to 110th Street.
† By 1870 the cost approached $9 million.

ply to improve the look of the property. As one friend observed, "[Olmsted] moved the barns. . . . He brought the road in so that it approached the house by a graceful curve, he turfed the borders of the pond and planted water plants on its edge. . . . Thus, with a few strokes and small expense he transformed the place from a very dirty, disagreeable farmyard to a gentlemen's house."[5] As sound as his native instincts were, however, the Manhattan park was an enormous task, the scale of which was beyond anything either he or Vaux had taken on before.

Both men favored the style of the English landscape garden. The geometric formality practiced in Renaissance Italy and in the seventeenth century by men like André Le Notre, landscape designer to King Louis XIV, had not suited the designers and occupants of the eighteenth-century English country house. Rather than harnessing nature into symmetrical curves, precise plantings, pools, allées, and gravel walks as the French did, the English looked to capture a countryside idyll. Tabletop flatness gave way to sloping lawns and rolling hills, winding paths, groves of trees, and meandering streams. This was nature tamed but in a manner that was picturesque, in imitation of the pastoral landscape canvases of painters like Claude Lorrain and Nicolas Poussin. These design principles had been transmitted to Joseph Paxton, who employed them at Birkenhead, and to Downing, who incorporated them into his books.

Some of the work Vaux and Olmsted did was conceptual, and they devised fresh answers to the unique challenges posed by the topography. One essential question was how to integrate the required east–west crossings for city traffic into an overall design, and the partners came up with a clever solution. They decided to submerge the through roads in eight-foot-deep trenches that resembled the ha-has of British landscape gardens. A convention of the eighteenth-century English pleasure ground, the ha-ha, sometimes rendered *Ha-Ha!*, was a deep boundary ditch that kept domestic animals, as well as the beasts of the forest, from the manicured grounds closest to a grand country house. Below-grade through roads would permit traffic to cross the park unseen and allow park visitors to enjoy deeper vistas. This approach dovetailed with the partners' notion of lining the park's perimeter with trees to screen views of the growing city's surrounding streetscapes; there weren't many houses flanking the park in the late 1850s, but everyone knew the northward development would continue. Olmsted and Vaux sought to enhance a sense of separation from the hustle and bustle of Manhattan, making the park seem like an escape to a rural oasis.

As they formulated a design, they saw in the unimproved acreage of the park an opportunity to practice the art of landscape. Together Olmsted and Vaux imagined that sweeping slopes, the Reservoir, and grand-scale gardening would characterize the Upper Park; the Lower Park would feature a long and rocky hillside. Other elements would include ornate bridges, hills and dales, and forests that mimicked wild country. To accomplish it all, uncountable cubic yards of earth and stone would have to be moved and regraded. Everything was to be subject to the main idea—they were creating scenery—and the whole would be bound together by a carefully calculated circulation system of roads and paths.

The particulars had to be rendered onto a competition drawing, a plan ten feet long and two feet, three inches wide, scaled one hundred feet to one inch. The plan required much drafting, and unsuspecting visitors to the Vaux household in those weeks were regularly put to work on the large sheet, which lay across a series of abutting tables in the parlor. "There was a great deal of grass to be put in by the usual small dots and dashes," Vaux's son Downing remembered, "and it became the friendly thing for callers to help on the work by joining in and 'adding some grass to Central Park.'"6 Thousands of trees also had to be indicated.

The designers supplemented the ground plan with a series of twelve presentation boards. These juxtaposed simple sketches of the existing scrubby undergrowth against richly rendered views of how the same vistas would look in the years ahead, contrasting the present raw terrain with tree-lined avenues, expansive greens, lakes, gardens, and occasional buildings.

Here again they found guidance in English sources, adopting the style of presentation drawings from some of the great landscape designers of eighteenth-century gardens, such as Lancelot "Capability" Brown, the man who gained his nickname by promising to bring out the "capabilities" of a landscape. They imitated Humphry Repton's Red Books too, which employed before-and-after watercolors of unimproved landscapes and their future appearance.

For the most part, Vaux himself executed the pencil and water-color drawings. As an apprentice architect in London years earlier, he had supported himself rendering illustrations for printers, but here, too, friends offered assistance. One among them was Vaux's brother-in-law, painter Jervis McEntee, a sometime student of the artist Frederic Church. The plan, together with Vaux's renderings and McEntee's oil sketches, collectively and elegantly represented a shared vision of how the muddy and scarred scrubland would be altered. As Olmsted later observed, "It would have been difficult to find another body of six hundred acres upon the island which possessed less of . . . the desirable characteristics of a park."[7] But its conditions had also made the land affordable.

The competition required specifications for materials and estimates for the cost of building roads, plus a "well digested written description." This work fell to the well-practiced writer Olmsted, who wrote in the practical terms that members of the board—men of business rather than artists—would comprehend. His gifts as a writer were invaluable as he made the case for the park's design ("a single work of art"), the construction plan ("improvement of the ground"), and, in particular, for the political and social goals. "It is one great purpose of the Park," Olmsted wrote, "to supply to the hundreds of thousands of tired workers, who have no opportunity to spend their summers in the country, a specimen of God's handiwork that shall be to them, inexpensively, what a month or two in the White Mountains or the Adirondacks is, at great cost to those in easier circumstances."[8]

Olmsted arranged for the report to be professionally typeset and printed. The team labored on the various pieces until the last possible minute—and beyond. When Olmsted and Vaux arrived late at the board offices on deadline day, March 31, 1858, only the janitor remained to take receipt of Park Competition Plan No. 33. "The Greensward Plan," so dubbed by its creators, was the last submission to the competition. It was also the most complete, polished, and persuasive entry.[9]

Olmsted delighted in the work. "I am greatly interested in planning the park with Vaux," he enthused in a letter to his father.[10] And for him, the collaboration seemed an entirely logical development on his superintendency of the park, a management job at which he excelled. That spring his workforce approached a thousand men as they took on the preliminary work of reshaping just the southern section of the park. The board, impressed with his good work, raised his salary to $2,000.

He wanted to win the competition. He wanted to pursue this new work, which felt like a fortuitous merging of virtually everything he had previously done, from his short stint as an apprentice surveyor to his work as a shop clerk, from his farming labors to his assiduous reporting when he saw firsthand how people less well-off lived. The task also drew upon his growing sense that the American landscape could not be separated from the national dream of democracy, an aspiration that he viewed as imperiled by the South's adherence to slavery.

This was more than a matter of design. He saw landscape—and parkscapes in particular—as an antidote to the stresses of city life and, in a larger sense, as a mode of social reform. "The Park," he wrote in his description for the board, "is intended to furnish healthful recreation for the poor and the rich, the young and the old, the vicious and the virtuous."[11] He believed the poor in particular "need an education to refinement and taste and the mental and moral capital of gentlemen."[12] Thus, to Olmsted, parks were a positive force that could even help maintain order among the rowdiest elements of society.

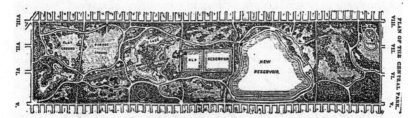

A much-simplified version of the Greensward Plan appeared in several of the New York papers after Olmsted and Vaux were declared the winners of the $2,000 prize in the Central Park design competition.

When the day of judgment came, the Central Park commissioners needed nine ballots to decide upon winner, runner-up, and third- and fourth-place finishers. On April 28, 1858, they awarded the prize to Plan No. 33. Vaux and Olmsted split the purse.

Olmsted's sudden turnabout in fortune was remarkable. Not so many months earlier, he had despaired of succeeding at anything, having abandoned work as a dry-goods clerk, merchant sailor, farmer, and nurseryman, and then failed as a publisher. In his letter to his dying brother on September 11, 1857, the day the board debated his hiring as superintendent, Olmsted had ruefully written, "What else can I do for a living?" A new answer had emerged.

With the plan formulated and the contest concluded in their favor, the self-effacing Vaux offered to withdraw. Olmsted dismissed the idea, insisting Vaux's presence was vital, that he did not regard himself as a designer. The board put Olmsted in charge, creating for him the office of architect-in-chief of the Central Park; Viele was relieved of his duties as head engineer. Olmsted was given a raise in pay to $2,500, while Vaux got a daily stipend and the title of consulting engineer.

For many months, the job consumed Olmsted's every energy. True to his word, he skillfully managed a rapidly growing labor force, which by October 1858 had expanded to twenty-five hundred men. With the coming of December, many laborers were let go for the winter, but not before the completion of much of the seven-mile stone wall that would enclose the roughly eight hundred acres, broken at intervals by the park's eighteen entrances.

Olmsted surrounded himself with experienced foremen. With water and sanitary management a priority, agricultural engineer George Edwin Waring Jr. oversaw the installation of more than twenty miles of earthen drain tiles, buried at three feet or more beneath grade. The sound of blasting regularly echoed, and despite Olmsted's precautions—including a flag system that warned of impending explosions—one man died. Given that more gunpowder would be expended in the park's construction than would be used by the armies at the Battle of Gettysburg a few years later, the death toll might well have been much greater.[13]

Central Park required a vast engineering effort, including plumbing works for the lakes and, as pictured here, the distribution system for water from the park's large reservoir.

W. H. Grant became Olmsted's road expert, managing the construction of the system of roads and paths, which included three types of discrete byways within the park. In addition to the transverse roads, there would be "drives" (carriage roads), "rides" (for horses), and "walks" (for foot traffic). Everywhere one turned new elements were needed, including retaining walls, curbs, and gutters.

Vaux designed a mix of buildings, but his thirty-four bridges and archways, variously of brick, stone, and iron, would win him wide admiration. Of varied and picturesque designs, handsome and serviceable, elegant and understated, the bridges blended into the undulating landscape. They served the eye as well as the wheel, hoof, and foot.[14]

The plan also called for vast new plantings, and much of the horticultural responsibility fell to head gardener Ignaz Anton Pilat and his crew. A quarter million trees and shrubs would be planted. Nursery areas were established within the park for trees, both native and imported species, which awaited the shaping of the park's new topography. By Olmsted's estimate, 10 million cartloads of earth would be shifted by horsepower, making the grading a major challenge. Olmsted supervised the process himself, square yard by square yard.

In mid-October 1858, he watched the planting of the first tree. Specimen trees were for show, and Olmsted also employed an array of common evergreens and deciduous trees of varying textures and colors to define the open and forested areas.

The administrative team in charge of the park included Olmsted (far right), Calvert Vaux (third from left), and Olmsted's sometime nemesis, comptroller Andrew Green (far left). The men are standing atop the Willowdell Arch, one of Vaux's bridges.

Though he attempted to remain staunchly apolitical, Olmsted faced daily battles with the inevitable requests from both the humble and the powerful for jobs, favors, and other considerations. He fought off attempts from several quarters to alter the park's rural character; typical was the proposal by two new commissioners for two straight lines of trees to run the entire length of the park, north to south, to divide in it half.[15] In resisting such proposals, Olmsted enlisted the help of journalist friends to make his case to the public. One who defended the Greensward Plan in print was Richard Grant White, an erudite young critic whose writings in *Putnam's Magazine* had gained him notoriety. A dozen years later, Olmsted returned the favor, providing White's son personal entrée to Richardson. Over the course of an eight-year apprenticeship, Richardson would turn young Stanford White into an architect.

A few weeks into his work at Central Park, Olmsted had received a letter from the bedridden John Olmsted. "I have not many days, the Dr says," his brother wrote.[16] Even before his words reached New York, he died, on November 24, 1857, just thirty-two years of age.

His grief for his dead brother changed Olmsted. He had been a light-living young man in his thirties who was still trying out different careers; as one friend said of his ricochet ways, "One thing is curious, disappointments never seem to trouble him."[17] But John's death seemed to inspire a new seriousness, and Olmsted threw himself into his job as superintendent of what was to become Central Park; his winning codesign of Central Park opened a new professional portal, and he walked determinedly into the new arena, freshly committed to what became his life's work. He understood instinctively its importance. "As the first real park made in this country," he wrote to a journalist friend, the Central Park would be "a democratic development of the highest significance & on the success of which, in my opinion, much of the progress of art and esthetic culture in this country is dependent."[18]

A parting request in his brother's last letter also played a role in Olmsted's new life path. Writing of his wife, who was at his side as he died, John beseeched his brother, "Don't let Mary suffer while you are alive."[19] Olmsted knew he must honor the plea from his much loved brother, but what the obligation meant was not immediately clear. As Fred carried on with Vaux, devising their design, winning the competition, and commencing work on the Greensward Plan, Fred and John's father tended to family matters in Europe. He had crossed the Atlantic in late 1857, hoping to see his son a last time, but arrived too late. When he returned with Mary in the new year, he settled the widow, along with her and John's three children—five-year-old John Charles, Charlotte, age three, and infant Owen—at Fred's Staten Island farm.

Throughout Mary's marriage to John, Fred had been a constant in her family's life. They resided much of the time under the same farmhouse roof; when Fred went off on his writing junkets to the South, Mary and John had tended to the business of the nursery. Now, with John gone, Fred and Mary shared the same painful sense of loss, an emotional vacuum that brother-in-law and sister-in-law came increasingly to fill for each other.

As a younger man, Olmsted had been "a good deal with the ladies," as his father put it, but after the painful end of an engagement, he had settled into a decade of playing the role of what he himself called an "old bach."[20] But as summer gave way to fall, he and Mary grew closer. She chose to relocate to Manhattan, where he witnessed her signature on the lease for a brownstone, in October 1858, on East Seventy-Ninth Street. The house stood within walking distance of his park office.

In the months that followed, the two would agree to marry, thereby honoring John's deathbed request that he "[not] let Mary suffer while you are alive." After more than decade of casting about in his working life for a path that suited him, Olmsted took on new, more intimate responsibilities, becoming stepfather to John, Charlotte, and Owen, by then ages seven, four, and two, on June 13, 1859, when he and Mary took the vows of marriage, with New York's mayor, Daniel Tiemann, presiding.

Mary had long experience with loss, having been orphaned as a child. Growing up in her paternal grandparents' household in New York, the slight, blue-eyed girl held her own in the company of such guests as the formidable Daniel Webster, senator of Massachusetts,

and William Cullen Bryant, whose wife was her godmother. As an adult, she shared both Fred's intensity and his candor, unafraid to speak her mind both about their lives and, increasingly, his work. As his wife, she took charge of the house that the park commissioners provided, part of the former convent at Mount Saint Vincent, which still stood within the park's boundaries. The two settled into a partnership and more.

Pictured here in 1863, Mary Cleveland Bryant Perkins twice became Mrs. Olmsted: initially as the wife of John Hull Olmsted, then, after John's death, when she married his brother, Frederick Law Olmsted.

The Central Park welcomed the general public for the first time on December 11, 1858. The Lake, a meandering man-made body of water not far from Eighth Avenue, fed by a new underground drainage system, had frozen over. Although just three hundred skaters came to test the ice that first Sunday, the few became the many as word spread. A week later, Olmsted and Vaux lost count as they welcomed perhaps ten thousand New Yorkers to the park. In the course of that cold winter, ice-skating became the city's most popular outdoor activity, with an estimated hundred thousand people visiting the park on the busiest winter days. Olmsted's plan for engaging the populace was working.

Over the course of 1859, Central Park received some two million visitors. A security force helped manage the crowds. Along with so much else, Olmsted insisted that policing fell within his province, and he fought to keep city police out in favor of "Park Keepers." Dressed in gray to distinguish them from the men in blue, they did more than maintain the peace. Charged with protecting the plants and educating the public, more than a dozen keepers, hired by Olmsted himself and mounted on horseback, went about their jobs, per Olmsted's instructions, "in a quiet, reserved and vigilant manner."[21]

On-site every day, Olmsted was both designer and builder, supervising everything, and as he watched, the picturesque English-style landscape that originated in his mind came to life. One section in which he took particular pride was the Ramble, a stone-strewn, thirty-seven-acre mix of crags, rock faces, a stone arch, a watercourse, and even a cave. It was a landscape sculpted under Olmsted's instructions by park workers and planted with hardy woody species like azaleas and rhododendrons. The Ramble opened in the summer of 1859, as progress gradually moved northward in what would be a nearly two-decade march to completion. For Olmsted, however, the Ramble was his park's finest moment. He had constructed a place where city folk could experience a mountainous trail accompanied by the sound of a stream, fed by a pipe, that splashed over a muttering waterfall.

The park was a revelation to visitors and played a role in the coming of age of the City of New York. To Olmsted's great satisfaction, his fellow New Yorkers regarded the park as their own, but his utter devotion to making it also took a growing toll on his health. A bout of typhoid in the spring of 1859 left him with little resistance, and in September, the recently married Olmsted fell ill again. Suffering from insomnia, headaches, and digestive discomforts, he could barely rise from his bed. Though his doctor prescribed a mix of medications—"effervescents, quinine, bitters & grapes"—the blue pills he provided, which contained mercury, worsened Olmsted's nausea and exhaustion.[22]

The Central Park commissioners gave Olmsted a six-week leave of absence and ordered their most valuable man to go abroad. They presented him with $500 to pay for the trip, which they envisioned as a mix of rest cure and working holiday, during he which would tour European parks. Departing at the end of September, and leaving his family behind, Olmsted landed in Liverpool in early October. News of Central Park had long since reached Europe's park makers, and Olmsted's new notoriety provided him with access to Joseph Paxton, designer of both Birkenhead and the Crystal Palace, the revolutionary glasshouse that had dazzled the world several years earlier with its

Olmsted, not yet forty, during the construction of Central Park.

twenty acres of interior exhibition space beneath an unprecedented expanse of glass. As always, travel energized Olmsted, and he met with Sir William Hooker, director of the Royal Botanic Gardens at Kew, and visited Chatsworth and Windsor Forest before moving on to Brussels and Paris. He viewed the Bois de Boulogne no fewer than eight times before returning to England, where he made still more stops at fine homes and private parks, and then proceeded to Dublin and Phoenix Park. Never truly off duty, Olmsted found time to purchase trees and shrubs for his own park. Though his trip was hardly restful, he arrived home a week before Christmas with a new and invigorating appreciation of what he, Vaux, and their vast crew were accomplishing in New York.

"In the earliest flush of dawn," Olmsted reported, John Theodore Olmsted entered the world on June 14, 1860, "with a great cry."[23] The new father was elated, but the arrival of another mouth to feed prompted Fred Olmsted to cast about for work beyond the bounds of Central Park. He and Vaux found takers—in New York, in Hartford, potentially in Brooklyn—but the overworked Olmsted would soon pay a terrible price.

On Monday evening, August 6, 1860, Fred harnessed up the buggy after his day's work at the park. He helped Mary, who held seven-week-old John Theodore in her arms, into the seat beside him. He planned a relaxing ride in the open carriage, heading north to the wooded acres of Washington Heights in Upper Manhattan. He and Vaux had been invited to create a plan for laying out an undeveloped eighteen-hundred-acre expanse north of 155th Street. This would be his chance, Olmsted hoped, to offer an alternative to the monotonous gridiron system elsewhere in Manhattan, which he regarded as dreary and inflexible ("it presents," he argued, "a dull and inartistic appearance").[24] The family excursion would double as a test ride too, since Olmsted was thinking of buying the unfamiliar mare in the traces.

The easy and contemplative ride came to a sudden and catastrophic end when he lost the reins. In that dimly remembered moment, the horse bolted. As the mare sped around a corner, the hurtling buggy struck a lamppost, and one of its wooden wheels broke into pieces. The buggy teetered, and Olmsted, rising in an attempt to regain the reins, was thrown clear, landing in a heap at the side of the road.[25]

According to his later recollection, "after a moment (which, for all I knew, had been a century), I recovered consciousness."[26] His first thought was of Mary. She appeared in his line of vision, along with baby John. Neither was hurt, but as Mary reached her husband's side, she saw he was gravely injured.

His left knee and thigh had taken the full force of the landing, striking an unforgiving outcropping of the same Manhattan schist that constituted the bedrock of his park. The jagged ends of his left femur, broken in three places, protruded from his torn trousers. Waves of pain left him helpless. The baby clutched to her chest, Mary ran to a woman she saw framed in a nearby doorway, begging for her help. The stranger took the infant John and ordered a servant to remove a shutter from one of the tall windows. Several among the gathering crowd lifted the prone Olmsted onto the makeshift stretcher, then carried him indoors.

"I was near to swooning from the pain of the movement," Olmsted recalled. "Things turned black and I thought I was dying."[27]

The next day, a horse-drawn bier ferried Olmsted home. The symbolism was lost on no one. His several doctors debated the wisdom of amputating the mangled limb; if they did not, they feared that infection might well kill the patient. In the end, they decided that surgery posed an even greater danger to this man, of doubtful health even before the recent event, now doubly weakened. Olmsted might live a week, they predicted, his odds of surviving his injuries perhaps one in a hundred.

The doctors clearly underestimated Olmsted's recuperative powers. The father would survive. Unexpectedly, his firstborn child would not. John Theodore appeared unscathed by the crash, only to fall suddenly ill. All symptoms pointed not to physical injury but to an acute intestinal infection. On August 14, a week after the accident, the two-month-old succumbed to cholera infantum, one of the age's familiar killers of children. Mary, bereft and inconsolable, took to her bed. For many weeks, she would suffer intense headaches, dyspepsia, and the lowest of spirits.

Despite his injury and the shocking loss of his son, Olmsted refused to abandon his work. He ordered maps and plans of Central Park spread on his bedroom floor, and though barely able to rise to a sitting position, he studied his great project. The impatient Olmsted summoned park workers, and they improvised a means of getting their housebound architect-in-chief into the park. With his leg extended before him in its splint, Olmsted rode in a makeshift litter chair like a minor Turkish pasha, issuing orders and asking questions.

He regained his strength slowly. Ten weeks after the accident, he reported to his father, "I gain a little more power of locomotion and am just today venturing to unseat & seat myself."[28] His immobilized leg interfered with everything, from dressing to simply turning over in bed, but the advent of crutches gained him some independence. He used his time in confinement to write to friends and drafted an essay on community design. His bones knit slowly, the knee remained stiff, and six months would pass before he discarded his crutches, having relearned how to walk, "with a terrible dip & swing."[29] Olmsted's left leg would remain two inches shorter than the right for the rest of his life, leaving him with a permanent limp.

As if his injury and the death of his son were not enough, Olmsted began to feel control of the park project slipping away.

One of the commissioners, Andrew Green, served as Central Park's comptroller. Their relationship had begun well; Green had been an outspoken supporter of Olmsted's during the deliberations concerning whom to hire for the superintendent's job in September 1857. He had grown up on his family's bucolic Green Hill estate in Worcester, Massachusetts, and though a lawyer by profession, he possessed an affinity for nature and a sympathy for park making. But Green was also an overzealous financial manager, and over time, with the park's purse strings within his strict control, he became a frequent and frustrating obstacle.

"I have found," Olmsted confided in a friend, "that I [can] not act in the smallest detail, absolutely and literally, [to] direct a matter involving an expenditure of 12½ cts. without [taking] the trouble to see Mr. Green personally and perfectly satisfy him that the said expenditure was unavoidable. The practical effect is that my hands are often tied just where it is of the highest importance . . . in the last touches, the finish of my work."[30] Olmsted couldn't so much as order the cutting of a lawn or the relocation of a nursery tree without Green's approval.

Though Olmsted resented Green's interference from the start, the man had further consolidated his control over park operations during Olmsted's European absence and his convalescence after the carriage accident. To Olmsted, the situation bordered on the untenable. He felt that Green not only undermined his authority but stood in the way of what he called his "*creative fancy*." As he explained to the entire park board, "the work of designing necessarily supposes a gallery of mental pictures, and in all parts of the park I constantly have before me . . . a picture [that] I am constantly laboring to realize."[31] And as he told Vaux, the endless quibbling with Green had become "a systematic small tyranny" amounting to "slow murder."[32] By early 1861, he could take it no more and submitted his resignation to the commissioners.

At a meeting of the board on January 22, Olmsted aired his grievances. No one wished him to leave, and the group managed to mollify him—even Green acknowledged he had been excessively controlling—and Olmsted withdrew his letter of resignation. But changes in the larger landscape of American politics were also unfolding around them.

Abraham Lincoln's election to the presidency the previous November left the nation confronting the fault line of slavery once and for all. South Carolina had seceded from the Union as 1860 ended. Mississippi, Florida, Alabama, Georgia, and Louisiana followed in January, Texas in February. The widening chasm threatened to result in war, a conflict Olmsted had already foreseen, writing to a friend in December, "The sooner we get used to the idea, the better."[33]

The moment of no return occurred with the bombardment of Union-held Fort Sumter, off Charleston, South Carolina, on April 12, 1861, and its surrender the following day. The fall of Sumter produced a surge of patriotism across the remaining United States. In Manhattan, no one could doubt that New Yorkers were ready to join the fight. The rush to buy American flags quickly exhausted the supply. A crowd overwhelmed Union Square to cheer Major Robert Anderson, Fort Sumter's last Union commander. Men young and old rushed to join up when Lincoln asked for seventy-five thousand volunteers.

Although many thought the war would be over quickly, Olmsted did not. He estimated the Civil War would "last 2 or 3 years and cost the North 600 millions of dollars."[34] Though lame and often ill, the thirty-nine-year-old Olmsted wanted to do his bit and told his father he was contemplating enlisting in the navy. He formed a home guard of his Park Keepers and drilled them on Sundays. Then, in June, a summons came from a trusted friend, a Unitarian minister named Henry Bellows, proposing a job better suited to a man of Olmsted's abilities. "I want to see you in regard to the *Resident Secretaryship* of our Sanitary Committee," Bellows wrote.[35]

With tens of thousands of recruits pouring into Washington, the inadequacy of the U.S. Army Medical Department was evident. Even if administrators in the army did not, Bellows, president of the commission, and its other founders understood what poor sanitary conditions, insufficient food, a lack of hygiene and of screening for contagious disease would mean for the health of the U.S. Army. The lessons of the British fight in Crimea a few years before were well known, where the death rate from disease among soldiers had been more than double the toll taken by enemy fire. To prevent the needless loss of lives, a man of Olmsted's capacity was needed to manage what would become a large-scale effort. Frustrated at the park and eager to join the war effort, Olmsted accepted the appointment, on June 20, 1861, as head of the newly established Sanitary Commission.

The job required him to move to Washington, D.C., and he sought and received a leave of absence from his Central Park duties. He left behind his wife and children, too, in order to serve his country. But he departed with the consolation that "the rude and fundamental work needed to the realization of the design was . . . in great measure done."[36] For the foreseeable future, he would do his duty at a time of war, setting aside his muse, listening not to his "creative fancy" but using his gifts for management and logistics as a quartermaster-at-large in support of many thousands of sick and wounded Union soldiers.

Chapter Four

MAN WITHOUT A COUNTRY

He was the Paul Bunyan of American architecture: a man
who in his own lifetime assumed legendary proportions.

—LEWIS MUMFORD

No tutor taught Olmsted journalism. He never took a course in
either horticulture or design. His school-of-hard-knocks training as
a seaman and farmhand enhanced a native instinct for deploying
men on a work site, but beyond the childhood basics, his formal
education consisted of his single semester auditing courses at Yale.
The ultimate autodidact, Olmsted taught himself landscape architecture, a field he came to define.

Richardson followed a different course in pursuing his profession. In the summer of 1859, he made a twelve-day Atlantic crossing
by steamship, traveling with Harvard classmates James Rumrill and
Frederic d'Hauteville. After landing in England, the three friends
spent what was left of August touring England, Scotland, and Ireland. Then, in September, Richardson sailed across the English
Channel, bound for France's Ecole des Beaux-Arts.

Since no American college offered professional training in the
art of building in the pre–Civil War era, a would-be designer in the
United States had little choice but to work as an apprentice to a carpenter or builder. But in Paris, at the *Section Architecture* of the
Beaux-Arts, Richardson found a fine alternative. Established in
1819, it had its own faculty and a unique curriculum. It occupied a
set of buildings on Paris's Left Bank on the site of a seventeenth-
century monastery. Charging no tuition, the Beaux-Arts welcomed

not only French students but men from around the globe. Only one American practitioner preceded Richardson, a New Yorker named Richard Morris Hunt, who had attended earlier in the decade.* To gain admission, Richardson was required to provide two documents. One was a birth certificate, since the school accepted only students between the ages of fifteen and thirty. The second, a printed form to be completed by a qualified architect, declared the applicant ready to pursue architectural studies. On September 14, 1859, the minister plenipotentiary of the United States affixed his signature to the former (undoubtedly Richardson's Harvard connections helped, not least his ties to the Adams family). The French architect Louis-Jules André signed the latter.†

With his name entered on the school's rolls, Richardson's official status became that of *aspirant.* That gained him privileges at the school's library, access to a collection of plaster casts of architectural ornaments, and permission to attend lectures. But he was not yet an official student, since becoming an *aspirant* amounted to only the first step up the Beaux-Arts' hierarchical ladder. His was a provisional admission that required he pass a battery of entrance examinations before being entitled to call himself an *élève.*

Richardson's timing seemed excellent, since the next scheduled tests began two weeks after his preliminary acceptance. Administered entirely in French, both orally and in writing, the exams would test his knowledge of pure mathematics (algebra and plane geometry), drawing, and descriptive geometry. As a child of New Orleans, a largely bilingual city, Richardson was less intimidated by the French than by the descriptive geometry, a branch of study that formed the basis for rendering three-dimensional objects on paper and with which he had no experience. It involved two-dimensional drawings known as *plans* (views of the elements of a structure from directly above); *sections* (drawings revealing details of the house's construction, floor levels, and other vertical elements as if the structure had been guillotined along a vertical axis); and *elevations,* which

---

* Two other Americans had studied architecture at the school, but neither went on to practice. The first woman admitted, American Julia Morgan, would not enroll until November 1898.
† "Minister" was the accepted title for accredited United States representatives to foreign nations until the late nineteenth century, when "ambassador" came into common use.

delineate the face of a building from the point of view of an observer
looking straight on from a horizontal vantage.

Richardson's preparation and performance disappointed: he
failed two examinations, one in drawing ornaments, the other in
mathematics. Hence his name did not appear among the fifty-six candidates accepted that November. The young man would have to wait
a full year for the next round of examinations, and John Bein's notion
that his stepson's European sojourn might last "six or nine months"
was quickly forgotten.

Always a creature who enjoyed his comforts, Richardson found the
pleasures of Paris to his liking. According to a social friend from
Harvard then studying music in Europe, "regular remittances of
money from New Orleans enabled him to live with ease."[1] Richardson shared a suite of rooms and the services of a housekeeper with
another student a kilometer from the Ecole. But he spent much of
the time at the atelier of his *patron*.

The pedagogy at the Ecole des Beaux-Arts bore little resemblance to Richardson's Cambridge experience. If he wished, he might
attend lectures devoted to architectural history, theory, perspective,
and mathematics. But attendance was not compulsory, and exams
based on the lectures were few (only in the sciences) and easily
enough prepared for without classroom time. Few *élèves* attended lectures, aside from the highly practical classes devoted to methods of
construction. Richardson and his fellow *aspirants* were more likely to
be found in independent ateliers, practicing and learning the basics
of design.[2]

Richardson had sought out as his *patron* Louis-Jules André, a
well-regarded Paris-based architect. André had been a student at the
Beaux-Arts, winning its highest honor, the coveted Grand Prix, in
1847, which permitted him to pursue architectural studies in Rome
at the expense of the French nation. After returning from his fellowship, André had opened a studio for Beaux-Arts students. Richardson would pursue his new craft under André's tutelage.

Architectural ateliers like André's were an essential adjunct
to an *école* education. At their assigned drawing boards, novices

gained exposure to the art of architectural rendering. As they earned the trust of older students, the less experienced men—the *nouveaux*—were invited to help with their elders' drawings. Eventually, when the new men went to work on their own designs, they would gain from the critiques of André on his occasional visits and the advice of the *anciens*, the older students, some of whom might have been pursuing their studies for five or even ten years. The atelier blended the sort of camaraderie Richardson enjoyed at Harvard with the tutorial atmosphere of the academy.

In preparing to retake the admissions tests, Richardson worked not only at the essentials of design but also at learning the inner workings of the Ecole des Beaux-Arts. Competition ruled at the architecture school's base of operations, the Palais des Etudes, located on the rue Bonaparte, and many men fell by the wayside along the trail to the top. In a typical year, roughly half of the hundred-odd *aspirants* gained formal admission to the second class, and over the course of the next several years, only about half of those *élèves* would perform well enough to rise to the first class. Thereafter, an even smaller coterie of the very best students competed for the Grand Prix, awarded to a single student per year and always to a Frenchman. The Ecole des Beaux-Arts aimed to winnow out the mediocre and reward the remarkable.

Performance in the *concours d'émulation* determined success or failure. Once a month, the professor of theory at the Ecole issued an assignment, or *program*, for a specified building. Usually expressed in a few words, the programs varied widely, ranging from such structures as an almshouse to a public market, a slaughterhouse to a medical school.

The *concours* were, quite simply, contests. They were of two kinds, the *esquisse* (sketch) and the *projet*, offered in alternate months. In a *concours esquisse*, students had twelve hours to consider the program *en loge*, at work in an *école* cubicle. Typically the *esquisse* assignment involved a small structure or part of a larger one, such as a façade. Before leaving the building, each student was required to submit a single drawing, the *esquisse*. Although he might converse with his direct competitors in the *concours esquisse*, consultation with either his *patron* or outsiders was forbidden.

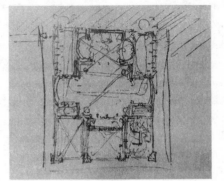

A Richardson esquisse *dating to July 1863 and his student days in Paris. Assigned to design "a casino over a hot spring," Richardson came up with an orderly, symmetrical plan of the sort the jury at the Ecole des Beaux-Arts expected.*

The task was to produce an original and rapid architectural solution, one that, whatever its eventual complexities, could be read at a glance. That was the Beaux-Arts way. When submitted, the sketch was entered in a registry by an *école* guard and assigned a number. The competition was anonymous.

A *projet rendu* (project rendering) took an assigned program further. Once again, the student submitted a preliminary *esquisse* in the allotted twelve hours but then proceeded to his atelier with a tracing of the sketch he had submitted. The competitor could then consult with his *patron* and peers on the *projet* over the next two months as he developed his design and prepared finished drawings. The rules required that the mature design remain true to the essentials of the original conception. If the drawings of the *projet* were adjudged to differ significantly from the preliminary *esquisse*, the student would be declared *hors de concours*, disqualified from the competition.

A jury of Beaux-Arts faculty reviewed each completed *esquisse* or *projet* submission and rendered a verdict. If a given submission was deemed satisfactory—the majority were not—the student gained a credit, or *valeur*. A few competitors gained a superior mark.

For much of 1860, Richardson worked to improve his drafting, regarded as primary to the architect's craft, since he was not yet eligible to enter the *concours*.* The following October, despite a brief

---

* Two of Richardson's drawings from this period survive. One is a crayon sketch of a standing male nude, based on a plaster cast made from an ancient Roman sculpture; the other, a pen-and-ink copy of a Giovanni Battista Piranesi engraving of an interior.

illness and his occasionally faltering French, he repeated the entrance exams. This time he passed, and on November 20, he was admitted to the second class of the Beaux-Arts.

Richardson took part in the next *concours* and, in the coming months, submitted sketches for four *esquisses* and designs for two *projets*. In none did he earn a passing grade, but the Beaux-Arts' standards were high, and the work difficult and unfamiliar. He was in good company, as few fresh *élèves* performed well in their initial competitions.

Richardson was paying his dues in every sense, in effect a lowly apprentice who paid for the privilege. He remitted fees to the atelier for the cost of rent and compensating the *patron*. The facilities were modest, with tall windows that permitted good light but also cold drafts. The hours spent drawing, in a room with no hot water and only smoky coal stoves for heat, were sometimes uncomfortable and a challenge for Richardson, who was, at best, an adequate draftsman.

Yet he found time to enjoy the people and the city around him. "Richardson was an excellent companion . . . fond of pleasure and society and always ready for a dinner-party or a dancing-party," remembered one friend. Even so, "[he] never allowed these things to interfere with the serious performance of his work; and many of his friends of that time will remember he not infrequently returned late to his rooms after a party to finish the night in study; or to his atelier when an exhibition of plans or drawing was in preparation."[3]

Within a matter of months, however, the war on the other side of the Atlantic would cast a cloud of gloom over Richardson's artistic life.

As the news filtered in about the Confederate bombardment of Fort Sumter in April 1861, Richardson went about his studies, enrolling in the *concours* for May and submitting an *esquisse* in June. But events at home presented him with an impossible choice, and after a summer of soul-searching, he decided he had to return to the United States.

He paused in London to visit Henry Adams, who served as amanuensis to his father, Charles Francis Adams, President Lincoln's minister to the Court of Saint James's. Henry sympathized with his friend; as he put it, the Civil War put Richardson into "a horrible position." In the young Adams's view, "his family and property are in New Orleans. He is himself a good Union man . . . but he does not want to do anything which will separate him from his family or make them his enemies."[4]

With the United States at war with itself, friends, cousins, colleagues, and even brothers enlisted in opposing armies to fight over the right to enslave people. For the twenty-three-year-old Richardson, the nation's division was personal. Since venturing north to enroll at Harvard, he had not returned to Louisiana, despite the financial support he had received. He maintained an affectionate correspondence with various family members, but finally decided he could not take the slaveholders' side in the conflict. He chose to go to Boston.

That city had become home for him after Julia Hayden had accepted his proposal of marriage in 1859. When the paddle steamer *Arabia* docked in the port of Boston on October 17, 1861, Richardson wanted nothing more than to go to Julia at her parents' home in Cambridge. Instead, his American dilemma confronted him squarely: Louisiana's secession, as Adams had warned him, rendered his passport invalid, changing his status from U.S. citizen to that of enemy alien.

After gaining provisional entry, Richardson spent the winter looking for work in the Massachusetts capital. He found nothing suitable, not least because he felt suspended between North and South: he could no more take an oath of allegiance to his fiancée's nation, the United States of America, and thereby disown his early life and family, than he could join the Confederate States of America in order to fire minié balls at Cambridge friends serving in Abraham Lincoln's army. He considered a return to New Orleans, but northern friends advised that doing so would irretrievably damage his long-term career prospects. He saw little choice, and by mid-March 1862, having bade Julia farewell once more, he was again in Paris, a man without a country.

Back at the Ecole des Beaux-Arts, he devoted himself to his studies. As he wrote to Julia, "I am just waking up to the value of time, and, feeling I may be called away at any moment, I try to make the most of my days."[5] He submitted an *esquisse* for the April *concours*—the assignment was an assembly hall for a legislature—but his entry was disqualified.

Richardson admitted to being "nervous and anxious" about the ill news that reached him from the city of his birth. By spring 1862, New Orleans was under siege. A battle near Shiloh Church outside Memphis drew precious gunboats away from the defense of the Mississippi River, leaving the Confederacy's most important port exposed to an oncoming flotilla of Union warships. Richardson wondered from afar at the fate of his mother, stepfather, and two sisters. His younger brother, William Priestley Richardson, also held a place in his thoughts, since Billy, following a path different from his own, had withdrawn from Harvard and returned home to join the Confederate ranks. Stationed near Shiloh, he wore an officer's uniform in the Thirteenth Louisiana Infantry.

Richardson clearly recognized the jeopardy his hometown faced when, on April 17, 1862, he penned his weekly letter to his fiancée. "I see that operations have been commenced against New Orleans." That meant another likely setback. As Julia phrased it, "What effect would the capture of New Orleans . . . have on [you]?"[6] Their letters were forever crossing, given the time lapse for delivery, with a fortnight or more required for a missive to cross the Atlantic.

As the eldest son in a prosperous family, Richardson knew only ease and privilege. But if New Orleans fell, the family fortunes would be ruined. Richardson's Paris life, dependent on his allowance from home, would surely get very much harder. As he told Julia, resignedly, he envisioned the end of his "hopes of receiving great aid from anything that [he] may have in New Orleans."[7]

Richardson faced penury, a prospect for which his earlier life had hardly prepared him. Within a matter of days, he learned that indeed his comfortable circumstances were no more.

"I burned with shame when I read the capture of my city and I in Paris," the forlorn expatriate wrote to his betrothed on May 16, 1862. "What is to be the end I do not see."[8]

He learned from his banker in Liverpool that he could expect no more money from his family. "From this moment," he told Julia, "I am dependent on myself and on myself alone."[9] Needing to find cheaper accommodations, he rented a room on the "not very attractive Rue Mazarin."[10] *Patron* André, aware of his pupil's need for money, arranged drafting work for Richardson in the office of architect Théodore Labrouste, then the chief architect for Paris's hospital agency.

"But continue my studies I *must*," he assured Julia. "I don't care about the want of money, but the time taken from my studies I regret."[11] His financial difficulties seemed to inspire a new appreciation of his vocation. "Every day," he mused, "I find new beauties in a profession which I already place at the head of all the Fine Arts."[12] More telling still, he earned his first *valeur*, or credit, from the Beaux-Arts jury that autumn for his design of a sculptor's house and studio.

Richardson now lived a divided life, earning a wage during the day at Labrouste's office, competing in *concours* when he could spare the time. To serve his twinned tasks, he established a regime. "I rise before eight, take a cup of coffee in my room, go to my office and remain there till half past five or six P.M. I then go to my room and dress for dinner. I dine about seven P.M. (for thirty-five cents). After my dinner I go to my room some, and think . . . until nearly nine. Then to my studio until eleven P.M."[13]

Richardson, the picture of the well-dressed young man-about-town, in a carte-de-visite image taken in Paris in 1861.

Tight finances required that he sell some of the books from the library of architectural volumes he had begun to assemble in more comfortable days, but Richardson refused to dress the part of the impoverished student. He had an account at Poole's on London's Savile Row, and on his stops in London while going to and from the United States in 1861 and 1862, the fashionable tailor provided him with such bespoke attire as "a fancy buck skin lounging vest" and "a blue milled melton lounging coat" with "silk sleeve lining."[14] Nor did his friends abandon him. One of his traveling companions in his first European days, Frederic d'Hauteville, offered to lend him the considerable sum of $500. "I give you 25 years to pay it in, or if that wont do take 50-years."[15]

Henry Adams regularly came to visit. "As often as [I] could," Adams reported, "[I] ran over to Paris, for sunshine, and there always sought out Richardson in his attic."[16] Richardson had further economized, taking up residence in a garret overlooking the rue du Bac. Although Adams professed to like nothing French but the food, he enjoyed the good company of Richardson and his flatmate, a talented Frenchman named Gustave-Adolphe Gerhardt, and their enthusiastic talk over dinner at the Palais Royal. "[The] overflow of life"—his evident enthusiasm and joy—"made Richardson so irresistible."[17]

Despite an occasional social respite, Richardson invested most of his considerable energies in learning to be an architect. He grew fond of his *patron*. The unexcitable Louis-Jules André took a restrained approach to critiquing his students. On periodic visits to the atelier, "he would pass quietly from table to table, from stool to stool, speaking little, never taking a pencil nor making a sketch, content with a wave of the hand or rub of the thumb." According to one *élève* who would go on to win the Rome prize, "in a silent language he would show us what had to be developed, enlarged, reduced in order to give a better look and nobler proportions . . . with a glance he would judge our sketches and show us the way to further development."[18] André encouraged his American pupil, helping nurture in Richardson a taste for "bigness" and "largeness of detail," and "all-embracing arches."[19]

The student began to make measurable progress at the Ecole des Beaux-Arts. Richardson didn't adopt every aspect of the French method—he wondered about the utility of color presentation drawings—but he passed examinations in mathematics and gained credits in materials *concours* for wood, stone, and iron construction,

and one each in *construction générale* and perspective.[20] He would enroll in thirty-eight *concours* and gain credit for nine. His was a record
comparable to those of other students, many of whom, like him,
worked at least part-time to earn an income. Participation in as few
as one or two *concours* per year permitted a student to remain on the
rolls, even if he never accumulated enough credits to gain promo-
tion from the second to the first class, which Richardson never did.
But the prestige of the place was invaluable, as any former student
could list himself as *un ancien élève de l'école des Beaux-Arts*. The association guaranteed respect.

Richardson's time working as an apprentice in the atelier of
Théodore Labrouste proved valuable too. Labrouste entrusted his
American junior with making preliminary drawings for the Hospice
des Incurables at Ivry, a large facility for the gravely ill poor. Richardson found other work in the offices of Jacques Ignace Hittorff, per-
forming the role of site superintendent during the construction of
the rail terminal Gare du Nord.

His friends saw how much his years abroad matured him. Two
fellow students at the Beaux-Arts believed the demands of working
and studying had actually played to Richardson's advantage. Englishman R. Phené Spiers, with whom Richardson would remain on
amiable terms the rest of his life, saw benefit in "all day working in an
office . . . and every evening in his Atelier, . . . and probably by this
accident were laid the foundations of his future career. The practical
work of which he acquired a knowledge in the working-office and on
the works," Spiers believed, gained Richardson an advantage over
those "who go to Paris to learn the art only."[21]

Fellow student and flatmate Gerhardt put it more plainly. "Mis-
fortune gave him a maturity of mind which is rarely exhibited by
young men of his age."[22] The once-privileged young man faced long
days of work and study after his allowance ended. But that also
meant he gained valuable working experience drafting and supervising construction. His life in the capital of the Second Empire also
provided him with an intimate familiarity with the streetscapes of
Paris and the nation's taste for neoclassicism.

When Robert E. Lee finally surrendered to Ulysses S. Grant at
Appomattox in April 1865, Richardson faced a new choice. He

could stay in France, become a citizen, and compete for the Rome prize. His brother, Billy, having survived the war, wrote to him in July urging his return to New Orleans, saying, "We all look to you for grand things" and "wish for your return to our midst."[23] Certainly new building would be required in New Orleans as it resumed its role as the gatekeeper to the Mississippi. His fiancée and his many friends in Boston beckoned too. Yet when he sailed for the United States in October 1865, Richardson chose a destination where he could be his own man and make his own way. New York would be the place where he launched his career.

Chapter Five

❦

CALIFORNIA DAYS

I felt the charm of Yosemite much more at the end of a week than at the end of
a day, much more after six weeks . . . and when, after having been in it, off and
on, several months, . . . I said, "I have not yet half taken it in."

—FREDERICK LAW OLMSTED

Frederick Law Olmsted's tour of duty as secretary of the Sanitary
Commission was hard fought but, in the eyes of most observers, an
extraordinary success. "Would that . . . Olmsted [was] Secretary of
War!" mused one influential New Yorker and a founder of the commission. "I believe that Olmsted's sense, energy, and organizing
faculty, earnestness, and honesty would give new life to the Administration were he in it."[1]

The task Olmsted took on posed an immense challenge. One
day into the job, he made his first survey of army camps on the outskirts of Washington. He found crowded and filthy conditions. The
soldiers habitually urinated wherever they wished, and the standard
practice of covering the previous day's toilet trench with six inches
of dirt was routinely ignored. The food, consisting of salted beef,
hardtack, and crackers that required immersion in water to be chew-
able, was rarely complemented with fruit or vegetables. Worse yet,
he saw few doctors at the ready and next to no medical supplies. He
aimed to address each of those matters.

Straightaway, however, Olmsted encountered a major obstacle
in the person of Surgeon General Clement Finley, the man in charge
of the U.S. Army Medical Department and, in theory, a partner of
the Sanitary Commission. In the coming weeks and months, Olm-

sted would repeatedly file detailed reports and recommendations with Finley and others in the government, but even after the Union Army's disastrous failure at the First Battle of Bull Run, in July 1861, they fell on deaf ears. The famously parsimonious Finley wanted to spend as few dollars as possible and certainly didn't want to invest in an effort run by an outsider. Olmsted recognized Finley's type, labeling him a "self-satisfied, supercilious, bigoted blockhead."[2]

Olmsted met Abraham Lincoln that fall in a vain attempt to get his organization on an even footing with the Medical Department. The conversation failed to produce results, but Olmsted wrote to his stepson John, who was back in New York, to share his observations. "I went to the White House to-day and saw the president," he told the nine-year-old. "He is a very tall man. He is not a handsome man. He is not graceful. But he is good. He speaks frankly and truly and straight out just what he is thinking. Commonly he is very sober but sometimes he laughs. And when he laughs he laughs very much and opens his mouth very deep."[3]

By the end of 1861, Olmsted had frustratingly little to show for his efforts on behalf of the commission. In his private life, he did have a fresh source of great happiness: on October 28, 1861, Mary had delivered a healthy baby girl. But the new arrival would be a distant joy for the most part. Though he sped to New York, arriving shortly after her birth, the delighted father could stay in New York only two weeks before returning to his work in Washington. Fred favored naming the child Content, but eventually the parents settled upon Marion.

In the new year, the Sanitary Commission finally got the opportunity to demonstrate its worth. The Peninsula Campaign aimed to capture the Confederate capital of Richmond, and the army's bold plan called for Union forces to attack Richmond from the south. That required moving the entire army by water to Fort Monroe, near the mouth of the James River, before marching north along the Virginia Peninsula to launch the assault. The invasion began in April 1862, by which time the incompetent Finley had at last been relieved of his duties. Olmsted thus became responsible for the floating hospitals.

He converted a flotilla of ordinary ships, among them the *Ocean Queen*, a side-wheeler that once belonged to Cornelius Vanderbilt. Their decks became separate wards for the care of soldiers with different ailments. He established a receiving hospital in a sea of tents on an abandoned plantation near White House, Virginia. At his orders, the Sanitary Commission, which relied upon civilian volunteers and contributions, brought clothing and hospital supplies to supplement those provided by the "deplorably insufficient" Medical Department.[4] By the time the invasion failed and the Union Army retreated in late summer, after having come within five miles of Richmond, Olmsted and his corps had cared for and safely evacuated back to northern cities some ten thousand soldiers. The Sanitary Commission demonstrated how essential it was to keeping alive both battle casualties and those suffering from typhoid and other diseases.

Mary and the children were still in New York, and for several weeks that summer Olmsted became concerned when she stopped answering his letters. Their correspondence resumed once he learned that his letters had been lost, since the family had relocated from their home at the Mount Saint Vincent convent, which had been turned into Central Park Hospital. That August, with the Peninsula Campaign wrapped up, Olmsted returned to New York, totally exhausted by his intense labors, and spent a recuperative week surrounded by family. At Mary's insistence, he agreed that his health and her workload as a single mother with a baby and three other young children demanded the family come together. He rented a house in Washington, D.C., and by November the six Olmsteds were residing on G Street.

With the Sanitary Commission's reputation on the rise, Olmsted embarked on an inspection tour of Union forces in the West, departing in February 1863. He met Ulysses S. Grant, with whom he felt an immediate camaraderie, based in part on a common resentment of politicians who too often interfered in their operations. Olmsted was back in Washington when the brutal three-day Battle of Gettysburg commenced, on July 1, and on hearing of its many casualties, he swung into action to provide relief. The first supply train to arrive in Gettysburg brought medical supplies, eggs, shoes, butter, crutches, and other goods that Olmsted had hurriedly purchased in Philadelphia. He wasn't far behind.

Under his guidance, the Sanitary Commission emerged as the largest charity ever created in the United States. He ran the operation in the only way he knew. "He works like a dog all day," reported one Sanitary Commission physician. "[He] works with steady, fever-ish intensity till four in the morning, sleeps on a sofa in his clothes, and breakfasts on strong coffee and pickles!!!"[5] But after two years, a familiar pattern emerged. First, his round-the-clock commitment to his work brought him to the verge of physical and mental collapse. Second, some of the commissioners to whom he reported took to interfering, just as some of the park board members had done in New York. Olmsted found once again that as soon as he demon-strated he could do the job as no one else could, he was bombarded with quibbles concerning expenses and an endless series of trivial demands. He began to wonder aloud whether he ought to resign.

The enervated Olmsted worried about what he would do next. In his absence, Vaux, too, had found working with Comptroller Green impossible, leading the partners to resign in May 1863 from their posts at Central Park. On his western inspection tour for the Sanitary Commission, a stop in Chicago had inspired thoughts of landscape commissions elsewhere; Olmsted thought a municipal park would serve that city well but also recognized that such thinking was purely speculative in wartime. He considered returning to publishing and even developed a prospectus for a weekly publication that would re-semble the *Atlantic Monthly*. He shared his thinking with Charles Dana, a publishing veteran he knew from his Dix and Curtis days, but his friend expressed doubt as to the viability of such a venture.*

Then, a few days later, in early August 1863, he received a letter marked "Private." Dana was passing along a job opportunity that he himself had turned down. The Mariposa Company, a large mining operation in northern California, needed a manager, and in this time of war, good candidates were few. The business had recently been acquired by eastern financiers, among them New York mayor George Opdyke.

Olmsted expressed interest in the job and traveled to New York for an interview. His solid New York reputation served him well, and

---

* Ironically, this, the most enduring of Olmsted's publishing ventures, was the one with which he had the briefest involvement. The *Nation* magazine did result from his brainstorming in 1863 with the man who became editor, E. L. Godkin, and his friend Charles Eliot Norton, but by the time its first issue appeared, in 1865, Olmsted had long since decamped to California.

after just one session with him, Opdyke and other investors offered him the position. Deciding whether to take it proved harder.

Henry Bellows tried to persuade him to stay, insisting "The country can not spare you at such a juncture."[6] Olmsted himself weighed his sense of duty to the Union, on the one hand, with the heavy burden of debt he carried, since he had still to repay the obligations incurred from the failure of his earlier publishing venture. His substantial family expenses argued for accepting the generous offer of a house with room for him and his family, $10,000 a year in salary, and five hundred shares of stock in the Mariposa Company. The chance to go west was tantalizing too for a man who liked nothing better than travel. He spent more than two weeks polling his friends and family, including his father and Mary. "I think," he wrote to her, "you had better be considering what you want me to do for you—where and how you will live, &c."[7]

In the end, the offer was too good to refuse. On September 1, 1863, Olmsted resigned from the Sanitary Commission. He would leave the Civil War behind and head for gold-crazy California.

Just getting to his new posting took Olmsted nearly two months, but the travel time offered at least one compensation. On stepping off the steamship that carried him on the trip's first leg, from New York to the Isthmus of Panama, Olmsted gazed upon a tropical landscape unlike any he had ever seen.

"Simply in vegetation it is superb and glorious and makes all our model scenery . . . very tame and quakerish," he wrote to Mary, who would stay east until Fred had made suitable living arrangements for the family in California. He was on an eye-opening adventure the likes of which he hadn't known since boyhood summer trips with his family. "I don't know when I have had such a day of delight," he mused.[8]

On board the three-masted SS *Constitution* for the Pacific Ocean portion of his trip, Olmsted was less impressed with the dull and dry landscape he saw as the steamer passed through the Golden Gate into San Francisco Bay. But this junket wasn't about scenery, and after meeting with Mariposa Company bankers in San Francisco, he set off for his new fiefdom. Getting there involved another steamship ride, this one over inland waters to reach Stockton, the closest decent-size town to Mariposa. To cover the last hundred miles he rented two horses and a coach, which carried him across the long, flat San Joaquin Valley, then into the hills, where a narrow and precarious track followed dry creek beds and climbed toward the great mountain vistas of the Sierra Nevada. Eventually he reached the Mariposa estate, which got its name from a cloud of monarch butterflies (*mariposas*) that Spanish explorers had observed a half century before.

Since an initial Mexican land grant known as Rancho Las Mariposas had been made in 1844, the seventy-square-mile estate had been owned by a series of proprietors. For more than a dozen years, the explorer and soldier General John C. Frémont held title—it was from Frémont that the Mariposa Company had purchased the property—and during that time, gold had been discovered in California. A United States territory at the time the first flakes of gold were spotted in a tailrace at John Sutter's sawmill in 1848, California underwent a dramatic transformation, becoming a state in 1850 and soon welcoming more than a quarter million people from all over the world. Most came to get rich.

As early prospectors expanded their search for gold deposits from the original strike at Coloma, Frémont's holdings, more than one hundred miles away, were found to be within the southern limits of the lode. Miners and settlers flooded into Mariposa, an irregularly shaped parcel that extended roughly eight miles north to south and eleven miles across at its widest point. The new arrivals established mining camps, the county seat of Mariposa, and the company town of Bear Valley.

On arrival, Olmsted took up occupancy in a closet-size room in a ramshackle inn. The landscape surrounding Bear Valley varied from barren moorlands to rolling hills dotted with oaks, with only a hint of green in the Sierras relieving the golden brown of withered vegetation and dusty red soil. New England had never looked like this.

Olmsted, who knew little about mining, educated himself about his new business. He crawled down mine shafts. He worried about the water supply, so essential to processing mills, and examined the company's books. At best, mining was a hit-or-miss affair: some got rich, others not, and every streak eventually came to an end. The Mariposa landscape he surveyed reflected good luck and bad, with many mines in disrepair and mills sitting idle. More worrying were ledgers that revealed losses in the range of $80,000 per month and a large debt that the New York investors had not disclosed.

He made the best of an increasingly difficult situation, devising many economies and, after cutting their pay, even settled a miners' strike. He was good at this job of managing the mining and milling operations, but in November 1863, he left the community of Mariposa for an upland expedition, one that would serve both his obligations to the company and his own hunger for scenery.

More than a decade before, late in the winter of 1851, a band of one hundred militiamen had marched into the Sierra Nevada. They were a select force, part of the Mariposa Battalion, mustered to track down a party of Miwok and Yokuts. The natives had attacked a trading post on the Fresno River the previous December, leaving three men dead.

Heading northeast, the company made slow progress, trudging through five-foot snowdrifts. They had no map—no white man had ever set foot here—but guided by a Miwok scout, they followed the waters of the Merced River.* Their objective was a rumored Native American encampment in a "deep valley." Individual soldiers took turns at the head of the column, packing the heavy snow to open a passable trail.[9]

When they reached their destination, they found a woman so old that, according to their guide, "when she was a child, the mountains were hills."[10] But on March 27, 1851, despite the blanket of snow, they found something more remarkable.

They walked into "a valley of surpassing beauty, about 10 miles in length and one mile broad." According to one soldier, "Upon either side are high perpendicular rocks, and at each end through

---

* There is disagreement regarding the first non-native person to wander into the Yosemite Valley—another vague account dates to 1833—but the March 1851 arrival of the Mariposa militiamen was certainly the first well-documented visit.

which the Middle Fork [of the Merced River] runs, deep cañons, the only accessible entrances to the Valley. The forest trees . . . are of immense height and size."[11]

Through low clouds, one cliff in particular caught the eye of Lafayette Bunnell, the battalion's twenty-seven-year-old medical officer. The sheer granite face rose toward the heavens, and in the shadow of the slanting winter light of late afternoon, El Capitan, as it was soon known, evoked "a peculiar exalted sensation [that] seemed to fill my whole being, and I found my eyes in tears with emotion."[12]

In an era when poets and scientists alike spoke reverently of the sublime, the sight left the half-frozen soldiers filled with wonder. The notion of "sublimity," described by Edmund Burke in his *Philosophical Enquiry into the Origin of Our Ideas of the Sublime and Beautiful* (1757), had wide currency for many decades. Burke and his contemporaries believed that the sight of the sublime evoked a powerful sense of awe that mixed attraction and terror, producing such paradoxical epithets as "terrible delight" and "savage beauty." Bunnell didn't put it in such terms, but he surely understood the concept.

Word of the "discovery" drifted slowly east.* In 1855, the first band of tourists glimpsed the valley's towering waterfall. The same year, an early lithograph of "Yo-Hamite Falls" went on sale in San Francisco.[13] In 1856, the magazine *Country Gentleman* dubbed the place *Yo-hem-i-ty* and called it "the most striking natural wonder on the Pacific."[14] By the end of the decade, rough-and-ready inns were rising in the vicinity, though the Yosemite Valley remained accessible only by horseback.

Olmsted understood that water, a commodity essential both to the mining business and the future of the arid region, was in short supply. Wading into the muddy Merced that autumn, he found the river barely cleared his boot tops. After deciding that only a canal could assure a reliable water supply, he embarked on an engineering foray to seek headwaters for a canal he wished to propose to the company.

---

* Native Americans, in particular the Ahwahnechee people, needed no introduction to the Yosemite Valley; their occupancy of the place extended back many centuries.

Heading into the hills, he and his pack train soon reached the end of recognizable trails. But their exploration took them into Mariposa's giant sequoia grove and, on his return to Bear Valley a few days later, Fred described the unimaginably large trees in a letter to Mary.

The *Sequoia gigantea*, he reported, "don't strike you as monsters at all but simply as the grandest tall trees you ever saw. . . . You feel they are distinguished strangers [who] have come down to us from another world." The canopy reached a height of 250 feet, and Olmsted wrote to Mary that the Mariposa Grove was among "the highest gratifications peculiar to [this] country."[15]

His days in Mariposa provided Olmsted with new insight into frontier life. Bear Valley was a churchless place where, on Sundays, "services consist of a dog fight" attended by many cheering and gambling denizens of the town. He could detect no sense of community in the "roving adventurers" around him, an ever-varying population of men prone to drunkenness and fighting.[16] Yet, on raising his eyes to the horizon line, he could see an extraordinary wilderness, one he had only begun to explore.

He contemplated El Capitan, which he could just glimpse in the distance from one of the Mariposa mines. In another letter home he described "the white cliff of Yo Semite" as thirteen times the height of Trinity Church's spire, referencing the church that was then New York's tallest building, at 284 feet.* In such juxtapositions, he recognized a paradox: his natural park in New York helped civilize a city through a simulated wilderness, but here, in truly wild central California, the wildness of the unsettled Sierras seemed more civilized to him than the mining town.

Alone during his first months, Olmsted missed his family, telling Mary, "I long for the children & you here."[17] In spring 1864, Mary traveled west with Charlotte, John Charles, and Owen, as well as Marion, now two, following the same route via Panama that Fred had

---

* In the same vein, Olmsted would describe the effect of his first glimpse of the great stand of sequoias in the Mariposa Grove as "one of the most impressive sights I ever saw—coming over one like St. Peter's" (the sight of the papal basilica in Rome had profoundly impressed him a half dozen years earlier). FLO to Mary Olmsted, October 17, 1863; FLO to Edwin Lawrence Godkin, July 24, 1864.

taken. Waiting for their ship to dock in San Francisco, Olmsted, feeling poorly once again, consulted a physician. Perhaps predictably, the lonely man suffered a mix of illnesses, and the doctor thought he knew why. "Dr. Ayres," Olmsted wrote to his father, "finds my heart is enlarged. The disease is incurable but not necessarily fatal."[18]

When the diagnosis reached physicians he knew from the Sanitary Commission, they disagreed, and their skepticism proved right. With the healing presence of his wife and family, together with the proximity of Yosemite, Olmsted's worries about his heart faded as he regained his strength.

Later in life, when he looked back at the Mariposa days, Olmsted would remember his time in the Sierras with great fondness. In particular he enjoyed two long Yosemite sojourns in the company of his family. The first began on the morning of July 14, 1864.

The Olmsted party left behind the intense heat of the valley, where the thermometer hovered near one hundred degrees day after day. California was in the third year of a severe drought and, with many streambeds dry, mining at the Mariposa estate had come to a virtual standstill for the season; with little to manage, Olmsted could afford to be away from estate matters for a time. The six family members set out for the South Fork of the Merced, accompanied by Miss Harriet Errington, a teacher who had come west with Mary and the four children; a Black man, Henry Bell, who acted as guide, groom, and cook; and two friends, geologist William Ashburner and his wife, Emilia. The well-equipped caravan consisted of ten saddle horses and two carriages, with a mule train following.

After covering some forty miles in a two-day climb through hill country to an elevation more than a mile above sea level, they made camp "in a valley with bold, craggy granite mountains around [them] and in the midst of the finest pine and fir forest in the world."[19] Beneath the cover of colossal trees and adjacent to a stream, they raised tents, including one for bathing; arranged chairs; and even scattered carpets on the forest floor. Although Olmsted returned to Bear Valley for periodic visits to tend to business matters, his family would remain in the mountains for seven unbroken weeks.

A short distance away stood the six hundred giant sequoias of the Mariposa Grove. These cinnamon-colored trees tested the visitors' imagination. "I have no simile," Mary Olmsted wrote to Calvert Vaux, "to convey to you an idea of the effect these trees produce on one." Nonetheless, she described them. "The color of the bark is . . . light tan and the sides are in great fluted lines. They are like cathedral columns or gigantic organ pipes."[20] Mary and the children had never seen anything like the "Grizzly Giant," a tree that, according to young John's measurement, was ninety-one feet in circumference.[21] The sequoias were not the only giants but shared the forest with Douglas firs and sugar pines that reached more than two hundred feet high.

The campers dined at a rough table under canvas, eating trout from the nearby stream and venison purchased from passing hunters. Having tried grizzly meat at one dinner, Miss Errington observed, "I came to the conclusion that bears of all sorts ought to be shot but not eaten."[22]

"The women have tents, the boys and I sleep out," Olmsted noted. "It is warm, but not excessively so at noon and cool enough at night to make us who sleep out careful about our fire and blankets, but we don't suffer."[23] To his friend clergyman Henry Bellows, he acknowledged something of the wonder he felt. "The night scene— those noble shafts lighted dimly by our camp-fire, [is] one of the most sublime I have seen."[24]

Olmsted had been apart from his family for much of the preceding three years, and these months in California became a time of reacquaintance. He observed with pride as Mary, a woman bred in town but newly free of the rigors of Victorian decorum, "gained quite wonderfully in courage," showing no fear in "dash[ing] up the steepest declivities, where I a little prefer not to follow."

To his father in Connecticut, Olmsted wrote of the children, with whom he was able to spend more time than his East Coast work had ever permitted. His eyes opened to the precocious Charlotte, age nine, "a nice young woman, simple, straight-forward and self possessed," who had become her elder brother John's "master in everything." Owen, his seventh birthday a few weeks away, remained "the perfect cub," a curious boy who was into everything, "[more]" prone to fall anywhere but on his feet than ever." Little Marion, the baby of the family and not yet three, tottered about as she hungrily imbibed language of all sorts, including the German, French, and Spanish she heard in the polyglot community at Mariposa. As for Olmsted, he took better care of himself, "giving myself less to do, I go to bed earlier and rise with more regularity."[25]

For the children, this expedition was an adventure, one that brought to mind *The Swiss Family Robinson,* a book they read that spring after friends back East sent them a copy. The fictional story of a shipwrecked family making the best of a strange life in uncharted territory seemed not so far removed from their experience as they moved into an unfamiliar, even mystical locale. In mid-August, the Olmsteds left the great wood, packing up to relocate even deeper into the wilderness, this time in the Yosemite Valley, for the second part of their summer adventure.

Unlike the unsuspecting soldiers who stumbled upon the place thirteen years earlier, Olmsted approached with foreknowledge. He had never been there—fewer than a thousand non-natives had—but he had read a number of first-person accounts of the isolated valley, including one by newspaperman Horace Greeley, who wrote of his 1859 visit, "I know no single wonder of nature on earth which can claim superiority over Yosemite."[26] But even people far away no longer had to rely on mere words. They had pictures to examine, courtesy of the new medium of photography—in particular, the starkly beautiful albumen prints of Carleton Watkins.

Born in Oneonta, New York, in 1829, Watkins moved to California in his early twenties. After working as a carpenter in Sacramento, he caught on as an assistant to a daguerreotypist. The medium of photography was barely a decade old, and Watkins soon began calling himself a "photographicist." He moved on from the one-of-a-kind daguerreotypes, positive images on silvered metal plates, and ambrotypes, on glass.[27] New glass negatives permitted multiple prints of a single image, broadening the market for pictures from the few who wanted portraits of themselves to the many who might purchase prints of urban scenes and rural landscapes.

Having become a view man rather than a portrait taker, Watkins had set out to record the beauties of Yosemite in 1861. He carried a new camera, an unusually large one made to his specifications by a local cabinetmaker to accommodate eighteen-by-twenty-two-inch negatives. He fitted his "Mammoth Camera," as he called it, with a special landscape lens. He hoped its wide-angle view would enable him to record the vast rock formations that constituted the backdrop of the Yosemite Valley.

The journey from his studio at the corner of Clay and Kearny Streets in San Francisco wasn't easy. With no cart path to travel the last forty miles, Watkins relied upon a dozen mules to carry his equipment along a narrow trail. The load included two cameras—the Mammoth and another to record stereographic images—as well as tripods, a dark tent, quantities of chemicals, processing trays, and numerous sturdy wooden cases carefully packed with the four-pound glass plates. He and an assistant required blankets, cooking kettles, foodstuffs, and all manner of other goods to sustain themselves for a period of weeks. All told, they packed some two thousand pounds of equipment and supplies.[28]

Making pictures involved much more than planting a tripod and snapping a camera's mechanical shutter. The state of the art was wet-plate photography, a time-limited process that, in the field, began in the dark tent, where a glass plate was coated with a syrupy mixture called collodion that contained silver nitrate. The collodion was then sensitized with other chemicals, and the plate, still damp, was inserted into the camera. After Watkins exposed it by removing the lens cap for several seconds, the plate, in its special lightproof holder, was returned to the dark tent, where it was developed and fixed. All this had to be done before the emulsion dried, typically within fifteen minutes.

Shooting first in the Mariposa Grove and then in the Yosemite Valley, Watkins employed both cameras to make images of the Grizzly Giant, El Capitan, Half Dome, the Cathedral Rocks, and other memorable natural sights. After returning to San Francisco, he sent thirty of his mammoth prints and a hundred stereographs to the East Coast, prior to Olmsted's departure for the West Coast. The pictures were met with an eager audience at the Goupil gallery in New York, where Ralph Waldo Emerson expressed his admiration for the giant prints. Oliver Wendell Holmes, a noted poet, essayist, and early proponent of photography, hailed them as "a perfection of the art which compares with the finest European work."[29]

An early Carleton Watkins image of Yosemite's towering El Capitan.

Photography exercised a new power over the American imagination. Photographs on view at the Mathew Brady Gallery that season altered the public perception of the Civil War. The bodies stacked after the September 1862 Battle of Antietam, reported the *New York Times*, "[brought] home to us the terrible reality and earnestness of War."[30] In contrast, Watkins's images conveyed a dreamier reality of sights few easterners had seen. The new nation had always prided itself on its natural wonders. Thomas Jefferson cited the extraordinary scale of the woolly mammoth and bragged that weasels were larger in America than in Europe. But Watkins's pictures offered hard evidence of American grandeur. A man pictured at the foot of the Grizzly Giant looked Lilliputian. There was a Brobdingnagian waterfall. To some, these unspoiled places brought to mind the paradise of Genesis before the fall; to them, the place looked like an American Garden of Eden.

Artists who examined Watkins's pictures saw spectacular pictorial possibilities. Painter Albert Bierstadt, a New York acquaintance of Olmsted's and one of the notables who had recommended him to the Central Park board years before, was inspired to spend seven weeks at Yosemite in 1863, working on preliminary sketches of its wonders. The resulting canvas, the luminous *Valley of the Yosemite*, was a sensation when it went on display in New York in April 1864.

In making his photographs, Watkins employed no tricks. Rather than emphasizing the picturesque, he strove to convey an impression of what he witnessed. His uncluttered composition offered straightforward views, tightly framed so as to exclude flanking forests, the river below, or other landscape features. His lens captured the planes of granite cliff faces, illuminated by the brilliant light. The nature of the collodion process meant that few clouds were recorded, but that served to bring the monumental stone walls forward.

Olmsted was familiar with Watkins and his work. One of the photographer's earliest commissions had been to make more than fifty views of the Mariposa estate that Olmsted now managed. He admired Watkins's photos so much he purchased two sets of the Yosemite images and sent them back East to his most trusted confidants, his father and Calvert Vaux. Having sensed that he and Watkins shared a sixth sense for landscape, Olmsted now wanted to lay his own eyes on Yosemite and explore the immense glacial gash for himself.

After an easy morning's ride due north, Olmsted got his first, inperson glimpse of the Yosemite Valley. Along with Mary, three of the children, and their servant Bell, Olmsted arrived at the rim on Sunday afternoon, August 14, 1864. With the return of the horses to the Mariposa Grove, the rest of the party would join them two days later.

Standing at the rocky precipice today known as Inspiration Point, Olmsted looked down into the great gorge. He could see the Merced River a thousand feet below, meandering peacefully through green meadows and sheltering trees. When he looked up, great variegated mountains rose like sentries around the perimeter, softened by wisps of smoke, the sunlight catching the ash in the air. For generations Native American inhabitants had used fire to manage forest and grasslands, partly to encourage the growth of black oak trees, prized for their acorns, which thrived in open sunlight.[31] White fleecy clouds overhead added to the atmospheric effects.

Olmsted and company descended slowly on a steep trail to reach the floor of the long, narrow valley. They chose as their camping place a spot beside the quiet waters of the Merced. John, a month short of his twelfth birthday, noted in his journal, "We have very steep mountains all around us [and] we are . . . in full sight of the Yo-Semite falls."[32] Its three-tiered drop of 2,425 feet made it the tallest waterfall in North America.

The sight resembled nothing Olmsted had ever seen, a natural fortress of "half a mile of perpendicular or overhanging rock." Yet he didn't find the place "frightful or fearful." Its quietude reminded him of home, "as sweet & peaceful as the meadows of [Connecticut's] Avon."[33]

For a man accustomed to shaping pastoral scenes with composed vistas of meadows and lakes and copses of trees, this immense place could not help but remind Olmsted of human limitations. Still, even if this landscape defied the hand of man, molded by infinitely greater natural forces, Olmsted understood it would require the intervention of men to preserve it for future generations.

In the spring of 1864, John Conness, a second-year senator from California, directed the attention of his colleagues in the upper house to a quiet place on the other side of the continent. Buttressed by a set of Carleton Watkins's stereographs, he presented them with a draft bill calling for the protection of the Mariposa Grove and the Yosemite Valley. He explained from the Senate floor that he spoke on behalf of gentlemen "of fortune, of taste, and of refinement"—one of whom included "Fred Law Olmsted"—and that "there were no other things like [Yosemite] on earth."[34]

Despite the nation's preoccupation with the war—Washington more nearly resembled a military depot than a national capital—the Senate approved Conness's unprecedented legislation, as did the House of Representatives. The law granted to the State of California 60.4 square miles of federal land, encompassing both Yosemite Valley and the Mariposa Big Tree Grove. It charged the state with preserving the land for "public use, resort, and recreation," but the words that meant the most were "inalienable for all time."[35] California's governor was required to appoint eight commissioners, in addition to himself, to plan governance and anticipate the future. Though precise strictures remained to be specified, the intent was clear: this Edenic piece of California was to be preserved forever. The law was a founding moment, a key precedent for the national parks movement in the years to come.

The bill landed on the president's desk. In all likelihood, Conness showed the Watkins images to Mr. Lincoln, his friend and political ally, and on June 30, 1864, the president affixed his signature.

As required by the statute, California governor Frederick Low named a mix of men to sit on the board, none of whom would be compensated. Some had political and business connections, others possessed expertise in geology and mining. He placed Olmsted at its head.

Olmsted took action the moment he heard the governor had made his role official. At his own expense, he dispatched two surveyors to start mapping the boundaries of the Yosemite Valley. He wanted to get a draft plan underway before the storms of winter. He didn't have to be told that the pristine territory faced real and immediate dangers. He had ridden past steam-powered sawmills that already dotted much of the route from Mariposa to Yosemite, one less than five miles from the Mariposa Grove.[36] He grasped that mining interests could hardly be far behind—whatever the fortunes of the Mariposa Company, men would always be seeking the next strike. With sheep already grazing on nearby slopes, farms and homesteaders were also beginning to encroach.

But the task wasn't a simple matter of prohibition, as the grant mandated that the new reserve be made accessible for "public use, resort, and recreation." Roads to and through Yosemite would be required for the transport of tourists, because at present, access could be gained only after a horseback ride of forty miles, much of it single file along narrow trails. Olmsted instructed his surveyors to make their map with lines of access in mind.

Over the course of the ensuing eleven months, he would sharpen his thinking. "I am preparing a scheme of management for the Yosemite," he wrote to his father, "which is far the noblest public park, or pleasure-ground, in the world."[37] Although this new scenic reservation was vastly different from Central Park, circumstances back East did inform his thinking. He had observed the evolution of his native region's landscape as virtually all of New England's virgin forest had been cleared. The quiet of the woods and pasture was forever shattered by the locomotive. While the Hudson Valley had inspired a school of painters, including Bierstadt, to record pastoral America, the bucolic places they worshipped were increasingly criss-crossed with railroad lines and dotted with industry. The wildness and wilderness that men like his father had known and cherished as boys was becoming harder to find, and despoiled streams and smoky skies were commonplace.

In consultation with other members of the board, Olmsted worked at what was, in effect, a manifesto. The document that emerged was largely his work, since none of the other commissioners brought to the task the mix of vision, pragmatism, and experience Olmsted did. In the absence of any precedent for setting aside federal land as a "scenic reservation," the job required original thinking, and Olmsted settled into the task of setting parameters and explaining an underlying philosophy.

Although the Yosemite Act specified no deadline for a park plan, Olmsted knew all too well the power of politicians, having experienced their interference in New York during his Central Park days and later in Washington when he headed the Sanitary Commission. This time, however, he looked not to yield to their power but to harness it. On learning that the Speaker of the House of Representatives, Schuyler Colfax of Indiana, was taking a cross-country tour to California and planned to stop in Yosemite, Olmsted set out to make him a sponsor of the park. An invitation sent through channels worked, and on August 7, 1865, after a four-day journey from San Francisco, Colfax arrived at Yosemite.

The Speaker drew a crowd, as his entourage of seventeen was among the largest to visit since the Mariposa Battalion fourteen years earlier. Olmsted had inserted himself into the company of twelve men and five women, which also included East Coast journalists Albert Richardson of the *New York Tribune* and Samuel Bowles of the highly respected *Springfield* (Massachusetts) *Republican*, and several members of the commissioners.

After pausing to look down on the splendors of what Bowles called "the Happy Valley," the Speaker headed for the valley floor.[38] The descent required two hours, going "down, down, among sharp rocks and dizzy zigzags," followed by much ferrying of equipment to the campsite. Once they reached the riverbed of the Merced, they found the view stunning. The "stupendous wall" of surrounding cliffs, Richardson of the *Tribune* noted, "confuse[s] the mind. By degrees, day after day, the sight of them clears it, until, at last, one receives a just impression of their solemn immensity."[39]

Olmsted waited a day for his visitors to acclimate; then, on Wednesday, August 9, he convened what would be, in effect, the last meeting of the Yosemite board. But the voluminous report Olmsted had written—eight thousand words long—was clearly aimed at a larger audience.

He began reading the fifty-two-page document. During the "darkest hours" of the Civil War, he told his audience, the images of Watkins and Bierstadt "had given the people on the Atlantic some idea of the sublimity of the Yo Semite."[40] In response, Congress had wisely acted to preserve the place. The report described in detail what made the great chasm unique, with its own mini-climate, rich vegetation, waterfalls, and snowy peaks in the distance. "The deepest beauty of nature, not in one feature or another . . . but all around and wherever the visitor goes, constitutes the Yo Semite the greatest glory of nature."

Like a barrister arguing a case, he shifted to the matter of conservation. He talked business first, citing the "obvious pecuniary advantage" in sights "that are attractive to travellers." He pointed out the example of the Alps, where tourism brought prosperity to innkeepers, farmers, and transportation businesses. A more accessible Yosemite, he suggested, would become a similar source of wealth for the state and even the nation.

He moved to the matter closest to his own heart. As he saw things, one duty of a republican government was to enhance its citizens "pursuit of happiness" by setting aside "great public grounds for the free enjoyment of the people." Echoing his pitch for Central Park almost a decade earlier, he explained that "it is a scientific fact that the occasional contemplation of natural scenes of an impressive character, particularly if this contemplation occurs in connection with relief from ordinary care, change of air and change of habits, is favorable to the health and vigor of men and especially to the health and vigor of their intellect." The countryside, the rural, and the un-

Olmsted on the floor of Yosemite (second from left, seated) with his audience of politicians—among them Speaker of the House Schuyler Colfax—and journalists in 1865.

spoiled were, he argued, quite simply health-giving. They might even make people who experience them smarter.

The surroundings silently reinforced his words. Olmsted spoke not in some sweltering interior space, but on the floor of the valley where the men and women were subject to what Olmsted called "the power of scenery." Just as he described it, they sat surrounded by "the miles of scenery where cliffs of awful height and rocks of vast magnitude and of varied and exquisite coloring, are banked and fringed and draped and shadowed by the tender foliage of noble and lovely trees and bushes, reflected from the most placid pools, and associated with the most tranquil meadows, the most playful streams, and every variety of soft and peaceful pastoral beauty."

He added an American slant to his argument. In Great Britain and Ireland, he pointed out, more than a thousand parks existed, but they were private parks. The price of their maintenance exceeded the cost of the national school system, yet regular access to the properties was limited to "less than one in six thousand of the whole population." As a bastion of democracy, Olmsted insisted, the United States must be different. It ought to be a nation where "the choicest natural scenes in the country . . . [are] laid open to the use of the body and of the people."

He got specific concerning Yosemite's future, recommending a road leading to it and a carriage drive inside the valley. Giving access "at a moderate rate" was essential for people of average means to make the journey, yet a balance needed to be struck between access and overuse. Nothing should be done that damaged "the natural conditions of the ground and presenting an unpleasant object to the eye in the midst of the scenery."

To these powerful Republicans, no doubt more than a little of what Olmsted said rang true, with its mix of patriotism and pragmatism. One man who got wind of the speech confided in a mutual friend that he regarded Olmsted as a man who "looks far ahead . . . with broader, deeper notions" than those around him.[41]

The document Olmsted read to his audience brought the commission's work to an end. Having made a set of recommendations, he and the other members of the board resigned, terminating the Yosemite commission. They passed the baton back to the politicians, whose turn it was to act—or not—upon the legislative actions suggested in the report.

Olmsted made some minor edits and corrections to the working draft after writing to Carleton Watkins to ask his advice on behalf of the commission.[42] Then he forwarded a clean, fair copy to the legislature that bore the title "Preliminary Report upon the Yosemite and Big Tree Grove." He assumed that the recommendations would be published in order to engender public discussion.

However, no money had been allocated to print it. Then a further obstacle emerged when two members of California's geological survey, both of whom had served on the commission, worried that monies appropriated for Yosemite—Olmsted's report recommended an expenditure of $37,000, mostly for building roads—might reduce the survey's budget. In the end, the report was tabled, and no would see it in print in its author's lifetime. Always a careful keeper of records, however, Olmsted stowed the thick sheaf of hand-written sheets into a file for posterity.*

Yet his contemporaries would not be left entirely unaware of his argument, because Olmsted had so wisely timed his presentation to coincide with the visit to Yosemite of influential easterners; his message would not be forgotten. Their days in the woods left his listeners with striking memories, and a fortnight later, addressing a grand banquet given in his honor in San Francisco, Speaker Colfax demonstrated that he had been paying attention. He recommended to his audience of wealthy and influential San Franciscans that their state ought to put in place "wise legislation" concerning Yosemite.[43] If they did, he predicted, the place would be visited by thousands. Others who had accompanied Colfax would write about their journey. Samuel Bowles's memoir appeared the following year. After their "week in the [Yosemite] woods," he wrote, "we [were] glad to see the washerwoman, but we lament that no more, save in memory, shall these eyes behold these scenes of infinite beauty and sublimity."[44]

Albert Richardson's account of Yosemite's wonders followed a year later. An evocative writer, he described the view from Inspiration Point, where one looks "down into Yosemite as one . . . would view the interior of some stupendous roofless cathedral, from the top of one of its roofless walls." He reported on the wonders he saw, detailing the towering walls (El Capitan, he thought, should be called "Mount Abraham Lincoln"). He concluded that, "on the whole, Yosemite is the most wonderful feature of our continent" and admitted to envying Olmsted, "who with his family, with horses, tents and books, remained for several weeks, moving from day to day, and encamping wherever fancy dictated." Richardson understood and approved of the emerging plan to set aside "pleasure grounds for the people of the United States and their heirs and assigns forever."[45]

If he had chosen them himself, Olmsted could have picked no better voices to spread his park philosophy. Even if his report

---

* The report would appear eighty-seven years later, when Laura Wood Roper, subsequently the author of *FLO: A Biography of Frederick Law Olmsted* (1973), published it, in *Landscape Architecture*, in 1952. She had come across the document in the Olmsted files in Brookline, Massachusetts.

remained unpublished, these men helped assure Olmsted's ideas had buoyancy.

For Olmsted, the weeks in the Sierras were therapeutic, and he reported to his father, "I [gain] health constantly while in the mountains." During this time away from his duties at Mariposa, Olmsted and a small party of men, including stepson John, hiked—although in Fred's case, his game leg meant he rode—high into the Sierras. They reached an elevation "over 12,500 feet above the level of the seas—and a thousand feet or more above the line of perpetual snow and of tree and shrub vegetation." The journey wasn't without inconvenience. "Every morning I found the water in my canteen under my pillow frozen," noted Olmsted, but in general he found the "Yo Semite . . . more beautiful than we had been led to anticipate."[46]

The youngest members of his family also thrived in this unspoiled landscape. Mornings were spent under the discipline of Miss Errington, reading and learning French; they spent afternoons catching butterflies, picking wildflowers, bird-watching, and shooting in a wilderness worthy of Paul Bunyan.[47] "I wish you could see the children," Olmsted wrote to their grandfather. "They all look so well."[48]

The family would remain in California for another year, and as a man who took his work to heart, Olmsted would take personally the continuing failure of the Mariposa mining business. The goal of the business was simple: extract gold from the earth. But the cost of employing hundreds of men and of maintaining and running mines and machinery, no matter how carefully Olmsted trimmed and conserved expenses, was exceeding the value of the gold mined. Earnings would go up briefly in November 1864 when, with the return of the rains, the mills resumed running. But a series of bad months followed as the veins beneath the seventy-square-mile grant in the Sierra Nevada foothills continued to underproduce. By early 1865, Olmsted's pay, dependent upon profits, diminished before ceasing altogether. He spent much of the late winter in 1865 in San Francisco dealing with bankers, trying to salvage what he could before the business collapsed.

Luckily, new possibilities presented themselves. A landscape commission came his way to design the twenty-acre Mountain View Cemetery in Oakland. He accepted the job and earned a $1,000 fee. His work on Mountain View was also a timely reminder of the joy he found in design, a skill he had set aside to administer the Sanitary Commission and the Mariposa mines. He welcomed an invitation from the trustees of the College of California, a new institution in an as-yet-unnamed town north of Oakland, for which he developed a preliminary plan for a campus, a residential development, and a park. The commission to design what would become Berkeley was Olmsted's first chance to think through a community from inception, and it inspired him to ponder even greater possibilities in landscape design.*

In a series of letters from the East Coast, Calvert Vaux made a persuasive case for his friend to return to New York. He offered two incentives: First, they might collaborate on a proposed new pleasure ground in Brooklyn, and second, though their work with Central Park had formally ended in 1863, Vaux was trying to get himself—and, in absentia, Olmsted too—rehired to proceed with the park's construction. Not one but two significant park jobs could come their way.

Thus a mix of circumstances helped point Olmsted back in the direction of landscape architecture. In an unexpected way, his thinking about Yosemite, both the experience of the place and the challenge posed by its preservation, became a driving force in Olmsted's recommitment to the land.

Olmsted's California obligations drew to a close. His inability to save the foundering Mariposa Company weighed heavily, and the stress no doubt contributed to the deterioration of his eyesight and his almost constant headaches. But his transparent and careful negotiations with the bankers helped him emerge with his reputation intact

---

* Although Olmsted's plan was not fully implemented, traces of it can still be glimpsed alongside later contributions from the landscape architecture firm that would bear the Olmsted name into the next generation and beyond.

as he readied for the long journey home. Together with his family, in October 1865, he boarded a Nicaraguan steamer in San Francisco bound for Panama; a second sea journey followed, traversing the Gulf of Mexico and then north to New York.

In the larger scheme of his life, the West Coast time can be seen as little more than a two-year detour, a time in exile. Yet the weeks spent with his family in the shadow of the great trees with the cinnamon-colored trunks were among the healthiest and most inspirational of his entire life. They reminded him of a deep need that he had suppressed in accepting the Mariposa job for monetary reasons.

"I love beautiful landscapes," he wrote to Vaux, "better than anybody else I know." He believed more strongly than ever that park making amounted to social engineering, that parks spread democratic ideals. If he couldn't quite bring himself to call himself an artist ("I don't feel strong on the art side," he admitted to Vaux), he would acknowledge that Central Park, whatever its challenges, had improved the lives of people across the social spectrum.[49] His California time had brought him full circle, allowing him to realize that, if his finances permitted, he wanted to return to the work of landscape design.

After his exposure to Yosemite, Olmsted possessed a new and richer appreciation of the diversity of the unspoiled American landscape. Conserving that extraordinary valley would never truly be an Olmsted project in the way that many parks, campuses, and other commissions would, but the report he read to the assembled body of politicians, journalists, and his fellow commissioners laid out the philosophical foundations for preserving unspoiled places. His work would have a profound and national impact in the years to come, and in time, his big thoughts concerning the American wilderness would provide the underpinning for the national parks movement. In California, as at Central Park, Olmsted demonstrated an extraordinarily rare capacity to set aside the self-interest of the present in favor of the well-being of future generations.

Chapter Six

NEW NEIGHBORS IN NEW YORK

Mr. Richardson [is] a gentleman trained in the most thorough French technical
school familiar with European roads and Sanitary Engineering and of highly
cultivated tastes with a strong practical direction.

—FREDERICK LAW OLMSTED, 1870[1]

The name Olmsted meant something in New York. Although he
lacked a college education, his work as a writer and publisher in
the 1850s had gained Fred Olmsted standing among the city's
intelligentsia. The making of the universally admired Central
Park greatly elevated his status. On his return to New York in late
1865, despite a lengthy absence, his remained a celebrated name
in America's largest city.

In contrast, when Henry Hobson Richardson arrived that au-
tumn, after almost six years in Europe, he was an unproven stranger.
A number of large, brassbound boxes announced his presence at a
rooming house in Brooklyn. Stacked in the hall and marked both
Paris and Etat Unis, the cases were packed with Richardson's profes-
sional library, including essential works by French architect Eugène
Viollet-le-Duc and medievalist John Ruskin, the British author of
Stones of Venice and *Seven Lamps of Architecture*.

Richardson pursued his one American job prospect, with a
builder named Roberts whose path he crossed in Paris. Based in
Brooklyn, Roberts—his first name is lost to us—had suggested a
partnership should his Beaux-Arts-trained countryman return to
America. Roberts proved good to his word, but the partnership

ended after barely six months. Apparently, their notions of the business differed, since Richardson wrote to his brother, "Mr. Roberts & I part good friends," despite "the complete want of sympathy between us."[2] Effective May 1, 1866, the architect went into business for himself.

Richardson fared better in finding suitable accommodations. He made the acquaintance of a woman who, along with her grown son, resided two doors down the hall at the same boardinghouse. One day she asked Richardson, as a man with expertise in buildings, to inspect a home she hoped to buy on Staten Island. On seeing it, he not only approved of the "pretty little house" but, that very evening, approached her with a proposition.

"Mrs. P.," he said, "I want you to take me as a boarder."[3]

He had impressed her with his fashionable clothes and "indescribable air of ease." She observed that he took long walks and cold baths and "had the look of a man in perfect health and with much physical vigor." She did notice his stutter, though that distracted her less than his preference for speaking French.

Still, she hesitated. "Why, Mr. Richardson, I know nothing about keeping boarders."

"No matter if you do not," he replied. He would be happy, he told her, so long as she served him coffee "so strong that you can never wash the cup white after using."

An understanding was reached, and Richardson took up occupancy in the rear parlor of her house. He studied his architectural texts and regaled his landlady and her son with stories of Paris and of Europe's cathedrals, palaces, and ancient sites. He readily admitted that his stay in Paris had been possible only given the generosity of his family and then his friends. He confided that he planned to marry Julia Hayden of Boston when his financial circumstances improved. Then, just a few weeks into his stay, he told her he could no longer afford to pay his rent.

Mrs. P. saw something in this "cultured gentleman—for gentleman he was, in every sense of the word"—and chose to be generous. "Do not be troubled," she said. "Something favorable will turn up after a while. Stay on with us."

Richardson, too, remained hopeful. "[I] am prepared for a hard time for some months," he wrote to his brother, "but have confidence in ultimate success. All I want now is an order."[4]

On January 9, 1865, Calvert Vaux had written to Olmsted in California, "You may be interested in the Brooklyn affair."[5] The matter in question concerned the creation of a major new urban oasis.

The notion of a park for the city of Brooklyn was hardly new. With the enthusiastic public embrace of Manhattan's greensward north of Fifty-Ninth Street, a consensus quickly emerged on the other side of the East River: being the competitive younger sibling that it was, Brooklyn, then an independent city, also needed such a park.* In 1859, as it had done to establish Central Park, the State of New York authorized the creation of the Brooklyn Park Commission.

The new commission considered several options for the park's location before settling on three hundred acres surrounding a city reservoir on one of Brooklyn's highest hills. It retained Colonel Egbert Viele, Olmsted's old boss at Central Park, to draft a scheme for the Mount Prospect site, and Viele delivered a "Plan for the Improvement of Prospect Park." That proposal had been mothballed in 1861 when the outbreak of the Civil War led to a construction moratorium.

In late 1864, with a Union victory seemingly assured, James S. T. Stranahan, president of the Brooklyn Park Commission, restarted the process. A railroad builder, former congressman, and owner of the Union Ferry Company, which connected the city of Brooklyn with Manhattan, Stranahan was, according to the editors of the *Brooklyn Eagle*, "a man of grand ideas; his confidence in the future . . . boundless [and] nothing appears impossible to him."[6] In Stranahan's opinion, the proposed site was too small. He also thought Viele's plan was unimaginative, since the West Point–trained engineer envisioned few changes to the existing landscape, such as lakes and lawns of the sort that Olmsted and Vaux had designed into Central Park.

---

* Brooklyn would not become a borough of New York City until January 1, 1898.

Stranahan, wanting a second opinion, saw an obvious and available source just across the river and reached out to Calvert Vaux.

"Stranahan induced me to go over the other day," Vaux told Olmsted in his January 1865 letter, "& examine the site with him."[7]

While the two men walked together on a wet winter Saturday, Stranahan told Vaux he wished "to increase the boundaries . . . some considerable extent."[8] Vaux, who had already examined the site on his own, immediately offered two suggestions: to shift the proposed parkland to the west and to add considerable acreage to the south. That would push Flatbush Avenue, a well-trafficked artery that bisected Viele's plan, outside the park boundaries; add more than two hundred acres to the total area; and result in a self-contained park.

When Vaux wrote to Olmsted to describe his conversation, he enclosed a crude sketch. Rough as it was, it indicated a "Hilly Region," a "Proposed Pond of say 40 Acres," and the "Principal natural Entrance from Brooklyn."[9]

The Olmsted–Vaux transcontinental correspondence in the months that followed would regularly circle back to the proposed park in Brooklyn. Another recurring topic was the former partners' possible reengagement with Central Park. But Vaux's overarching concern was his earnest wish to persuade Olmsted to resume their collaboration—in Brooklyn, Manhattan, and wherever else they could find landscape design work.

Olmsted liked the idea but wavered. "My heart really bounds (if you don't mind poetry)," Olmsted wrote in March from San Francisco, "to your suggestions that we might work together [again]."[10] But he also acknowledged a grave concern that, with his considerable family expenses, he might not be able to earn a decent living making landscapes.

Vaux refused to take no for answer. He wrote repeatedly, not always waiting for Olmsted's replies at a time when a month or more was usually required for a letter to reach the opposite coast. Alternately wheedling and demanding, he even invoked the Almighty in support of Olmsted's return to landscape architecture: "He cannot have anything nobler in store for you."[11]

During the weeks Olmsted spent preparing his Yosemite report on the West Coast, Vaux gained two hard-won victories in New York.

In June 1865, with the war recently ended, the Brooklyn Park commissioners engaged him to plan their park along the enlarged lines he had outlined to Stranahan. Then, on July 26, 1865, the Central Park commissioners reappointed "Messrs Olmsted & Vaux . . . Landscape Architects to the Board." Though Olmsted hadn't formally agreed to partner again with Vaux, he soon would, lured by the work he loved and persuaded by the two important jobs. Much later Olmsted acknowledged the essential role his friend had played twice in reorienting his life toward landscape architecture. "But for his invitation," he admitted, "I should not have been a landscape architect. I should have been a farmer."[12]

On November 22, 1865, Fred, Mary, and the four children finally steamed through the Narrows into New York Harbor aboard the *Ericson*, exhausted from a journey that consumed forty-one days, including the rail crossing of Panama. On the quay stood Calvert Vaux, who had found rooms for the family at Mrs. Neeley's boardinghouse, located on East Fourteenth Street, a convenient walk from Vaux's home on Eighteenth Street.

Once again in the same city, their business began anew at Vaux's offices, at 110 Broadway, as Olmsted, Vaux & Company, Landscape Architects. One task demanded their immediate attention. Vaux's preliminary survey had met with approval almost six months earlier, but now the reunited partners needed to deliver a detailed plan for the new Brooklyn park. They had a mere six weeks before the due date of January 1, 1866.

In the absence of paid work, Richardson kept his spirits up by seeking the company of the most imaginative of his New York peers. In a city where the arts rested in the hands of a few, he found what he desired at the Century Association.

The social club occupied a converted dwelling on East Fifteenth Street. The principal founders of what was originally called "The Century," led by William Cullen Bryant and painter Asher Durand, wanted a place of sociability for a hundred of New York's "authors, artists, and amateurs."[13] According to its constitution, the club, founded in 1846, was to be a meeting place for "the cultivation of a taste for letters and the fine arts, and social enjoyment."[14] With the club approaching its twentieth anniversary, its membership, no longer limited to one hundred members, tilted toward moneyed men of business, though the names of professionals in the arts also dotted the rolls. On Richardson's club visits, he was likely to encounter painters Albert Bierstadt, Jervis McEntee, and Frederic Edwin Church; publisher George Palmer Putnam; and numerous architects, including Calvert Vaux and Richard Morris Hunt. Another member, Frederick Law Olmsted, had pledged on the same day as Vaux in 1859.

The Century was a place for drinking, smoking, and conversation among the main men behind the first wave of high culture in the United States. With his mix of New Orleans gentility, Harvard pedigree, Ecole des Beaux-Arts bona fides, and, in particular, his gift for conviviality, Richardson rapidly passed muster, becoming a member in 1866. But he also saw the irony of his role as a man-about-town. "Look at me, I wear a suit made by Poole, of London, which a nobleman might be pleased to wear *and—and—and—*" he observed in his rapid stammer, "*and* I haven't a dollar to my name."[15]

Despite new friends, these were hard days for Richardson. His mother, age sixty-three, died in New Orleans, though he chose not to take the long journey to the city of his birth to mourn her. He found consolation closer to home, in visits to Boston, with fiancée Julia Hayden. To pay his bills, he sold a collection of books from his college years, which he had left in storage in Massachusetts. "With the proceeds of the sale," reported a friend, "[Richardson] prepared for another trial of patience."[16]

On workdays, he took the ferry from Staten Island to Manhattan and walked up lower Broadway to the Trinity Building, where he occupied an office lent him by Emlen T. Littell, a promising young architect.[17] Though two years Richardson's junior, Littell had already built an impressive stone Gothic church on Madison Avenue.* But the two men were not partners, and as Richardson approached his one-year anniversary back in the United States, he remained utterly without professional prospects.

---

* The Church of the Incarnation, completed the previous year, still stands at the corner of Madison Avenue and Thirty-Fifth Street.

His first big opportunity came to him not through New York connections but via what Henry Adams called Richardson's "valuable friendships at college." One of his mates in Cambridge had been James Rumrill, who had joined Richardson on his British Isles tour after graduation. Three years later, in 1862, the friends had reengaged when Rumrill and his new bride, Anna, sojourned in Paris during a yearlong wedding tour.

The son of a gold-chain manufacturer based in New York, Rumrill had married the daughter of Chester W. Chapin, a power in the vital western Massachusetts city of Springfield. Though born a farmer's son in nearby Ludlow, Chapin had worked his way from the factory floor to ownership of steamships that linked Springfield to Hartford, New Haven, and New York. By 1866, he also served as president of the Western Railroad, the busy line extending west from Massachusetts to Albany and beyond. In 1863, Chapin's new son-in-law became Western Railroad's corporate secretary.

The Rumrills and the Chapins attended Church of the Unity, a modest wood-framed structure with a temple façade that resembled many other New England churches nestled into the towns that dotted the Connecticut River valley. But the church's congregation had expanded with Springfield's prosperity, which was based in part on munitions manufacture, since Congress had established the U.S. Armory there in 1794. Recognizing the need for a larger house of worship, the Unitarian Society invited several local architects to submit designs in the summer of 1866. Though some of the building committee objected to an "untried man," Richardson got a place in the competition at the insistence of his influential friends.[18]

He also lacked construction experience—no Richardson design had yet been built in America or anyplace else—but that didn't daunt him. Nor did the even larger disadvantage that he had no experience in the Gothic style. His Beaux-Arts training had emphasized the classical, drawing on the grand traditions of imperial Rome and the Italian Renaissance. His French friends Julien Guadet and Gustave Gerhardt each had won a Grand Prix de Rome with designs for broad, precisely balanced buildings with façades lined with columns and arched windows. Richardson's work at the *école* had been in the same vein, which positioned him poorly for the tastes of post–Civil War America, where

Protestant elders expected churches in the Gothic Revival style with its characteristic pointed arches. The competition judges in Springfield surely imagined an English-school spire that aimed at the sky. Richardson saw such a steeple daily as he strode past grand Trinity Church on his way up Broadway to his office in downtown Manhattan. The work of British-born Richard Upjohn, the large-scale stone edifice was separated from Richardson's offices only by Trinity's churchyard. Yet Upjohn's house of worship offered no obvious inspiration, since Richardson's task wasn't to design a cathedral but rather a parish church.

He looked instead to his library and undoubtedly refreshed his imagination with a dose of John Ruskin, the self-anointed archbishop of the Gothic. But as Richardson worked at his proposal in the fall of 1866, he brought to the competition a discipline that his more experienced competitors did not. The ritual of the Ecole des Beaux-Arts *concours* was ingrained in him: from an *esquisse* he knew how to produce a polished presentation of a *projet*. Time and time again in Paris, he had put the power of his imagination to work with rigor and precision. He understood that paper plans either persuaded the judges or they didn't.

Richardson himself was a religious skeptic, but perhaps the spirit of his great-grandfather Priestley, an early Unitarian minister, looked over his shoulder as the young architect designed a spiritual place. He chose local Massachusetts stone—soft Longmeadow brownstone, trimmed with Monson granite—and designed a tall, square tower that faced the street. A rose window, fifteen feet in diameter, would light the nave, and two dozen pointed-arch Gothic windows would line the sanctuary walls. Open timber trusses defined the ceiling. At the rear, behind a bank of organ pipes, would be a space for the Sunday school.

The design was a plainly stated response to the congregation's needs. He showed the drawings to Mrs. P., who thought "Mr. Richardson's work was good, for he put his soul into it."[19]

He traveled to Massachusetts when the winner of the competition was to be decided. As the judges reviewed the plans and specifications on November 6, 1866, Richardson waited down the hall, just as Olmsted had done nine years before during the Central Park competition. Upon learning he had won, he burst into tears. "That is all I wanted," he exclaimed, "a *chance*."[20]

Olmsted required no convincing that Brooklyn needed a fine public park. An assortment of villages and farms extending east on Long Island was now a rapidly expanding city. He saw a fresh opportunity for him and Vaux to expose Brooklyn's inhabitants to a world like the Connecticut countryside of his boyhood, with forest and field, streams and lakes.

Since its incorporation as city in 1834, Brooklyn's population had exploded from twenty-five thousand to nearly four hundred thousand people, and Olmsted, as a sometime Brooklyn resident and New Yorker, had witnessed much of that growth. Half the inhabitants were recent immigrants, a rough majority Irish, the rest mostly German and English. Many lived in evident poverty.

The docks area near Atlantic Avenue, the Erie Basin, and Red Hook had developed rapidly after the steam ferry connecting Brooklyn and Manhattan had begun operating in 1814. The completion of the Erie Canal in 1825 had helped make New York's harbor the busiest in the nation, and Brooklyn soon became the nation's third-largest city after New York and Philadelphia. In 1855, Brooklyn had consolidated with inland Williamsburg and Bushwick, which became Brooklyn's eastern district, and wetlands were being reclaimed along the Gowanus Creek to the south. Just as the people of Manhattan had moved north into less populated areas, Brooklyn's streetscapes continued to encroach upon the open lands and villages farther east.

In the winds and snow that swirled in December 1865, Olmsted surveyed the potential parkland firsthand. Despite his uneven gait— he often carried a walking stick for stability—he repeatedly explored the unfamiliar acreage, sometimes alone but often with Vaux, viewing both the original site, which flanked Flatbush Avenue, and the larger alternative that Vaux had proposed.

That expanded site incorporated a diamond-shaped area to the west of Flatbush Avenue from the area delineated in Viele's first plan, as well as substantial undeveloped land east of Ninth Avenue and south to what was then Franklin Avenue.* The task of the Olmsted, Vaux & Company report would be to justify the expanded borders and describe the varied park spaces the partners proposed to create. The Brooklyn commissioners also needed cost estimates before construction could begin.

Olmsted had no difficulty making the case for Vaux's larger alternative. Even in strictly geometric terms, the angular footprint appealed to his taste for the irregular. Unlike Central Park's rigid rectangle, the bounds of the proposed Brooklyn park looked like a half-full burlap bag, with lumpy corners and asymmetries. And the banishment of all city streets from the interior, submerged or otherwise, meant an uninterrupted parkland with unbroken scenic views.

Like much of inland Brooklyn, the area, which was roughly a mile wide and a mile and a half north to south, remained undeveloped. Some rugged terrain on the eastern edge had been the site of Revolutionary War skirmishes, where American colonists had fought British regulars at Redoubt Hill and Battle Pass during the Battle of Brooklyn. Olmsted walked country roads that ambled through farmland, past harvested fields and cattle grazing on nearby slopes. At the north end, Vaux showed him an expanse of level ground he imagined could become the Green, a great lawn whose crescent shape meant expanding vistas for those walking its paths. To the south, they looked at low-lying land where Olmsted envisioned a skating pond larger than the one in Central Park. "A gymnasium," Vaux labeled it in a letter to Stranahan, "for the healthy development of the young citizens of Brooklyn in winter."[21]

Olmsted took in all that he saw and imagined an antidote to the city around it, a place that would offer its visitors the healthy illusion that they were truly in the country.

Perhaps the most painful lesson Olmsted learned at Central Park concerned the bureaucracy. In his experience, most of those chosen

---

* Ninth Avenue and Franklin Avenue would become today's Prospect Park West and Parkside Avenue, respectively.

to serve as municipal commissioners tended to be "good and well intentioned directors, estimable men." However, experience also told him that, when it came to envisioning parks, they tended to be unsophisticated and even wrongheaded.

"There [might] be no better men for the usual business of a board of hospital trustees," he observed, "but the best board of hospital trustees would commit what the law regards as a crime, if they assumed the duties of physicians and nurses." Meanwhile park commissioners, Olmsted complained, imagined themselves landscape designers, despite possessing "no more sense in this respect than children."[22]

He used his well-practiced writing skills to educate the Brooklynites, both the commissioners and the general population, and Vaux complemented the text with an elegant and precise scale drawing. The accompanying report would bear a weighty title: "Preliminary Report to the Commissioners for Laying Out a Park in Brooklyn, New York: Being a Consideration of Circumstances of Site and Other Conditions Affecting the Design of Public Pleasure Grounds."

A purity of purpose informed Olmsted as he sat down to render a description of Prospect Park, and he wrote furiously. The report—in its final printed form almost ten thousand words long— spoke in terms far beyond the task at hand. Although Olmsted had spent a combined four years at the Sanitary Commission and the Mariposa Company, his mind had never ceased milling the grist of the landscapes he had seen. In California, his city park expertise had been sought in Oakland, Berkeley, and San Francisco. He had been further inspired by Yosemite, and his thoughts had returned to Central Park with regularity.

He began with broad strokes. The pleasure of parks, he wrote, is "the feeling of relief experienced by those entering them, on escaping the cramped, confined and controlling circumstances of the streets of the town; in other words, *a sense of enlarged freedom* is to all, at all times, the most certain and the most valuable gratification afforded by a park."[23]

To leaven the lesson, he resorted to an anecdote credited to the fabulist Aesop. One day a fellow Athenian upbraided Aesop for engaging in childish games with a group of boys. In response, Aesop laid an unstrung bow before his critic. "Tell us what the unstrained bow implies," he asked. After a pause, the man admitted he had no idea.

With a smile, Aesop explained. "If you keep a bow always bent, it will lose its elasticity presently; but it if you let it go slack, it will be fitter for use when you want it."[24] Olmsted thought Aesop's moral applied to his work, that the amusements and scenery in a city park would offer its citizens a place of release for the "unbending of the faculties."[25]

The essential ingredients for Prospect Park remained the same as Central Park's, primarily meadows ("greensward"), woods ("groves"), lakes ("waters"), and "corridors of well-mannered woods." But instead of an enclosing wall around the whole, the partners decided upon an embankment, much of which would be twenty feet high, a ridge of earth half-camouflaged by bushes and vegetation, punctuated at intervals by arched entrances to the park. Although overlooks within the park from such heights as Vanderbilt Hill would offer distant vistas of New York Harbor and a sweep of ocean, the "boundary arrangements" would, for the most part, "shut out of view that which would be inharmonious and counteractive to our design."[26]

The designers planned a scheme of traffic separation like that in Central Park, with five miles of carriage roads, largely at the perimeter; four miles of bridle paths; and almost twenty miles of pedestrian walks. They anticipated all seasons. Since their park in Manhattan had made ice-skating a popular pastime, their lake would accommodate large Brooklyn crowds in winter. The earth beneath park carriageways would be properly prepared so the snowmelt and spring rains wouldn't render them impassable. A steam-powered pump would circulate water through an elaborate system of pools, streams, and the lake.

They proposed an open-air concert area. Performances would take place on an island, and the sound carrying over the waters would be heard by perhaps ten thousand people in a shady glade to the south and by those on horseback and in carriages listening from an oval concourse to the north.

Olmsted acknowledged, "We cannot have wild mountain gorges," but he proposed a ravine and waterfalls.[27] Even if the highest point in the park was a mere 168 feet above sea level, Olmsted saw no reason not to incorporate a sense of drama.

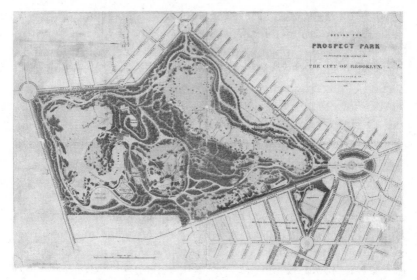

The plan for Prospect Park, Brooklyn, as published in 1868.

Although the partners worked all hours to finish the proposal, Olmsted, Vaux & Company ran late. The commissioners extended the deadline, and some January nights saw oil lamps burning until midnight at Vaux's house. Olmsted continually suggested elaborations to the plan while Vaux worked at polishing the drawing. Even when Olmsted completed his handwritten manuscript, more time was needed to typeset the text for proper presentation.

When it was finally done, the report was a tour de force. It offered philosophical arguments: "Experience shows," the document argued, "that the great advance which a town finds in a park, lies in the addition to the health, strength and morality which come to its people."[28] But it was also a practical plan tailored to realizing a public park at the Brooklyn site, complete with rustic shelters, ornate bridges, arbors, and pavilions. It would be a place where the people of the city could come together.

Finished copies were delivered in mid-February 1866, and the partners celebrated with valued friends. At Vaux's house, they raised glasses of orange-juice punch and claret in toasts to a job well done. Months would pass before the commissioners acted, but on May 29,

1866, Vaux and Olmsted learned the job was theirs, and on July 1, officially, they assumed management of park construction.

The task of completing the 526-acre park, including the Green, the Ravine, and the Lake, would require seven years, though the first section of the Prospect Park grounds—some of the East Drive at the north end of the park—officially opened to the public on October 21, 1867. During construction, elements would come and go. The planned Zoological Ground disappeared and an Upper Pool was incorporated into the plan. Olmsted, Vaux & Company provided a series of elaborate topographical maps to guide construction. A crew of some eighteen hundred men, many of them immigrants, worked as laborers, carpenters, gardeners, stonemasons, and blacksmiths. A newfangled rock crusher and a steamroller imported from Liverpool helped shape the park's paths. A well was dug and a boiler house built to power the waterworks that fed the park's streams and ponds. Vaux designed bridges and rustic shelters.

Both Olmsted and Vaux knew they could make another fine city park, certain that the second time around they would do it even better. They would later agree: Prospect Park was their masterpiece.

After spending most of her twenties as a bride-in-waiting, Julia reached the end of her eight-year engagement after Richardson won the Church of the Unity competition. Eight weeks later, his confidence reinforced and the church's money in his pocket—it was no nest egg, but it made him solvent—Henry Hobson Richardson married Julia Gorham Hayden, in Boston, on January 3, 1867. The big day was organized quickly—as Julia's mother observed a few days later, "If we had had more time, we should probably have managed better."[29]

The Richardsons began their married lives together with a train ride that took them to Springfield to visit with their friends the Rumrills. With the coming of spring, ground was to be broken for construction of the Church of the Unity, and Richardson found the circumstances for talking business auspicious. Chester Chapin, Jim Rumrill's father-in-law, planned to invest some of the profits from the rail line he operated in new offices on Springfield's Main Street. Although Richardson had never designed such a building before—not many had, in a day when few businesses had large numbers of office employees—he embraced the notion of a commercial structure for the Western Railroad with varied spaces for officers, secretaries, and clerks, as well as a public area for greeting customers. No agreement would be announced until the Springfield newspapers reported the news of Richardson's second commission two months later, but on returning to New York in mid-January, the young architect had good reason to believe another important job was within reach.

The couple moved into a cottage on Staten Island in the Clifton neighborhood. Trunks of blankets, household goods, and some fine engravings, including one of Richardson's great-grandfather Joseph Priestley's, arrived from Boston, but money remained tight. Richardson pursued other work, including a Connecticut chapel and a home for friends on Staten Island, though neither would be built. John Hayden sent his daughter a draft for $1,000 to help with household expenses.

With the railway office commission freshly in hand, Richardson immersed himself in his work; that spring he was known to labor until five o'clock in the morning. Once again, he wanted to build with stone, this time local granite. Richardson based his office building design on a mode he knew from his Paris days. Called the Second Empire style, its most obvious characteristic was a steeply pitched and dormered roof. In the course of Paris's building boom in the 1850s and after, which had been engineered by Baron Georges-Eugène Haussmann, the mansard roof had become a defining presence on the new boulevards.[30] New and fresh to Americans, the Second Empire style was becoming fashionable in the United States. Richardson put it to use for his client.

In his rendering of the elevation for the three-story railway offices, Richardson lined the building with pedimented and arched windows along its 110-foot-long façade, details he found in engravings in architecture books, including *Edifices de Rome moderne*, a book he had purchased in Paris.[31] The building set no new precedents, blending as it did elements Richardson knew from his Ecole des Beaux-Arts days, but designing it took a toll on the young architect. Julia wrote to her mother that her husband had become so preoccupied with his work, "he had a headache & kept talking in his sleep about the staircase."[32] Late in the month, he took an overnight visit to Springfield to present the plans. They met with approval.

In early February, a letter to Richardson had offered another proof that his architectural practice held real promise. The sender, Charles Learoyd, knew Richardson from their Harvard days, when the young men made music, played cards, and drank ale together.[33] Now Learoyd was rector at Grace Church in Medford, just north of Boston, and he, along with Shepherd Brooks, a major contributor to the building project, invited Richardson to submit a design for a new Episcopal church.

The competition drawings for Grace Church in Medford would test Richardson's creativity. The proposed house of worship in the town would be smaller and simpler than Springfield's Church of the Unity, though in most ways, Richardson would again follow English country-church conventions, complete with a ninety-foot tower.

This time he could not present his plan in person, but his absence didn't matter. On March 21, 1867, a day after the post delivered Richardson's sketches to Medford, Reverend Learoyd wrote back to his friend, "We were all struck by [the plans] and unanimously agreed that there was more genius and originality in them than in any we had seen."[34] Learoyd admitted the five-man building committee worried the design might be beyond their budget, but after minor modifications to the plan in the interests of cost, Richardson would be officially awarded the commission.

The design for this house of worship varied in many particulars from the Church of the Unity, but in honoring the wishes of one wealthy parishioner, Richardson revealed a fresh instinct for designing in a way that bonded his building to its place. A recently built stable belonging to one of the church's main benefactors had incorporated the plentiful glacial stones that seemed to sprout from the New England earth. Pleased with the cobblestone look of her new barn, Mrs. Ellen Shepherd Brooks (Peter Brooks's mother) suggested that the new church should also incorporate such "bowlders of New England."[35] The logic of employing local materials was hardly new. Henry Wadsworth Longfellow, who resided a few miles away in Cambridge, had recently extolled the ancient notion in a poem: "That is best which lieth nearest— / Shape from that thy work of art."[36]

Richardson had been trained to design buildings in the language of classicism, but his American clients were pushing him to move beyond what he knew in order to satisfy their tastes. He had yet to develop an individual style, but here at the Medford church, he incorporated the idea of native "bowlders" in a way that not only met with the approval of his clients but felt right to him. Though he chose cut, quarry-faced granite for door frames, window surrounds, and buttresses, the larger areas of the walling would consist of weathered boulders, rounded and variable in size, laid not in courses but with a random look to resemble a farmer's fieldstone wall. The glacial stone, unimproved by human hand, conveyed a solidity and strength, its crudeness softened by the careful geometry of the granite bordering. No one in André's atelier had taught Richardson how to do it, but his blend of the manufactured and rugged worked, and was the first small step toward a personal style that could be both an expression of his own vision and reflect his native land. He stowed the bowlder notion for future use.

With three significant commissions to his credit, Richardson was suddenly busy, both with designing and with the periodic visits required to supervise the construction sites at the three Massachusetts jobs. But Julia meanwhile had another matter on her mind. In April 1867, she confided in her mother that she might be with child. "I am anxious to hear if your hopes are realized!" the grandmother-to-be wrote back. "When I told your Father you took tea *to my delight* he said a Dislike of coffee is one of the *first symptoms*."[37] Julia would indeed go into confinement late that fall, with her mother at hand. The baby, named Julia Hayden Richardson, arrived on November 25. By then, Richardson's architectural practice had gained further momentum, as well as a new partner.

On October 1, 1867, Charles Dexter Gambrill and Henry Hobson Richardson established Gambrill & Richardson, Architects. Both were Harvard graduates, though their time in Cambridge had not overlapped, since Gambrill had preceded Richardson by five years. When they joined forces, Gambrill was already a recognized figure in New York with a decade of business experience, having apprenticed in the

offices of Richard Morris Hunt before going into a partnership with
another Hunt protégé, George B. Post. Yet Gambrill left Post in order
to align himself with the promising Richardson, whose personal mag-
netism and sophisticated training were winning him attention.
The partners shared offices at 57 Broadway. Though the name
of Gambrill, the elder of the two, was listed first, Richardson would be
the dominant partner. In a pattern common among architectural
partnerships, one man—Richardson—handled the design side while
the other mostly tended to office matters and construction management. Richardson's verve as a designer won him substantial commissions; Gambrill brought the practical experience of a man with
existing contacts with American builders and suppliers. The arrangement freed Richardson to become, as his biographer later put it,
"an independently creative artist," to open new doors and find new
clients.[38] And to make new friends, one of whom was Frederick Law
Olmsted.

Richardson could only gain from an association with Olmsted's
good name and reputation, and in time their personal friendship and
professional collaboration would significantly alter both men's lives.
Yet, oddly, neither left a record of when or how they first encountered
one another. Both arrived in New York in autumn 1865 as the nation
sought to forget the cataclysmic Civil War and the horror of Abraham
Lincoln's assassination just a few months before. By early 1866, both
men resided on Staten Island, after Olmsted decided his Manhattan
landlady, Mrs. Neeley, charged too much, and he and his family
settled into a rented house in the Clifton neighborhood, where the
Richardsons already resided. Both men regularly took the same ferry,
launched from Vanderbilt's Landing, to Manhattan.

They may have crossed paths earlier in Brooklyn, Richardson's
first New York residence and the site of Olmsted's big new project,
Prospect Park. Almost certainly their acquaintance, whenever and
wherever it began, was enhanced by shared time at the Century
Club. By June 1866, Alfred Bloor, an architect at Olmsted, Vaux &
Company, lunched regularly with Richardson and Gambrill. Bloor
met often with Gambrill at meetings of the American Institute of
Architects, where Bloor was secretary of the New York chapter, Olmsted an honorary member, and Richardson a dues-paying member.

Richardson's office was a one-minute walk from Olmsted's on lower Broadway. Whatever its origins, however, the Olmsted-Richardson connection would gradually become of far greater import than Richardson's professional marriage of convenience to Gambrill.

If their meeting was unavoidable, it was far less certain that Olmsted and Richardson would become dear friends. Separated by education and age, they had been on opposite sides of the era's defining divide. Richardson's prosperous merchant family had owned enslaved persons, while Olmsted's voice had been essential in the antislavery movement. Olmsted was intense, solemn, self-contained, imperious, and quick to anger; even those who loved him acknowledged that he, a perfectionist, could at times be testy, temperamental, and tactless. Richardson seemed to like—and, in return, to be liked by—everyone he met, as he embraced the world with tears and laughter. He was, everyone said, the kindest and warmest of friends.

The men would find they shared as much as they differed. Each believed deeply in his work. Both looked at the world in three-dimensional terms—or even four-, as times past and future would figure into their designs. An essentially apolitical man, Richardson had chosen to absent himself abroad in order to avoid a war in which he had friends and intimates on both sides, while Olmsted accepted a job on the other side of the continent in a misbegotten attempt to secure financial stability for the family that he had largely inherited from his brother. But by the time they repatriated to New York, their nation had entered a new era of recovery and reconstruction, and both men arrived with something to prove. Soon they would begin to enrich the American landscape together, when they embarked on a common project in Buffalo, New York.

Chapter Seven

Mr. Dorsheimer, Buffalo Benefactor

Here is your park, almost ready made.

——FREDERICK LAW OLMSTED

Late in the summer of 1868, an up–and–coming Buffalo lawyer named William Dorsheimer invited both Frederick Law Olmsted and Henry Hobson Richardson to his city. He would offer each of them a commission, and in doing so, Dorsheimer accidentally assumed the role of go-between. An Olmsted park design for Buffalo and a Richardson-designed house for Dorsheimer would be the first in a series of public and private collaborations that would link the three men over the course of the next two decades.

After emigrating from Germany at seventeen, Dorsheimer's father, Philip, had made his fortune as a hotelier, then served as New York State's tax collector and treasurer. By the time his father died, in the spring of 1868, the younger Dorsheimer had already held the rank of major during the Civil War and served as a U.S. district attorney. He cared deeply for Buffalo, a city he had called home since settling there after college, and he believed that two of his fellow Centurions, Richardson and Olmsted, could make the place better.

A distracted Olmsted arrived first. In addition to ongoing work at Prospect and Central Parks, he now consulted with educational institutions, including Vassar College, in Poughkeepsie, New York; the new university in Ithaca, New York, later Cornell University; and the National College for the Deaf and Dumb, which would become Gallaudet College, in Washington, D.C. He fielded requests for publishing projects and charity work, but above all, Olmsted, Vaux & Company was in demand to consult on city parks, having received invitations from Philadelphia; New Britain, Connecticut; Newark, New Jersey; and the nation's capital. Yet another landscape assignment awaited him in Chicago, but on his way there, Olmsted made a stop in Buffalo.

On Sunday afternoon, August 16, 1868, Olmsted climbed into William Dorsheimer's open carriage for the purpose of viewing "some properties in the suburbs of Buffalo, with a view to their fitness for a Park."[1] The drive started at the city's center, Niagara Square. No fewer than six streets angled away in all directions from the little green dotted with tall trees. A number of fine dwellings surrounded the square, including a tall-chimneyed Gothic Revival mansion occupied by Buffalo's First Citizen, former U.S. president Millard Fillmore.

A tall, portly, and convivial man, Dorsheimer took pleasure in talking about his city as he directed the carriage westward toward Lake Erie. Once the men reached the waterfront, they gazed at length at the lake, cogitating on the Canadian shore in the distance. What Olmsted saw was enough for him. Turning to Dorsheimer, he told him, "the beautiful view of the lake and river" would be "extremely desirable to secure."[2]

Back in the carriage, they followed the city grid north, driving past a plot of land Dorsheimer had purchased three months earlier and on which he planned to build a house. They were bound for the rolling acres of Forest Lawn Cemetery, the closest thing Buffalo had to a park. As Olmsted listened to Dorsheimer's narration over the course of the two-and-a-half-mile ride, he saw around him a new and emerging city.

In little more than a half century, a village in a near-wilderness had become home to more than a hundred thousand people. The transformation had begun when the Holland Land Company, which owned most of the former Iroquois lands west of the Genesee River in western New York, hired a surveyor named Joseph Ellicott to plan a city next to Buffalo Creek. Ellicott was one of a handful of men on the continent with the experience to do the job, since he had staked out the bounds of what had since become the nation's capital, along with his brother, Andrew, and the French engineer Pierre L'Enfant. In 1804, Joseph Ellicott handed the Dutch investors who owned the Holland Land Company his scheme for what he called New Amsterdam. Though the name did not last, Ellicott's plat for what became known as Buffalo soon filled with houses and inhabitants.

A natural port situated at the origin of the Niagara River, which in turn connects Lakes Erie and Ontario, Buffalo's geographic advantages had been further enhanced by the completion of the Erie Canal in 1825. Buffalo had become the American Constantinople, hard by a watery crossroads, welcoming westbound settlers who boarded lake steamers. The city's growing pool of laborers processed a flood of coal, lumber, and other goods headed east. After a rail line paralleling the canal opened in 1843, Buffalo became a rail hub too, a point of convergence for nearly twenty rail lines that connected the Upper Midwest and Canada with New York City and the East Coast. In the 1860s, spurred by the wartime economy, local factories boomed, producing stoves, shoes, fertilizer, and machinery. Its advocates would soon claim Buffalo was the busiest port in the world.

All the smoke and congestion, as well as the immense grain elevators that lined the shore, marred the view. To one visitor, English novelist Anthony Trollope, the grain elevator was "as ugly a monster as has been yet produced."[3] Olmsted could clearly see the city needed, as one Buffalonian expressed it, "public breathing spots more attractive and more accessible to the common man."[4] The heavy traffic of goods and passengers bound for points east and west meant profits and tax revenues. Prosperous Buffalo, Dorsheimer and others believed, could afford to pay for the creation of a fine, Olmsted-designed park.

Just north of the cemetery, Olmsted asked Dorsheimer to halt the carriage. They were at elevation, looking down upon a vista of undeveloped land, a mix of deep woods and meadows dotted with trees. This spot had not been in Dorsheimer's thinking, but he was pleased to hear Olmsted say, "A very trifling expense could impart to it a park-like character."

In case he hadn't been clear enough, Olmsted put it another way.

"Here is your park," he said simply, "almost ready made."[5]

Gambrill & Richardson, Architects, welcomed a range of clients. One of the first, the Century Association, wanted new gallery space to display art made by the club's members. But after their work on churches and office buildings, by 1868, Richardson's first full year of partnership with Charles Gambrill, most jobs entering the office involved designing houses and homes.

In April, Richardson's Harvard cohort once more brought him business when his friend Benjamin Crowninshield asked him to design a town house. Having established himself in New York in the dry-goods business, Crowninshield planned to return to Boston, and his decision to buy land in the Back Bay, the city's newest neighborhood, made the commission a particular challenge.

Boston in Colonial days had resembled a paint splatter, a peninsula that extended into the waters around it. Only a narrow spit of land called Boston Neck saved it from being an island in Boston Bay. But the rapidly growing state capital had long since outgrown its watery footprint, and the city had been gradually filling in inlets at its perimeter, among them West Cove, begun in 1803, which created the area around Charles Street at the base of Beacon Hill; Mill Pond to the north; and East Cove in the vicinity of the Long Wharf. The Back Bay was the latest and largest reclamation project, a 450-acre expanse of marshy and brackish shallows that lay behind a long dam lining the Charles River.

Begun in 1859, the Back Bay landfill required long trains that chugged in daily to carry immense quantities of gravel and stone from nearby Needham. Block by city block, the fill was dumped on top of what had been the basin of the Back Bay, raising the grade of the land by some twenty feet. Crowninshield's lot, at the intersection of Marlborough and Dartmouth Streets, was in 1868 at the leading edge of the landfill. Building on newly created land required wooden pilings, tree trunks driven into the earth to provide a stable foundation, for Crowninshield's tall house and all those around it. No. 164 Marlborough would be Richardson's first—but not last—encounter with the blue clay that lined the Back Bay's bottom.

During Richardson's time abroad, an *architecture suburbaine* had evolved in the French capital. Houses built for the emerging middle class, many designed by students from the Ecole des Beaux-Arts, were typically built of brick and capped with mansard roofs shingled with slate. Richardson himself had competed in one *concours* for which the specified program was a *petite maison bourgeois*.[6] For his friend Crowninshield, Richardson adapted the manner of the French Second Empire, as he had done for the Springfield office building.

Richardson decided the same mode suited him, and on Staten Island he set about designing and building a house with a mansard roof for his growing family. After a winter of sharing their rented cottage with an infant daughter and the nurse who helped care for her, the Richardsons decided they needed a larger dwelling. On April 3, 1868, they took title to a parcel of land on a ridge overlooking the Narrows, the tidal strait separating Brooklyn and Staten Island. The new projects listed in the Gambrill & Richardson ledgers suggested a growing and profitable architectural practice, and Julia's father reached into his own coffers to help pay for the new home, built on just under an acre and located a ten-minute walk from the ferry landing. The timing was sound: soon after the house was completed, at 45 McClean Avenue, Julia gave birth to a son, John Cole Hayden Richardson.

For the exterior, Richardson borrowed detailing from the newly popular Stick style, which used clapboard cladding and bands of flat boards to suggest the posts and beams of the internal wood-frame structure. He specified tall chimneys and an iron roof crest, which gave the house imposing height. In using familiar elements, his design set no new precedents, but the growing influence of his neighbor Olmsted did distinguish the house. A pair of large porches, or piazzas, enhanced the sense of connection between the interior and the surrounding landscape. Tutored by Olmsted, Richardson demonstrated a new sense of how to think about buildings from the inside out, reversing the classical practice in which the balance and symmetry of the exterior determined much about the configuration of rooms inside. With his usual exuberance, Richardson celebrated moving-in day by lighting roaring fires in all the fireplaces, earning the disapproval of his conservative father-in-law.

Richardson's next house design would be a significant creative departure. Client Richard Codman's Boston Brahmin family traveled in the same social circles as Julia's parents, and Richard, together with his bride, Susan, had met up with the architect in Paris in 1865.* On returning home from Europe after a two-and-a-half-year wedding trip, Codman purchased a small cottage in West Roxbury, a rural town ten miles southwest of downtown Boston, and reached out to Richardson to design him a new house on the property.[7]

Although not a wedding photo, pictured is Richardson's bride, Julia Gorham Hayden.

This time the architect's floor plan departed radically from the norm. Instead of treating the entry passage of the house as a vestibule for sorting and greeting visitors, Richardson enlarged both the dimensions of the room and its usage. The "Hall," as he labeled it on his rendering, ran the full thirty-three-foot depth of the house. At the far end of the twenty-two-foot-wide space, he placed a large fireplace with built-in recessed benches. Dining and drawing rooms would flank the hall, but the big and open central room at the core of the dwelling would function as the primary living area.

The unobstructed openness was unexpected, a departure from the era's typical floor plan of boxy rooms. Rooms at the time usually had discrete purposes, but Richardson brought fresh thinking to the

---

* The Codmans had been married that April at Boston's King's Chapel. "All the churches in the city were draped in mourning at that time," Codman remembered many years later, "because of the assassination of President Lincoln. Without my knowledge my ushers asked to be allowed to take down the draperies for the occasion, offering to put them up again after the ceremony. This being refused they simply took them down and, so far as I know, did not put them back up again." Codman, *Reminiscences of Richard Codman* (1923), p. 17.

flow of this proposed home. The tall hall would have an entrance at one end, with a chimney and a stair at the other. It would provide entry to the house; it would be its central circulation space, a room the Codmans passed through to reach the dining room or ascend the stairs; and it would be a common living space, focused on the hearth that was the heart of the house. The latter would be a large inglenook, then increasingly popular, a recessed fireplace with built-in seats on either side of the firebox. People would inhabit the common space together; its plan was simple, the flow informal. But this wasn't the sort of configuration that a well-to-do householder like Richard Codman expected.[8]

Radical as it was, the clients embraced the design, and with Richardson's plans in hand, Richard Codman sought estimates for construction. However, when the costs added up to double the sum he wished to spend, Codman balked—and promptly abandoned the whole idea of building a house. He wasn't put out with Richardson; he paid "the architect's commission cheerfully." He had enjoyed the process and told Richardson he was grateful. "I had all the fun of building," he explained, "without having to pay for it." Richardson's notion of eliminating walls and opening up the floor plan of a traditional house would be set aside for another day and another client.

After his Buffalo visit, Olmsted caught a terrible cold. He blamed a drafty passenger carriage, which he compared to an icebox in a letter to his wife, Mary.[9] He felt so poorly that he took to his hotel bed in Chicago, but he recovered enough that, a few days later, on Saturday, August 22, 1868, he boarded a night train back to Buffalo. He had promised Dorsheimer he would return to resume discussions of the proposed park.

On arrival, however, he was greeted by the unwelcome news that, without his knowledge, more than two hundred of Buffalo's "leading citizens" had been invited to hear a public address from him two days later on "the matter of a public park." Although his voice was little more than whisper, he wrote to Mary, "there was no help for it."[10]

Together with a laborer and an assistant, he spent Monday and Tuesday making the rounds of the possible park sites he had seen with Dorsheimer. With picks, shovels, and a horse-drawn cart, Olmsted's team dug test pits to determine soil quality and drainage. When the men of the city gathered Tuesday evening, former president Millard Fillmore chaired the meeting, and Dorsheimer introduced the featured speaker. Despite being troubled by a lingering cough and a sore throat, Olmsted spoke for a full hour.

He prefaced his plan with caveats. He told the gathering that he had had insufficient time to develop his thinking fully. Furthermore, he warned, they should understand that making a park was a challenge: the task was to create "a work of art" that would require decades to mature.

The next day's *Buffalo Evening Courier & Republic* reported that Olmsted proposed to design a place of "contrast, change, recreation and relief from the turmoil of the city." To accomplish that he planned to create a "variety of scenery, undulations of surface, freedom of motion, and a harmony of design."[11] To anyone who knew Central Park or Prospect Park, the description was familiar and reassuring.

Then, the paper reported, Olmsted had surprised everyone. His proposal for Buffalo called for not one but *three* parks. The first, consisting of thirty or more acres, would occupy a ridge east of town; set back three miles from Lake Erie, the site afforded a panoramic view of what Olmsted called "the extent and the prosperity of Buffalo." A second inland park on the rolling terrain he had spotted the week before would be immediately north of Forest Lawn Cemetery. It would be the largest of the three parks, between three and four hundred pastoral acres, taking advantage of the many "particularly perfect park trees," while adding a man-made lake using the waters of Scajaquada Creek. The third park, located at the shoreline and thirty to forty acres in size, would have a grand vista of the expanse of Lake Erie, the Canadian shore, and the rumbling waters at the mouth of the channel that fed the Niagara River, which, twenty miles downstream, tumbled over the famous falls.

Olmsted's was a city-specific approach, tailored to the conditions at Buffalo. And there was more. He also wanted to link the parks and the city with broad avenues. Earlier in the year, he and Vaux had tried to persuade Brooklyn's park commissioners to

create what the partners called "park ways." He told his Buffalo
audience he imagined a series of stately thoroughfares, "180 to
200 feet wide, with a pleasure drive in the center, flanked with
trees and walks, and a traffic road on the side." Miniature parks in
themselves, these parkways would be functional, beautiful, and
accessible to those walking, on horseback, and in carriages. At
the center of certain intersections, ornamental islands of earth
and stone could provide settings for statues, monuments, and
fountains.

Before ending his talk, he offered an assessment of possible
costs. He thought the overall price would be moderate and very
likely recouped in future assessments of rising real estate values.
"Parks," he said, "pay a city even in a pecuniary way."

Although he had devised a complex plan for a city he hardly
knew, working in hotel rooms and on train cars, in barely a week's
time and during borrowed hours, his unrehearsed proposal went
over very well with Dorsheimer and company. "The solid men of
Buffalo," as Olmsted called them, were virtually all converted on the
spot, "pleased & encouraged" at what they heard.[12]

The Buffalonians' enthusiasm left the usually cautious Olmsted optimistic. "I think it will go," he wrote to Mary.[13] Indeed, on
October 1, he would complete a plan that, though subject to miscellaneous modifications, resulted in an enduring system of parks and
parkways for the citizens of Buffalo very much as Olmsted first envisioned them.

In early October 1868, Richardson also fell ill. His ailment was
more than a cold, but the cause was unclear. Seemingly in good
overall health, the young man, who had turned thirty the previous
month, spent several days in his bed, unable to work. To make
matters worse, his sickness meant he let Olmsted down, unable to
deliver the promised sketches for what was to be their first professional collaboration.

An important supporter of Olmsted's from his Sanitary Commission days, Alexander Dallas Bache had died the previous year of "soft-

ening of the brain."* Bache's wife, Nancy, and Mary Olmsted had been dear friends, and the two men had held each other in high personal regard. "What a grand heart he has," Bache said of Olmsted. "Is not goodness after all the bestest of qualities?"[14] A circle of Bache's friends wished to honor his accomplishments as head of the U.S. Coast Survey, which mapped much of the East Coast, by marking his place of burial in Washington's Congressional Cemetery on Capitol Hill. They sought Olmsted's assistance and he, in turn, invited Richardson's participation. The job was small, with a budget of $2,000, but significant because it offered Olmsted both the opportunity to honor an old friend and to work with a new one for the first time. Thus, Richardson's apology: "I have been unable to attend to the Monument to be erected to Mr. Bache."[15]

By mid-November, Richardson had recovered enough to hand over two drawings, an elevation and a perspective. The proposed monument was spare, consisting of an engraved marble coffin set on a tall, plain plinth of granite. The design—true to the charge given for a "simple, permanent and severe" tomb—was soon approved and plans begun for its execution.[16]

While designing Bache's monument, Richardson also started the job of designing Dorsheimer's mansion on Delaware Street in Buffalo. In October, Richardson produced a design for a stately but sedate house, with an exterior of red brick and gray sandstone trim. Dark gray slates would hang on the steep pitch of the mansard roof. The look was unmistakably French, honoring both Richardson's time in France and his client's Gallic tastes. ("There is no department of human activity," Dorsheimer believed, "in which France is not honorably distinguished.")[17] The home would suit a man of means who looked to improve his city not only with the park program but also as a founder of both the Buffalo Historical Society and the city's fine-arts academy.

* In today's terminology, the cause of death was likely a cerebral hemorrhage. A scientist of note in his own right, Bache could trace his lineage back to another man of genuine curiosity, his great-grandfather Benjamin Franklin

Laid out in Joseph Ellicott's 1804 plan for Buffalo as one of the avenues radiating from Niagara Square, Delaware Street would become, in Olmsted's visionary plan, the main parkway from downtown to what he called "The Park," the largest of the three proposed greenswards. Olmsted imagined Delaware Street becoming a Parisian-style boulevard with double rows of elm trees, a vision that would soon be realized.* When author Mark Twain, on the verge of worldwide fame, took up residence at No. 472 several years later, the locals knew Delaware as "The Avenue."

Richardson labored over the details of the house, which needed to be large enough to accommodate a substantial domestic staff and for the gregarious Dorsheimer to entertain his friends. A semi-octagonal bay overlooking Olmsted's parkway and a pair of generous parlors on either side of the entrance hall would be essential to the design. Outside Richardson specified decorative panels between the first- and second-floor windows with carved rosettes and stylized triglyphs. He added a course of red tiles near the crest of the roof and, late in the process, a piazza.[18]

The house clearly impressed not only Dorsheimer but other Buffalonians. In 1869, the rector of Christ Episcopal Church traveled to Manhattan to request a plan for a new church just a block south of Dorsheimer's home. Richardson would not be awarded the contract—he came away with only a small fee of $250 for his sample designs—but he gained a new advocate, physician James P. White, who argued for Richardson at the vestry meeting where another architect's design was chosen.[19] White would soon play a role in gaining Richardson his first truly major commission, one that gave the architect both a chance to explore some unexpected ideas of his own and to draw Olmsted into the project. The task—an "insane asylum" for Buffalo—would cement the Olmsted–Richardson connection once and for all.

In Colonial America, caring for "distracted persons" tended to be a private family matter. In the Revolutionary era, almshouses were con-

---

* In time, "The Park" became known as Delaware Park, the shoreline acreage as "The Front," and the acreage in East Buffalo as "The Parade."

structed in growing cities to provide shelter to individuals "disordered in their senses," as Benjamin Franklin described them. Usually the mentally ill were housed side by side with the poor and the infirm.

In the first quarter of the nineteenth century, the earliest free-standing asylums specifically for people with mental disorders were established in the United States. These new institutions tended to be small and funded by private and philanthropic moneys, which meant people of modest means were not able to afford care. By mid-century, however, even politicians recognized the need for a larger and better governmental solution to the "lunatic problem" that was growing rapidly along with the country's population.* Madness had become society's problem, with a growing number of the insane "stroll[ing] abroad about the streets or country."[20] But a new body of thinking, common to pioneer psychiatrists, many of whom were members of a new organization called the Association of Medical Superintendents of American Institutions for the Insane (AMSAII), held that "insanity, of all diseases the most fearful, is . . . among the most curable."†

The best scientific thinking of the day considered "insanity" to be a disease that occurred in the absence of natural laws governing human behavior. Doctors believed that patients were inherently good and might be cured through "moral management" or "moral treatment." This consisted of a regime of good daily habits, including healthful foods and ample exercise; the inculcation of a sense of personal responsibility; and a reasonable work schedule. Baths (warm and cold) as well as certain medications (opiates and laxatives) might also be prescribed.[21]

The right setting was essential to the cure. The ailing patient needed to be removed from his or her usual habitat—typically the city, with all its ills and distractions—and resettled into a new and healthy way of life in an asylum. Proper treatment in such places, doctors believed, could result in as many as three out of four of patients returning

* The term *lunatic problem*, uncomfortable as it may be in our time, was common in Olmsted and Richardson's. In understanding the nineteenth-century context of "insane asylums," I have frequently drawn on Gerald N. Grob's thorough study, *Mental Institutions in America* (1973).
† Samuel B. Woodward, quoted in Grob, *Mental Institutions in America* (1973), p. 165. The AMSAII would become the American Psychiatric Association in 1921.

to their communities as functional members of society. (Those who
have analyzed surviving records have found they were not far off the
mark, though the ratio may have been closer to two in three.)[22] State
governments were paying for few public buildings at the time, but
among them were state capitals, prisons, and insane asylums.

Dr. White, who had helped found Buffalo Medical College two
decades before, shared the belief that mental illness could be cured.
Though it was not his field—he practiced gynecology, another emerging medical specialty—he first broached the notion, in 1864, of a state
institution for the insane in Buffalo. The legislature had not acted, but
White was not one to give up easily, and his repeated appeals eventually won support in Albany. On March 13, 1869, an act passed authorizing the Buffalo State Asylum for the Insane in western New York.
Dr. White was named a member of its first board of commissioners.[23]

The timing proved propitious. Richardson's local reputation
was freshly burnished by the appearance of a second Buffalo lawyer
on the Gambrill & Richardson client list. Asher P. Nichols, who owned
a lot adjacent to Dorsheimer's on Delaware Street, wanted a generous home for his family, guests, and servants; coincidentally, he would
also be invited to serve on the board of the Buffalo asylum. Richardson's
related professional experience didn't hurt: his first Paris job, working in the drafting room of Théodore Labrouste in 1862, involved
preliminary work on the Hospice des Incurables, a two-thousand-bed
hospital at Ivry."[24]

Since the calming effect of nature and the discipline of outdoor work were thought to be part of the treatment of the mentally
ill, the grounds of the proposed Buffalo hospital were also important. That meant the commissioners needed a landscape designer as
well as an architect. Already making regular journeys to the city as
the architect of the new parks, Olmsted too brought mental health
credentials. He had consulted on landscape plans for the Bloomingdale Asylum in Manhattan and the Hartford Retreat for the Insane,
and he had laid out the grounds for the Hudson Valley Hospital for
the Insane in Poughkeepsie.*

---

* The Bloomingdale Asylum was located on what is today the campus of Columbia University.

Olmsted embraced the mission of the asylum, which aligned with his own fundamental belief that serene landscapes could exercise a calming and even rejuvenating effect on city dwellers faced with urban disorder and density. "The home grounds of a retreat for the insane," he wrote, "are probably those which favor an inclination to moderate exercise and tranquil occupation of the mind, the least desirable those which induce exertion, heat, excitement or bewilderment."[25] A suitable natural setting, he believed, might help the confused mind find new calm, a new equilibrium.

By December 1869, Richardson was aboard a train for Buffalo to meet at the Buffalo Club with Olmsted and the men in charge of the Buffalo State Asylum for the Insane.[26]

This Buffalo assignment resembled no other in Richardson's American experience. The project was more akin to a design *concours* at the Ecole des Beaux-Arts. He was handed a chance to rummage about in his own imagination to devise a solution to a concrete problem.

While many aspects were not yet standard, a generally accepted basic program for asylums had been developed by a doctor named Thomas Kirkbride. A Philadelphia Quaker, Kirkbride had been among the thirteen charter members of the Association of Medical Superintendents of American Institutions for the Insane. Humane care was one of the organization's stated goals, and at their first meeting, in 1844, the reform-minded founders had resolved that whenever possible, the use of restraints should be avoided. The task had fallen to Kirkbride to translate the "moral treatment" of the insane into an architectural schema, and after long study of existing care facilities, in 1854 Dr. Kirkbride published *On the Construction, Organization, and General Arrangements of Hospitals for the Insane.*

In the intervening years, the Kirkbride Plan, as it was known, had become the standard, specifying a strictly functional architectural template. The building or buildings had to be large enough to accommodate hundreds of patients. In Kirkbride's view, the two most essential elements were a large administrative building at the center and a matched pair of separate patient wings (one for male patients, the other for female) extending from either side of the central block.

The wings, in turn, would be divided into wards that reflected patient classifications based upon the nature and seriousness of their disturbance or, as Olmsted soon expressed it, "for so placing the violent and noisy patients, that the quiet and convalescent would escape disturbance or annoyance from them."[27] The main building would house offices and quarters for the superintendent and his family. Additional patient pavilions could be added, as necessary, to the wings. The overall character was to be homelike rather than institutional, with sitting rooms, dining rooms, and individual bedchambers for each patient. Set amid the calm and quiet of a constructed countryside, the facility was intended to be a retreat in a scenic setting.

Yet, despite these elements, the standard template almost entirely lacked specificity. It did prescribe a hierarchical building or set of buildings but did not determine their materials nor their shapes, colors, or detailing. The Buffalo commission thus was an almost unfettered opportunity for Richardson to apply original thinking in creating an unusual freestanding community. The expenditure would be very large—the construction cost eventually ballooned to more than $10 million.

Richardson tentatively sketched an elevation in a notebook, one that consisted of a mansion-like main building flanked by a series of cottages on either side that were linked by covered walkways.[28] In a subsequent variation, he added a pair of small gables at either end of the administration building's long hip roof. Had this been a *concours esquisse*, however, Richardson would have been declared out of the competition because his final design, still several incarnations down the road, varied greatly from the early drafts.

In another round of sketches, Richardson veered toward Victorian Gothic, giving the end gables turrets with conical caps like a medieval castle. But the biggest change he made was the addition of a bulky, cathedral-like central spire with a large rose window of stained glass. Richardson had seen elements of church architecture used in medical institutions in France, but his assemblage resembled nothing he had done before. The sketches satisfied neither the architect nor his clients; as one observer later wrote, this conception was "a characteristically youthful attempt to cram all one's ideas into a single paragraph."[29] Further cogitation on the building's elevation would be required.

Turning his attention to its footprint, Richardson consulted Olmsted. Richardson wanted to improve upon the principles of the Kirkbride Plan, and his friend suggested he break the line of the façade: Rather than line up the administration building and the pavilions as if they were on a city street, why not set back each pavilion, one to the next? To do so would increase privacy, Olmsted argued.[30] Richardson embraced the idea and went one better. He proposed linking one patient building to the next with curved corridors with quarter-circle footprints. This would offer increased light and air circulation to improve the patients' quality of life. Along with fireproof iron doors in the corridors, the separation would reduce the risk of a fire spreading from one ward to the next.

The setback design altered how the building would be seen from every angle. The receding wings would make the wide structure less monolithic from the front. At the rear, the open arms of the approaching wings would create a courtyard as well as embrace the agricultural acreage in the middle distance. Most dramatic of all would be the bird's-eye view of a precisely symmetrical structure that wasn't linear. The eleven independent structures—ten pavilions, five on either side of the main block—assumed a flattened V formation that bore an unmistakable resemblance to a skein of geese in flight. A great building had been collaboratively conceived.

When in Buffalo, Richardson and Olmsted found comfortable accommodations at Mr. Dorsheimer's completed house.[31] A three-way friendship seemed in the making, but more important, the two designers were finding that two heads worked better than one.

Together they walked the asylum property, which, by state statute, had been provided by the city of Buffalo, along with a supply of water, in perpetuity. The commissioners had identified a two-hundred-acre site consisting of a picnic ground bounded by undeveloped farmlands that extended south from Scajaquada Creek to Forest Avenue.

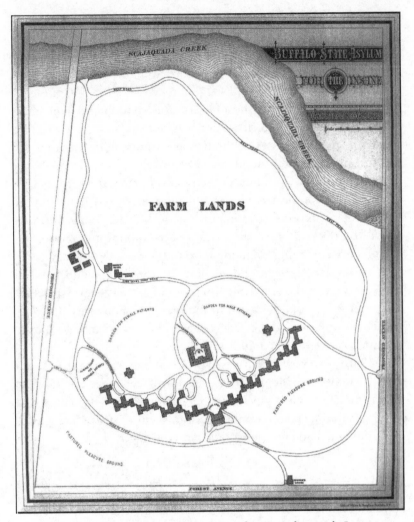

The Olmsted plan of the grounds for the Buffalo State Asylum for the Insane, dated 1871. The whole is anchored by the immense, wingéd footprint of the main hospital building.

Located three miles north of Niagara Square, the hospital property also abutted the largest of the reserves in Olmsted's park plan, making neighbors of parkgoers and asylum patients. If anyone objected to this proximity, the newspapers chose not to report their complaints. Instead, there was a general acceptance that the good work of the hospital in promoting the true interest of the insane need not be exiled to the backstreets of the town. A grand insane hospital would be a source of community pride.

When Olmsted gazed upon the asylum property, he didn't see just rolling acres of meadowland. He noted the gentle undulations, especially the several ravines that ran east–west across the property. That meant bedrock, but Olmsted saw that its contours also represented opportunity; he was about to give Richardson a tutorial on the art of integrating a building into its site.

One of the project's oddities would be the sheer breadth of the building with its twenty-two-hundred-foot wingspan. In particular, Olmsted worried that in an emergency, lifesaving minutes might be lost if fire engines had to drive around the building to reach the opposite side, a distance of up to a half mile along a curving roadway. His solution was to put one of the ravines to practical use. Olmsted measured a fourteen-foot drop, similar to his below-grade road in Central Park. A building constructed over such a ravine could have "subways" beneath "for the passage of wheeled vehicles from front to rear."[32] Richardson recognized the wisdom of the idea and incorporated the subways into his plan.

Olmsted suggested another improvement. Everyone's first instinct had been to plant this proud building with its long face parallel to the road, and Richardson was laying out the patient pavilions with bedchambers on the north side of the building to permit generous windows along the broad corridors and dining and living rooms that lined the south elevation. However, "as to the position of the buildings," Olmsted proposed a pivot: the long sequence of structures, otherwise unchanged, should be built "in a line *diagonally* to the line of the street."[33] Instead of squaring its shoulders to Forest Avenue, the hospital's façade would face slightly southeast. The result, Olmsted explained, would be the maximum amount of mood-enhancing daylight for both wings during the winter months. Richardson and the commissioners quickly adopted the idea.

With the building's situation in the landscape decided, Olmsted worked on the larger landscape plan. He employed a traditional European conceit for grand buildings, treating the south-facing entrance façade differently from the garden façade that looked north. As Olmsted imagined it, the approaching visitor would proceed through a "pastured pleasure ground" of broad lawns punctuated by occasional stands of shade trees. To the rear, he specified a larger expanse of "farm lands" extending all the way to Scajaquada Creek. He expected the acres devoted to tillage and pasturage to perform double duty as both a source of food for the institution and a place of healthful labor for patients.

The existing perimeter avenues ran straight, but within the bounds of the asylum grounds, Olmsted gave the roads and drives graceful curves. A carriage path would meander along the margins of the rear of the property and the creek for peaceable rides in what amounted to a self-contained countryside. Thick hedges and fences at the borders would screen the hospital grounds from prying eyes, enhancing the sense of privacy, safety, and seclusion for patients. At the front, Olmsted specified breaks in the tree line along Forest Avenue to permit passersby a perspective view of the soaring towers and handsome façade of the hospital building.

Richardson and Olmsted agreed the building must be constructed of stone.[34] Several sources seemed plausible, but the two men looked for the best and most practical source, finding it in Orleans County, some fifty miles away. The town of Medina sat aside the Erie Canal and gave its name to a sandstone quarried there. This brown stone could be laid up randomly or cut precisely, and Medina's earthen color would help blend the vast structure into its setting. It could also be shipped directly to the site, arriving on barges on the Scajaquada.

The commissioners signed off on Richardson's site plan—with Olmsted's improvements incorporated—on July 7, 1871. With ground as yet unbroken, Olmsted's siting suggestions had not cost a cent but had made the nascent building better.

A century earlier, in April 1770, Joseph Priestley, man of science, made another of his discoveries, this time concerning a property of India rubber. "I have seen a substance," Priestley wrote, "[that is] excellently adapted to the purpose of wiping from paper the mark of black lead pencil."[35] His great-grandson Henry Hobson Richardson had learned to trust erasers, as his own first instincts evolved.

With the final design of the building not yet settled upon, Richardson returned to the drafting table. First, he eliminated the steeple-like tower and rose window of the main hospital administrative building. Then he raised the mass of the building to three stories, topping it with a steep-roofed attic from which sprang two spires. At first, his towers didn't match, but in a subsequent sketch, Richardson drew them as twins. This new approach looked less like a church and more like a European rail station.

Richardson had begun to move beyond his usual sources and influences. As he said to New York friends, "It would not cost me a bit of trouble to build French buildings that should reach from here to Philadelphia, but that is not what I want to do."[36] He had already done so with his houses for Crowninshield, Dorsheimer, and himself. He had also tried English Gothic for his Medford and Springfield church clients, but neither seemed quite right in Buffalo.

His fellow *élèves* at the Ecole des Beaux-Arts would have immediately recognized the new basic shape of the asylum as a descendant of the European town hall. But its entryway would have been less familiar to his classically inclined classmates, consisting as it did of a set of three arches that hearkened back to the manner of medieval French churches. As he prepared to wrap his Buffalo hospital in the humble brown stone that he and Olmsted favored, Richardson had moved to the Romanesque, a building style named earlier in the nineteenth century by English cleric William Gunn. Eleventh- and twelfth-century buildings of this style were typically built of stone with barrel vaults, thick walls, and round arches rather than the pointed arches of the later Gothic style.

Richardson chose to turn down the visual volume typical of his own highly decorated age. The window, door, and other trim at the Buffalo State Asylum would be understated, and he noted in his sketchbook, he wanted to "depend upon simple & monumental effects."[37] His inclination was a well-ordered building that invoked a simpler time, an era that carried an aura of spiritual enlightenment. The uncoursed, textured stone he wished to use had a nativist American character that he thought suited the European precedents.

Inside this noble refuge, Richardson added a chapel on the top floor beneath the steeply pitched roof, along with quarters for doctors and staff on the second and third levels. An apothecary, library, and matron's office were laid out on the ground floor. A basement tramway would carry food to the pavilions. He designed service structures to stand behind the main building, including a large building to house the laundry and workshops, along with a pair of greenhouses to serve the women's and men's wings. His final design, published in 1872, changed little during construction, but the big building—it would be triple the length of Saint Peter's in Rome and would take ten minutes to walk end to end at a brisk pace—required many years to build.

The landscape, too, required time to mature.* At the main approach to the hospital, an Olmsted curve arched in from Forest Avenue, revealing a perspective view of the administration building. Initially the visitor saw barely half of Richardson's immense façade, with the opposite wing hidden behind the central block. When the proposed dense plantings of trees and shrubs eventually matured, the formidable structure with its towers and the interplay of roof planes would become but one element in a series of picturesque views.

This big project had important business ramifications for Gambrill & Richardson. Their first payment for the Buffalo State Asylum was a substantial $5,000. The job would require multiple draftsmen to execute countless working drawings, men who would remain on the Gambrill & Richardson payroll for years to come. The teamwork pleased Richardson, who, while in Paris, had reveled in the shared creativity of the atelier. Richardson was a man of collaborative inclination, and the Buffalo job also gave him a chance both to put his head together with Olmsted's and to assemble an architectural team.

The city of Buffalo provided extraordinary opportunities for both men. As Olmsted entered his prime, he got his first chance to create a complex of parks and parkways that would define an emerging city. By 1874, he was also designing Parkside, a suburban devel-

---

* By the time landscape work began late in the decade, Olmsted and Vaux's initial drawings had been lost. Olmsted prepared a new scheme that was, no doubt, a mix of the remembered and the reimagined.

With Olmsted's mature plantings around it (this picture was taken ca. 1900), the great mass of Richardson's asylum softened. The hide-and-seek character of the glimpses from the curving drives only added to the appeal of this unique hospital facility, one unlike any built before or since.

opment that wrapped around the Park, laid out in the graceful curves he favored. It would become the city's most prized neighborhood. For Olmsted, the Buffalo parks and parkways were a fulfillment of his goal to make city life better for all its inhabitants.

With his career still finding its first momentum, Richardson gained a powerful advocate in Dorsheimer, as well as his largest and most important commission to date. Together, he and Olmsted accomplished something remarkable at the asylum by unifying buildings and grounds. The almost unimaginably large structure looked timeless. Given its sheer breadth, the hospital might have resembled a fortress, but thanks in no small measure to Olmsted rooting it in nature, the safe, therapeutic place would betray no air of incarceration.

Chapter Eight

THE FALLS AT NIAGARA

[When] the eye catches the falls, the imagination is instantly arrested,
and you admire in silence.

—ANDREW ELLICOTT

Unlike the Yosemite Valley, the trio of towering waterfalls at Niagara
in western New York was not an indigenous secret. Samuel de Cham-
plain, one of the earliest explorers from the Old World, heard of the
extraordinary natural wonder from his guides and wrote of it in his
Voyages and Explorations. Numerous firsthand accounts followed, and
a stylized engraving appeared in France in 1697.[1] The place was difficult to reach, but the French, English, and Americans who did get
there found themselves struck dumb at the sight of Niagara's tum-
bling waters.

The Niagara River drains Lakes Superior, Michigan, Huron,
and Erie, which together account for roughly one-fifth of the world's
fresh water supply—and the sight of such a stupendous volume of
falling water casts a spell. Early visitors heard the roar of the waters
through ancient trees, and almost invariably, they reported that
their minds overflowed with thoughts of God, Death, or Nature.
The rising mists blurred the vision, and the sheer scale of the place
conveyed a sense of sublime beauty and power.

There was something distinctly American and almost proprie-
tary in how visitors reacted. Writers and artists embraced the line of
the three cataracts known as Horseshoe, Bridal Veil, and American
Falls at the Canada–United States border. James Fenimore Cooper employed the falls in the climactic scene in the first American

historical novel, *The Spy*, published in 1821. Over the decades, hundreds of artists attempted to capture Niagara Falls on paper, on canvas, and in prints, among them such accomplished painters as John Trumbull, Edward Hicks, and Thomas Cole. Visiting in 1820 for the express purpose of sketching the site, the great naturalist John James Audubon came away admitting defeat. "I give up my vain attempt," he wrote. "I will look on these mighty cataracts and imprint them where they alone can be represented,—on my mind."[2]

One could appreciate Niagara only in person, and with the completion of the Erie Canal and the arrival of rail service to Buffalo, tens of thousands of visitors flocked to what previously had been a place of pilgrimage for the few. That meant "improvements," including a network of paths, stairways, and footbridges to provide access to the vistas. Terrapin Tower, a circular stone cylinder constructed with an observation deck at its top, offered panoramic views from nearby Goat Island. Profit-minded businesspeople built hotels, museums, inns, and saloons to serve the tourists. Many industrial entrepreneurs arrived, too, to take advantage of the water power. One English gentlewoman complained her first view was marred by "an enormous wooden many-windowed fabric, said to be largest paper-mill in the United States. A whole collection of mills disfigures this romantic spot."[3] Among some discerning folk, a once-pristine natural wonder began to seem very much at risk. In a lecture at the Century Club in 1869, painter Frederic Edwin Church warned his fellow members that the great natural wonder at Niagara Falls rapidly approached ruin.

His investigations in western New York had begun much earlier. Like the Olmsteds, the Churches had been among Hartford, Connecticut's earliest settlers. Frederic's father, Joseph, though trained as a silversmith, had proved a wily investor. But the adolescent boy veered away from mercantile trades towards the arts, and Joseph Church, with some misgivings—he would have liked his only son to become a physician—used his influence to persuade the best-known American painter of the day, Thomas Cole, to take on the eighteen-year-old as his pupil in 1844.

An English expatriate, Cole was something of a pied piper; he would inspire the loosely linked fellowship of artists that, in time, came to be known as the Hudson River School. Cole had given up portraiture in Ohio to paint the landscape of his adopted land, seeking from his base in Catskill, New York, in the Hudson Valley, to record "the wild and great features of nature: mountainous forest that know not man."[4]

Between 1844 and 1846, Cole instructed Church on drafting and painting techniques. He also encouraged Church's inclination to travel widely, to hike beyond the beaten path, to look with great intensity at what he saw, and "to make his brush his only walking stick."[5] After mornings in the studio, teacher and student spent afternoons exploring the countryside, sketch pads in hand. Cole believed that "to walk with nature as a poet is the necessary condition of a perfect artist."[6]

During Church's period of study with his generous and good-spirited mentor, the young artist began to gain recognition in New York City. Paintings of his selected for exhibition were widely praised and sold for handsome prices in what had become the nation's art capital. He chose to relocate there in late 1847 and would carry on Cole's legacy after the older man's death a year later, at just forty-seven, of pneumonia. Church soon won new admirers, membership in the prestigious National Academy, and important clients for his canvases.

He traveled extensively to sketch in New York, New England, and the Canadian Maritimes, and the resulting paintings portrayed mountain scenes and seascapes. He demonstrated a remarkable gift for retaining "the minutest details of the general or specific character of tree, rock, or cloud," according to one critic.[7] His precise painting and an intuitive spiritual sense for the continent enabled viewers of his paintings to feel they had been transported to places they might never otherwise see.

In 1851, Church took an extended journey to Virginia, Kentucky, and the Mississippi River. On his way home, he detoured to Niagara's falls. What he glimpsed there so deeply impressed him that he headed for the falls again and again, including three visits in March, July, and October 1856. During his summer stay, he found accommodations with friends at a nearby cottage. "He is intoxicated with Niagara," reported one member of the household. "He rises at sunrise and we only see him at meal times. He is so restless away from the Falls that he cannot keep still, always feeling as if he were losing some new effect of light." He excused himself during evenings to return to the falls to observe the scene lit by the moon.[8]

The studies Church made on-site added to a thickening portfolio. Working in pencil and occasionally in oils, Church sketched the falls from several perspectives: at the base looking up; from each of several precipices looking across; from nearer and farther away; when nearby trees were barren and in full leaf; after a fresh snowfall. Ultimately, Church sought a point of view that earlier artists had not chosen, wanting to capture more of the magic of the falls themselves.

In his Manhattan studio in October 1856, Church closed in on how to compose his picture. His would be a more intimate view than his predecessors' paintings, and by the end of the month, he completed an oil sketch. Painted on a canvas nearly three feet wide but just twelve inches high, the panoramic view encompassed all three of the falls, with Goat Island at the center. He illustrated little of the scenery on either side and just a thin band of sky. In the ensuing weeks, Church completed a second oil sketch, this one on two sheets of paper, in which he shifted the view slightly in order to make Horseshoe Falls the picture's dominant element.

In December, Church permitted the public to view the second sketch in his New York studio at 497 Broadway. It thrilled onlookers, not least the critic of the *Crayon*, a new art magazine that had quickly become a gossipy must-read in the New York art world. According to the *Crayon*, Church in his new view "more fully renders the 'might and majesty' of this difficult subject than we ever remember to have seen . . . on canvas." The editor added a note of encouragement. "We shall look forward to the picture to be made from this sketch with much interest, as we believe Mr. Church intends to reproduce it on a more extended scale."[9]

The normally staid artist—as one female admirer put it, his was a "refined, quiet, almost a Quaker manner"—worked feverishly.[10] In an intense six weeks that winter, he stood before his canvas, applied his pigments, then strode back to regard his work from a distance. Those who saw him at work thought he might walk miles each day in his studio. His efforts produced a wondrously detailed canvas nearly eight feet across and almost four feet high. In fact, he produced *two* of identical size. "On one he experimented till his critical eye was satisfied with a line or an object." Only then, having tested the effect of his color and brushstrokes in rendering a detail, did he transfer them to the final painting.[11]

When Church put the painting on display late that spring, *Niagara* rapidly gained the status of a "Great Picture," a term that meant something particular at that time. Certainly it implied the work in question might be an artistic masterpiece, but to the art-conscious public, the announcement of a Great Picture was also an invitation to view it and be transported.

Following the then-current British practice of exhibiting a canvas in a one-man, one-painting show, Church's *Niagara* went on display in May 1857, at the gallery of his New York dealers, Williams, Stevens, and Williams. He had already sold them the painting, reproduction rights, and the right to put it on display for a great deal of money—$4,500—with the understanding that, on resale, he would get half the purchase price.* The curious paid the not-inconsiderable sum of twenty-five cents to see what was billed, in handbills, pamphlets, and advertisements all over town, as the city's latest attraction. Thousands of people came to look. Leaving the bustle of lower Broadway behind, according to the *New-York Daily Times* account, the viewer passed through the gallery to a small back room, "and behold! there is the marvel of the Western World before you."[12]

Everyone seemed to agree they got their money's worth. In the darkened studio, they stood before the great horizontal canvas, many for an hour and more. Encouraged to bring opera glasses, people forgot where they were. In the gaslit room, one couldn't hear the water or feel the spray, yet art connoisseurs and gawkers alike felt as if they stood at the precipice of the falls. Church's chosen vantage—there is no foreground—left the viewer wondering whether he or she might be standing in the rushing water. One's instinct for safety was tested by the threat of gravity, a sense of vertigo,

---

* Church's *Niagara* would sell twice more. One buyer would go on to become the first president of the Metropolitan Museum of Art. The second, acquiring the canvas at auction for $12,500, was William Wilson Corcoran, who was in the process of establishing the museum that bore his name in Washington, D.C., where the painting would hang until 2014, when the Corcoran's collection was donated to the National Gallery of Art.

Niagara (1857) is perhaps the greatest of Frederic Edwin Church's "Great Pictures," both majestic and large, at nearly eight feet in length and almost four in height.

and the seemingly unconquerable power of the water. This was Nature's scene, with the mad rush of the falls heightened by the flicker of a rainbow and a streak of sunlight. The only evidence of humankind, the diminutive Terrapin Tower on the left-hand side of the canvas, was utterly dwarfed by the expanse of water.

The picture was a hit. In a matter of weeks, some eleven hundred subscribers agreed to purchase either an artist's proof of the

work (a chromolithograph) for thirty dollars or a signed print for twenty dollars. The painting crossed the Atlantic, and by summer, Londoners rushed in droves to see it. One visitor mattered more than most, and the reigning arbiter of taste, John Ruskin, fell under the spell of *Niagara* too. Church's use of light so impressed him that Ruskin insisted upon examining the gallery's windows to be certain he wasn't witnessing an optical trick rather than an inordinately skillful use of pigments, washes, and glazes. On its return from abroad, the painting toured other American cities, including Philadelphia, Washington, Richmond, and New Orleans. It toured England a second time and, in 1867, won a medal at the Paris International

Exposition. Few disagreed with the assessment that it was "the finest picture yet done by an American."[13]

Church became American landscape painting's chief ambassador. He could confide quietly on gazing upon a seascape by England's J. M. W. Turner, "I never talk about art—I do not know enough about it."[14] But as Turner's heir—Turner having once bound himself to the mast of a ship in a great gale to experience the power of nature—Church chose to stand not at a safe distance from the falls and capture a traditional easel painting but rather at the brink, inviting the viewer to join him.

Selling in the tens of thousands, prints of *Niagara* became very much the fashion. As one obituary writer remembered many years later on the occasion of the painter's death, "Who does not remember when a chromo[lithograph] of Church's *Niagara* was considered a very handsome wedding present?"[15]

Church himself returned to Niagara—he would paint the place again, though less memorably—but he could not help worrying how much industry and commercialization encroached on Niagara Falls. When he chose to speak of it to his artistically inclined brethren at the Century Club, perhaps no one could have been better attuned to his plea than his fellow Centurion, Frederick Law Olmsted.

Olmsted's first impression of the falls dated back decades. Family journeys had taken Fred to Niagara Falls at the age of six, again at twelve, and for a two-day visit after he turned sixteen. As a boy and an adult, Olmsted observed on his occasional visits the changes wrought by the arrival of the railroad and the construction of the first mills. But the wonders at Niagara remained unseen by Richardson until his friend took him there on August 7, 1869.

Both men had traveled to Buffalo to check in on their respective projects. Olmsted planned to present a park proposal the following Monday, which would be unanimously approved. Richardson wanted to inspect construction progress at William Dorsheimer's Delaware Street house. Work on the insane asylum was still in the future.

Although four years his senior, Olmsted had met Frederic Church, a distant cousin, a quarter century earlier, when their paths had crossed at Hartford Grammar School. Much more recently, as Olmsted later recalled, his cousin had called "my attention . . . to the rapidly approaching ruin of [Niagara's] characteristic scenery."[16] This trip to Buffalo offered a chance to visit Niagara and to consider Church's worries. Dorsheimer joined Olmsted and Richardson, and the three checked into Cataract House, a hotel in the village of Niagara Falls with a broad piazza and a commanding view of the rapids.

That afternoon, they crossed the iron bridge to Goat Island, the small landmass of some sixty acres that appeared to rise from the waters at the precipice between Bridal Veil and Horseshoe Falls. They rambled in the island's forest, examining what Olmsted—and horticulturalist friends like Harvard's Asa Gray—believed was the richest variety of indigenous vegetation in the United States. Meandering along rough paths that penetrated the unspoiled forest of vine-draped trees, Richardson and Dorsheimer wiled away hours in the woods. On Sunday they explored the vicinity in a carriage, listening to Olmsted rehearse his argument for the site's preservation. He believed they must do everything in their power to promote the idea that the falls and their surroundings should be secured for the public not as a park or pleasure ground but as a reservation. "He pointed out to them the danger of the practical obliteration of the Falls as a natural spectacle."[17]

They drew other men into the scheme at an impromptu meeting in Dorsheimer's room at the Cataract House, including the hotel's owner and the man whose family owned Goat Island. Having been persuaded by Olmsted's plan, the group began the work of raising public awareness and lobbying for state ownership of Niagara. Despite these early efforts, these "reservationists," as they were soon known, would need years to achieve their goal.

Some people, such as the aspiring young novelist Henry James, quickly grasped the value of such a project, writing in the *Nation*, "Why should not the State buy up the precious acres? It is the opinion of a sentimental tourist that no price would be too great to pay."[18] The politicians were much slower to adopt Olmsted's and Church's thinking. The New York State Legislature took no action until Canada's governor-general, Lord Dufferin, joined the campaign in 1878 after a meeting with Church. Only then did the state government take the notion seriously, led by Dorsheimer, by then elected New York's lieutenant governor. He managed to get a survey authorized, with Olmsted as codirector.

The resulting report made a solid case, pointing out how disfigured the natural site had already become, its shores lined with shops, stables, baths, houses, hotels, and ugly signage. The plan gained momentum as others rallied to the cause, lending their names in support. They included senators, college presidents, and the likes of Emerson, Ruskin, and Oliver Wendell Holmes. One crucial supporter proved to be the newly elected governor of New York, Grover Cleveland, a recent mayor of Buffalo, who put his signature to a bill that formally created the New York State Reservation at Niagara Falls in 1883. Two years later, the Niagara reservation welcomed its first visitors, as the park took shape. A scheme for a parkland on the Canadian side was in the works too, and in 1888, it would open as Queen Victoria Park.

The buildings and fences within the new park's boundaries were destroyed, since the guidelines Olmsted provided forbade all man-made structures, including statues and monuments. Carefully laid out paths and carriage drives would serve the large flow of visitors. The underlying principle, as Olmsted put it, was that the reservation become "a spot reserved, and sacred to what divine power has already placed there, rather than a proper field for the display of human ingenuity or art."[19]

On the occasion of their marriage, in 1867, the demands of his work and a shortfall of funds meant that Henry and Julia Richardson did not take a wedding trip. Eight years later, however, the Richardsons joined Mary and Fred Olmsted on a leisurely loop west and north, with stops in Buffalo, Montreal, Quebec, and New Hampshire's White Mountains. The days would be remembered as the Richardsons' belated "wedding journey."[20]

The Olmsted and Richardson friendship—and their *ex officio* partnership—was evolving. The Buffalo State Asylum for the Insane was the most notable shared project to date, but the two had also collaborated in writing a development plan for the Staten Island Improvement Commission. After being appointed to head its "committee of experts," Olmsted insisted upon having Richardson on his team, writing to the commission chair, "Mr. Richardson [is] a gentleman trained in the most thorough French technical school familiar with European road and Sanitary Engineering and of highly cultivated tastes with a strong practical direction."[21] Together Olmsted and Richardson drafted a fourteen-point plan in 1871, "Report to the Staten Island Improvement Commission of a Preliminary Scheme of Improvement." They addressed such issues as ferry access, the water supply, sewage disposal, flood planning, and the scenery and byroads in one of New York's most desirable suburbs. Although the local villages failed to agree upon how to proceed—few of the proposed improvements were made—the document survived as an early and important attempt to address the growing problem of regulating urban development.

Richardson and Olmsted also shared a second monument project. In 1874, Olmsted invited Richardson to contribute to the redesign of Niagara Square in downtown Buffalo. He wanted a central memorial to the city's soldiers and sailors who had died in the nation's wars. Richardson proposed a handsome arch reminiscent of Paris's Arc de Triomphe. The arch would never be built, since those charged with the fund-raising failed to collect the estimated $50,000 construction cost. But Richardson's specifications contained a clue as to how much Olmsted was beginning to influence his thinking, even in his selection of building material. The architect specified that stones selected for construction should be rough enough to enable vines to find purchase, a harbinger of the melding of structure and situation that would appear often in their future collaborations.[22]

In 1872, Olmsted formally ended his partnership with Calvert Vaux. Though they remained friends, they no longer saw their business futures in the same way. "Mr. Vaux's ways are not my ways," Olmsted admitted to their mutual friend Alfred Bloor, "and I could not fit mine to his."[23] He had begun to think Vaux too hard-driving; his working relationship with Richardson was different. Never formalized by an any legal arrangement, it was based on simple trust, on mutual creativity, and on sensory perceptions as much as pure reason.

In describing their attachment much later, Olmsted recalled the 1875 journey the two couples took together. When they passed old French farmhouses in Quebec, Richardson was quick to describe their virtues, pointing out to Olmsted "how much more pleasant they were than such cottages as we were accustomed to, in which so much more had been done to please."[24] Unsophisticated as the country dwellings might be, Richardson's well-trained eye enabled him to assess plain, vernacular buildings with the same acuity as an Ecole des Beaux-Arts jury.

At Niagara, the men's roles were reversed. "I have never seen the like of it, even in a school-boy," said Olmsted. "The whole-heartedness with which he gave himself up to enjoyment for the time being was the most interesting circumstance of the journey." Richardson put himself in his friend's hands. "This is a matter in which you are an expert," he said. "I will not take off the least share of your responsibility." Their first day at Niagara they walked for several hours, but without taking in the view of the falls. Olmsted consciously chose to delay the big reveal.

When Richardson finally took in the vista of the falls, Olmsted remembered, his friend sat "for hours in one place contemplatively enjoying the beauty, . . . taking quiet pleasure and laying up pleasure." Olmsted admired Richardson as a man who found plain joy in simply looking; for his part, Richardson had intuited his friend's belief that scenery must be absorbed in solitude.

The United States was entering a new phase, with its population moving rapidly to cities. Olmsted was acutely attuned to this shift in balance and, in particular, to its most worrisome consequences. Too often progress meant running roughshod over the landscape, thanks to a growing desire for manufactured goods and the rapid development of towns and cities. But Olmsted, Richardson, Church, and other like-minded people set about ensuring that, in the interests of civilization, Nature would not be brought to her knees.

Chapter Nine

RICHARDSON DESIGNS
A DUOMO

We have chosen Richardson of New York for our church architect,—the best of
all competitors by all means. He will give us something strong and good.

—PHILLIPS BROOKS

While Richardson carried on his collaboration with Olmsted in Buffalo, another major commission, this one in Boston, brought him
within walking distance of national fame. The work came to him officially in June 1870, when he won a quiet competition to design a
new house of worship for the long-established congregation at Brattle Square Church. The job, which took him to the familiar confines
of the Back Bay, would be a stepping-stone that led directly to his
most enduring monument, Trinity Church of Boston.

Richardson knew Boston well, both from his college days and
after supervising construction of the mansard-roofed town house on
Marlborough Street for Benjamin Crowninshield. As the seaport
city spread inland, more and more people were choosing to live in
the new and fashionable Back Bay neighborhood, and the well-to-do
parishioners of Brattle Square Church joined the trend. They
wanted to separate themselves from their deteriorating downtown
neighborhood, just a block from the rough and tumble of the waterfront, and the elders had acquired a building plot on the corner of
Commonwealth Avenue and Clarendon Street.

Richardson's design for the site was chosen over those of
several competitors, a decision reached with the aid of Benjamin

Crowninshield's father, a leading underwriter of the project. But even before Gambrill & Richardson officially got the job, the prospect of the Brattle Square Church architectural fees prompted Richardson to consider adding a full-time draftsman to the staff. The leading candidate, Charles Follen McKim, arrived at his interview at the Gambrell & Richardson offices armed with more than the sketches under his arm. The twenty-two-year-old Philadelphian had just returned from three years of study at the Ecole des Beaux-Arts. Olmsted was a friend and a sometime business associate of his father, abolitionist James Miller McKim, and the younger McKim had spent time the previous year in Great Britain under the tutelage of architect R. Phené Spiers, a dear friend of Richardson's from his own Beaux-Arts days.[1]

With his office docket already busy with the enormous Buffalo State Asylum, Richardson needed a skilled draftsman with real architectural training. The new hire would join the partnership's other employee, the auspiciously named Charles Hercules Rutan, an eighteen-year-old brought aboard a year earlier for four dollars a week. Rutan was showing real promise under Gambrill's tutelage in engineering and construction management, but he was no more than a competent hand at construction drawings.[2] Someone was needed with the talent and training to elevate the firm's draftsmanship.

Richardson liked what he saw. "My d-d-dear fe-fellow . . . we are in the competition for the Brattle Square Church in Boston," Richardson told McKim, "and if we win—I'll take you on."[3] Days later, the impulsive Richardson decided he wasn't going to wait. McKim was right for the job, whatever the firm's finances. Ambidextrous Charles McKim thus came to occupy the head draftsman's table, at a salary of eight dollars a week, launching a career that would carry into the next century.

After construction of the new Brattle Square Church began in 1871, it attracted attention; as one contemporary reported, no other building site in recent memory "compelled half the notice" of the Brattle design.[4] The church Richardson envisioned was neither large nor surprising, with a footprint in the shape of a cross and a time-honored rose window that would overlook Commonwealth Avenue. But people were struck by the tall shaft of its corner bell tower. Richardson's campanile, which stood almost apart from the main nave, was unexpected in a city of churches with steeples that tended to sprout symmetrically from their roofs.

The Brattle Square Church put Richardson's originality on display. Its design differed from his earlier churches. No longer quoting the Gothic of the English parish, Richardson replaced narrow pointed arches with broad, round ones that, at the base of the Brattle church's tower, defined a *porte cochère* for the carriages of arriving parishioners. His individuality was emerging, and his shift in style offered a fresh inkling, also on view at the Buffalo State Asylum, of a growing inclination to borrow from the Romanesque style.

Two years would be needed to complete construction, in part because of the added time required to execute the bas-relief sculpture that decorated the tower. Confident in his own skills, Richardson welcomed the contributions of others, even well after a design had been agreed upon. On meeting Frédéric-Auguste Bartholdi in New York in 1871, he invited the Alsatian sculptor to work on the Back Bay church. A French citizen, Bartholdi was in the United States to promote a plan for a great monument to Franco-American friendship and American independence, which fifteen years later, would become the Statue of Liberty, overlooking New York Harbor on a base designed by Richard Morris Hunt. But his first American work was the frieze of Brattle Square Church.

Richardson revised his original design to provide an opportunity for Bartholdi to display his talents, and a team of carvers near the top of the 176-foot tower worked from sketches and plaster models provided by Bartholdi. Along with his originality, this was a second important Richardson trait that emerged at the Brattle Square Church: he found the company of other artists congenial, and his frequent embrace and encouragement of them to enhance his architecture would become a hallmark of his career.

Directed by a young Welshman named John Evans, the artisans high above the street on wooden scaffolding chiseled a soft, iron-rich conglomerate called puddingstone, quarried in nearby

Brattle Square Church tower, with its dramatic, carved-in-place frieze of saints and worthies, in a rendering published at the time of the building's completion.

Roxbury, giving human shapes to blocks of stone. Although each side of the tower represented a sacrament, many of the faces of the celebrants were recognizable not as biblical characters but as notable men of the time. The likenesses included Emerson, Longfellow, Abraham Lincoln, and Massachusetts senator Charles Sumner. In addition to these larger-than-life figures, trumpeting angels with gilt horns stood guard on each of the four corners. One Boston wag could not resist dubbing the building the "Church of the Holy Bean Blowers," referencing the common Boston Saturday night meal.

While Richardson's professional career showed signs of robust growth, his personal health was worrisome. He was barely into his thirties but had developed a painful hernia, possibly a lingering complication from a minor accident in his Paris days; he habitually wore a truss. Having gained weight, the graceful lad his Harvard friends remembered moved more awkwardly, and even his tailored London suits could not camouflage his added bulk. Nevertheless, Richardson's work schedule would only intensify.

In 1872, many Bostonians walking along Commonwealth Avenue paused to admire the new Brattle Square Church and its tower. One was a local boy, sixteen-year-old Louis Sullivan, who recalled years later being mesmerized by Richardson's new structure.

Sullivan had left Boston English High School to enroll in the School of Architecture at the Institute of Technology, today's MIT. The man in charge of the architectural program at Tech, William Ware, was a disciple of Richard Morris Hunt. His new school, established in 1867, offered the first full architectural curriculum in the United States. Ware had designed the program, loosely based that at on the Ecole des Beaux-Arts, but Sullivan found that neither Ware nor his teaching mode suited him. He thought the professor amiable but ponderous (he carried himself, said Sullivan, with the "pose and poise of cultural Boston"). When Ware lectured, his face half-obscured behind a full beard, he never looked his pupils in the eye. He was a conservative Brahmin with a slavish respect for the orders of Greek and Roman classical architecture. In his drafting classes Sullivan dutifully rendered the Corinthian, Doric, and Ionic with great care—he was already an excellent draftsman—but Ware's almost religious devotion to the orders seemed to Sullivan "quaint." He thought they were "mechanical and inane . . . stultified . . . lack[ing] in common sense and human feeling."[5]

Sullivan wanted to place his faith not in the old method but in "freedom." During his first year at Tech, he got a taste of what he desired two blocks north and one west of the school's home base. Brattle Square Church became the fount of Sullivan's new "architectural theology." It had been "conceived and brought to light," Sullivan observed, "by the mighty Richardson."[6]

The shapes he recognized, and the squared-off ashlar stone he knew. But Richardson's rejection of symmetry, the sculptural frieze, and the rounded arches turned Brattle Square Church into a beacon for Sullivan. Richardson had the courage to mix elements of the French Romanesque and the Renaissance Italian, but above all, Sullivan saw, the church was original. Richardson won in him an important convert, another man who would bring fresh thinking to American architecture.

On March 12, 1872, as the Brattle Square Church was rising, the morning mail brought Richardson a significant letter from Boston. Written in a copperplate hand, the unexpected invitation neatly filled a large sheet of lined white stationary. The letter began with what was now a familiar refrain. "You are requested to furnish designs for the erection of a church."[7]

The senders, two Bostonians acting on behalf of the Trinity Church Building Committee, offered a few particulars. "It is desired to seat on the floor 1000. Persons, and 350. in the galleries. . . . No Columns, Well Lighted, warmed & ventilated with good acoustic qualities." An organ and a parish building would be required but no basement. The cost should "not exceed $200,000-dollars." Unlike his Medford and Springfield houses of worship, or even Brattle Square, this clearly would not be a modest parish church.

As one of six invitees, Gambrell & Richardson would be competing with the best architects in the country and the most established professionals in Boston and New York, including the redoubtable Richard Morris Hunt of New York and Boston's Peabody and Stearns. Richardson's Brattle Square Church had probably gained him entry into the competition, thanks to the admiration it had garnered and its location, barely two blocks away from the Trinity site. He possessed the least experience of the group, and the deadline, jotted at the foot of the page, was short. "Plans to be sent in on, or before May 1, 1872." He had just six weeks.

Though Richardson could hardly predict the outcome, he did understand that the freshly opened letter he held in his hand represented a major opportunity. But seated in his office near Manhattan's southern tip, the unruffled and unintimidated Richardson, on an otherwise unmemorable morning, simply went about doing what he loved best. He turned the letter over to its blank verso, picked up his pencil, and let it speak. In short order, he rendered in graphic form his first, rapid-fire thoughts in an *esquisse*. Two notions came to him, and in a few pencil strokes, he produced thumbnails of a pair of rudimentary floor plans. One he rejected because, given the commission's proscription of columns, a traditional basilica church with a long nave and generous flanking aisles would not be acceptable. But the other jotting clearly contained the germ of an idea that might suit the site very well.

This floor plan had the plus-sign shape of a Greek cross with four short arms of equal length. Richardson noted the church's

Richardson's thumbnail of Trinity Church's plan—a crude crisscross of pencil stokes—was an almost immediate epiphany that would be realized in the years to come as a great stone edifice.

ninety-foot breadth, the width specified in the letter, which was consistent with Trinity's recently acquired plot at the corner of Saint James and Clarendon Streets in the Back Bay. The architect's simple yet full-blown conception had come to him in an instant. As one young friend explained, he had "a rare intuitive sense that enable[d] him to strike at the foundation and grasp the whole of a truth at once."[8]

Patrons constitute a distinct class of architectural co-conspirators. Without them, great buildings remain lines on paper, since architects rarely have the wherewithal to build their dreams. The best patrons are not merely bystanders with deep pockets but creative forces in their own right, and at Trinity Church, two men were poised to play this essential role. Phillips Brooks, rector of Trinity, would be the client, while Robert Treat Paine, chair of the building committee, would function as the project's banker and overseer. Both born in 1835 and scions of Boston, they grew up as friends in the same downtown neighborhood and went on to earn their Harvard degrees in the class of 1855.

From there their paths diverged. A brief stint as a teacher at Boston Latin ended badly after Brooks found he could not control a roomful of thirty-five sixteen-year-olds; he resigned rather than face boys he termed "the most disagreeable set of creatures without exception that I ever met with."[9] Within a year, he had followed in the footsteps of numerous divines in both the maternal and paternal lines of his family, deciding to become a man of the cloth. After theological studies at the Episcopal Divinity School in Alexandria, Virginia, and his ordination as an Episcopal priest, he discovered that not all of his parishioners at Philadelphia's Holy Trinity Church welcomed his radical abolitionist stance. In time, he won them over, as his carol, "O Little Town of Bethlehem," rapidly became a Christmas standard, and his sermon on the occasion of Abraham Lincoln's death in 1865 was widely published.* By age thirty, he had emerged as a churchman of national stature, and in October 1869, Brooks accepted an invitation from the elders of Trinity Church to return to Boston.

Within months, he gained a significant convert. Having come to hear his old friend preach, Robert Treat Paine left King's Chapel, where he and his wife had married, giving up Unitarianism to be confirmed as an Episcopalian and a Trinity parishioner.

Paine's early adulthood had been very different from that of Brooks. The great-grandson of a signer of the Declaration of Independence, Paine attended Harvard Law School for a year, then traveled to Europe with his family. He continued law studies in Dresden and Paris, then joined an established law practice in Boston. His specialty in real estate law aided him as he assembled a fortune, with savvy speculations

---

* According to church organist Lewis Redner, whom Brooks asked to put his words to music, Redner awakened in the night hearing the sound of angels singing the melody, which he quickly jotted down. Brooks memorably said of Lincoln, "In him was vindicated the greatness of real goodness, and the goodness of real greatness."

in Michigan copper mines and railroad stocks as well as riskier Nebraska land bonds. Having succeeded in his single-minded quest to become wealthy, Paine decided he "was not willing to devote the last half of [my life] to the mere business of making money."[10] Retiring at age thirty-five, he launched a decades-long effort to improve the living conditions in Boston's slums, which involved the construction of hundreds of houses. He thus acquired an appetite for architecture.

Called to the pulpit at Boston's Trinity, Phillips Brooks arrived with ambitions. Trinity's existing church stood on an "ancient site" at the corner of Bishop's Alley and Summer Street, in a neighborhood where shops and the "noisy appliances of trade" had replaced most of the houses and gardens.[11] His parishioners voted in favor of a move, and Trinity soon acquired a location that would give the church immediate prominence. It overlooked Art Square, where the building for Boston's new Museum of Fine Arts was under construction on an adjacent site. Eleven men, including Paine, were named to a building committee.

Two weeks after receiving the invitation to compete for the Trinity commission, Richardson traveled to Boston to call upon Phillips Brooks, hoping to take the measure of the rector's expectations before submitting the firm's entry. Richardson was aware that his own personality—his exuberant charm, the passionate manner that had always attracted people to him—was part and parcel of what he, as an architect, had to sell, and he knocked on the door of Brooks's home on the evening of March 25, 1872.[12]

Richardson was tall for his time, at six feet, but the man who rose from his dinner table to greet the architect stood an imposing six feet four. Brooks knew and admired Richardson's work at the Brattle Square Church, and two Brooks cousins had played a role in commissioning Richardson to design Grace Church in nearby Medford. Brooks was no architectural novice himself, having overseen the completion of the new church for Holy Trinity in his Philadelphia days. Arriving well into construction, he had insisted the original tower design be changed, and the revised result had pleased him.

This time, exercising control from the start, Brooks held very firm notions about what he wanted. Trinity needed an impressive building, one that would help ensure that America's leading intellectual and cultural city remained a center of faith. As he explained to Richardson, he didn't want a building that was merely showy. He envisioned a great Episcopal monument, but one with an auditorium scaled to the human voice.

For Brooks, the rites and rituals and the show of the sacraments were less important than the sermon, and even his powerful voice might not reach the length of a long nave. Nor did Brooks want a high altar that resembled a great stage, remote from his flock. Despite his earlier failings as a teacher, he wanted to offer an accessible spiritual education. "Preaching," he believed, "is the communication of truth by man to men."[13] The churchman also admitted he didn't much like steeples and that he felt a strong obligation to welcome those who couldn't afford pew fees.

Better informed by the visit, Richardson returned to New York to resume work on the competition drawings. Meanwhile, Paine and Brooks made scouting trips to New York to visit Saint Thomas, Saint Bartholomew's, and Saint George's churches, continuing their architectural education. Informed, experienced, and thoughtful, they both wanted the right man to design the perfect church.

They would also be prompt in their decision. In early June 1872, Richardson burst into the morning parlor of a neighbor's home. Brandishing a roll of drawings, he announced exuberantly, "I've got it! I've got it! I've got it!"

"I see you have," the lady of the house observed, bemused at the man's boisterous interruption of her family's quiet breakfast. "But *what* is it you have?"

"I've got the Church!" Richardson exclaimed. "Trinity Church—in Boston. I've got it!"[14]

In the same way that Central Park established Olmsted, making him the central figure in American landscape design, Trinity Church would elevate Richardson to the position of the most admired architect of his era.

Another young man who sought work in Gambrill & Richardson's New York offices would contribute mightily to Trinity's design and execution. Olmsted again did the introductions, after his art critic friend Richard Grant White asked him to arrange an interview for his son Stanford.

Born in 1853, Stanford White was barely beyond boyhood, as evidenced by the ghost of a mustache adorning his upper lip. The freckled and redheaded lad, who went by Stanny, proffered his sketchbook. Examining the drawings, Richardson's trained eye detected a genuine ease and felicity with pencil and paintbrush. White had limned churches, houses, and landscapes, and his renderings were detailed, atmospheric, and varied.

The meeting unexpectedly turned out to be more than a matter of courtesy, since Gambrill & Richardson did need another draftsman. Unlike Charles McKim, however, who arrived after three years of training at the Ecole des Beaux-Arts, Stanford White had previously demonstrated no particular vocation for architecture. He admitted to dreams of becoming a famous painter but only after meeting John La Farge, another friend of his father, had a different path opened to him. La Farge advised him to forgo the difficult course of making it as a painter and try architecture instead.

The personable young man exuded energy and confidence, but more important, as Richardson could discern from his sketchbook, he possessed both an intuitive grasp of buildings and the ability to record them in a lively way on paper. These were rare and valuable skills at a time when accurate, elegant presentation drawings were important to winning commissions. Though Stanny could not claim any drafting or engineering training, Richardson recognized how useful his artistic skills might be in winning over clients. He hired him on the spot. When the time came to carry out a series of redesigns for Trinity Church, Stanford White was ready.

When the Trinity Church Building Committee chose his design, its members knew something that Richardson did not: The church

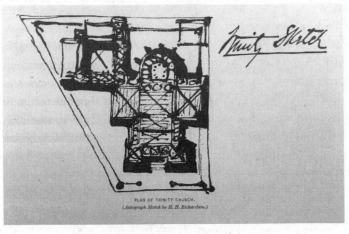

PLAN OF TRINITY CHURCH.
(Autograph Sketch by H. H. Richardson.)

*Richardson's autograph sketch, executed in June 1872, for the
enlarged site with the chapel added on the upper left.*

would not be built as rendered in the competition drawings. The
winning design would have to change, though neither Paine nor
Brooks could know how much or how many times.

In the preceding weeks, Paine had jumped at the chance to
acquire a triangular piece of adjacent land to the Trinity plot from
another church member; that meant the original 90-by-248-foot
rectangle at the corner of Clarendon and Saint James would assume
a trapezoidal shape. The added property would nearly double the
site to slightly more than an acre, permitting the addition of an attached Parish House. Employing his legal and real estate experience, Paine persuaded the city to eliminate the passageway between
the two parcels, and with a lithograph of the enlarged site in hand,
embarked on a "begging campaign" to raise the money needed to
close the deal.[15]

Where another architect might have been miffed that the
ground beneath his proposed building quite literally had expanded,
Richardson instead saw opportunity and quickly produced a fresh
esquisse. In his rudimentary sketch, the basic configuration of the
church remained a short-armed cross with a central tower. The Parish House rested to the north, coupled to the church by a cloistered

passageway. The result was a dense mass of conjoined structures that nearly filled the enlarged site.

That summer Richardson fell seriously ill. The episode, his worst yet, continued into the autumn, but no doctor could offer a clear diagnosis to explain the fatigue and other discomforts that left him unable to rise from his bed. Assuming he would recover, Brooks continued to hold services in Trinity's 1828 church on Summer Street, just as he had since arriving three years earlier, and Paine went about his fundraising campaign. No new drawings appeared from New York, but the building committee remained patient—until the great Boston fire of November 9, 1872.

The Saturday night was cold and the wind blustery, when at 7:22 P.M., somebody pulled the lever of one of Boston's fire-alarm boxes. Flames in the basement of a commercial warehouse on Summer Street shot up the building's wooden elevator shaft to the upper floors. Then still an architecture student, Louis Sullivan happened to witness one of the first outward signs of the fire when he saw "a small flame curling from the wooden cornice."[16] The fire leapt to adjacent buildings, and by the time Boston's engine companies contained it, twelve hours later, the inferno had consumed almost eight hundred buildings, including the existing Trinity Church.

Its tower had collapsed, leaving only blackened and crumbling walls. With its church in ruins, Trinity's congregation was suddenly homeless. Brooks arranged for Sunday services in Huntington Hall, at the Institute of Technology, and for weddings at Emmanuel Church. The fire also prompted Brooks and Paine to climb aboard a southbound train to visit the still-ailing Richardson in New York. They wanted to assess the architect's ability to complete what he had begun. Time had become a new imperative.

Once in New York, they took an afternoon ferry to Staten Island. The busy Richardson household now included four children under six, including a second daughter, Mary, born in 1871, and two-month-old Henry. Adapting to his illness, Richardson had begun working from his bed. After going over drawings for several hours, the Bostonians departed, relieved and reassured that the plans for the new Trinity Church were "nearly completed."[17] On February 17, 1873, detailed drawings arrived in Boston, along with Richardson himself, who presented them at a building committee meeting.

In a series of subsequent submissions—more new plans arrived in April, another batch in May—the central features of Trinity evolved. The church's footprint remained roughly as long it was wide, but Richardson shortened the tower. The man he most needed to please, Phillips Brooks, liked what he saw, but committee members raised a "question of safety."[18] They worried that the great octagonal tower, an immense superstructure of stone, might sink the finished church into the "made land" of Boston's new Back Bay neighborhood.

The underlying geologic strata were the concern. Deep down there was rock, but immediately beneath the surface were thirty feet of fresh fill and below that the muddy bottom of what had been the bay, a layer of blue clay, then hardpan. While the surface looked like solid ground, everyone wondered how much the mix would compress under the weight of a major stone edifice.

Extraordinary measures would have to be taken to prevent the church from settling into the mud, but the problem was certainly not new. At the house Richardson designed for Ben Crowninshield, wooden pilings had been driven into the ground, a stabilizing technique in use all over the Back Bay. But the challenge at the Trinity Church site was vastly greater because of the sheer bulk of the church and its generous Parish House.

On April 21, 1873, pile driving began at the site of the future Trinity Church. The first of a veritable forest of spruce trunks, each roughly a foot in a diameter, were driven into the gravel and clay. A clerk recorded the location and depth of each piling, some of which went down thirty-five feet. He noted "the weight of the hammer with which it was driven, the distance the pile sank at the last three blows, and height from which the hammer fell." Using these data, a contour map would be made of the "bearing stratum."[19]

Though the casual observer might detect little progress that summer, hundreds and hundreds of posts were being submerged below grade, the first of what would eventually be forty-eight hundred pilings. The most critical were at the four corners of the church's crossing, where immense horizontal timbers would be anchored to the dense grid of pilings using mortise-and-tenon joints. The result—in effect, four fixed wooden rafts—became the foundations for the building's main piers. The wood beneath would be flooded and disappear beneath the church, since wood that remains constantly immersed in water does not rot. On top would be pyramidal stacks of stone that Gambrill & Richardson draftsmen had carefully drawn and dimensioned to support the church that rose above. It was an elegant solution to the most muscular of tasks.

While the site preparation was underway in Boston, Richardson revised the design yet again to allay the committee's fear of subsidence. By his calculations, lowering the tower's height would decrease its weight more than nine thousand tons to about seven thousand. He also lowered the main building's height, a proposal his draftsmen delineated in a new set of plans. But a team of consulting engineers hired by the building committee remained fearful, and the committee rejected the revised plan and then its members collectively resigned.[20] In their place, a three-man executive committee, led by Paine, assumed responsibility.

After Richardson delivered another revised plan in September, the decision was made to seek preliminary construction cost estimates, but this brought more bad news. Even the lowest of the estimates soared well above anyone's expectations. The once hoped-for construction cost of $200,000 suddenly seemed ludicrously low. Stunned at the expense—the bids ranged from $355,000 to $640,000—the vestry halted all work except the pilings to support the main walls.

With the project paused, even the usually positive Paine had his doubts, seeing "no escape from the necessity of abandoning the plans."[21] But Richardson invited a fourth man into the inner circle. The author of the lowest estimate, Orlando Whitney Norcross, soon emerged, along with Paine, Brooks, and the architect himself, as one of the four men critical to realizing Trinity Church.

Unlike the other three, O. W., as he was known, possessed no Harvard degree. Born in 1839, he had spent his early years in Maine, where his father, Jesse, operated a sawmill. But the family's fortunes shifted when Jesse left for California to try his luck as a forty-niner and went missing in the gold fields. He never returned.[22]

Together with his brother James, O. W. spent his teen years as a journeyman carpenter, working in and around the prosperous port city of Salem, Massachusetts. When the Civil War began, he enlisted in the First Massachusetts Heavy Artillery and put his mechanical skills to good use building bridges and roads for the Union Army. After discharge, in 1864, he and James joined forces as builders. Their reputation for skill and integrity led to an 1866 commission for a church in Leicester, taking them to central Massachusetts. In 1868, they established headquarters in the rapidly growing industrial city of Worcester. There they first encountered Richardson, who had been commissioned to design the new Worcester High School in 1869. Their collaboration continued on other Richardson projects, including the Hampden County Courthouse in Springfield, Massachusetts, in 1871. Richardson nurtured a bond of trust with O. W. in particular, one he could use in maturing the Trinity Church design. For Norcross Brothers, as for Richardson, the new church would provide a career lift unlike any other.

A short, sturdy man with the hands of a laborer, O. W. functioned as the outside man for Norcross Brothers. While brother James managed the office and kept the books, O. W. met architects and clients and inspected building sites. He did the estimating of the material and labor costs, and already had a reputation for keeping his men busy by underpricing competitors ("Orlando," noted one contemporary credit report, had few peers in "figuring on contracts, closely and with safety").[23] Facing an uproar at Trinity's high costs, Richardson asked Norcross to sharpen his pencils.

At a glance, they made strange bedfellows: Richardson tall and patrician, Norcross stocky, with a protuberant nose and a cartoonish walrus mustache that almost obscured his mouth. Norcross was a determined temperance man, while Richardson liked nothing better than a quaff of champagne. But the two had become "strong personal friends" and Richardson got what he hoped for.[24] O. W. honed his bid, already the lowest by far, another 20 percent. Paine and the others at Trinity agreed to terms, and after the signing of a construction contract on October 10, 1873, Norcross Brothers opened an office at 79 Huntington Avenue, in Boston, to manage their big new project.

Some architects insist their work is utterly original. Frank Lloyd Wright, born during Trinity's construction, would be one such. Although his designs often mimicked Richardson's arches and borrowed from the man he trained with, Louis Sullivan, Wright liked to say he was indebted to no one.

By contrast, Richardson's generous spirit permitted him to admit that he owed something to someone for almost everything he did. Though no copyist, he nonetheless was alive to stimuli, past and present. At Trinity, where the ground rules changed often, Richardson repeatedly ransacked his library and photo collection for a solution to the too-tall and too-heavy tower. He particularly admired a Romanesque church, Saint-Paul-in-Issoire, in southern France, which he knew from photographs. But he also consulted the archive he carried around in his head, his own store of architectural memories, many of which dated from student days and his time in Europe.

Among them was a mental picture of the English village of Hooton near Liverpool, which he had visited in 1861. There he had seen a nearly finished parish church, another Saint Paul's, designed by engineer and architect J. K. Colling. Its plan was a Greek cross, with a short nave and shallow transepts. The apse that protruded at the rear was round. A dome hovered over the crossing and a rose window lit the nave. The church's exterior was an earthy polychrome of stone. The overall manner was Romanesque, and Colling's church, though hardly a cathedral, bore an unmistakable resemblance to Richardson's first conception of Trinity.

One difference, however, was significant. In Gambrill & Richardson's winning presentation drawings, Trinity was topped with a tower and a spire that soared above the roofline, with a combined height more than one and a half times the height of the nave. In contrast, Saint Paul's tower was much shorter. Reaching into the depths of his memory more than a decade later, Richardson found a piece of his Boston puzzle in James Colling's church.

On April 15, 1874, he presented still another set of sketches to the building committee. He had lowered the church walls another six feet, on top of the four-foot reduction made in his 1873 revisions. The tower was simplified, as the lantern that had been its topmost feature was now gone. The rose window had disappeared too, replaced with a series of arches, and the apse had shrunk.[25] His sketches were preliminary but pleased the client. "I am glad to say," Brooks wrote to Richardson, "how pleasant the sketch of the new tower struck me when I saw it."[26]

Over a period of several more months, Richardson had continued to refine his design, balancing his own instincts with the concerns of the building committee and its engineers. The setting around the church site was evolving too. The neighborhood consisted of half-empty lots dotted with a few plain-faced town houses of four or five stories, but it was changing with the construction of two other

The tower at Trinity Church as drawn by Stanford White, in April 1874. Roughly as wide it was high, the new tower, its footprint square, consisted of a two-story cube with small corner towers and a pyramidal roof.

new churches, including Brattle Square Church, as well as the Museum of Fine Arts. Richardson, with his Beaux-Arts training in urban planning, understood that Trinity and its Parish House needed to be a part of this urbane conversation.

The design solution for the tower came to him when, once again remanded to his sickbed by fatigue, he received a sheaf of photographs from his painter friend John La Farge. An image of the Old Cathedral in Salamanca, Spain, was "like a spark to tinder." On seeing its tower, Richardson exclaimed, "This is what I want."[27]

Richardson might also have known the church from a book on his shelves, *Some Account of Gothic Architecture in Spain*, by British architect George Edmund Street. "Better than the lantern of any church," Street had written in 1865, the Salamanca tower solves "the question of the introduction of the dome to Gothic churches."[28] In search of a solution, Richardson also reinvigorated an earlier—and unexecuted—design of his own. Just a month before receiving Trinity's invitation, Gambrill & Richardson had lost a contest to design a new Connecticut capitol, but the firm's entry had featured a cross-shaped floor plan with a low, square central tower.

All these sources—St. Paul's, Salamanca, the Hartford capitol proposal—floated into Richardson's head. He also had the help of the gifted Stanford White, who would produce a mesmerizing perspective drawing. Executed under Richardson's guidance, it played a role in persuading the committee the solution had finally been found for its newly earthbound building. Possessed of the rare confidence to second-guess himself, Richardson would later acknowledge that he preferred the much-revised finished version to his original conception. "I really don't see why the Trinity people liked them [the 1872 competition drawings]," he admitted, "[or] why they let me do what I afterwards did!"[29] What emerged was what Richardson himself called "a free rendering of the French romanesque."

Chapter Ten

~

BUILDING TRINITY CHURCH

[Richardson] was obliged . . . to throw over-board in dealing with the new
problems all his educational recipes learned in other countries.

—JOHN LA FARGE

Julia delivered a fifth child, Philip, in February 1874, but the continuing series of journeys to Boston kept Richardson from his family for
days at a time. Construction at Trinity was proceeding at full speed,
and he needed to attend building committee meetings, conduct frequent inspections, and promptly certify Norcross's bills. With other
new work pending in New England, the moment seemed right for a
change. Richardson decided to make Massachusetts his home.

Richardson would not move the family to the city proper but to
Boston's outskirts, as he had done in New York. He settled Julia and
the children into a comfortable suburban house, at 25 Cottage Street
in Brookline, rented to him by his old Harvard classmate Ned Hooper.
Richardson knew the town, having entered a competition for a town
hall design in 1870, although his plan was not selected. The village of
just eight thousand residents retained the qualities Andrew Jackson
Downing had ascribed to it after a visit more than thirty years before.
The rolling hills west of Jamaica Pond, Downing had written, resembled "a kind of landscape garden, . . . so inexpressively charming as
the lanes which lead from one cottage, or villa to another . . . give it
quite an Arcadian air of rural freedom and enjoyment."[1]

Erected as a farmhouse in 1803, the family's new abode resembled one of the planters' mansions that Richardson knew from his
Louisiana childhood. Although its hip roof respected the local New

England vernacular, its wraparound, two-story porch echoed the Caribbean style typical of Louisiana's River Road. The large house, complete with servants' quarters and many bedrooms, suited the Richardsons' expanding family. The generous plot of more than two acres would suit another arrival, a great mastiff named Rover. Richardson rarely did anything in a small way.

From Brookline he sent his rough sketches to the Gambrill & Richardson offices, where his draftsmen worked at more polished drawings. But this cumbersome process occasioned delay, and Norcross, for one, worried about the absence of timely drawings. "No work can be done economically," he complained, "without knowing what will come up the next week."[2]

Richardson found an expedient. A draftsman—usually Stanford White—would board a train in New York with freshly executed plans to be carried north. "Tall, lank, red-haired, freckle faced, with interest and enthusiasm expressed in every feature and every movement," he would be both delivery boy and apprentice. He had become Richardson's favored draftsman, since Charles McKim, essential to the early designs of the church, had departed to launch a practice of his own in a small office adjoining Gambrill & Richardson.[3]

When in Boston, White was deputized to make any further changes to the plans. During these sojourns, he lived at Richardson's house, sometimes for a week at a time, working under the watchful eye of the man he called "the Great Mogul." White told his mother, "Thanks to Richardson and his committees, I feel as if I had been standing on my head all week." He also became keenly aware of his mentor's health. "How Richardson can be, I can't tell; for, setting aside all brandies, gins, wines, and cigars, he seems to subsist chiefly on boiled tripe which he insists upon calling the 'entrails of a cow.'"[4] The energetic young man couldn't help but notice Richardson's increasing girth—he now weighed well over two hundred pounds—and his uncharacteristic, if occasional, listlessness.

Other draftsmen sometimes came to Brookline, evoking memories of the Atelier André in Paris. As one architect friend reported, "[Richardson] soon found that he could do his best work in the quiet and retirement of his own home."[5] The home at 25 Cottage

Street became a teaching experiment, one that brought out his mentoring skills.

In the good hands of O. W. Norcross, construction at Trinity proceeded apace. Per the orders of the building committee, the Parish House (also called the Chapel) would be built first. The smaller building anticipated the big church, built of a matching mix of stone. The walls would be of random-size, rough-cut granite, quarried in Dedham, Massachusetts, set in red mortar. A reddish-brown sandstone was chosen for the trimming and cut stonework. It arrived by rail from East Longmeadow, Massachusetts, a hundred miles west.

By November 1874, after a mere eight months, Norcross Brothers completed the Parish House. Trinity's Sunday school began meeting in the new space, and for the first time since the fire, normality began to return to a congregation exiled to strange quarters. By then the church's walls were well aboveground, and four derricks were hoisting the large stones, some of them two tons or more, as the walls rose higher. Access to the towers was made possible by scaffolding, massive freestanding superstructures of timber. By mid-spring 1875, the walls had risen two stories, and in June the walls stood more than fifty feet in height.[6] On July 27, the main arches at the crossing were completed.[7]

Nonetheless, the process wasn't always smooth, and the men managing it were learning one another's limits. On a July day, Paine interfered once too often. After he issued an instruction to workmen—without consulting Norcross—word reached O. W. The usually self-contained contractor hotly warned Paine that if he interfered again, he would be banished from the work site.[8]

The Trinity project, news of which spread far beyond Massachusetts and Manhattan, gave Richardson a new visibility in his profession. But his network of old friends still played a key role in getting him assignments.

Almost two hundred miles west of Boston, in Albany, William Dorsheimer, recently elected New York State's lieutenant governor, had a problem. A report in May 1875 by the senate finance committee found the new state capitol building was vastly over budget, with an estimated cost of $4 million ballooning to $11 million. Two builders from New York claimed that the interior walls were being constructed of a dangerously inferior quality of brick.[9] Construction was lagging too, and after six years, an empty shell stood just two stories high, less than half its proposed height.

In search of a solution, Dorsheimer called upon Richardson and Olmsted. Together with a German-trained and New York–based architect named Leopold Eidlitz, they would serve as a three-man architectural advisory board. Dorsheimer charged them with examining the building, which had been designed by Thomas Fuller, a British-born architect and author of the palatial Parliament House in Ottawa. He wanted the trio to recommend a way forward.

They delivered a damning twenty-eight-page report in March 1876. If the present plan were carried out, they believed, the interior would be ill lit, its interior arrangements inconvenient, the roof irregular and too complicated. They saw structural flaws, and in their view, the exterior would be banal. They even second-guessed Fuller's choice of the Italian Renaissance style. They adjudged the building a hodgepodge that would require "a very decided remodeling of the design above the third floor."[10]

Despite the report's careful documentation, the entire architectural profession was soon embroiled in a controversy surrounding the building's future. Perhaps the loudest voice was Richard Morris Hunt's. He spoke for many in the profession when he expressed shock and outrage at the nearly unprecedented recommendation by Eidlitz and Richardson to change the building's style mid-construction. Hunt also thought it was unethical to alter another man's design. He coauthored a widely distributed "Remonstrance," calling the proposed change a "direct antagonism to the received rules of art." Eidlitz and Richardson recommended the upper stories be Romanesque, and Hunt thought the mere suggestion exhibited bad manners. He termed the proposed melding of Renaissance and Romanesque "absolutely inharmonious."[11]

Albany politicians took turns supporting and undercutting the plans of Dorsheimer and his advisers. Olmsted was somewhat sympathetic to those who protested, admitting to a confidant that he worried the finished building might have a "patchwork character."[12]

Typically, Richardson chose not to respond—his public pronounce-
ments were rare—but he privately offered Olmsted and Dorsheimer
a stylistic argument for those opposed to changing styles.

"I do believe," he wrote, "that the building can be well finished
in Francois 1st or Louis XIV which come under the head of Renaissance."[13] For him this wasn't an either-or choice between Renaissance
and Romanesque: harmony and good taste should rule. Richardson
and Eidlitz got to work redesigning the building, while Fuller lob-
bied the American Institute of Architects for support. But the controversy quieted, and Dorsheimer, as chairman of the New Capitol
Commission, bulled ahead. Fuller was asked to resign, and Eidlitz,
Richardson & Co., a temporary architectural partnership created
specifically for the project, was retained to complete the job in Albany's Capitol Park, aided by the measured mediation of Olmsted.

In his early fifties, Eidlitz was a seasoned architect, with work
that ranged from Saint George's Episcopal Church in New York to
Iranistan, an extraordinary Moorish mansion capped with an onion
dome built for circus impresario P. T. Barnum in Bridgeport, Connecticut. Eidlitz and Richardson divided the design responsibilities
at the Albany capitol. Although the floor plan couldn't be changed,
the complexity of the structure meant much could be. Eidlitz began
with the larger Assembly Chamber while Richardson took on the
Senate and Executive Chambers, the State Library, and the Court of
Appeals. Eidlitz got the eastern stair, Richardson the western.

Olmsted meanwhile sorted out the existing contracts with
builders and suppliers. Dorsheimer supervised, monitoring the delicate balance of the lavish designs Richardson and Eidlitz produced
and the budget, which remained the project's main political liability. The four men became an effective team, meeting regularly in
Albany to inspect progress. On more than one occasion, when Richardson had been at his New York offices, the four men traveled together on the night steamer from Manhattan to Albany. "There was
never so much wit and humor and science and art on that boat before or since," *New York World* writer Montgomery Schuyler said of
the conversations he overheard while churning north on the Hudson. Richardson would rhapsodize in his passionate manner, and
Eidlitz, in his German-accented English, would interrupt, offering

"I have already begun sketching on the dormers & roofs & know that something good can be done," Richardson wrote to Olmsted, on March 26, 1876. This photograph, taken nearly a decade later, shows the largely completed exterior of the Albany capitol.

his own propositions. Missing nothing, Olmsted would, "at critical points [offer] a mild Socratic inquiry always of high pertinence." And Dorsheimer "hover[ed] on the circumference of the discussion like a genial chorus."[14] Many years later Olmsted, too, would recall warmly "our all-night debates."[15]

The most admired room in the finished building would be the Senate Chamber. Richardson entrusted much of the work to Stanford White, who produced lush and detailed drawings. White wrote to his sculptor friend Augustus Saint-Gaudens, "Between us, I think we have cooked up something pretty decent. . . . The whole room is to be a piece of color."[16]

Beneath the oak beams that lined the ceiling fifty feet above, White and Richardson blended gray Knoxville granite, dark yellow Siena marble, Mexican onyx, columns of Scottish red-brown granite, and gilded-leather upper walls. The floor covering was a flowered carpet. They designed the tall clocks, elaborate paneling, and red-leather and mahogany chairs, one of which, larger than the others, would accommodate Dorsheimer's three-hundred-and-fifty-pound girth. Richardson's goal—blending the opulent with the simple to achieve serenity—was widely admired.*

From Brookline, Richardson wrote to Olmsted regularly in New York, providing updates on progress in Albany. The easy comradeship the families shared as Staten Island neighbors had ended, but family news filtered into the men's conversation, and their letters invariably closed with affectionate regards sent from one man's wife to the other. The Olmsted family had expanded when, after years of trying (a second son tragically died just hours after his birth, in 1866), a healthy son of Olmsted's own, Henry Perkins Olmsted, arrived on July 24, 1870. The baby thrived, but his name sat uneasily with Olmsted, who never got in the habit of calling him by his Christian name, more often referring to him as "Boy." Worrying about his professional legacy, Olmsted, by then aging into his fifties, began thinking about the boy as an heir in more than a legal sense. Thus, the child, before reaching school age, became Frederick Law Olmsted Jr., abbreviated by the family to Rick.[17]

In their correspondence, Richardson confided in Olmsted concerning his medical condition, which showed no sign of lessening. "You will be interested to know that Dr. Hodges made a partial examination of me to day," he reported. His body tended to swell with accumulated water weight, and "finding my parts very much engorged," he told Olmsted, the doctor "has ordered me to my bed for one week when he will make a careful examination." In a way that he did with no other friend, he went further. "He intends to do for me all that one can for another. . . . I may be obliged to submit to an operation but will object and resist anything that endangers my life on account of my wife and babies."[18]

---

* The worries over cost overruns that prompted the change in architect were more than realized under Eidlitz and Richardson. Perhaps the best-known architectural element in the New York State Capitol is Richardson's Great Western Stair—better known by its popular nickname, the "Million Dollar Staircase"—which cost that and more. Its 444 steps reached a height of 119 feet. Some fourteen years were required to complete construction, which included seventy-seven carved stone faces of prominent Americans.

During this time, the couple also welcomed another child, their sixth and last. Richardson was in Albany at the moment Julia gave birth, on July 10, 1876. Dining with his capitol collaborators, he was overjoyed to hear the news and proclaimed the child would bear the name of the men around him. He was christened Frederick Leopold William Richardson.[19]

In Boston, the exterior of Trinity Church neared completion. Walls of quarry-cut gray granite melded with arches, columns, and other details, shaped and carved in the muted brown sandstone. Fired-clay red tiles roofed the tower, an earthy contrast to the charcoal-gray slate of the lower pitched roofs. With the last stone laid in July 1876, the massive church, a mix of textured surfaces and restful colors, possessed an unexpected quietude.

Inside, however, the look would be anything but understated. There Richardson's subtle language of stone would give way to a colorful conversation of an entirely different kind. From the outset, the architect had envisioned what he called a "color church."[20] Rather than the "cold, harsh effect of stone," he imagined "a rich effect of color in the interior," one that "could not be obtained in any practicable material without painting."[21] This wouldn't be merely an explosion of color. Even in the initial presentation drawings, Richardson hinted at a decorative program with huge portraits of seated and standing apostles and prophets bringing the weight of biblical history, and he knew precisely whom he wanted to hire to bring the worship space to vibrant life.

Richardson and John La Farge had met in Manhattan in 1866, when Charles Gambrill's then partner, George B. Post, introduced them. Post told La Farge that Richardson was "a clever man who would make his mark." For his part, La Farge thought the design for the Springfield church he saw on Richardson's drafting table was "striking." La Farge told Post, "*That* looks like the beginning of genius."[22]

Three years apart in age, the two men had much in common. Having returned to America something of a Parisian, Richardson spoke French with La Farge, who, though a native New Yorker, had learned the language as a child from his émigré parents. La Farge had studied in France, toured its medieval cathedrals, and trained in the studio of academic painter Thomas Couture during an 1850s grand tour. On returning home, La Farge had continued his painting studies in Newport, Rhode Island, with William Morris Hunt, brother to architect Richard Morris Hunt.

For decades, La Farge would keep a studio on Tenth Street in Manhattan, sharing the building with Frederic Church and other artists. He was tall and slim, typically dressed in black, and spoke in a deep and sonorous voice. He, too, was a member of the Century Club, though he favored dining alone. A fastidious man, he shrank from shaking hands but, like Richardson, possessed a large gift for friendship. Among his most valued companions were Henry and William James (the former fondly remembered La Farge's advice that he give up painting to become a writer). Henry Adams, who met La Farge while both were teaching at Harvard in the early 1870s, thought he was, quite simply, "the best conversationalist of his time."[23]

During their New York days, La Farge and Richardson rapidly formed a mutual admiration society. They saw a good deal of each other, often meeting on Staten Island, where La Farge enjoyed "day and night hospitality." After seeing wall panels of fish and flowers that La Farge had painted for a Boston dining room, Richardson proposed they work together. "[He] made me promise," La Farge reported, "to accept some decorative work in the first building that he might control throughout."[24]

When the Brattle Square Church commission came to him in 1870, Richardson thought it the perfect vehicle for such a collaboration. To the disappointment of both men, however, the church ran out of money, and La Farge never joined the team.* Now, six years later, the architect, once again laid low by his still undiagnosed disease, summoned John La Farge to his bedside in Brookline. He wanted La Farge to decorate Trinity with murals characteristic of the Romanesque churches that had inspired it.[25]

---

* Rather than La Farge murals, the congregation chose a less expensive stenciling scheme. That said, La Farge remembered playing an indirect role at Brattle Square Church. When Richardson visited his studio, La Farge introduced him to Bartholdi, who subsequently designed Brattle's signature frieze. Among the faces the French sculptor depicted overlooking Commonwealth Avenue were likenesses of Richardson and La Farge.

"Like many other great men [Richardson] was a mighty eater and drinker," La Farge recalled. "A pitcher of milk, a pitcher of champagne, a pitcher of water—everything was done on a large scale."[26] Perhaps it was no surprise, then, that the job his friend offered him would be the largest painting ever attempted by an American artist.

Only one other American work could justly be spoken of in the same breath. A fresco, titled *The Apotheosis of George Washington*, completed in 1865, lined the dome of the United States Capitol. But its artist, Constantino Brumidi, had spent years planning his "canopy" and another year painting General Washington and his angelic host. In comparison, the schedule at Trinity would be absurdly short.

In the summer of 1876, Richardson laid the enormous task before La Farge. The artist had never attempted anything like it: he was to cover some twenty thousand square feet, an area almost five times that of *Apotheosis*, and the Trinity Church Building Committee wanted it done by Christmas. Richardson warned there was little hope of "pecuniary profit," calling upon his friend's "true enthusiasm . . . for the highest exercise of a painter's talents."[27]

Both logistics and cost made the notion of fully illustrating the upper levels of the church unlikely at this late date, so initially Richardson did not tell the building committee of his conversations with La Farge. Paine and the rest had already accepted that, for "reason of economy" they would have to settle for "the simplest treatment."[28] But to Richardson, a plain coat of paint on the plastered interior wasn't acceptable, and he and La Farge quietly set about assembling a proposal to present to the committee. La Farge would take virtually no fee beyond expenses. The builder's scaffolding offered a significant economy, since the painters could use the staging already in place inside the church, sharing it with the builders as they completed the roof tiling and window installation.

La Farge devised a specific plan for the immense job. Aside from the prevailing color of the church—Richardson and Phillips Brooks specified a "red effect"—the scheme was his to invent. He visited Trinity twice in late August, and at his request, Gambrill & Richardson forwarded him measured drawings of the transepts, apse, ceiling, nave walls, and moldings.

In mid-September, Richardson submitted La Farge's plan to the building committee. "I hereby propose to execute the decoration of the auditorium of Trinity Church," La Farge had written, "in general conformity with the sketches submitted herewith." He asked for just $8,000 and agreed to complete the work by December 20.[29] His sketches featured six giant saints, together with a series of elaborate panels for the tower and upper walls of the nave. He would engage a painting firm to complete the coloring of all the walls and ceilings. He would hire a half dozen fine painters to help him complete the figures. One of those was the young Irish artist Augustus Saint-Gaudens.

On September 15, the building committee approved the proposal. The completion date loomed, barely three months away.

On Wednesday, September 24, 1876, the walls began to turn red.[30] The figurative and ornamental work would start later, so in these early days, La Farge came and went as the church took on the hue of what Richardson called Pompeian red (La Farge himself preferred "Persian red"). The artist visited the building site when necessary but spent many hours sketching out preliminary drawings in his Newport studio while his team of painters executed the groundwork. In mid-October, he moved to Boston for the duration.

La Farge chose encaustic paint, using a formula given to him twenty years before by Henry Le Strange, the painter of a dramatic tower ceiling at England's Ely Cathedral. Mixed on-site, it required melting wax into pine turpentine, alcohol, and costly imported Venetian turpentine, an oil distilled from the European larch tree. La Farge thought the expense justified. "I was asked how long the paint would last, and I told our anxious committee that it would last when the city of Boston no longer existed."[31]

La Farge and his team began their work high in the tower, applying their brushes to open areas defined by the building's moldings, pilasters, and arches. The illustration program was ambitious, starting with sixty-four ornamental patterns recessed into the panels of the coffered ceiling, 103 feet above the floor. Next came the upper tower walls that framed the windows, which would feature symbols that looked like they came from the pages of a medieval illuminated manuscript. Among them were the Ox of Saint Luke, the Lion of Saint Mark, the Eagle of Saint John, and Latin crosses. A dozen scriptural scenes would decorate the lunettes over the windows.

La Farge provided the other artists with paper cartoons covered with scaled gridlines and scrawled notes, but the hurried schedule meant that one day's work often came from his pencil only the night before. The manner of the painting was primitive, the illustrations highlighted by a red and gold background. The assistants worked as they would have in a Renaissance or Baroque workshop—a *bottega*, La Farge liked to call it—executing the work in the master's style. "The aim," said La Farge of Raphael's workshop, "was the work itself, and not who did this or that part."[32]

The painters often had an audience of people who came to crane their necks upward. The onlookers couldn't see a great deal as they peered between staging timbers to assess progress, but in early November, one of those on the church floor got dangerously close to the action.

On Thursday, November 2, the Reverend Brooks treated himself to a trip to the Back Bay to survey progress on his magnificent new church, close to completion after so long. As was his habit, he had delivered his midweek sermon the night before at Trinity's temporary meeting place. Now he found the ubiquitous Paine noting progress in his detailed log while teams of Norcross's and La Farge's men busied themselves high above.

One of the workers in the tower nudged something near an opening in the scaffolding floor. Precisely what happened in the next few heartbeats is variously remembered. The object in free fall—by one account, it was a plank, though La Farge thought it a box—plummeted toward the floor. It accelerated directly toward Phillips Brooks.

Paine shouted out a warning, and Brooks had a second, perhaps two, to react. As Paine coolly noted later in his diary, "Mr. Brooks had a narrow escape from being killed, a box falling down the Tower Inside & he just escaped by jumping aside."[33] The preacher barely avoided the fate of becoming the first man buried within Trinity's walls.

On November 24, 1876, the dismantling of the staging began on the uppermost level of the tower. Though the painting proceeded at a remarkable pace, a mix of problems presented themselves. The firm hired to redden the lower walls quit, and another contractor had to be found. Although the building committee had promised the building would be closed up and heated for the painters, the installation of the five furnaces took longer than expected.[34] Then the delivery of the windows brought objections from La Farge. The yellow tint of the glass clashed with his color scheme; it was, he said, "more than atrocious."[35] Richardson took his side in the dispute, but their alternative—a fish-scale pattern of yellow, olive, and red glass—meant another delay in sealing out the elements.

As November drew to a close, Richardson wrote to Olmsted in New York about the New York State Capitol project, apologizing for his absence. Though he knew his presence was needed in Albany, he said, "I cannot leave Trinity just now." La Farge insisted he be on hand for approvals, but Richardson assured Olmsted the end was in sight in Boston.

On the following Wednesday, Norcross sent formal word that the church building itself was substantially completed, though the same could not be said of the painting. La Farge and his crew needed more time. According to his revised schedule, the simpler work would be done by January 6, though completing the "purely artistic portion . . . the figure painting" would take the rest of the month.[36] With the painters still working their way down the walls of the tower, the building committee had little choice but to extend the completion date.

When Richardson wrote again from Brookline, on December 15, he was elated. "[La Farge's work] is glorious," he told Olmsted. He wished he could share his joy with his New York friend. "I'd give a [great] deal if you could come and see Trinity."[37]

The frantic weeks of work that followed were, in La Farge's memory, a "jamboree." Despite fighting off illness, he and the other artists worked in the cold and windy church dressed in overcoats and gloves. After the other paintwork was largely completed in early January, the team of artists faced the daunting job of completing the six full-length figures that stood guard at the crossing. As La Farge and Brooks had agreed, these eighteen-foot-tall holy men were Isaiah, Jeremiah, a youthful King David, an aged Moses, and Saints Peter and Paul (the last would be painted by Saint-Gaudens). With the date for the church's consecration ceremony set for February 8, the tenacious La Farge tested his limits.

He required the help of an assistant to climb the ladder to his perch because an acute episode of lead poisoning ten years earlier had left him unsteady on his feet.* "Slung on a narrow board sixty feet above the floor of the church," he remembered, "with one arm passed around a rope and holding my palette, while the other was passed around the other rope, I painted on my last figure." He worked for twenty-one of the final twenty-four hours before the deadline of 7:00 A.M., February 1, 1877.[38]

Only after the exhausted La Farge descended could the last of the scaffolding be dismantled. The staging had risen with the building; no one had seen the interior of Trinity without the rough-cut framework that filled the crossing. As the timbers were lowered to the ground—the last were stacked in the yard on Saturday morning, February 3—curious onlookers found their way in.

On Monday, the *Boston Transcript* published the first public assessment:

> The grand exterior dimensions of the church somewhat prepare one for the spaciousness within. But only seeing can realize the superb beauty of the decoration, rich yet not garish, elaborate and not "piled on," magnificent in splendors, yet noble and dignified, artistic yet religious and fitting for the place. Its richness is beyond compare, because there is literally

---

* In keeping with the ill-informed medical practice of the time, La Farge was variously diagnosed with malaria, rheumatism, neuritis, and neurasthenia; his numerous symptoms, which included insomnia and eye strain, were also attributed to lead poisoning, a plausible but uncertain diagnosis. Some have suggested his ailments were more likely somatic or stress-related. La Farge himself described his ailments in correspondence with Henry Adams. See also Adams, "John La Farge, 1830–1870" (1980), pp. 259ff.

nothing like it this side of the ocean. Trinity is the first church
in this country to be decorated by artists.[39]

The anonymous commentary would be the first of countless
enthusiastic notices in the days and years to come. But only four
days remained until the church's first public ceremony when many
worthies of Boston were scheduled to walk the length of the nave for
Trinity's consecration. Before then, the church interior had to be
cleaned, floors finished, carpets laid, and the organ installed. Under
Richardson's guidance, the young draftsmen at Gambrill & Richardson had designed the furniture and fittings for the interior. The details matched the architecture of the church, thickly proportioned
and incorporating medieval iconographic details like trefoils and
quatrefoils. Black walnut was the material of choice for wainscoting,
doors, and trim, ash and oak for the stairways.

Norcross Brothers' workshops supplied the architectural woodwork, but the 238 pews, manufactured according to a drawing by
Stanford White, were milled across the river at Osborn's Mill in
Cambridgeport. The shop specialized in church furniture, and its
workers varnished Trinity's seating a rich reddish-brown to complement the red paint scheme of the walls.

Phillips Brooks wanted his church to welcome not the few but
the many, so Richardson had designed galleries, located above the
church floor in the facing transepts; they would be open to the public, requiring no one to pay a pew tax or fee to attend. The number of seats in the galleries, a total of roughly four hundred, was
larger than the total congregation at many houses of worship. To
the consternation of some, the liberal Reverend Brooks welcomed
not just Episcopalians but even Unitarians to his consecration
ceremony.

The completed structure unmistakably embodied Richardson's
first imaginings as he had expressed them in a quick sketch five years
earlier. The floor plan, as designed and built, could be understood at
a glance, still a cross with four equal arms. The roof of the massive
building sloped as it ascended, dominating its Back Bay streetscape as
if it were a monadnock, the geographical phenomenon of a hill that
stands noticeably above its surroundings. As the praise heaped upon

it would demonstrate, the building, at once richly detailed and plainly symbolic, met and even exceeded everyone's expectations.

Trinity made the name H. H. Richardson famous, but Boston's Episcopal duomo would also promote the many men who built it.* In part, this was because O. W. Norcross used the Boston contract— and a quasi-partnership with Richardson—to pioneer a new business model. Until 1872, Norcross Brothers had identified itself, like many firms, with the descriptor "Carpenters and Builders." But that year, as it undertook the construction of Trinity, it rebilled itself as *Norcross Brothers, Contractors and Builders.* The swap of one word signaled a large change.

In practice, it meant Norcross Brothers put a wide variety of skilled workmen on its payroll. Rather than subcontracting various jobs to masons, carpenters, and other tradesmen—a large job might require the help of twenty-odd outside contractors—the firm's own crews did virtually all the work. This was a new way of organizing a work site, one that required the estimating genius of Norcross to make it work.

O. W. took another large step in the company's transition by developing captive sources of supply. Over a period of years, Norcross Brothers leased or opened its own quarries, and with interests in at least fifteen granite, sandstone, and marble companies located all over New England and as far afield as Georgia, the firm emerged as a dominant presence in the building materials industry. Norcross Brothers had captive brickyards too, and at its headquarters in Worcester, strategically located near the Union Railroad yard, there were shops for cabinetmakers, machinists, painters, and blacksmiths, as well as one for the superb stone carver John Evans, whose firm, Evans & Tombs, had operated out of adjacent quarters in Boston and regularly subcontracted with Norcross. When one hired Norcross Brothers, one got the nation's first "general contractor."[40]

---

* Although Trinity Church was never formally designated a cathedral, it functioned as such for the Massachusetts Episcopal diocese for many years. The other architects in the competition each walked away with only a $300 kill fee for their trouble.

O. W. Norcross was much more than a builder. Though lacking any formal training as an engineer, Norcross possessed a gift for innovation. He prepared carefully. Though he had never before built a church of Trinity's scale, he took himself to Montreal to study large stone churches. When Richardson was asked to design unique buildings in new forms to suit new needs—as he would soon undertake to do with libraries and train stations and even early high-rise city buildings—he looked to Norcross, drawing upon his skills as a problem-solver. Over the years Norcross accumulated more than a dozen patents for building-related inventions.

This builder-architect partnership went beyond the men at the top. After a year at the Institute of Technology, young Glenn Brown went to work for Norcross Brothers in 1876 "to obtain some experience in actual building." Just one week into his employment, he was elevated from carpenter to clerk-of-the-works at the Cheney Building, a Richardson-Norcross office building in Hartford, Connecticut. "The clerk's work was varied," Brown would recall. "All duplication of drawings was done by tracing, and [the clerk], at least with Norcross, did most of such duplication. Of the architect's drawings he made full size shop drawings, with patterns for stone work details of carpenter's and mill work." That meant, Brown explained, "the [Norcross] office was in reality a working Branch of the Architect's office."[41]

Even the best architects require translators. Drawings become buildings only when a knowledgeable builder turns them into material orders and instructions, ideas into budgets and estimates, contract dates into sequential schedules for tradesmen. In the best circumstances, coordination and communication is tight between designer and builder. Despite more than a few disagreements along the way, Richardson and Norcross settled into a highly productive working relationship during these years.

Another reason the Richardson-Norcross collaboration worked was neatly explained by the consulting engineer at Trinity. Norcross was, in his experience, "ingenious and resourceful and while desirous of making money . . . ready to subordinate the financial profit to excellence of results."[42] For both men, the building mattered most.

Phillips Brooks and 106 other churchmen representing various congregations in the city entered the west doors of Trinity Church punctually at 11:00 A.M. on the second Friday in February 1877. Leaving the bright, clear morning behind, they processed past a packed house of honored guests, including the city's mayor and the governor of Massachusetts. According to Trinity's records, among those in reserved seats just off the middle aisle were "the architects, artists, and builders of the new Church."[43]

To the reporter for the *Boston Traveler*, Trinity was "a fitting cathedral for the present and future."[44] Visitors that day—and since—compared the "colored mist" of the church to Venice's San Marco. Others believed the church's beauty lay in what some called its "pre-Gothic, pure Catholicism."[45] But no one doubted that Boston had a new and memorable monument.

The long service was punctuated by music provided by a quartet of solo voices and forty choristers. Worshippers looked skyward

The completed Trinity Church, with a pile of scaffolding stacked in the rear.

where an immense wrought-iron chandelier resembling a crown, which Richardson called a "corona," lit the proceedings. The nave was not yet finished, and in the coming months La Farge would complete more murals on its walls. The plan allowed for many of the plain tall windows to change in time; John La Farge was embarking on a new career as a stained-glass maker, and an array of stained-glass windows would eventually tint Richardson's glorious interior. These memorial windows would come not only from La Farge but the British workshops of Edward Burne-Jones, Henry Holiday, and the renowned firm of Clayton & Bell. By the turn of the twentieth century, one writer would declare the place a "Gregorian chant of color."[46]

The total cost of the new Trinity ran much higher than expected, just short of $750,000, though the sum included the land, foundations, stone structure, interior fittings, and painting. Richardson's fee, including expenses, was just under 1 percent of the overall cost. Paine went about retiring the added debt as the congregation settled into its rites and rituals.

The United States had recently celebrated its one hundredth birthday, and the nation's arts were coming into their own. The exhibition in Philadelphia of Thomas Eakins's *Gross Clinic*, a powerful and graphic depiction of a surgical procedure, conveyed much about the caliber of both the country's arts and its sciences. Mark Twain's *Tom Sawyer*, another cultural event of the centennial year, had become an immediate classic and was already being pirated around the world. Trinity Church was another American moment to celebrate.

In Boston, Trinity became an immediate and defining landmark, the only structure in the city that competed with—or perhaps even outshone—Charles Bulfinch's Massachusetts State House. People came from across the country and around the world not merely to pray but to look upon Trinity; they still do. Richardson had opted for the quiet profundity of simple, timeless forms, calling his church "a pyramid; the apse, nave, and chapels forming only the base to the obelisk." But he also made the place subtly American, with oak leaves and acorns carved into the capitals.[47] Brooks had wanted a church for rich and poor alike, a house of worship where the display of faith was secondary to the messages as delivered by the human voice.

The church presided over an expansive public space that, in the next decade, would come to be called Copley Square. On the south side of the plaza stood the Museum of Fine Arts, and Charles McKim would be commissioned a few years later to design a new Boston Public Library building to face Trinity Church across Huntington Avenue, which then ran diagonally across the square.*

Richardson created a house of worship where Phillips Brooks's flock came to celebrate its faith. Fittingly, the first infant to be baptized after Trinity's consecration was Robert Paine's infant daughter, Lily. But Richardson's church amounted to something much greater too, as it was quickly recognized as a defining moment in American architecture.

Trinity resembled no other church. On the exterior, it was a respectful rethinking of the Romanesque; inside, Richardson simplified the medieval elements in order to assemble a soaring interior space that, with its mix of color and rich detail, was a revelation on the American scene. His design inspired imitation, and soon the growing cities of Kansas City, Omaha, and Minneapolis gained monumental buildings that were unmistakable copies of Trinity Church—even though one was a pumping station, another a rail station, the last a public market. In a way that no other building in the United States ever had, Boston's Trinity Church would become a global destination, a church that was both of the Old World and a democratic house of worship.

The city would continue to evolve around Trinity, making it the centerpiece of one of the America's most memorable urban plazas. But from the start, as one astute observe remarked on first viewing, "Trinity look[ed] as though its site had been planned for its sole sake."[48] Undoubtedly, that insight delighted both Richardson and Olmsted, the friends and designers who would soon embark on a series of innovative collaborations that melded buildings designed by the former to landscapes shaped by the latter.

---

* The urban plaza we know today did not exist until the 1960s, when Huntington Avenue was truncated short of Copley Square.

Chapter Eleven

BOSTON DAYS

The root of all my work has been an early respect for and enjoyment of scenery,
and extraordinary opportunities for cultivating susceptibility to its power.

—FREDERICK LAW OLMSTED

Like Richardson, Olmsted received a summons to Boston. His invitation came in 1874 from a man named Charles Sprague Sargent, and together they would create the Arnold Arboretum, America's first public open-air collection of shrubs and trees.

Born to wealth, Sargent had not been keen to follow in his father's footsteps as a banker and railroad investor. Instead, after graduating from Harvard, where he placed eighty-eighth among the ninety men in the class of 1862, he settled for managing Holm Lea, the family estate in Brookline. Amid the mix of woodland, pasture, and cultivated dales at Holm Lea, a property he had known since boyhood, he found his calling as a gentleman horticulturalist.

In the early 1870s, no one in the emerging field of horticulture had academic standing. There were noted gardeners and a few landscape designers—most prominently Olmsted—but horticulture, as distinct from taxonomy, remained a rich man's hobby. Sargent brought a new seriousness to the work, diligently learning the Latin names of plants and how to distinguish the subtle differences between species on his 150 acres in Brookline. He absorbed the theories of landscape gardening as he went about managing the rambling landscape of Holm Lea, which lacked the usual manicured flower beds or gardens. The work suited Sargent's temperament, and his family agreed that he preferred the company of trees and plants to people.

To his Harvard friends, Sargent's preoccupation with Holm Lea seemed at best a hobby, at worst a dead end with no future prospects.[1] Then, in 1872, Sargent was appointed an assistant to one of Harvard's great scholars, botanist Asa Gray, even though Sargent as an undergraduate had conspicuously avoided Gray's famous natural history course.* Gray had been among those who had recommended Olmsted for the job of superintendent at Central Park almost fifteen years earlier, and the word of this internationally recognized man of science had carried real weight with the park commissioners. Now, at age sixty-two, the overcommitted Gray had asked President Charles W. Eliot of Harvard for staff assistance, and Sargent, one of the four new men Eliot assigned to Gray, took over supervision of Harvard's Botanic Gardens. Word of Charles Sargent's work at Holm Lea had gotten around—he had made the family estate, in effect, a horticultural laboratory—and despite his lack of academic credentials, at thirty-one he was given the title professor of horticulture.

For much of the next year, Sargent received firsthand tutelage from Gray, and in 1873, Sargent's responsibilities expanded when he inherited a yet-to-be-realized horticultural project that bore the name of its benefactor. At his death in 1868, a New Bedford whaling merchant named James Arnold had left the college a $100,000 bequest designated for the establishment and support of an arboretum. Arnold wanted an open-air study collection of indigenous and exotic trees, shrubs, and herbaceous plants, but when Sargent was put in charge, no arboretum yet existed. Arnold's money simply had not been sufficient to pay for all that needed to be done.

Now bearing the added title of Arnold Professor of Dendrology, Sargent proved quite capable of thinking like a businessman. Aware that discussions were underway to create parks in Boston, Sargent devised an innovative public-private partnership. In 1874, in a preliminary letter to Olmsted, whom he knew and admired, he laid out his scheme. Another benefactor had bequeathed to Harvard a

---

* Among his many distinctions, Asa Gray was an early Darwinian. Before the publication of *On the Origin of Species*, Gray corresponded with Darwin, addressing botanical queries from Darwin that centered on their shared skepticism of the received wisdom that species were immutable. Later Gray would confront the obloquy of churchmen and academics alike when he defended Darwin's thinking.

farm located in the village of Jamaica Plain, six miles from Cambridge, and Sargent made it his target. "An arrangement could be made," he wrote to Olmsted, "by which the . . . 130 acres could be handed over to the City of Boston on the condition that the City should spend a certain sum of money in laying out the ground and . . . leave the planting in my hands in order that the scientific objects of the trust could be carried out."[2] If the proposal were put in place, he argued, the city could legally pay for roadways, fencing, and policing. Harvard would establish and manage the site as the Arnold Arboretum, and the resulting scenic space could be open to the public, free of charge, every day of the year. Sargent wanted Olmsted's approval—but also his help, as he had yet to sell the concept to Harvard and the politicians in Boston.

Sargent wasn't the only Bostonian in need of landscape advice. As the nation's best-known park maker, Olmsted had already had numerous conversations about possible park plans for Boston. In 1870, he had come to town to deliver a much-discussed paper in which he made a familiar argument, warning of the risks to a city's quality of life if the surrounding countryside were gobbled up by uncontrolled development.[3] A park bill had promptly been drafted and passed by the legislature, but it failed to gain final approval in a referendum that November. Philosophical about the setback, Olmsted wrote to a friend, "Better to wait a few years than adopt a narrow local scheme."[4]

Boston was expanding exponentially, its population having quintupled in the second and third quarters of the nineteenth century. The city was in the process of annexing a number of nearby villages to the south and west, including Roxbury, Dorchester, Brighton, and West Roxbury. (Brookline was not among them, as its citizens had rejected the idea of consolidating with the city in an 1873 ballot). As the city expanded, new dense street grids and row houses rose, seemingly at random and often amid once-pastoral towns— just as Olmsted had predicted.

After a growing political consensus led to passage of the Park Act in 1875, he was asked by the new three-man park commission to consult informally on a skein of parks not so different from his nearly completed Buffalo system. He prepared a memorandum describing a series of elements, including frontage along the Charles River embankment, a park farther afield in West Roxbury on undeveloped land around Jamaica Pond, and linking parkways like those in Buffalo. Though the commissioners offered him no official role, the city published a plan that clearly reflected a good deal of Olmsted's big-picture thinking. The proposal then languished again in the absence of appropriations.

As Olmsted's informal agent in such Boston matters, Richardson, with many powerful and progressive Bostonian friends, kept him informed.[5] After years of hesitation, the city finally came up with funding, though the moneys were woefully inadequate, since the great fire of 1872 and the economic depression that had begun the following year still limited the city's resources. But in 1878 the city began acquiring properties along the Charles River embankment near the Back Bay. The acreage was the cheapest available, the plots mostly fenland intercut by the Muddy River and Stony Brook, mudflats and marshes no one else wanted. With deeds freshly in hand, the city sponsored a competition, hoping to find a local man to plan the park, but even the best of the unremarkable submissions, devised by a florist, satisfied no one, with the *American Architect and Building News* dismissing it as "childish."[6] At last the city formally asked Olmsted for a plan.

He had been away, having spent the winter of 1878 in Europe, stopping in familiar places like Birkenhead and traveling around Italy. He dispatched his stepson John, now twenty-six and in his third year working as an apprentice in the Olmsted office, to survey the site. The task would be more than a matter of making a new parkland with pretty plantings, because the fens posed a major civil-engineering challenge. Once a receiving basin for the Back Bay, the designated hundred-acre marshland was now a pestilential swamp, poisoned by runoff, including raw sewage, from the growing towns of Roxbury, Dorchester, and Brookline. High tides in the adjacent Charles River complicated matters, causing a backflow of salt water into the river's freshwater tributaries. Worst of all, the toxic mix of salt and sewage had killed off most of the native flora and fauna.

Having had already built his share of ponds and watercourses in Central Park and elsewhere, Olmsted immediately recognized the primary problem was hydraulic. He devised a multipart solution, starting with a Charles River water gate to regulate tidal ebb and flow. He proposed a smaller pair of gatehouses upstream to control the fresh water that spilled from the Muddy River and Stony Brook. In between, he envisioned burying conduits to resolve the sewage problem, as well as setting aside some twenty acres of low-lying land that, in times of flooding, could be under water. The rest of the acreage would then be a mix of restored saltwater marshes and the park ground Bostonians wanted, complete with bridle trails, footpaths, and the several avenues that transited the area. The project, when realized much as Olmsted first envisioned it, would be known as the Back Bay Fens.

After Sargent first wrote to him in the summer of 1874, Olmsted hesitated. "A park and an arboretum seem to be so far unlike in purpose," he told Sargent, "that I do not feel sure that I could combine them satisfactorily."[7] But over time, Sargent convinced him to try, and by the summer and autumn of 1878, Olmsted was juggling plans for two atypical parks, one the Back Bay Fens, the other the Arnold Arboretum. He also continued to nurture hope that he might be put in charge of a larger scheme based on his 1875 plan, in which the fens and the arboretum would become precious parts of a string of Boston green spaces.*

Working with Sargent, Olmsted immediately grasped that creating an arboretum was a different kind of assignment than any he had taken on before. It also had particular appeal to him since, along with boulders and bushes and babbling brooks, trees were among the most precious tools of the landscape craft. He agreed to do the initial design work for no fee, just the out-of-pocket costs of an accurate survey and contour map.

Yet again, he started with a less-than-auspicious site. Even Sargent himself recognized the property was "a worn-out farm partly covered with native woods nearly ruined by pasturage and neglect."[8]

---

* Later, when the plan was realized, it would be picturesquely dubbed the "emerald necklace."

Its best features included Hemlock Hill, a rocky knoll capped by a stand of old evergreens, and a second eminence, Bussey Hill, which had a panoramic view of Boston. But the rest of the land was a mix of bog, undrained meadow, and thickets.

In designing the arboretum, Olmsted set himself two goals. In park-maker mode, he wished to welcome a public seeking a quiet respite from urban life. But his client dictated that the arboretum also had to be a teaching tool, which Sargent called a "museum of living trees."[9] Sargent wanted the organizing principle to be plant families, with species grouped in sequence, so "a visitor driving through the Arboretum [is] able to obtain a general idea of the arborescent vegetation of the north temperate zone without even leaving his carriage."[10] Trees would be planted near their relatives for ease of comparative study. That meant Olmsted's task was to blend a scientific garden into a parkscape. The roadways and pathways, lined though they were with specimen trees and bushes, had to look natural.

In 1879, after much consultation with both Sargent and Asa Gray, Olmsted completed his initial design for the Arnold Arboretum. The sinuous curves of a meandering carriage road would loop throughout the acres, providing the longest possible route, alongside which the tree collections would be planted. Many conversations ensued regarding the placement and grouping of trees, but the city and Harvard would not consummate their purchase and lease arrangement until 1882, and only when the road was well underway did permanent plantings begin, in 1885, with beeches, ashes, elms, and hickories (*Fagus, Fraxinus, Ulmus,* and *Carya,* respectively). Dozens of drawings would emerge from Olmsted's office, shuffling the distribution of the tree collection.

Olmsted brought his artistry to the Arnold Arboretum, and Sargent would return the favor, advising Olmsted on the selection of trees and plantings for the Back Bay Fens. The two perfectionists became friends and, in the not-so-distant future, would be Brookline neighbors.

Henry Hobson Richardson ate and drank with abandon. Any of his old friends or fellow clubmen at the Century could report that was nothing new, but by the late 1870s, those who knew him before the Civil War saw a changed man. In early middle age, the lad who might once have been cast as Hamlet more nearly resembled Falstaff.

His weight approached three hundred pounds, but Richardson wasn't merely stout. Nor could overconsumption alone account for the fact his face frequently looked flushed and swollen. He could no longer scale a ladder on a building site because of his added bulk, and for reasons that still were not altogether clear, he was regularly confined to his sickbed. He would spend a full three months in 1879 working from his bedchamber.

Although Richardson steadfastly refused to accept that his health might interrupt his work, business at Gambrill & Richardson had slowed along with the nation's economy. When La Farge had begun painting Trinity's interior in late 1876, the country was still emerging from a deep economic downturn triggered in the United States by the Coinage Act of 1873, which ended bimetallism, the practice of pegging the value of the dollar to both silver and gold, relying instead solely on the gold standard. Europe had fallen into hard economic times too, and the ripple effects included falling prices for grain, cotton, and silver. The so-called Long Depression meant new construction in the United States had come to a near standstill.

By the time this picture was taken, in 1879, Richardson's tailors were forced to cut much larger suits to clothe his portly figure.

Income still came in from continuing term work at the Albany capitol and the Buffalo hospital, keeping Gambrill & Richardson solvent, but those jobs were drawing to a close, and though admiration for Trinity spread, Richardson did not have long-term clients to fall back upon. In Boston, he remained a new man in town, having moved to Massachusetts less than three years earlier.

In late 1876, Richardson wrote to Olmsted twice worrying about his next job. He still had one large hope, since his firm, along with several well-respected Boston competitors, had entered another design competition. The nearby town of Woburn, Massachusetts, recipient of a large legacy for the purpose, planned to build a public library, and the generous budget would represent a plum assignment. "Have heard nothing from Woburn," he wrote in November, and in December, reporting in again, "Nothing positive from Woburn yet."[11] At last, in January, better news arrived: the library commission was his.

The chance to design the Winn Memorial Library in Woburn meant more than a handsome fee. The very idea of the public library was new, a manifestation of how democracy was changing social norms in the United States. The nation did not have a history of libraries open to everyone, and Richardson would thus have to come up with a fresh approach. A public library would not be just a storage space for the book collection of a rich man or a college but rather a building suited to a public purpose. As Olmsted had done with his parks, Richardson would have to wrestle with a new concept, and for the first time, but not the last, he would devise a new paradigm. As critic Lewis Mumford observed, looking back a generation later, "Richardson was the first architect of distinction in America who was ready to face the totality of modern life."[12]

For centuries, in Colonial America as in Europe, education was largely a tool of the church, the titled, and the rich. One royal governor of Virginia, Sir William Berkeley, saw schooling as a sliding scale: it ought to be a matter, he thought, for "every man according to his own ability in instructing his children." He saw nothing wrong with a system in which the well-to-do remained the well informed and most of the less privileged stayed illiterate. Doing otherwise, Berkeley explained, would only foster "disobedience and heresy" and risk discontent amongst the lower sort.[13]

A century later, another Virginia governor saw the matter quite differently. By 1778, the United States was in full rebellion. Thomas Jefferson, the duly elected chief executive of the Commonwealth of Virginia, proposed dividing his state into "little republics," each a half dozen miles square and with its own school to teach reading, writing, and arithmetic. At a time when a third of the population couldn't read, Jefferson and his like-minded contemporaries regarded educating the electorate—then limited to White men—as essential to the American experiment in democracy.* Lexicographer Noah Webster went further, famously asserting that education must be "the most important business of society."

Jefferson's proposed legislation for his state, "A Bill for the More General Diffusion of Knowledge," never became law, and the idea of universal public education was slow to gain momentum. In 1837 that began to change, when legislator Horace Mann resigned his office to become secretary of Massachusetts's newly created Board of Education. Mann launched a campaign for "common schools," echoing the ideas of Jefferson and Webster. "A republican form of government," he said pointedly, "without intelligence in the people, must be, on a vast scale, what a mad-house, without superintendent or keepers, would be on a small one."[14]

Mann thought educating the poor as well as the rich was the responsibility of the state. Believing teachers should be professionally trained, he founded the first state-funded teacher's college or "normal school." His ideas spread nationally with the assistance of a publication he edited, *Common School Journal*, and by 1870, laws in every state mandated education for children.

The public library traveled a parallel path. Book collections dated back to early civilizations. The greatest assemblage of books in antiquity, in Alexandria, Egypt, was hardly the first collection of bound volumes when it burned in 48 B.C.E., in a conflagration believed to have been ordered by Julius Caesar. But for many centuries, through the Middle Ages, the Renaissance, and the Enlightenment, libraries remained largely the province of monarchs, the nobility, universities, and the church.

In Colonial America, a man could count himself rich if he possessed a handsome house, stylish clothes, and a private library, though most book collections then consisted of dozens or, in a handful of in-

---

* Data on eighteenth-century literacy rates are limited, but most historians agree that literacy was highest in New England (perhaps 90 percent or more), while in the South nearly half of Whites could neither read nor write. A tiny minority of the millions of Blacks in bondage received any formal education.

stances, a hundred or more volumes. By the nineteenth century, newly established colleges, literary societies, mercantile and mechanical institutes, athenaeums, and parishes in the United States had begun to accumulate institutional collections of books, but here Jefferson surfaced once again. A fanatical bibliophile who assembled three major book collections in his lifetime, he sold the largest of his collections, consisting of more than six thousand volumes, to the nation after the burning of the U.S. Capitol by the British in 1814. His books had become the core of the Library of Congress. When he welcomed the first students to his "Academical Village," in 1825, he broke with centuries of precedent by specifying that the Rotunda, the central building at the University of Virginia, a half-scale copy of the Pantheon in Rome, would be a library, not a chapel.

Yet access to books was slow to reach beyond fee-paying members, scholars, and the well-connected few until the early years of Olmsted and Richardson's adulthood, when the idea of the public library emerged. At the time, no major American or European city had a lending library. The case for such an institution was made by men like George Ticknor, a sometime Harvard professor, literary scholar, and disciple of Jefferson; and Edward Everett, a former governor of Massachusetts, who would later become a U.S. senator and the nation's secretary of state. The two founded the Boston Public Library in 1852 because they believed library privileges should extend to the average person. They wanted to build upon Horace Mann's common school movement, arguing that books, as Ticknor put it, had the power to "affect life and raise personal character and condition."[15] They wished to carry on the good work done in inculcating values and virtues in public schools, aiming to extend, as Everett said, the "happy equality of intellectual privileges, which now exists in our Schools, but terminates with them."[16] Free libraries would allow adults to continue their education on their own. The very notion of lending books was relatively new; for centuries, in the Middle Ages and beyond, books in Europe had literally been chained to their shelves, readable only in situ.

In Woburn, prompted by a $300 gift from a man named Jonathan Bowers Winn, the town fathers had established one of the first public libraries in the United States in 1854, located in a room in the town hall, with a small collection also financed by Winn. Such modest quarters were typical of early public collections, which generally occupied secondary spaces in post offices, schools, or even commercial locations like apothecaries. Winn had made his fortune in the leather business, but he worked first as a schoolteacher and throughout his life held books and learning in high esteem. Although a weak constitution led his only son, Charles, to withdraw from his college studies, he, too, was a curious man who "spent most of his years in travel, finding a change of scene and climate a partial relief from pain," and would visit "every habitable portion of the globe."[17] Upon his death in 1875, at age thirty-seven, two years after his father's, the peripatetic Charles left a significant bequest to honor his father's name. The stated purpose was the creation of "the ideal public library."[18]

Construction was barely underway in Woburn when in September 1877, Richardson got another commission for a library, this one in North Easton, Massachusetts. Two more library designs would follow for nearby towns—Quincy, in April 1880, and Malden, in 1884—and another for the University of Vermont, in spring 1883. All five of these libraries (as well as a sixth design for East Saginaw, Michigan, which was rejected) were established in honor of wealthy men.* Few towns possessed funds sufficient for such projects, so civic-minded Yankee men of means stepped in. Their altruism was also informed by the potential gains of a better-educated workforce. As a U.S. senator observed at one library opening, "the well educated operative does more work, does it better, wastes less, [and] uses his allotted portion of the machinery to more advantage and more profit."[19]

Several hundred public libraries existed by the time Richardson entered the Woburn competition in 1876, but almost none occupied a building of its own. As Richardson went about putting his personal stamp on this new building type, the freestanding public library, he was designing warehouses of knowledge accessible to

* In addition to Jonathan Winn, the libraries would honor Oliver Ames, a manufacturing and railroad magnate from North Easton; Thomas Crane, son of Quincy, who trained as stonecutter but later leveraged a successful stone yard in New York into substantial real estate holdings; Elisha Converse, founder of Malden-based Boston Rubber Shoe Company, which employed more than two thousand workers; and Vermonter Frederick Billings, who, after making his pile in railroads and serving as president of the Northern Pacific, retired to his home state.

all but that would simultaneously be "architectural ornaments," as Charles Winn put it, to America's capitalist class.[20] For Richardson there was an added bonus: the opportunity to collaborate with Olmsted again, since his friend would soon shape the surrounding landscape for several of the commissions. Together they would create welcoming and accessible temples of learning.

The Winn Memorial Library in Woburn was the first and by far the largest of Richardson's half dozen libraries, with a 78-foot stair tower that rose above the massive 163-foot-long edifice. Its plan reflected the wishes of George Champney, chairman of Woburn's building committee and its future librarian, who first put on paper a general idea of what the interior of the building should be. He requested an entrance vestibule, a "Reception Room," "general Reading Room," and "Reference and Study Room," along with "a Room in the center for the Circulating Department" to hold the books.[21] Champney also specified small rooms for the trustees and the librarian and a basement containing the cataloguing room and water closets.

Since the Winn legacy included a collection of fifty oil paintings, the design would also have to incorporate an exhibition space, plus a "Cabinet Room" for fossils, minerals, and stuffed birds belonging to one of Charles's uncles. Richardson was thus tasked with creating a lending library comprising roughly ten thousand volumes for Woburn's population of some ten thousand citizens, as well as a natural history museum and an art gallery. This mix of demands added up to an especially interesting *concours projet.*

The most essential space would be the book room. During Richardson's years at Harvard, Gore Hall had been the college library. Completed in 1841, its footprint was an elongate cross, with a nave that rose thirty-five-feet to a vaulted ceiling. Though it resembled a small-scale Gothic cathedral, Gore Hall had no side aisles but rather a sequence of alcoves that flanked the 140-foot-long central space. Two stories tall and lined with shelves, the alcoves held the library's book collection.

The use of alcoves was not unique to the Harvard library, having been pioneered by Christopher Wren at Trinity College, Cambridge, in the seventeenth century and more recently adapted for new libraries at Brown University, the Boston Athenaeum, and other New England institutions.* Shelved alcoves had also been used in Paris's Bibliothèque Sainte-Geneviève, which had been the talk of Paris when Richardson arrived there to study, and at New York's Astor Library, located mere blocks from Gambrill & Richardson's New York offices. But no books were lent from any of those libraries. At Woburn, the books would come and go.

Richardson's solution for controlling the flow came from church architecture, a variation of a rood screen, which segregated the book stacks from the patrons. He added a delivery desk, from which a librarian could manage the process, procuring books from the collection and handing them over to patrons as if ministering to a flock.[22]

Richardson's repeated reworkings of his Trinity Church plans in the preceding years had not been wasted. Like the linguist learning a new tongue by articulating unfamiliar phonetics, his experiments with the Romanesque had given him fluency. The book room in Woburn would resemble a basilica nave, rising high to a barrel vault. At the opposite end of the building, Richardson added an octagon that, from the exterior, might easily be confused with a church apse but would become the natural history museum. A large central block stood between the book room and museum, fronted by the tall stair tower that, again in an ecclesiastical echo, resembled a campanile. A broad entry arch abutted the tower, providing access to the vestibule, gallery, and reading rooms.

While his design was highly functional, splendid detailing would also characterize the finished library. Richardson and his draftsmen designed spindle friezes and matching chairs. The alcoves lined with books were defined by arcades with arches that sprang from pilasters with carved oak-leaf capitals. Elsewhere the carving featured botanically correct specimens of elm and horse chestnut leaves and a mix of flowers. The ceiling was a ribbed barrel of butternut wood, and

---

* Among them was Williams College, where book alcoves lined all eight walls of octagonal Lawrence Hall.

the warm space was lit by a ribbon of windows high on the walls. The exterior was composed of tawny granites and cream-colored sandstone, cut and carved and blended. Rough quarry-faced blocks became checkerboards and two-tone arches. Carved foxes and owls looked down from corbels and cornices, inhabitants of a magical, medieval construction. All of this evidenced not only the design insights of Richardson but the talents of carver John Evans and the skilled draftsmanship of Stanford White.

The Winn Library barrel vault and book alcoves in Woburn, Massachusetts, along with Richardson-designed library chairs and tables. The view is of the building's axis, through to the gallery and museum at the vanishing point.

Located on the site of what had been the Winn homestead, the new library consisted of recognizable elements, but by aligning the book room, delivery room, gallery, and museum on one axis, Richardson gave the interior a grand scale, a sense that to look along its *enfilade* of aligned openings was to telescope human knowledge. The *Woburn Journal* reported that the new library was "the most perfect of any in New England," crediting in part the building committee because they "allowed the master hand of the architect to have full sway."[23]

An out-of-town visitor, Frederick Billings, also liked what he saw. As the benefactor of a new library planned for the University of Vermont, Billings decided he wanted one very much like Woburn's. To hire Richardson, he decided, was "really the proper thing to do."[24]

With his reputation on the rise, a mix of new work now coming to him, and his ongoing collaboration with O. W. Norcross, Richardson gained the confidence to make a final break with Gambrill. His partner had remained in New York when Richardson moved to Boston

*The just-completed Winn Memorial Library in Woburn, with its mix of shapes
and rooflines and polychrome pattern of stonework.*

four years earlier, and in 1878, the firm of Gambrill & Richardson
ceased to exist. Richardson became an independent practitioner, entirely his own man.*

Beginning in 1878, the Olmsted family summered in Boston. His
work at Central Park hadn't ceased, but neither had the ongoing
travails of New York politics. Olmsted's old nemesis, Andrew Green,
had become one of Manhattan's most powerful men as the city's
comptroller, and they saw almost nothing the same way, with Olmsted still focused on social and aesthetic issues while Green valued
efficiency above all else. A long series of budget cuts had limited not
only new plantings and landscape effects but basic maintenance.

---

* Two years, later Gambrill, suffering from liver trouble and financial setbacks, held a gun to
his head, killing himself at his offices at 87 Broadway.

From Olmsted's perspective, heedless occupants of city hall regularly installed incompetent appointees with whom he had to deal, and he found himself wearying of the city itself, increasingly uncomfortable with what he described as its "roadside exhibitions of excessively bad taste, shabbiness or slatternliness."[25]

The prospect of grandchildren also led the Olmsteds to shift their gaze to Boston, after the 1878 marriage of Charlotte, the stepdaughter Olmsted affectionately called "Charlotty," to a Boston physician. The existing combination of family and work—for Sargent, at the fens, and with Richardson—made New England's biggest city attractive as a new permanent home.

In January 1880, Olmsted enlisted Richardson's help in another bureaucratic battle. A major thoroughfare, Boylston Street, passed through the construction site of the Back Bay fenland, its existing broad roadbed higher than the other routes to and from the western suburbs. For Beacon Street, Commonwealth Avenue, and even the Boston & Albany Railroad, inconspicuous low bridges across the Muddy River would be sufficient. But Olmsted recognized that well-trafficked Boylston Street would "dominate everything & be seen from the Charles River to Parker Hill." Therefore, he argued, a bridge of "rustic quality" and "*picturesque* in material" was essential.[26] He wanted a highly visible bridge that looked like it belonged in its setting.

When he said as much to the city's engineer, the response was unsympathetic. Impatient and persistent, Olmsted went over the man's head, appealing to the Boston park commissioners. The design of the Boylston Street Bridge, he argued, could not be left to "the habitual drift of the Engineering mind." He suggested a possible solution. "I wish you would consider whether you could not let me have Richardson's assistance?"[27] Olmsted's request was promptly granted, and the bridge he and Richardson made together for the Back Bay Fens would be another joint tutorial on planning a structure in relation to its site.

At Olmsted's insistence, Richardson visited Central Park to examine three possible prototypes. Olmsted did not want a "beautiful iron bridge," which would be discordant amid the fens.[28] Brick or timber might do—but he and Richardson soon agreed, stone would be best.

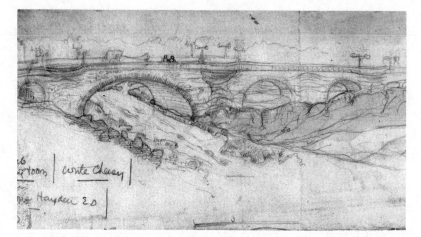

Thought to be a sketch by Richardson himself, this preliminary rendering of the
Boylston Street Bridge was drawn, in 1880, in pencil with a pale red wash.
The jottings in the lower left-hand corner are to-do notes in the architect's
recognizable handwriting.

The bridges they examined in New York had been designed by
Calvert Vaux, but they were undeniably Olmstedian, since everything in their great Manhattan park bore his imprimatur. The
bridges to which Olmsted drew Richardson's particular attention
were rustic. One was a narrow, doorway-like feature in Olmsted's
fondly remembered Ramble. All three bridges had been built of local
stone, roughly dressed on-site. Each looked as though it had been dry-
laid, with deep, shadowy joints. Despite the material's irregularity—no
two boulders were alike—the bridges were unmistakably solid and
durable, with a timeless, even primitive air.

Richardson had already experimented with found stone in his
early commission for Grace Church in Medford, Massachusetts. Yet
Vaux's rustic bridges and the one Richardson proposed for Boylston
Street were different. The Central Park bridge that particularly
caught Richardson's eye was the Huddlestone Arch at the north end
of the park, with its enormous, crude voussoirs and barrel vault. It
looked like the handiwork of giants.

Olmsted wanted "a single, simple, sweeping arch," and Richardson gave it to him.[29] The height and span had already been speci-

fied in Olmsted's plan dating to 1879, so the basic configuration was prescribed. Once a completed Richardson pencil sketch was in hand, the bridge would be approved.

But Richardson gave his friend something more, too. He designed a bridge that would both settle into its landscape and welcome it. He added voluptuous curves to the roadbed, with two sets of *tourelles*, half turrets that corbelled out from the sides of the bridge. They amounted to platforms from which pedestrians could view the naturalized holding basin, an Olmsted transformation of a watery wasteland to welcoming urban park.

Richardson's busy mind at work, here in a preliminary sketch for the Crane Library, in Quincy, Massachusetts. It is annotated with to-do notes, among them, "write Olmsted." The latter would plan the library's landscape.

Richardson's best buildings were different from the picturesque designs of his peers. At a time when other designers were applying standard machine-made materials to the eclectic and evolving styles that came to be called Victorian, there was nothing cookie-cutter about any Richardson work; so-called gingerbread never had much appeal to him. He relied upon a layering of surfaces; he melded dynamic parts. A Richardson building required no explanation, its flow and purpose self-evident even to first-time visitors.

At one of his most admired buildings, the Thomas Crane Public Library in Quincy, and at the much larger Converse Memorial Building in Malden, Massachusetts, the man who settled Richardson's buildings into their sites had been Olmsted. When considering the libraries a few years later, Richardson's biographer labeled them

The Converse Library, in Malden, Massachusetts, as settled into
its landscape by Olmsted.

"organic compositions."[30] That 1888 use of the descriptor *organic* anticipated the term's adoption in the next generation by Frank Lloyd Wright, whose most favored and oft-repeated rubric became the epithet "organic architecture." When Wright defined *organic*, he spoke of a structure "built of the thing and on it." In doing so, he was channeling the joint Richardson and Olmsted ethos.

Wright would be one of many indebted to Richardson. In 1890, when Andrew Carnegie launched his library initiative, his first library would be based on Richardson's Woburn Public Library.[31] Although not all of the more than two thousand Carnegie libraries that followed were Romanesque in appearance, the conception remained Richardsonian. The architect developed floor plans first; architecture for Richardson wasn't framing views *of* a building; he was concerned with creating a living experience *within*. In designing each landscape, Olmsted looked for the genius of a place and sought to employ it; as an architect, Richardson possessed an unusual capacity to think from the inside out, disregarding the streetside symmetry that was the hallmark of so many other architects of the era and the clichéd decorations of the day. His buildings compelled people to pay attention. As a younger architect would say of him at the turn of the twentieth century, he was "the one right and particular star on the architectural horizon in the United States."[32]

Olmsted's and Richardson's influential fusion of minds had yet to fully flower, but a new project in North Easton, Massachusetts, provided them with the perfect situation to raise their collaboration to a new level.

Chapter Twelve

◆

AMESTOWN

It is built of Bowlders ... but in a more eccentric way.

——M. G. VAN RENSSELAER

The shovel had been the making of North Easton, Massachusetts. When Oliver Ames forged his first one in a converted nailery near the Queset River in 1803, it was lighter than those of the British competitors. He further improved the design, adding the so-called Ames bend, which offset the blade, making the tool easier to use. His shovels met a ready market in Boston and beyond. Farmers and canal diggers swore by them, and by the late 1820s, with rail lines extending in all directions, so did the men laying the tracks.

Oliver Ames and Sons continued to thrive after second-generation brothers Oakes and Oliver II became partners in the shovel works in 1844. Among gold-digging forty-niners who raced to California, the prized Ames shovel sometimes stood in for hard currency. By then the town of North Easton, located twenty-five miles south of Boston, might well have been renamed Amestown. The family's mills dominated the village center, with wagon barns, tall smokestacks, dams, millponds, and factories of local stone. The biggest structure, the Long Shop, was more than five hundred feet long.

What had formerly been a hamlet of Yankee yeoman farmers had become an unplanned industrial sprawl. Tenements and two-family homes housed immigrant Irish laborers, who had arrived to restart their lives after escaping the Great Famine at home. A rum shop had been banished, and a company store opened. At peak production, the Ames operation would employ more than five hundred workers and manufacture 60 percent of the world's shovels.

The pattern of North Easton's streets was haphazard. Centered on the shovel works, the town center, with its crooked roadways and multiple dead ends, was halved by a rail line and boxed in on three sides by Ames family estates. But a short distance to the south, where Main Street made an arching turn to the east, one area remained relatively undeveloped. After the death of Oliver Ames Jr. in 1877, it would become an Olmsted oasis and an experimental station for Richardson, where they would test boundaries and soften the line between architecture and landscape. Over a period of years, Richardson's and Olmsted's practices would be bolstered by a total of twenty commissions from Ames family members, most of them in the town they dominated. Their Ames collaborations would also cement Richardson's and Olmsted's unofficial partnership.

Richardson's first Ames clients were Frederick and Helen Ames, the children of Oliver Ames Jr. Acting on behalf of their father, who left a $50,000 bequest for the purpose, they hired Richardson in September 1877 to build a public library, which would be a distillation of Woburn's Winn Memorial Library. Scaled down and less ornamented, the Oliver Ames Free Library required neither a gallery nor a museum, though a towering memorial fireplace, designed by Stanford White, would dominate the black-walnut-paneled reading room. A few years later, the overmantel would gain a bronze bas-relief bust of Oliver Ames Jr. by Augustus Saint-Gaudens.

The second Ames commission, which entered Richardson's office in February 1879, came from cousins. In honor of Oakes Ames, Oliver III and his siblings wanted a town hall, single community structure for lectures and fellowship to serve as a pedagogical extension of the library. It would be built on an adjacent parcel, just south of the library.

Olmsted had played little or no role in situating the Ames Free Library—and it showed. Richardson had dropped the building into its sloping topography, choosing to regrade the rising contours just enough to flatten an area for the library. This time, however, when it

A collaborative drawing labeled "Terraces and Steps for North Easton Town Hall, North Easton, Mass." With the draftsman's light penciling as a backdrop and the landscape plan added in bolder brown ink—most probably by Olmsted himself—the imaginations of Richardson and Olmsted engaged on the same sheet.

came to settling the Oakes Ames Memorial Town-Hall into its terrain, Richardson wisely brought in Olmsted.

The task reminded Olmsted of an earlier one. At Central Park, he and Calvert Vaux had installed an architectural folly called the Belvedere.* The similarities to the town hall site were many, among them a jagged outcropping and large glacial boulders littering the approach.[1] The Belvedere that Vaux designed resembled a minia-

---

* Follies, or "eye-catchers" as they are sometimes called, are fantasy buildings, typically with little or no purpose, common to grand landscape gardens and parks. In the case of Central Park's castle, the Belvedere was intended, as its name suggests, to take in the beautiful vistas of Olmsted and Vaux's park.

ture castle, standing alone above man-made Turtle Pond, with a panoramic view of Central Park. In contrast, the town hall overlooked a well-traveled street, the library, and a triangular intersection with an island where, Olmsted knew, the Ameses wanted a Civil War monument, a commission he hoped would come to him. His job was less to make this proud building stand apart than to make an earthly connection in the same way his patrons wanted to mingle their own fate with this town's.

Everyone involved agreed that, like Central Park's Belvedere Castle, the town hall should sit high on the knoll. Richardson's picturesque building would overlook Main Street, with a tall corner tower and a porch lined with an arcade. Low arches had become one of the architect's favorite design elements, great sweeping semicircles that sprang from squat columns. The almost pyramidal stone and brick building would loom over the adjacent library, which had been sited some twenty feet lower on the hillside. But Olmsted's key contribution would be in relating the memorial hall to the street.

O. W. Norcross's masons had raised the building's shell, and his carpenters were at work on the interior finishes. Richardson's office provided Olmsted with a plan and a street elevation of the building, and during their hours together that summer, Richardson and Olmsted discussed the solution.[2]

The entrance porch, shielded by the row of Romanesque arches, was a comfortable distance from the street. But perched on the bedrock, the building's main floor stood three stories above passing pedestrians and traffic, and the two men decided that although there was room for one, a straight, single-flight staircase of fifty-odd steps would be intimidating rather than welcoming. Furthermore, it might give the building a high-and-mighty quality in relation to the town that was the opposite of the message the Ameses wished to send.

A drawing of the next step in the process revealed Olmsted's special insight. He sketched directly on the pencil rendering provided by Richardson's office, limning the structure's geological underpinning like the many facets on a cut diamond. Into this rock outcropping he cut not a single run of stairs but series of shorter runs, each separated by a landing. Olmsted added shading for emphasis and sketched some foliage; the vegetation and a low stone wall would help camouflage the turns. The building lost none of its impressive height, but Olmsted rendered it approachable, with the rude, rugged stone of the site giving way to the refined and precisely finished building above. When completed, the Oakes Ames Memorial Town-Hall (sometimes shortened to Ames Memorial Hall) and its immediate landscape, dedicated in November 1881, conveyed a clear sense that Olmsted and Richardson's imaginations had worked in tandem.

Olmsted made a virtue of the setting, mingling the vegetation and the craggy rocks with Richardson's fine building. Between them, the two men transformed a rugged New England glacial drumlin that, until their arrival, had changed little since the prehistoric withdrawal of the Laurentide Ice Sheet. The building, though manmade, looked like it belonged on the rugged hill, and Olmsted's curving stone retaining walls with their undulating capstones added to the ensemble effect. The whole was a manifestation of Amesville's hierarchy. Its landscape, this time scraped by the hand of man, looked as timeless—and natural—as it had before Richardson, Olmsted, or any of the Ameses laid eyes on it.

Frederick Ames aspired to live "in the fashion of a country gentleman."[3] Well on his way to becoming Boston's largest landowner, he owned a fine city house in the Back Bay. His many railroad directorships often took him to New York and farther afield, but his most cherished place remained Langwater, his North Easton estate less than a mile from the Ames Free Library and Memorial Town-Hall.

Both his father and grandfather had been village wrestling champions, and Fred Ames was also a big man. As the first in his family to go to college, he had gained what he called a "fondness for extravagance . . . [during] my Cambridge days." He appreciated the arts, and the collection he and his wife, Mary, accumulated included paintings, among them a pair of Rembrandts and a Millet, plus

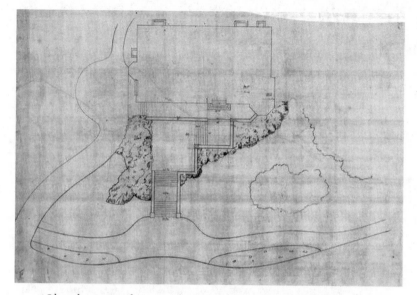

Olmsted incorporated no fewer than four landings and five sets of steps, no two the same, to naturalize the Oakes Ames Memorial Town-Hall.

museum-worthy carpets and tapestries, jades and crystals, and ancient Roman pottery.*

When Mary Ames expressed an interest in new quarters for visiting family and guests, Frederick Ames took up her request with Richardson. The architect recommended a building at Langwater's entrance, a traditional gate lodge. Although the eventual building would retain the name Gate Lodge, it would be anything but traditional.

The first proposed design looked like a plain Tudor barn, with a long roof and ample interior space for occasional visitors and servants. After looking at Richardson's sketch, however, Ames realized he wanted more of a statement. The lodge, Ames thought, should "function as an estate entrance of some impressiveness."[4] Warming to the task, Richardson designed a generous archway to

---

* In time, many of the Ames paintings and precious objects would enter the collections of Boston's Museum of Fine Arts.

straddle the entry road from Elm Street, one that would provide an easy pass-through for horse and carriage. He chose a Syrian arch design, a half-round curve that would spring from the ground rather than rest atop pedestals or columns.

The addition of the arch prompted Richardson to wonder whether a pendant structure on the eastern side of the arch would make sense, a second mass to frame the estate entrance. Ames didn't necessarily disagree, but, as he noted, "the function of the second structure was not early decided."[5]

The lodge had begun to resemble the Boylston Street Bridge, which was on the drafting boards at Richardson's offices in the same months. Both featured a great central arch. The lodge was to be built of boulders that, in the way of New England meadows, had appeared in nearby fields, heaved upward by winter frost. But Richardson soon had another idea.

One of Ames's chief avocations had become gardening. He approached horticulture with the same seriousness that he did his business. He contributed generously to the Massachusetts Horticultural Society and the Arnold Arboretum, and he was assembling a world-class collection of orchids in his greenhouses. Richardson's suggestion was to make the lodge's eastern wing a wintering house for some of Ames's cherished plants. It could be open to the rafters, with a great door through which carts and barrows could enter, bringing delicate plant materials for storage during the difficult New England winters.

One intriguing idea gave rise to another. A cylindrical stair tower, capped by a conical roof, got taller, melding into the main roofline. Olmsted's role in this design was informal, though his influence on the Gate Lodge is clear. The building screened the inner landscape of the estate from the street, and a visitor, on passing through the Syrian arch, beheld a new vista. To Olmsted, it looked like "a bridge," and would serve, like many of the bridges in Olmsted's parks, as a transition intended to reveal a different landscape.[6] As the name suggested, the Gate Lodge would separate the public road and outer world from the inner realm of the family. It was an Olmsted-like sleight of hand, and Richardson, already skilled in designing dramatic interior spaces, would use the technique repeatedly.

Ames and Richardson hired Norcross Brothers to build the Gate Lodge, but for O. W. and his masons, this was not a typical job. A multitude of details had to be worked out on-site, because the finished building would differ in many particulars from the architectural renderings Richardson's draftsmen provided. The big fieldstones, laboriously shifted by horsepower and men with ropes and levers, seemed almost to have a mind of their own, "demand[ing]," as Ames reported, "daily evaluation and decision as they were laid."[7]

No ordinary client, Ames understood the complexity of the process in aesthetic terms. "The boulders were placed with attention to the textural effects radiated by the brute coarseness of the medium," he noted. Other, more experienced critics would put it differently, among them Henry Van Brunt, one of Richardson's peers and a major Boston architect at the time. He called the completed Gate Lodge an "extraordinary piece of architectural athleticism . . . which might

The completed Ames Gate Lodge at Frederick Ames's Langwater.

have been piled up by a Cyclops . . . [a] specimen of boisterous Titanic gamboling."[8] It was a structure that compelled everyone who saw it, layperson and professional, to think about buildings in a new way. This was architecture derived as much from its materials as from the imagination; it was as if an intimidatingly large New England stone wall had been transformed into a dwelling.

This building, neither Georgian nor Greek, neither Gothic nor Richardsonian Romanesque, did not fit into a neat category. It was not truly vernacular, since no one could point to another building, near or far, that resembled it, though many would in the future, among them some of Frank Lloyd Wright's ground-hugging houses. It might best be described as geological, but whatever the label, the Gate Lodge was liberating for all three men: for Richardson, certainly, trained as he had been in the rituals of the Ecole des Beaux-Arts; for the disciplined businessman Ames; and for Olmsted, who, as a friend and adviser, saw the man-made fused with the natural. As he increasingly liked to do, Richardson drew upon natural colors and textures, and under Olmsted's influence, the line of demarcation between building and site blurred. The building appeared to have emerged from the earth upon which it stood.

Oakes Angier Ames, Frederick Ames's cousin, wanted to build a "memorial ground" to honor the Union dead. He and his cousins hoped it would become North Easton's focal point, and they summoned Olmsted to tell them how to go about it.

To begin, he dispatched his stepson John to prepare a survey. Arriving in North Easton in the fall of 1881, the younger Olmsted measured a dusty island defined by the triangular intersection of Main and Lincoln Streets. Ames Memorial Hall overlooked the designated site as did the town's high school, a bank, and the company store.

According to the plat John prepared, the three-sided ground, measuring roughly three hundred feet by one hundred feet, sloped precipitously. With a topography well suited to a sledding hill, this was, to most observers, far from the logical place for a monument. But Olmsted wasn't envisioning a usual commemorative marker such as a statue, arch, or obelisk. He proposed instead a bastion of boulders to honor the North Eastoners who had gone to war.

He summarized his thinking in a letter to Ames. "In very old times it was customary to commemorate important events by ... bringing together at a place agreed upon a great quantity of loose field stones and laying them up in a conical pile known as a cairn." They consisted of enormous stones, he explained, manageable only by many men, and small ones "brought by the hands of the youngest and feeblest of the community." In time, plants sprout around the cairn and "spring out of their crevices." By such means, wrote Olmsted, alluding to landscape markers around the globe, had some of "the oldest and most enduring monuments in the world" come to be.[9]

Olmsted proposed an unusually elaborate cairn for North Easton. A great retaining wall would rise some twenty-five feet from a green at the lowest point of the triangle. The top of the wall would form a parapet, behind which a terrace walk would offer a vista of

The bare bones of Olmsted's cairn, before its vegetation took hold. Note Ames Memorial Hall (middle distance, left) and the densely packed neighborhood of "shovel town."

*The archway and tunnel passing
beneath Olmsted's cairn, as recorded
a few years after construction in an
Olmsted Brothers file photograph.*

the surrounding landscape. At one end a flagpole would rise seventy-five feet above a curved, rampart-like tower. The stone assemblage would be surrounded by evergreens, vines, and shrubs, with its "crannies, niches and pockets" filled with foliage and flowers.[10]

Olmsted added a Richardsonian touch, a pass-through in the form of an arched opening with a stone stair that tunneled through the cairn beneath a vaulted ceiling of the same crude stone, supporting the promenade above. The structure, a mix of irregular stone and native vegetation, would become, said Olmsted, the centerpiece of a new "Town Square." At this "rockery," as many called it (though Olmsted disdained the name), he took his own turn at building with boulders. This vest-pocket park across from the Memorial Town-Hall was representative of what he did best, endowing the site with a shared sense of place, community, and historic memory.

On a winter Sunday in 1881, first light revealed a thick blanket of fresh snow. A guest in the Richardson household at 25 Cottage Street, Olmsted was enchanted by the crystalline brightness he saw out the window. He spied a horse-drawn snowplow and several laborers clearing the street, a process supervised by a town official on horseback. The tableau before him had set his resolve.

"*This* is a civilized community," he said, turning to Richardson. "I'm going to live here."[11]

Since ending his partnership with Vaux in 1872, Olmsted had run his business from the dining room of his home on West Forty-

Sixth Street in Manhattan, where Richardson, after moving to Boston, had been a regular guest on his trips to New York. Within weeks of Olmsted's resolution to move, the four-story house in Manhattan was out for lease, and by summer, he and his family were residing in a rented house in Brookline, once again practically around the corner from their friends, as they had been on Staten Island a decade earlier. For the Richardsons, the Olmsteds' move to Boston amounted to something of a reunion. Wives and children alike were overjoyed at being close neighbors again.

Olmsted and Richardson were both family men, with enduring marriages and multiple children. Neither professed any deep religious faith—Olmsted once quipped, "I have taken the boys to a Beer Garden Concert. I never took them to a church."[12] Their temperaments were complementary. As a man subject to periodic bouts of depression, Olmsted found Richardson's joie de vivre in the face of his chronic ill health revitalizing. By nature, Richardson was a collaborator. "He was constantly turning to Mr. Olmsted for advice," observed one contemporary, "even in those cases where it seemed as though it could have little practical bearing upon his design. And where it could have more conspicuous bearing he worked with him as a brother-artist of equal rank and of equal rights with himself."[13]

Reunited in Boston, Olmsted and Richardson thought together about architecture, not merely as buildings but as elements in the larger American context. Their collaborations encouraged Richardson in a way that his Beaux-Arts training had limited him, loosening the restraints on his imagination. Theirs was a shared passion for the local and a sense of connection to familiar places. Richardson's hearths anchored his houses, and their broad roofs spoke of protection. Both men favored exposed structure, an acknowledgment of the workman's hand, honest and true. Their palettes favored earthen tones, wood grains, stone textures, and a respect for the patina of time. Each possessed an abiding fondness for the permanence of stone; both employed crude and ancient rock to create meaning and beauty.

The work that Richardson and Olmsted executed in North Easton amounted to a fulcrum moment in Richardson's career and in the two designers' relationship. Frederick Ames in particular, a man of curiosity and abundant means, trusted them to do original work with a minimum of interference. But whether working for wealthy patrons like Ames or building libraries for the common folk, Richardson was designing buildings and Olmsted shaping landscapes that were site-specific, places that honored the rugged and pragmatic American character.

◆

Chapter Thirteen

THE MACHINE IN THE GARDEN

The railroad station, being the front door to the neighborhood, should
have the same artistic qualities as the front door of a public building
or a private residence.

——FRANK A. WAUGH

The label was new and so was the concept. Until a steady flow of
people began making the daily journey to and from a city, the word
commuter had no utility.

Prior to the Civil War, wealth permitted a few merchants and
gentleman farmers who owned both city dwellings and rural estates
to travel at will from town to country. But highly productive factories
concentrated in cities like Boston had begun producing wealth
not only for mill owners but for a better-paid and upwardly mobile
middle class. In the decades after the war, this accumulation of
means allowed a rapidly growing proportion of urban citizens to buy
homes of their own.

Without affordable transportation, the aspiring middle class
might have remained in place. But the growing network of rail
tracks allowed many people to escape cities like Boston, where the
population would triple between 1870 and 1920. Rail transport
made it possible to leave the smoke and din of the busy city for a
healthier home environment in a so-called "streetcar suburb." A
radical demographic change was launched, as tightly packed
downtowns fanned out, and traditional pedestrian cities became
suburban metropolises. By 1900, for example, Boston's radius would

extend some ten miles from the harbor and contain more than two dozen cities and towns.[1] The two-part city was evolving.

Many people wanted to work in one place and live in another, and one man at hand to facilitate the trend was named E. A. Richardson. Although he worked as a baggage manager for the Boston and Albany Railroad, E. A. (no relation to H. H.) yearned to be a horticulturalist. On his own initiative, in the early 1880s, he took on the task of improving the grounds at his assigned rail station in Newtonville, Massachusetts, a growing suburb eight miles from Boston Common. A sympathetic assistant engineer provided him with loam and sod. Members of the community offered seed, plant material, and encouragement. Richardson's fresh greenery and blooming flowers soon made his little station into a "bower of green" and "a haven of rest and shade to the waiting passenger." It was an exception along a route lined with cindery, unadorned, and "uniformly ugly station yards."[2]

Reports of E. A. Richardson's labors reached Charles Sprague Sargent. The Arnold Arboretum plan had become Sargent's lifework and was on its way to becoming an internationally recognized scientific institution and the nation's finest repository of woody plants from around the world. Sargent, his face largely obscured by a lush mustache and graying beard, maintained a sphinxlike calm in most interactions; as Olmsted said of him, "He is the most obstinate and implacably 'set' old man I have ever known." Nonetheless, Sargent liked the idea of the "railroad beautiful" and decided to expand on E. A. Richardson's public-spirited gesture.[3] As a member of the board of the Boston and Albany Railroad, thanks to his father, Ignatius, an early investor in railroad stock, Sargent possessed the clout to promote a railscape improvement scheme.[4]

He made the case to the board. With its new rail circuit to and from Boston's suburbs, the Boston and Albany, long a successful freight hauler, had begun to focus on the growing number of commuters who purchased ten-ride tickets at reduced rates (and hundred-ride tickets when the line began to sell them in 1883).[5] Sargent argued that if the railroad was looking to capitalize on the societal shift of commuting, it should develop more commodious stations. These would serve as an incentive for more people to move to the emerging suburbs, and that would surely be good for the railway's business. The argument was buttressed by a statutory requirement in Massachusetts that the railroad line, then the commonwealth's wealthiest corporation, reinvest some of its considerable profits in its business.[6] New station construction would be a means of doing so.[7]

The argument proved persuasive, and the Boston and Albany board developed a station-improvement plan in 1881. One beneficiary would be E. A. Richardson, who, after some months of more formal training at Mr. Sargent's arboretum, rose to become superintendent of a newly established Department of Station Gardens. The Boston and Albany elevated one employee's instinct to beautify one station into a much larger program, and the former baggage handler would eventually manage a company nursery that serviced dozens of stations, each with its own "railroad garden." But the men who turned the notion of the railroad beautiful into a national phenomenon were Sargent's near neighbors, Olmsted and the other Mr. Richardson.[8]

Richardson's friends thought he could design anything, and one true believer was James Rumrill. He had brought his influence to bear fifteen years earlier, helping the just-launched architect gain his first major commission for Springfield's Church of the Unity. In 1881, he lent his support again, this time as one voice in a powerful triumvirate. Now vice president of the Boston and Albany Railroad, Rumrill was joined by Sargent, who served on the B&A's building committee, and the railroad's president, Chester Chapin, Rumrill's father-in-law and another Richardson admirer.

Before Richardson, train stations tended to resemble buildings of different functions altogether. Paris's Gare du Nord, constructed during his years in Paris, consisted of a great triumphal arch flanked by symmetrical arcades of small arches; though it trumpeted the rail industry's success, it did not say *railroad*. London's Paddington Station was topped by a great hotel. Oddly, for structures that served an earthbound mode of transport, many stations in Germany and elsewhere pointed to the sky with clock towers, turrets, and pinnacles. A train terminal was more likely to look like an immense mansion or even a cathedral than a functional place to catch a train.

On the other hand, Richardson found no inspiration in the motley collection of existing rail structures along the B&A's commuter loop. Mostly constructed of wood, these boxy stations resembled ordinary houses. Some were larger, others smaller, but all looked to have been plunked down rather too close to the tracks. An hour's wait in such a station was said to be a "purgatory of discomfort and patience."[9]

Richardson's charge was to devise something better adapted to the purpose. What was needed was not a grand city building that expressed the prosperity of a great place, but something subtler to suit rural towns on the outskirts. The simple architectural program demanded only a welcoming and comfortable place for passengers to pause, quiet points of connection where people arriving on foot or riding in carriages came to catch a train. Commuters would get there in the morning to depart; later in the day, the process would be reversed when they returned home. On an average day, the B&A's typical customer would spend only a short time at the station, but in theory, making the transition pleasant would increase ridership. Richardson's concept would prove so influential he received contracts to design a string of suburban stations for the B & A, along with one built on commission for his reliable patron F. L. Ames to serve the Easton Branch Railroad, which linked North Easton with the metropolis of Boston.*

By Richardson's reckoning, the key element had to be the roof. Beneath would be a comfortable waiting room where, depending on the weather and the season, the travelers could choose to rest indoors or proceed to the shed-roofed platforms that lined the track bed on the building's opposite side. The commuters who arrived in private carriages would find added protection from the elements along the building's façade, since Richardson had incorporated a covered carriageway, or *porte cochère*.

Richardson's insight—*it's all about the roof*—led him to the design solution. He recognized the line of the ridge was key, and he drew it with the station house rising at center, with the platform

---

* Roughly thirty stations were designed by either H. H. Richardson or his successor firm, Shepley, Rutan and Coolidge, in Massachusetts and New York. Hundreds of others indebted to Richardson's conception popped up across the country before the end of the century.

*This simple elevation sketch renders the essentially horizontal character of the
Old Colony Railroad depot in North Easton, Massachusetts, and its passenger
sheds. The message, the meaning, is entirely in the roofline which seems to
compress the building.*

sheds flattening at both ends. The whole structure would look to be
hovering, long and low like a silhouette obscured by fog. The rise
and fall of the station and shed roofs would echo the gentle up-and-
down character of the surrounding New England horizon line. As
was second nature to him by now, Richardson was thinking in Olmstedian terms.[10]

When Sargent invited Olmsted to take part in the design of Greater
Boston's rail stations, he understood the logic of what he would
call the "permanently inviting suburb." The onslaught of big steam
machines was erasing the connection with nature. People saw the
world differently when the countryside whizzed by at train speed,
vanishing before it could be appreciated. Olmsted also observed
that he personally had already stopped at too many "shabby and
incommodious railroad stations" and immediately agreed to join
the design team.[11]

He applied his familiar approach. Gently curved trails and
footpaths to the station were laid out for convenience. For the
Auburndale Station, built in Newton in 1881, he designed densely
planted islands and a peninsula with a border of bushes to define the
route to and from the station. At Chestnut Hill, a large open area
next to the station became a generous green with tall trees at its
perimeter. At each of the station grounds he would design for the

railroad, he planned ample space for carriage turnarounds and un-
loading baggage.

He chose mostly indigenous New England species as plantings;
as usual, Olmsted avoided maintenance-intensive lawns and seasonal flower beds. Where the train ran in a crude cut in the terrain,
Olmsted planted shrubs and climbing wild roses to soften the apparent gash in the earth. He emphasized evergreens for visual impact
in winter as well as summer. He favored sturdy lilacs, and planted
willow trees so their great arching crowns would complement the
curving carriage approaches. Woodbine, Virginia creeper, Japanese
ivy, and other vines were trained to climb stone *portes cochères*. Although he might use an occasional hardwood to define a point of
entry, most of the rugged plants he chose grew low and accented
rather than overshadowed Richardson's stations. Olmsted's green
palette and his mixing of texture, form, and shape blended with his
friend's buildings and helped obscure workers' sheds and other utilitarian structures.

Commuters, Olmsted thought, left the city for the meadows and
the woods. When they completed their workdays, they would arrive at
welcoming stations that looked as if they belonged where they were.
As Charles Sprague Sargent explained, the whole effect was to make
the stations seem "part and parcel of Nature's handiwork."[12]

Elaborating upon the idea that begat the building, Richardson
sculpted the all-important rooflines using low-pitched hips and flattened gables. His roof planes would appear to fold into one other at
varying pitches with multiple valleys. According to one contemporary
commentator, "Richardson strove first of all clearly to express the
building's purpose," and the roof became a pure "expression of
temporary shelter."[13]

Wishing to give his buildings "a sturdy air of permanence," he
worked in his favorite medium, mixing square-cut, local granite for
the walls and brownstone window trim. The surfaces were left un-
polished. The slate roofs, capped with terra-cotta ridges, added to
the sense that these buildings had a certain geologic permanence.
The broad eaves of the waiting areas at the periphery, supported by

heavy wooden brackets and timber posts, left the bulk of the buildings in shadow, adding to the sense that the stations had been settled onto their sites long before.

Richardson's buildings were supposed to function as points of entry to towns that were still largely unsettled, and as a writer for *Architectural Record* would note early in the next century, his designs were intended to convey "an artistic character, expressing the standing of the suburb as a progressive and cultivated community."[14] *Engineering Magazine* reported that the stations also represented the proud and prosperous B&A Railroad corporation, since "nothing advertises a [rail]road better than tasteful station buildings."[15]

Most of Richardson's stations would not house such amenities as restaurants, which were more usual in the larger terminals that served long-distance travelers in hubs like Boston, New York, and Philadelphia. He did incorporate a mix of other spaces into his suburban stations, including restrooms, baggage rooms, and waiting areas. Typically, he located a ticket and telegraph office on the track side of the station, breaking the line of the wall with the swell of a bay window. Glazed with decorative bull's-eye glass, the protrusion permitted the ticket seller to look along the length of the track and see approaching trains.

Though the elements were much the same, his stations varied considerably in size. Given the mores of the Victorian era, the larger plans included separate waiting areas for women. But most of Richardson's station buildings were more intimate in size, just one room deep and human in scale. Always interested in the details, Richardson also designed drinking fountains, gaslight fixtures, and even benches, and where the budget permitted, his office provided renderings of carvings to decorate the exterior. Given his belief in the beneficent presence of a welcoming hearth, most of his stations had fireplaces.

Forgoing clock or bell towers, Richardson designed the horizontal look of the stations to suit their rural village settings, proud and welcoming yet subtle occurrences in the landscape. The task wasn't to design look-at-me buildings but to make stations that served as important points of entry for suburbanites. Their Richardsonian character implied permanence and quality, and unlike his

One Richardson's larger stations, in Framingham, Massachusetts, offered protection from the weather and immediate access to the tracks.

former apprentices McKim and White in their later rail stations, he performed no architectural pirouettes. He merely built uncomplicated stone boxes beneath spreading roofs.

Sargent expressed his satisfaction. "Until Richardson began to build rural railroad-stations," Sargent wrote, "none had been erected in America which deserve much consideration as intelligent and pleasing works of art. . . . He showed for the first time what such a building ought to be."[16]

At the turn of the new century, the magazine *House Beautiful* would describe Olmsted's and Richardson's integration of landscape and architecture. "The low stone station of the Richardson type nestles beside the track . . . and up and down the line of the road, the vista, once the train has passed, is as beautiful and peaceful as a country lane."[17] Richardson's firm would produce several dozen rail stations, while Olmsted oversaw the landscaping of perhaps three times that number. Over the course of a decade, the appeal of Richardson's and Olmsted's shared vision found favor in other regions too, extending to suburban Philadelphia and New York's Westchester County. Railroads as widespread as the Michigan Central, Norfolk and Western, and Union Pacific initiated landscape experiments, and Iowa and Illinois soon had stations that were admired for their "quiet picturesqueness" and their "pleasant, verdurous prospect."[18] People liked them for the "evocative juxtaposition of the mechanical artifact with the shapes, lines, colors, and textures of the natural setting."[19]

Such welcoming, parklike stations, whether in the Northeast, the Midwest, or even farther afield in California, helped provide a transition between city and country and an escape from what Richardson's and Olmsted's acquaintance and fellow Centurion Samuel

Clemens had called the "dusty and deafening railroad rush."[20] As Americans took possession of their landscape in a new way, the pair helped give form to the emergent American suburb.

As much as the American landscape dominated Richardson's work and day-to-day life, the idea of returning to Europe had been percolating in his mind for years. Olmsted reported that periodic journeys across the Atlantic refreshed his imagination, and Richardson felt certain that visiting some of the antique buildings he knew only from photographs would do the same for him. In the spring of 1882, when the Right Reverend Phillips Brooks asked Richardson to join him and several other gentlemen on a trip abroad, his answer, despite his unreliable health, could only be an enthusiastic yes.

His architectural practice was going great guns. In addition to several rail stations and libraries, he and his draftsmen were completing drawings for Austin Hall, the new building for Harvard's law school. Construction was well underway for the city hall in Albany, New York, and various private homes were also in the works. New and old clients competed for his services, but Richardson felt confident they would wait if he went off for the summer. The first long vacation of his adult life suddenly seemed both plausible and important.

After twelve demanding years in Trinity's pulpit, Phillips Brooks had decided he, too, needed a break. Granted a year's leave of absence by the church board, he would depart in June, bound for the port of Liverpool. Accompanied by a mix of parishioners and friends, Brooks planned a stop in London and an extended tour of France before going on alone to India and the Far East. By the time they sailed, the party had expanded to seven people, including a Boston lawyer named John Codman Ropes, Richardson, and the youngest member of the party, a draftsman in Richardson's office named Herbert Jacques.

Though Richardson's desired destinations were the medieval churches of France and Spain, the London stop would fulfill a second purpose. Julia was deeply worried that his health continued to deteriorate. Consultations with the finest physicians in Boston had at last produced collective agreement on a likely diagnosis. Richardson, they said, suffered from Bright's disease, but even if they were correct in identifying the cause of his problems as kidney failure, they offered neither a cure nor satisfactory treatments. In England he could seek another opinion from Sir William Withey Gull, an expert in Bright's disease whose research had produced new insights. If Richardson were absent for several months, Julia would have to tend to "the babies," as Richardson referred to his children, who now ranged from the eldest, Julia, age fourteen, to Frederick, age five, but the possibility of a lifesaving consultation with Gull seemed worth it.

When the men departed in mid-June, they did so in grand style, sailing out of New York Harbor aboard the SS *Servia*. A prototype for new luxury liners, the vessel had incandescent electric lighting and a double hull of steel, both firsts on a civilian ship, and the greatest number of first-class cabins. The generous appointments aboard included a men's smoking room, a ladies' drawing room, a grand staircase, and a large main salon. The *Servia* was truly an elegant hotel at sea, with three masts that permitted a large spread of sail to help propel the steamship. Under ideal conditions, it could cross the Atlantic in as few as six days. Ships like the *Servia* meant the trip went from hazardous hardship to leisurely cruise.

Much of Richardson's time at sea was spent planning the continental tour to come. Several of his fellow travelers, including Brooks and the Right Reverend William McVickar, who had become rector at Brooks's old Philadelphia parish, came to his stateroom to look over Richardson's architectural photographs of French and Spanish churches they might wish to see. Following a leisurely shipboard schedule ("I am eating 5 meals a day & sleeping splendidly," Richardson wrote to Julia), an itinerary emerged that included the Auvergne and southern France, followed by Italy and Spain.

On making landfall, they headed to London. Richardson made a long-overdue stop at Poole's, his Savile Row tailor, where his measurements needed radical adjustment. A truss maker came to him at his London hotel for a fitting. Richardson collected letters of reference from the United States minister to the Court of Saint James's, James Russell Lowell, and the ambassador's words would both open doors on the continent and please Richardson, whom Lowell called "our most original Architect."[21] More important, Sir William Gull of Guy's Hospital agreed to take his case, and an appointment was set for Saturday, July 8.

Earlier in the century, kidney disease or nephritis had gained the name Bright's disease from Dr. Richard Bright, who had been first to associate symptoms like Richardson's to kidney failure. Guy's Hospital in London had been a place of discovery, and several of Dr. Bright's colleagues had also lent their names to freshly understood diseases, including Thomas Addison and Thomas Hodgkin. Along with much else, medical practice was entering a new age. Where previously doctors relied upon guesswork and superstition, advances in pathology had led to recognition of germs as disease-causing agents rather than imagined "humors." A relationship was discerned between findings at autopsy and visible symptoms in the living and, just as more measured approaches to madness were being introduced, effective remedies were being developed for many other conditions.

Sir William Gull, now governor of Guy's, was a worthy successor to men like Hodgkin, Bright, and Addison, having saved the life of the Prince of Wales, the heir to the throne, who had been stricken with typhoid. His royal doctoring had gained him both the title of baronet and an appointment as physician-in-ordinary to Queen Victoria.

After their first meeting, Richardson reported to Julia that Gull made a "careful examination of my heart & said it was remarkably sound."[22] But the doctor wasn't certain about the diagnosis and wanted to see him again. Only on Richardson's third visit a few days later did Gull confirm the ailment as Bright's disease, based on urine tests, abdominal swelling, and dropsy—swelling due to water retention, now called edema.

Nonetheless, his time with Dr. Gull left Richardson feeling optimistic. "He told me abruptly that my trouble did *not* proceed from the heart," Richardson wrote to his worried wife.[23] Gull had not found the cardiac deterioration common to those with kidney disease, and best of all, he declared Richardson's case of Bright's "treatable." The doctor did preach prudence in the consumption of food and drink to relieve the pressures on the patient's overworked stomach and liver. Henceforth, decreed Dr. Gull, Richardson should consume "a drink of claret, lemon & warm water—*no* sugar" to ease the persistent thirst characteristic of Bright's.[24]

For Richardson, this was a great burden lifted. His sense of relief was such that, on departing London for the continent, he would largely ignore Dr. Gull's many advisories concerning "regularity of living."[25] He embarked on a virtual nonstop tour of cities and villages— in one span, he visited thirty-three towns in thirty-two days—during which he would indulge more than just his insatiable appetite for architecture. As his junior Herbert Jacques would report, "He was off on a holiday and was bound by no rules of health or diet, though they were all written for him and I was supposed to enforce them!"[26]

After London and a short stay in Paris, the tour progressed at what Richardson himself termed a "lightning rate." The cathedral at Chartres was an early stop. A journey of seventeen hours took them to Clermont-Ferrand, where, as at other towns in the Auvergne region of central France, "he studied [the churches] critically, but silently for the most part." At Nîmes they examined Roman remains, including the Maison Carrée, the temple that Thomas Jefferson had mimed in his Virginia capitol. But soon Richardson was once again "[drinking] his fill of the lovely eleventh-to-thirteenth century work" in the south of France.[27]

Their French days were memorable. McVickar, Brooks, and Richardson made a particularly noticeable threesome when they walked the narrow village streets. All three were six feet or taller (McVickar stood six feet seven) and, according to Richardson's calculation, they displaced a collective 912 pounds.[28] They made such a remarkable sight, as the story was later told, that one child, assuming the three Americans were giants in a circus freak show, inquired of them whether the dwarfs would soon follow.[29]

At Saint-Nectaire, Richardson plodded up a steep path to see a compact Romanesque "church in the clouds." The sojourners looked at cloisters, towers, ruins, and cliff-like streetscapes in Avignon and Arles before reaching Marseille, where they boarded a ship to head to Italy. There the tour continued at Genoa, Leghorn (known as Livorno), and Pisa. In Florence, young Jacques reported, "What with architecture, sculpture, and painting . . . Mr. Richardson's cup was full to the brim, and he would have stayed a year had he had his wish."[30]

"You should have seen the man in Venice!" Phillips Brooks wrote of Richardson to Robert Paine back in Boston. "The wonder is that any gondola could hold such enthusiasm and energy!"[31] Only in Venice and in a state of near collapse did Richardson slow the pace and write an account of the preceding three weeks, in which he admitted indirectly to overdoing things, telling Julia, "I expect to have artistic indigestion the rest of my life." He found Venice "a sort of dreamland." He reported that he and his fellows had hired a pair of gondolas for a week, and that he spent his days comfortably ensconced in his vessel, lazily exploring the great city on the lagoon. He offered assurances as to his health ("I am so well & am having such a splendid rest & only hope I can crowd everything into my time") but seemed resigned to a harder truth: "I can never have such an opportunity again."[32] Still, he would test his health further, as the Venice days were followed by another breakneck tour, now of sites in Spain, including the cities of Barcelona (which interested Richardson little), Saragossa, Madrid, Toledo, and Salamanca, along with dozens of lesser-known destinations. Seven cities in seven days brought them within reach of the French border and on to Paris.

Though his health was variable, Richardson's thirst for photographs was unquenchable. He understood that neither he nor Jacques had time to make drawings ("to attempt to sketch would be folly"), so he sought out photographs and books everywhere of the buildings he saw.[33] Images were already essential to his practice, and he was adding greatly to the reference collection for his own use and that of the men in his office.

As his biographer would note a few years later, "Mr. Richardson's enthusiasm carried him through as a traveler just as it did at home, and his wonderful vitality and endurance were never more fully tested."[34] He brimmed with renewed enthusiasm for the work he was doing, and his understanding of and reverence for the Romanesque grew even greater. He was "glowing with fresh ideas," as Brooks put it, some of them concerning a much-discussed porch addition to Trinity Church.[35]

He regretted that O. W. Norcross and carver John Evans had been unable to share what he had seen. Even though he had been mildly irritated when the bishop of Albany had interrupted his European vacation with an invitation to enter a competition, he nonetheless conceived a plan for the All Saints Episcopal cathedral. Caught up in the moment, he designed one based in part on the duomo he saw at Avila in central Spain.* Just as Olmsted did on his travels, Richardson could not help but pierce the thin veil of "vacation" to do the work he felt driven to do.

At his last stop on the continent, in Paris, Richardson revisited the Cathédrale Notre-Dame, the Louvre, and his old school. He looked up friends from the Ecole des Beaux-Arts, among them his former flatmate Gustave Gerhardt. Since winning the Rome prize in 1865, Gerhardt had continued to prosper. He operated both his own firm and, as *professeur-chef* at the Beaux-Arts, an atelier for *élèves*.

Circling back to Great Britain, Richardson gained insight into broader trends. His old friend Phené Spiers took him on an architectural tour of London, with a stop at Parliament to examine its heating and ventilation system, an innovative design that Richardson would later employ in a major commission in Pittsburgh. He visited William Morris, the man at the center of England's Arts and Crafts movement and toured his works at Merton Abbey. Invited to tea at Morris's home, Kelmscott Manor, Richardson found much in common with his fellow medievalist, as he did upon meeting ceramicist William De Morgan and painter Edward Burne-Jones. He shopped not only for himself but also for clients, purchasing a Persian rug for Fred Ames among other items.

In long talks with his French friends, Richardson found them much intrigued by his work and, according to Jacques, "not a little awed" by his accomplishments. However, he admitted to being less impressed with their designs, which he regarded as "the old cut-and-dried-course," designs very much as prescribed by the staid Ecole des Beaux-Arts. When he told them so, they defended their conservatism, arguing that public opinion and government policies meant that the

---

* Richardson's submission for Albany's Cathedral of All Saints, delivered the following March, would be rejected as too expensive and not sufficiently Gothic.

national taste was fixed and that there was little room in France for anything but the classicism they had learned together from Monsieur André. Richardson wasn't persuaded, however, and he argued passionately that they should be "working out *their own architecture.*"[36]

After a few last days in London, he and Jacques boarded the SS *Cephalonia* at Liverpool on September 27; one at a time, his other companions had gone their own ways in the preceding weeks. On landing in Boston, Richardson resumed the work of inventing a distinct architectural style for a country previously without one.

Chapter Fourteen

OF SHINGLE AND STONE

No sharply defined lines [should] mark the sudden transition
from the formality of architecture to the irregularity of nature.

—FREDERICK LAW OLMSTED

The gesture was quintessential Richardson. On April 6, 1883, he wrote
from Albany, updating Olmsted on shared concerns. He and William
Dorsheimer had dined with Governor Grover Cleveland a few days
before. The three talked of progress on the New York State Capitol
(too slow, thought Cleveland) and of the pending legislation to make
Niagara Falls a state park (the governor was "*strongly* in favor"). Only
after promising Olmsted more details when he returned to Brookline
did Richardson get to the real purpose of his letter.

After two years of renting, the Olmsteds contemplated a permanent home in Brookline, and Richardson made a proposal. "What I
write for is to ask you to wait til my return before deciding about moving or building—what would you say to building on my lot?"[1]

The spontaneous suggestion was heartfelt, if unfeasible—
Richardson didn't even own the property; Ned Hooper did. Julia, for
one, thought the notion "impracticable," but still, Richardson mused,
it might be "advantageous" to their increasingly entwined businesses.
Then the artist in him hijacked his own train of thought and he
quickly drew a plot plan that located a second domicile.[2]

"A beautiful thing in shingles?" he scribbled above the drawing.[3]

Olmsted soon chose another path and bought a house nearby.
But the intimate connection between the men, their work, and their
families gained a new permanence. As Rick, Olmsted's youngest child,

by then a teenager, remembered, "I was in and out of [their] house and office all the time, with father and with the Richardson children."[4]

After the dissolution of his New York partnership with Charles Gambrill in 1878, Richardson's home and office in Brookline had become one and the same. As if a household with six children wasn't busy enough, an array of young draftsmen was given the run of the house.

Richardson played at landscape design in his letter of April 6, 1883. He indicates his existing house on the left, a proposed one for Olmsted, and an altered carriage drive.

When Richardson had worked alone in Brookline, with occasional visits from Stanford White, the east parlor of the rented home had effectively been Gambrill & Richardson's satellite office. But a single room plainly would not be adequate for an independent and increasingly busy architectural firm, and with Hooper's permission, the house gained a one-story shed addition that angled off the parlor at the rear. At first, the new wing contained only a few drafting tables, but it expanded along with the business. The addition, accessed via a pair of French doors, grew longer, with a series of alcoves, each containing a large drafting table for one or two apprentices, a window, and a curtain for privacy. "The Coops," as the wing was affectionately known, also enclosed a business office and a large, open exhibition space to display renderings of the firm's works in progress.

The arrangement suited Richardson, since his health made working at home a necessary convenience. When Olmsted stopped by one day, he found his friend immobilized by one of his hernias, a circumstance that, to Olmsted, seemed "most irksome and depressing." But Richardson rose above it. "[He was] very lively in mind," said Olmsted, "with his draftsmen about him, directing a great deal of interesting work."[5]

In these suburban quarters, Richardson realized his dream of establishing an American atelier, and he became *le patron* to many young men, just as Louis-Jules André had been to him and other Ecole des Beaux-Arts students in Paris. Unlike their French counterparts, however, these American apprentices did not compete in educational *concours*. The draftsmen drew real buildings, worked out actual design problems, and rendered presentation drawings for clients and, eventually, working drawings, usually for Norcross Brothers.

Richardson's atelier differed from the French model in another way. "We children," his eldest daughter, Julia, recalled, "felt we shared in his work, even designs, as constantly ideas for a competition would come to him at the dining table, and we would be sent running for paper and pencils." When he climbed into his buggy for an inspection tour in Cambridge or Boston, "he always had some of us children with him and we reveled in it, he was so gay and full of fun."[6] The personal and the professional in Richardson's life were neither discrete nor separable. According to one young architect-in-training, "The life of the house overflowed continually through the office, bringing always good cheer."[7] By mingling home and work, Richardson assumed the role of paterfamilias to his apprentices, though always in the service of art. "Richardson's office was not an office in the present sense," remembered one of those apprentices, Charles Coolidge, some forty years later. "[It was] an atelier where one lived and thought art, and hours did not count."[8]

Stanford White was gone. He had taken a leave for a European tour in 1878, after which, as a confirmed New Yorker, he decided to join forces in Lower Manhattan with Charles McKim. But new men regularly arrived, most of them having completed the architectural program at MIT, since Richardson had an informal understanding with Tech that he would offer employment and training to the three best graduates in each class.[9]

He granted his apprentices surprising latitude. A new project typically began with a small drawing or two or three that Richardson left on a drafting table late the night before. Although "rude enough at first sight," such sketches were, one apprentice remembered, "very definite after all, these little drawings. As you studied them, it was as though you made out the walls and roofs and towers of some building looming through mist or smoke."[10]

Richardson's *esquisses* set a process in motion and, for the most part, ended Richardson's participation as a draftsman. He would instead invite one of his young men to try his hand. "Do what you can with it," he would say, "and then we will see."[11]

Apprentices were free to consult Richardson at any time. Always a patient critic, when faced with an unsatisfactory sketch he was known to say, "Let us look into the thing and see what is the matter." He often suggested the drafts-

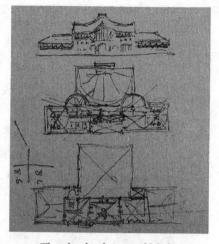

These thumbnails—most likely left by Richardson after an evening's cogitations for his apprentices to find in the morning—would become Austin Hall.

men compare their conceptions with other designs to be found in the many sources he had accumulated, pointing out a particular book or portfolio or even his own sketchbooks. He frequently instructed, "Study this building" or "Adapt that motive," or pointed to a set of photographs in the spirit of encouragement. According to Coolidge, the eventual result of these "small suggestions after the original sketch" would be a "final design . . . as much Richardson's as if he had drawn it himself which he never did. His method was not teaching but suggestions and inspiration."[12]

Richardson routinely made morning rounds, with stops at each drafting table, where he offered commentary, quickly penciled revisions directly on a drawing, or a fresh marginal sketch. Lunch was a daily tutorial. He organized Monday night dinners to which both current and former pupils were invited. But not every moment on Cottage Street was working time. Work was on occasion relieved by play, and during lunch hour (12:30 to 1:30), one draftsman might challenge another to a set of tennis on the lawn visible from the Coops' windows. Richardson organized musicales and other gatherings for

The Coops contained more than 4,000 square feet of studio space
for Richardson's many draftsmen, a sprawling space that connected
the house to Richardson's office.

the "best people & music," and sometimes a hundred friends and
neighbors came.[13] The exhibition room, its tables removed and replaced with chairs, became a performance hall, often for a string
quartet. At meals, he held the floor, discoursing on his life in Paris
and his views on art and architecture.

As one trusted former apprentice put it, "He was like a father
to his pupils and assistants, and held them to him by the cords of
personal affection as well as of professional admiration and respect."
He brought a particular passion to his profession: "Architecture was
his religion."[14]

Pranks were not unheard of, such as the day when two apprentices impersonated Richardson, buttoning one of his double-
breasted vests around them (together with three pillows); the pair
then marched around the office, mimicking their employer to the
amusement of "twenty or thirty jolly workers."[15] Nowhere else,
everyone in the business agreed, was there the generosity and creative alchemy of Richardson's drafting room, nor a man with Rich-

ardson's capacity to put his personal artistic stamp on the work of his firm.

The house belonging to the Misses Clark seemed perfect for the Olmsted family. A place of "rurality," a term Olmsted favored, it was within easy walking distance of both the Richardsons' home and Sargent's Holm Lea estate. Even from the street, the property looked like it had "capabilities," with a solid two-story wood-frame home and a good barn. The property, however, which was owned by sisters Sarah and Susannah Clark, wasn't for sale.

That didn't stop Olmsted. He had ample work in the vicinity and money in his pocket, both due to a freshly negotiated three-year contract with Boston for the city's new park system. He proposed building the unmarried sisters a new cottage at the rear of the roughly two-acre property and granting them life tenancy. Theirs was one of the more modest houses in Boston's most desirable suburban neighborhood, and the parties came to an agreement. For a generous $13,200, Olmsted would take title to 99 Warren Street.

By April 1883, landscape work was underway, and once the sisters' cottage was completed, the Olmsted family moved into the main house. With John, Owen, and Charlotte grown and gone, Fred and Mary shared the house with their twenty-two-year-old daughter, Marion, and her younger brother, Rick, age thirteen.

In its bucolic Brookline setting, the 1810 house possessed something of the character of Olmsted Hall, an ancestral property in England, which Olmsted had visited while researching his book *Walks and Talks of an American Farmer* a quarter century before. That farmhouse had been home to Nicholas Olmsted prior to his departure for the American colonies in the seventeenth century, and his great-great-great-great-grandson, a nineteenth-century man who favored the unpretentious, opted to call his new manse not Olmsted Hall but to borrow the name of his ancestor's English parish, Fairsted.

Once again, Olmsted tasked his stepson John to survey the two-acre Clark parcel, and the younger Olmsted recorded the structures and a few topographical features, including mature trees and an orchard past its prime. A new entrance to the property was needed, since the existing drive went directly to the barn at the rear of the lot, and father and son decided to add a loop to bring clients, friends, and visitors to the front door. They added a pedestrian path too, from Warren Street, to ease visits and errands by family and friends in the neighborhood. A secluded rock garden would occupy a corner of the property, screened by bushes and a perimeter fence.

The property's most dramatic feature was a deep depression in the front yard, a ravine that extended from one corner of the house to the road. It would become a secluded garden, defined by an outcropping of Roxbury puddingstone and a set of stone stairs that descended into the hollow to become a meandering path. Some of the aging apple and pear trees were eliminated, but most of the larger hardwoods kept, among them a majestic seventy-five-year-old, vase-shaped elm, a favorite tree of Olmsted's. A careful selection of oak, ash, elm, and other hardwoods were planted, along with cedars, pines, and birches. What had been a rather bleak landscape of collapsing fruit trees was richly planted and enclosed by a pole fence of spruce.

Fred left most of the work to John, though periodically he offered guidance. "I don't object to cutting away of certain bramble patches if brambles are to take their place—or anything that will appear spontaneous and not need watering or care. More mowing or dug ground I object to. Less wildness and disorder I object to."[16] Azaleas and rhododendrons, ferns, and viburnum abounded, and vines began to cover the house and climb the stone walls of the hollow.

Roughly a decade after the Olmsteds arrived, a reporter from Chicago saw the fulfillment of Fred's vision of "wildness and disorder." He wrote, "In no portion of the grounds is there any display of magnificence. Every shaded walk and every little rocky nook shows but a careful oversight of nature's own simple ways."[17] At Fairsted, Olmsted created a retreat from city life for his family and a business address embodying his ideals about how one's environment could be a civilizing force.

Like Richardson, Frederick Law Olmsted was in demand. In 1883 and 1884 alone, his firm, though fully engaged with the complex

*This ca. 1900 photograph shows the Fairsted manse amid
maturing plantings that father and sons introduced. They removed
the Clark sisters' collapsing orchard but saved one fine specimen
American elm. That vase-shaped shade tree, cherished as the
"Olmsted Elm," survived into the twenty-first century.*

Boston parks plan, had more than a dozen rail stations to landscape,
along with a half dozen jobs at schools and colleges, among them
Amherst College, the University of Vermont, and the Lawrenceville
and Groton schools. In addition, he committed to a mix of municipal
commissions, several residential subdivisions, and many private estates. Still other obligations in these years took Olmsted to ongoing

projects in Montreal, Albany, New London, Niagara Falls, and Washington, D.C.

Olmsted alone could hardly do justice to so many clients, not to mention to the personal vision that drove him. Having witnessed firsthand the workings of Richardson's office, he devised a variation for a modern landscape architecture practice.

John, his stepfather's office manager and only draftsman, had maintained the Olmsted presence in New York while the rest of the family summered and rented in Boston. But with the purchase of Fairsted, he, too, left Manhattan for Brookline. His arrival meant the Clark house would have to be adapted for both family and business. With Olmsted often on the road to meet clients and supervise projects in the works, the task of executing these "Home Improvements" was delegated to John, as were the design and construction of the cottage for the Clark sisters.[18]

The footprint of Fairsted's north parlor was extended ten feet to fit a large drafting table. The addition would be the first in an on-again, off-again building campaign that added a rambling set of structures over ensuing decades. The family gained a glassed-in conservatory that looked southwest from which to enjoy the landscape around the house and the Jack and Isabella Stewart Gardner property beyond. The elder Olmsted gained an office with a large table at its center for examining plans. Two walls were lined with bookshelves, largely for reference works and Olmsted's park reports. Among the room's decorations were framed reproductions of a few of the firm's plans, including New York's Greensward Plan, and photographs of John Ruskin and French horticulturist Edouard André.[19] As it did Richardson, working at home suited Olmsted. Both men were known to return to their offices after dinner and to work late into the evening.

Although the family would share Fairsted with the business, Olmsted intentionally kept a separation between the two, orienting family life to the south and west, the business along the road. Unlike Richardson, whose personality permeated everything he touched, Olmsted, as his son Rick put it, wanted to find "solutions of *other people's* problems, and definitely *not* opportunities for 'self-expression' for himself."[20] But as a pioneer, the senior Olmsted worried what would happen to landscape architecture after he was gone; he hoped he could keep working "until reinforcements arrive."[21] In the short term, he needed able hands to execute an ever-larger workload; in the middle term, he wanted to thoroughly instruct Rick; in the future, he hoped a new generation of well-trained men would carry on his work.

In May 1883, Charles Eliot joined the firm. He was the first non-family member but the son of an old friend of both Olmsted and Richardson, Harvard president Charles W. Eliot. The following year, a second apprentice came aboard, Henry Sargent Codman, nephew of Charles Sprague Sargent. And in another nod to the future, the firm's name changed when his father elevated John to the status of partner. As of 1884, the letterhead read "F. L. and J. C. Olmsted."

Like Richardson, Olmsted sought college graduates for his atelier. John had a degree from Yale's Sheffield Scientific School, Codman one from MIT, and Eliot was a Harvard graduate. But unlike Richardson's apprentices, most of whom arrived with degrees in architecture, these landscape men had gained only indirect instruction in their chosen profession (botany and horticulture at Harvard, engineering and drawing at MIT). Because no college program existed in landscape design, Olmsted found himself running what he called "a grand professional post-graduate school."[22] He prescribed books to read. He recommended a familiarity with good pictures and good architecture. He handed out assignments that, over time, grew more difficult. When he took Charles Eliot with him on working trips to visit clients and jobs, Eliot was expected, he wrote to a friend, "to gather principles and the practice of the profession. . . . I am to be of what service I can . . . chiefly in doing draughtsman's work, making working-drawings from preliminary design-plans."[23]

As a self-taught practitioner, Olmsted's method had been ad hoc and informal. His landscapes more often took shape in his head than on paper, and frequently on-site as he looked at the topography before him. But he also brought to the art of landscape an organized mind and years of experience in providing wartime medical supplies, managing a mining operation, and the making of large parks. He had learned along the way, but now aimed to train his heirs simultaneously in the paradoxical traits of the artist and the administrator, the dichotomy at the heart of landscape architecture.

His goal was to raise his "calling from the rank of trade, even of a handicraft, to that of a liberal profession—an Art, an Art of Design."[24] He insisted his men be better prepared than he had been.

A procedure rapidly evolved in the Olmsted office for managing workflow; it was Olmsted's own, less formal practices made standard. First came the essential preliminary visit to a site, with compasses and canteens in hand, and the preparation of a topographical survey. Once back in Brookline, Olmsted's notes, penciled on scratch paper, would be typed on the recently arrived typewriter (for years the job of copying them out neatly in pen and ink had been Mary Olmsted's).[25] A report and study plan would be prepared for presentation, and after consultation with the client, the plan finalized.

After the site was properly prepared, construction could begin and planting follow. But the Olmsteds' commitment did not end then, because Fred insisted upon supervisory visits over several years. This was no moneymaking expedient, since the follow-up fees were modest. Whether the job was a single-family home, which might involve fewer than a half dozen drawings, or a city park, like Boston's, that required more than twelve hundred, he would take work on only if the client agreed that the Olmsted firm would supervise construction and plantings and conduct annual visits thereafter. "We do not sell our drawings," he told one client. "They are our instruments for providing what we do sell."[26] This was also the only way to assure the client the result would be an Olmsted landscape.

"Upon the large table," a visitor wrote a few years later, "young artists . . . work[ed] busily over acres of grades and walks, and drives, and cunningly devised effects for nature's development."[27] As on nearby Cottage Street, Olmsted's atelier gradually filled with gifted and ambitious young men. For a dozen years, they would have the benefit of Olmsted in residence, where they could observe him doing what he did best. As his son Rick put it, his father's gift was "to approach each new problem that was presented to him . . . objectively, openmindedly . . . studying it for what it was to him, *a newly-met thing*."[28]

When he suggested to Olmsted "a beautiful thing in shingles," Richardson had a mode in mind. In a shift from the familiar Victorian styles of his earlier domestic work, he had for some years been experimenting with houses wrapped in wooden shingles. It was a manner especially well suited to the rural ideal of the new suburb.

The source was neither French nor English. Simple, wood-frame Colonial-era houses, many of them survivors along the New England shores, intrigued Richardson and his early draftsmen. In the 1870s, photographs of such Colonial houses circulated widely, as young architects took to gazing back into American history as the nation celebrated its centennial. There was something unexpectedly fresh about the unpainted siding and uncomplicated gable roofs, a simplicity that contrasted with the ornateness of other contemporary styles.

The Olmsted firm's apprentices taking a break for a photograph at Fairsted.

The first Richardson project to adapt shingle elements had been a summer home for William Watts Sherman in 1874. Designed with Stanford White's assistance, this "cottage"—in the sense of cottage as an escape, rather than as a small or plain dwelling—was located in Newport, Rhode Island, a once-prosperous port city then reemerging as a fashionable summer destination for the wealthy. The Watts Sherman House was a mansion with a difference, since Richardson incorporated several elements of early American houses, including a saltbox-shaped front gable and a massive center chimney. Most notably, however, its shingled walls, roofs, and even its window frames, per Richardson's instructions, were left unpainted, in order that the wood would weather naturally and the house "look as if it had been built for years."[29] With its broad front gable, the house seemed to sit lower on its site, and the blend of shingles, horizontality, and historical elements pleased the public.

Richardson was pioneering a new style, and over the years he would design a number of other Shingle-style homes for friends and family. One of them was a collaboration with Olmsted, constructed for the latter's stepdaughter.

At age twenty-three, Charlotte had married a Boston physician named John Bryant. Two years later, in 1880, the Bryants, by then parents of an infant son, decided to build a summer place. Olmsted and Richardson put their heads together to perform the fatherly and avuncular duty of devising a peaceful seaside home for the young mother, her husband, and their child. John and Charlotte owned a fine site, since his mother had distributed family land in Cohasset, Massachusetts, to each of her children. The family's roots went back four generations in the town, and as the eldest child, Dr. Bryant inherited the most picturesque parcel, a promontory known as Hominy Point. Hard by the channel that led into Cohasset Cove, the acreage possessed a spectacular view of open water and ships well out to sea steaming for Boston.

Olmsted began the design process with a survey of ground elevations indicating the contours of the land. Reached via shore-hugging Margin Road, the rugged topography rose from an inland wetland to the obvious building site, a wooded knoll, before dropping precipitously to the sea. A second drawing specified the sight lines from the property's apex, indicating nearby landmasses, which included several islands, one with a lighthouse. Using this guide to the viewscape, Olmsted and Richardson decided upon the location of the house's footprint. Richardson then sketched a floor plan, oriented such that the house's windows and porches would frame the best views.

The house stood on a foundation of rubble stone, rooting it to the site. Its entrance was a carriageway at basement level, from which a generous flight of stairs rose to the main floor. There the visitor was greeted by an embracing view of the seascape via sets of large windows. French doors provided access to a porch, and large pocket doors enhanced a sense of openness in the interior, despite multiple room divisions.

The entire exterior of the finished house would be covered with plain shingles, its roof surface broken only by rising chimney stacks of rough stone. With virtually no decorative detail or trim—even the porch posts were clad in shingles—the Bryant place would not call attention to itself. Olmsted's terraces and Richardson's porches fit into the folds of the granite outcropping undergirding the house. The walks and paths Olmsted laid out on the waterfront acres further tethered the Bryant home to its place. The house, its view, and its setting were one.*

Richardson designed a more modest Shingle-style summer residence on a wager. The client, a friend of Phillips Brooks, didn't need a home on the scale of the Watts Sherman or Bryant houses. The Reverend Percy Browne desired only a simple, contemplative dwelling overlooking the harbor in Marion, Massachusetts, just west of Cape Cod, and he laid odds that Richardson could not built one for less than $2,500.

In the end, Reverend Browne's 1882 house came in very close to budget and very much met expectations, sitting long and low, its length aligned with the water views. As one critic said, it was "so appropriate to its surroundings that it seems to have grown out of them by some process of nature."† Richardson's simple conceit of a membrane of shingles and few details would inspire countless variations and imitations. Many of them, like the Browne house, would have gambrel roofs, a Colonial form that had fallen from use before Richardson revived it for Reverend Browne.[30]

Though many did, not every client fell under Richardson's spell. One who felt imposed upon by his confident manner of working, Mrs. Mary Fiske Stoughton, a widow, pushed back concerning her new shingled home on Brattle Street in Cambridge. Her frequent

---

* In the year after the house's completion in 1881, a second son arrived. The birth of a third son, in 1883, would take Charlotte to the brink of madness. In her postpartum days, she experienced a "sudden failure in mind" and her husband committed her to an institution, where she would remain the rest of her life. FLO to Calvert Vaux, October 7, 1883.

† The writer of those words, Mariana Van Rensselaer, whom we will get to know shortly, knew the house well, as it was located very near her summer home and next door to that of her great friend Richard Gilder; the latter, as editor of the *Century*, gave her many pages in his magazine to write about buildings and grounds in general and Olmsted and Richardson in particular. Van Rensselaer, *Henry Hobson Richardson and His Works* (1888), p. 106.

objections culminated in three letters she wrote to him in a four-day period in July 1882. Returning from his trip abroad a few days later, Richardson found the handwritten missives awaiting him.

He thought her complaints unreasonable and promptly wrote to tell her so. He reminded Mrs. Stoughton that he had drawn upon his personal relationship with O. W. Norcross to persuade the Worcester construction firm to build her home. He pointed out, "You're getting your house for remarkably little money." Then he announced his departure from the job. "I think it best for all concerned that I should withdraw from any further charge of the erection of your house."[31] Richardson, who had already expressed a growing reservation about working for individual clients rather than on larger institutional jobs, felt he had no choice.

When the house on Brattle Street was completed the following year, the interior was more hers than his; Mrs. Stoughton had accepted his resignation and hired another man more willing to complete the job to her tastes. Nevertheless, the house as seen from the street was very much Richardson's and promptly became the talk of the profession.

The two-story home was on a lot that, until divided by his heirs, had been part of the late Henry Wadsworth Longfellow's expansive property. Built on the corner of Ash and Brattle Streets, the new house was a distillation of the Georgian and Gothic designs nearby. Richardson incorporated popular architectural tropes, among them a turret, bay windows, and intersecting gable roofs, as well as a porch. But he withheld the latter, making it a shadowed hollow within the mass of the house. Rather than calling attention to the eclectic elements, he cloaked the whole structure in a uniform skin of cypress shingles that conformed to the undulating shapes of the house. The shingles and the minimal trim were painted a uniform deep green.

The windows, grouped in twos and threes with numerous small panes, added to the horizontal feel, making the house look lower. The effect was unexpected. Rather than calling attention to itself, the Stoughton House occupied a quiet place, as if some somber, shy soul within wanted to engage on her terms, in her time, rather than inviting comment. A writer in *Inland Architect and News* described it as "a dear comfortable looking homestead."[32]

Mrs. Stoughton's Cambridge house, as photographed in the late nineteenth century.

The design would be recognized as a benchmark. "When Mr. Richardson built this house," wrote the author of *Artistic Country Seats* less than three years later, "he set the style . . . and since its erection, the use of shingles instead of clapboard has greatly increased, while the entire absence of all frivolous ornamentation of scroll-work, and other souvenirs of the 'Vernacular' architecture of former years, set hundreds of architects thinking."[33] Richardson's architectural peers admired the house's radical simplicity and its unusual avoidance of multiple colors. They not only liked what they saw, but many imitated it and in a multitude of places.*

Once more working in tandem with Olmsted, Richardson would create another precedent-setting variation on the Shingle style on a hilltop site not far away from the Stoughton House. Their clients

---

* Along with the Ames Gate Lodge, the Stoughton House also came to occupy a keystone place in virtually every survey text that recounts the story of nineteenth-century American domestic architecture.

were old friends, Robert Treat Paine and his wife, Lydia Lyman Paine.

As a child, Mrs. Paine spent her summers at the Vale, the Lyman country home in Waltham, ten miles west of Boston. Established late in the previous century by her grandfather, the estate featured a fine Palladian mansion amid a four-hundred-acre landscape with an English-style pleasure garden, woodlots, ponds, and even a deer park. When William Cullen Bryant first visited, he described the property as "a perfect paradise."*

On the occasion of the Paines' marriage in 1862, Lydia's father gave the newlyweds a portion of the Vale property, a hundred-plus-acre parcel on the slope behind the main house. There they had constructed a home for themselves, one that, with its mansard roof, resembled the early Second Empire homes Richardson built later in the same decade as he launched his career.

The crucible of the Trinity Church project in the mid-1870s established a kinship between vestryman Paine and architect Richardson. Lydia and Robert became regular guests at the Richardsons' dinner table in Brookline, a convenient carriage ride away, and by autumn 1883, the Paines were contemplating an architectural project of their own. They now had five children, and their Waltham country house felt cramped. A trip Lydia had made to Albany to view Richardson's work had helped decide the next step. She found the Albany capitol "superb," and Richardson became her architect of choice for a new house.[34]

One obstacle remained, however. Much as they liked one another, Richardson remained preeminently a man of artistic temperament, expansive and excitable, while Paine was the somber philanthropist. More to the point, Paine had been a constant, hovering, and sometimes intrusive presence at Trinity Church during construction. Furthermore, the unpleasantness at the Stoughton project a few months before had left Richardson with new reservations about working for individuals in general.[35] Committees were one thing; his experience was that differences among a gathering of

---

* Samuel McIntire, the Salem wood-carver turned architect, designed the Lyman manor house.

men could be addressed with sweet reason. But the concerns of private clients were too often dictated by inscrutable emotion.

Eager to proceed with their building project, the Paines invited Olmsted into the middle of the discussion. Richardson was off on a trip to inspect an out-of-town job when Robert Paine wrote to Olmsted in January 1884: "Sometime after Mr. Richardson returns we must meet and talk 'house.'"[36] Olmsted seemed a natural ally, since social welfare was at the core of his ideas about the value of parks and landscape, and Paine had devoted years to addressing the wretched living conditions of Boston's poor, writing and lecturing about social conditions, philanthropy, and "pauperism." In the end, though, the Paine property itself was what persuaded both Richardson and Olmsted to proceed.

Olmsted arrived to inspect the Paine acres. He took in the existing house, nestled into the hillside and surrounded by a tennis court, stable, henhouse, greenhouse, and croquet green. But his park-maker's eye drew him up the slope, lured by a stone outcropping the family called Glacier Rock. After limping his way to the crest of the plateau, he stood amid a stand of pines, studying the easterly view of the Charles River basin and the city of Boston. The existing house, halfway down the hill, left him unimpressed, but he saw what he needed to see.

"A new site [is] preferred by him," Lydia noted in her diary that night, "so we are all upset again."[37] The momentary upset soon gave way to a new understanding, and an enthusiastic Olmsted was eager to start fresh on the new site. Richardson put the sourness of the Stoughton job behind him, and the tandem of designers took the job. The Paines would ultimately not be hectoring clients, but the challenges of their desires and the possibilities of their property would test both Olmsted's and Richardson's capacities for original answers.

When Robert Treat Paine first conceived the layout of a new home for his family, he sat by a lake high in the Bavarian Alps. Although he was no draftsman, he applied his pencil to a page in his ever-present pocket diary. His experience at Trinity Church had shown him how a simple sketch could be the germ of something much greater.

The crude floor plan that Paine eventually handed to Richardson featured a pair of cylindrical turrets like those at North Easton's Ames Memorial Hall and the Gate Lodge, but it also omitted one rather major complication. Left unacknowledged was that Paine, a conservative and economical man, would never abandon the two-and-a-half-story box that had served his family for the better part of two decades. Despite appearing nowhere on that early sketch, the Second Empire structure would be part of the job, making this a renovation, a class of work Richardson rarely undertook. Furthermore, since everyone agreed that the current site was far from the ideal location, the 1866 house would have to be moved.

Richardson responded with his own drawing, one he prepared within a day of a site visit. It respected both his client's wishes to incorporate the standing structure and Olmsted's preferred setting. Richardson extended the south elevation, attaching the block of the Second Empire house to the west end of his design. The broad south façade of the combined old and new structures would overlook the Vale estate below. From Paine's sketch, he picked up the curved structures defining the east and west corners. He drew the first as a turret, the other as a bay window. But a close look at Richardson's rough floor plan revealed something else.

The added breadth of the house would be equally apparent inside. Richardson imagined an unobstructed east–west axis that ran the entire length of the house. He sketched very few partitions, leaving the first floor largely open. It recalled the unbuilt home for Richard Codman, but such a long and unobstructed space had few other precedents. Still, the Paines liked what they saw, and the open plan would change little in the more polished drafts to come from the Coops.

Over the coming months, Olmsted and Richardson would share a give-and-take that determined much about the final character of the house. While it was agreed the structure would be planted onto the chosen spot on the high ridge, its footprint oriented to take in the view, there were complications. On the north side, the first priority was logistics. Family and guests would arrive in carriages, so a suitable drive with a turnaround and covered carriage entrance, a *porte cochère*, were needed. The south side posed a different challenge. The sloping hillside would exaggerate the height of the two-story house, but Olmsted wanted, above all else, to avoid making it look like a prominent and alien object. His answer was a terrace that ran the length of the façade at the same level as the main floor of the house, which would function as a sort of plinth, providing a setback that eased the transition from the house to the slope it overlooked. A retaining wall at the base of the terrace would be constructed not of cut and squared stone but of crude boulders. Its resemblance to native New England stone walls would be clear.

Olmsted also gave the terrace a curvilinear outline that terminated with a pair of graceful arcs that were concentric to the cylindrical shapes at the ends of the house. The house footprint would then fit into Olmsted's landscape as rounded pegs into rounded holes. To further ease the transition to the fall of the hill, he located curving stairs within the semicircular ends of the retaining wall that descended to the existing grade of the hillside.

"House pretty much decided on," Lydia Paine wrote in her diary in July 1884, after more meetings with Olmsted and Richardson.[38] But the evolutionary flow of drawings from the offices of both men would continue into the winter.

One turret became three and then two, with the westward one neatly obscuring the joining of the old house to the new. A pitch of the steep hip roof dropped by half, giving the house a markedly lower profile. The notion of cladding the addition entirely in shingles shifted when boulder walls like those Olmsted specified for the surrounding retaining walls replaced the shingles on the surface of the first story and the corner towers. It was as if Olmsted's perimeter wall came to life, and the landscape began to envelop the structure. In the way that Olmsted's and Richardson's minds merged in planning it, the living landscape of the hillside and its new crowning element looked to become one.

Site preparation began in earnest in late 1884. Olmsted visited at the end of September to consult on the configuration of the terrace, then a week later to supervise the culling of trees. In the spring still more trees came down, many of them mature oaks. Removal of their huge root systems required blasting, and the Paine children thrilled to the loud cry of "Fire!" and, an instant later, the great reverberation of dynamite detonating.[39] But the family would not be on hand to watch the entire process.

In May 1885, mother, father, and all five children embarked on the SS *Etruia* from New York Harbor. In a surprising act of trust— even more than Brooks, Paine had been an on-site presence at Trinity Church—the family would spend four months in London, Venice, Paris, and the Alps, far from their construction project.[40] There was, however, a house-related rationale for the trip. Keen collectors of artistic objects, the Paines would acquire furnishings for their enlarged house on the hill, including Sienese marble fireplaces, neobaroque Venetian furniture, light fixtures, and hundreds of other items.

In their absence, the old house was moved. Relocating a house was no rarity, and in this case, after the structure was raised on a cribbing of railroad ties, it was laboriously dragged by oxen nearly a thousand linear feet and elevated twenty-three feet. Its cellar hole was then backfilled and leveled.

By early September, the stonemasons completed work on the walls and turrets. When the framing and sheathing was finished, the shingling began, and carpenters set to work inside. On a late August site visit, Richardson proclaimed he was "highly pleased with everything."[41] But when the Paines returned in mid-September, they found a house far from done.*

Lydia thought it "grave but interesting" and "very large."[42] Robert Paine quickly assembled a long list of questions for Richardson concerning drains, fireproofing, and the cost of painting the old house, now an ell largely hidden by the addition. He also found he had returned in plenty of time to supervise—and second-guess—the landscape work being executed.

After Paine entrusted his own gardener with the job of building the terrace wall without the on-site guidance of Olmsted, the latter objected. The work needed to be redone, Olmsted told Paine firmly. Otherwise, he warned, the terrace would be in "shabby in-

---

* Although Norcross Brothers remained Richardson's preferred builders, Paine chose not to hire the Worcester firm. The likely explanation is that after their disagreements on-site at Trinity Church, neither Mr. Paine nor O. W. Norcross was keen to tangle further.

congruity" with the walls of the house, "as different a thing . . . as chalk to cheese."[43] Paine reluctantly agreed.

The Paines dubbed their estate "Stonehurst" (in Old English, *hurst* means "wooded hill"). When completed in 1886, the house stood alone, with all signs of the previous dwelling erased and a new stand of specimen trees occupying the former barnyard. With the removal of five hundred feet of old stone walls, the lower field, once divided by the zig and zag of the walls, became an open meadow. Glacier Rock, now a larger expanse of bedrock scraped clean at Olmsted's orders, seemed to point at the newly uncluttered viewscape like the arm of a resting giant. Stones abandoned by the receding glacier dotted the landscape.

The collaborative conversations had resulting in a unique house. Olmsted's and Richardson's specifications read like a dialogue, with Olmsted positioning an outdoor "room" with great care at the center of the terrace where a carpet of brick pavers defined it. Richardson's "summer parlor" was flooded with light; the "autumn parlor" was a snug, carpeted, interior room with a sense of enclosing warmth.

The completed south terrace did precisely what its creators asked of it, providing a space of transition from the inside to the boundless vista outside. The planned stairs descending to grade had been replaced with grass ramps, further easing the transition. Uncharacteristically, Olmsted expressed pride in his accomplishment, admitting to Paine, "I have never done anything of the kind that I liked as much."[44]

On its singular site with a broad view of Boston, Olmsted had planted Stonehurst in the landscape: The grand mansion looked natural, immovable, even inevitable. At the level at which the boulders ended on the house walls, the first courses of shingles flared out before rising to the cornice, leaving an overhang that added a shadow line to camouflage the shift in walling material. As he had at the Watts Sherman House, Richardson specified the shingles be left unprotected and, darkening with each season, their color would approach that of the red sandstone lintels and window sills. Vines began to climb the walls, enhancing the sense that the house was in nature's grip.

A family photograph, taken in 1886, shortly after Stonehurst's completion.
The house is Richardson, the stonewall-enclosed terrace Olmsted.

A large sundial Richardson designed, mounted on one of the towers, further implied the harmonic interaction of site and structure. As Phillips Brooks, a frequent visitor to Stonehurst, would remark, "All [Richardson's] buildings took possession of the earth they stood on."[45]

On entering Stonehurst, proper Bostonians and European guests were shocked by the main hall. People were accustomed to houses that reflected class and social distinctions, and Richardson's unrestricted living places seemed as revolutionary in the nineteenth century as democracy had been a century before. This house had no barriers. There was no confining vestibule that screened visitors; instead, its living-hall plan was a continuous space to which every visitor gained entry upon walking in the door. The sight and the experience of the room was a shock, with its 50-foot depth, front to back, and 114-foot length. The expanse was informal, vast, even exposed, with circulation and living spaces combined. The expanse was unbroken by so much as a column, the result of a truss system that suspended the beamed ceiling from above.

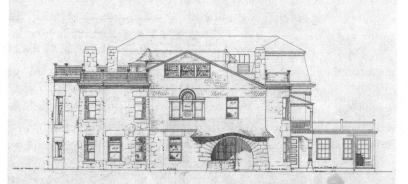

*This drawing of the east elevation of Stonehurst, found in Olmsted's files,
speaks for the complexity of Richardson's assignment. Though largely obscured, the
tall double-hip roof of the Second Empire wing can be discerned at rear. He
incorporated one of his signature Syrian arches on the first floor and a Palladian
window above, alluding to the Vale. Suggestive as this elevation is, the house
demands to be seen in three dimensions, with its curves and shadow lines, its
recesses and textures, and the way that Olmsted devised his own matching scheme.*

But Richardson's floor plan also anticipated the need for intimate spaces. He designed inglenooks, window seats, and stairway
benches for private moments and conversations. Robert Paine got a
study and Lydia Paine her "bow parlor," a cozy space half-hidden in
the base of a tower. The colors and textures also set a mood. The
ceilings were gilded between the beams, the walls were red and sten-
ciled. The architectural surfaces set off the exotic furniture the
Paines had brought home from their European tour. Richardson—
and the Paines—found ways to create rooms with few walls.

The stairway was the house's armature and an architectonic
sculpture. Partially enclosed by paneled wainscoting of quarter-sawn
red oak and nearly a hundred turned balusters (five per tread), the
three-run stairway rose to a landing, then again to a semicircular sitting room, and, finally, accompanied by a twisting handrail, reached
the upstairs hall. The whole was a tour de force that honored Richardson's specifications, which called for the woodwork to be executed "by a skilled artist in a spirited and artistic manner."[46] The

price for such workmanship was high: The total cost of Stonehurst was just under $40,000, including Richardson's fees of $2,945.02, at a time when the average wage earner made less than $20 per week.

The Paines went on to spend the rest of their lives in the home they came to cherish, surrounded by the work Olmsted had done to integrate the estate's pine trees, Glacier Rock, and the site's big boulders. They held annual picnics to which they invited inner-city families. By the time Robert Paine died in 1910, he and Stonehurst had claimed one another. As he faded away inside, a granddaughter chose to write to her sister from "his terrace where so many evenings we have all sat around & talked & laughed." The place, its trees and rocks, and "even the crows cawing around—all seems so full of him."[47]

With the Paine and Stoughton houses, as one critic of his day put it, Richardson "set the style, so to speak, for many other country houses."[48] His earliest domestic designs, such as the Second Empire town homes for Dorsheimer and Crowninshield, were good of their kind, but in a well-established manner based on French precedents. But in later years, at North Easton and Waltham and elsewhere, Richardson refined an architecture of place alongside Olmsted, designing unique structures that would be almost unimaginable anywhere else. As Phillips Brooks remarked, encountering such Richardson designs was to feel "the wind . . . of an elemental simplicity, out of the primitive life and fundamental qualities of man."[49]

Other architects would pay heed to Richardson's shingled experiments, both large and small, and, in particular, to the open plans he conceived, which would redefine how designers imagined interior space and how their clients inhabited it. As the leading twentieth-century scholar of Richardson wrote, "The geological inspiration at Stonehurst create[s] a sense of timeless continuity between house and site."[50] The American house would, quite simply, never be the same, thanks to Richardson and later architects who saw his work as a touchstone for new answers, with Charles McKim, Stanford White, and Frank Lloyd Wright prominent among them.

Chapter Fifteen

CITY OF CONVERSATION

This is the only place in America where society amuses me,
or where life offers variety.

——HENRY ADAMS

The cityscape of downtown Washington, D.C. posed very different challenges from rural New England, but both Olmsted and Richardson would do important work in the nation's capital. The former's labors on the U.S. Capitol grounds would prove timeless; sadly, Richardson's several mansions fared less well. None would survive intact into the twenty-first century, caught in the tides of rising real estate values, a society shifting away from live-in servants, and a new mobility with the arrival of the automobile.

In pursuing commissions in the city, both men gained friends among the Washington elite. Perhaps the most coveted social invitation in town was to the tall white house at 1607 H Street, where Mrs. Marian Hooper Adams, known universally as Clover, conducted her "talk parties."[1] Her charm, the wide-ranging wisdom of her husband, Henry, and the wit of their distinguished guests had won the Adams's drawing room an international reputation. No less a personage than novelist Henry James described their home as "that intensely lively Washington salon."[2]

The Adamses had moved to the capital in 1880. He was the grandson and great-grandson of presidents, she a privileged child of Beacon Hill, whose grandfather had been a Marblehead, Massachusetts, banker enriched by the China trade. They had spent much of the

1870s in Boston, where Henry had launched Harvard's Graduate Department (later, the Graduate School of Arts and Sciences). But with his decision to become a full-time historian, they rented the house on H Street so he could settle into the research for a multivolume history of the Jefferson and Madison administrations. For her part, Clover pursued her growing passion for photography, and her portraiture in particular rapidly gained recognition as she took pictures of friends and family as well as the personages in their circle. The couple opened the doors of their house on Lafayette Square with its view of the White House to such favored guests as eminent historian George Bancroft; Clarence King, an especial friend, who, as director of the U.S. Geological Survey, had mapped not a little of the American dominion; and a mix of notable Washingtonians, Bostonians, and other visitors to the nation's capital. It was a place for lively conversation but rarely political talk, as few senators were admitted. Washington deals were unlikely to be brokered at Clover Adams's table.

In early November 1882, a Washington assignment brought Richardson to dinner. Clover had made the rented house on H Street a gallery for displaying the art she purchased on her European travels, including drawings by Rembrandt and Michelangelo and more recent works by William Blake, John Constable, and J. M. W. Turner, together with an array of objets d'art, including ceramics, glass, and carpets. As her friend Mrs. Bancroft admitted to her, "My dear, I dislike auctions very much, but I mean to attend yours after you die."[3]

Henry's longtime friend Richardson also discovered at Clover's table that, according to her, his latest project, a large brick home at 1530 K Street for another Harvard classmate, had become "the object of much discussion and very opposite opinions."[4] Lacking in the usual Victorian details, it was dismissed by its detractors as plain. Although Clover called it "emphatically a gentleman's house," she still had not quite made up her mind. "[Though] the lines are very fine," she told her father in a letter home, "it is very stern and severe as a whole."[5] The lively discussion concerning the house seems to have planted a seed, however, one that would germinate in the coming year when Clover Adams decided she, too, wanted a Richardson house.

Olmsted quite naturally found a welcome place amid the stimulating company. Certainly any friend of Richardson's would be embraced by Henry and Clover, but Olmsted arrived in 1882 with an added advantage. He knew Clarence King, a confidant of the Adamses, since King had prepared the maps for Olmsted's Yosemite report in 1864.

Olmsted's presence in Washington that autumn concerned his ongoing project around the U.S. Capitol. Nine years earlier Vermont senator Justin Morrill, chairman of the Senate Committee on Public Buildings and Grounds, had invited Olmsted to rationalize the Capitol grounds. Until his arrival, they had evolved more or less haphazardly for three-quarters of a century.

The "Permanent Seat of the Government of the United States"—the city that would become Washington, D.C.—had been formally established by passage of the Residence Act of 1790, which provided for the construction of a new federal city near what was then the geographic center of the young country. When President Washington had visited the proposed site at a fork of the Potomac River, he saw a rugged and untamed wilderness. As he and Major Pierre Charles L'Enfant sat astride their horses at the top of Jenkins Hill in June 1791, they saw swamps, wooded thickets, meandering creeks, and a few scattered farmsteads. L'Enfant recognized the potential of the place, imagining generous boulevards that cut diagonally across a grid of streets, a "President's house," and, on the exact hilltop where Washington and L'Enfant conversed, a "Congress house."

By the time Olmsted had received his initial invitation to discuss landscape in the capital in 1873, Washington was a burgeoning city, and Thomas Jenkins's pasture had become known as Capitol Hill. The imposing United States Capitol was the centerpiece, with a great cast-iron dome, completed during the Civil War, that rose to a height of 288 feet. As grand as the sandstone and marble Capitol was, its immediate setting needed improvements suitable to the $16 million edifice. Another act of Congress, this one signed into law in 1874, elevated Olmsted from consultant to contractor.

No comprehensive landscape plan had previously been devised for the fifty-eight acres of the Capitol grounds. On inspecting the precinct, Olmsted found poor soil, a single tree of majestic proportions (the "Washington Elm," said to have been planted by the first president), a dozen other healthy midsize specimens, but little else worth saving. It was less a park than a confused welter of crossroads: Olmsted counted a total of twenty-one roads and forty-six footpaths entering the park.[6] The Capitol building itself had clearly outgrown the existing terracing, which had been laid out for a structure half its size.

The task was not just a matter of beautifying the surrounding parkland. The Capitol served as a national symbol of democracy; a place of business for the legislative branch; and the site for major events like presidential inaugurations. In Olmsted's judgment, the city of Washington also needed a public park for daily visitors.

Olmsted gave Morrill's committee an uncharacteristically symmetrical and formal "skeleton plan."[7] He cut the number of streets with access to the grounds to seven. In recognition of the city's hot summer climate, he proposed plantings of trees and shrubs to provide shady summer spaces. As usual, he avoided temporary flashes of color, favoring "greenness" in his choice of trees, shrubbery, and ground cover. In a first attempt at reimagining how the west front of the Capitol might be better integrated into the landscape, he proposed stairs to descend the steep slope.

Work had begun in 1874. Straight streets were replaced with curvilinear drives and paths that meandered in a precise pattern; when viewed on a map, they resembled the petals of a flower. He planned extensive regrading and drainage, with a foot of new topsoil to enrich the existing dense clay.

One result of his changes would be to frame unobstructed views of the Capitol. In Olmsted's mind, the iconic building should be seen and admired, emphasizing its important role in helping "form and train the tastes of the nation."[8] Congress had appropriated funds to carry out his plan, and by the time he visited the Adamses on H Street for the first time in the autumn of 1882, that first landscape plan had been largely implemented. But he was back in town to promote another scheme.

Over the years, Olmsted had rethought how the Capitol ought to occupy its space. Over eight decades, the city had developed east of Capitol Hill. That meant the elevation most people saw looked not at the picturesque Potomac River valley that lay to the west and

Olmsted's 1874 plan for the acreage around the Capitol. The outline scheme survives at eastern end of the National Mall.

Olmsted provided Senator Morrill and his committee with this perspective drawing to illustrate the new and grand double staircases he proposed for the west front, complete with strolling couples enjoying and admiring the United States Capitol.

south but at the cityscape in the opposite direction. The eastern orientation also relegated both the White House and the Washington Monument, the latter nearing completion after decades of delay, to what Olmsted called the Capitol's "back yard."[9] To him, that made little sense.

In his first overall plan for the Capitol grounds, he had proposed a pair of broad staircases on the west façade, with generous landings to ease descent to the grade nearly thirty feet below. But Congress had allocated no money for the staircases, and they remained unbuilt. Now he advocated an alternative plan that would enlarge the base of the building. When seen from the west, the Capitol looked like it teetered on its hilltop, so Olmsted proposed expanding the architectural footprint by laying a wide stone terrace. This broader base would serve the building as a pedestal does a sculpture, taking advantage of the elevation to make the Capitol appear on approach to possess its hill and look all the more impressive. The notion resembled the siting of Stonehurst but writ much larger.

Once visitors reached the new podium, Olmsted asserted, they would have an elevated viewing point, and the landscape west of the city would no longer be a "back yard" that "appear[ed] to tail off to the rear of the Capitol." Another advantage, Olmsted wrote, would be that "what has been considered its rear will be recognized as [the Capitol's] more dignified and stately front."[10]

Olmsted had worked his way up the federal hierarchy, writing to Edward Clark, Architect of the Capitol, then to individual members of Congress. To help sell the approach, he added another element to the plan. One hundred new rooms could be created beneath the proposed marble terraces on the north, west, and south elevations. The Capitol was badly overcrowded, and the new spaces could accommodate much needed storage, new offices for clerks, and congressional meeting rooms. To combat the argument of those who worried the terrace would obscure the building, he constructed temporary scaffolds that mimicked the size and shape of the terraces to demonstrate how the alterations would affect sight lines.

After much debate, the funds were appropriated in 1882. In the coming months and years, the job would bring Olmsted to town regularly to supervise progress, lobby for additional funding, and to fight off proposals that threatened to water down his plan. At one point he brought Richardson into the discussion, since the stamp of approval from Richardson, a man as widely recognized in the press and in his profession as Olmsted, carried real weight.[11]

The Adamses great friend John Milton Hay possessed many skills. As a young man, he had served as President Abraham Lincoln's personal secretary, and after Lincoln's assassination in 1865, he took up diplomatic posts in Paris, Vienna, and Madrid. Later, trying out journalism, he filed dispatches from the Great Chicago Fire in 1871, reporting, albeit inaccurately, that the conflagration had been started by a Mrs. O'Leary, who, lamp in hand, went "to the barn behind the house, to milk the cow . . . that kicked the lamp, that spilled the kerosene, that fired the straw that burned Chicago."[12] He published a much-admired book of verse and aspired to write the definitive biography of his old boss.* Among Hay's closest friends was Henry Adams, and their bond would result in Richardson's most important Washington commission.

The course of Hay's life had shifted at age thirty-five, when he married Clara Stone, daughter of Amasa Stone, a powerhouse Ohio railroad man and banker who had been an early backer of Lincoln. Mr. and Mrs. Hay traveled often, but more often than not, they lived luxuriously in Cleveland in a home Clara's doting parents had built for them. John helped manage his father-in-law's myriad business interests, and the couple welcomed two daughters and a son. But in his early forties, Hay had begun to suffer from bouts of dizziness and depression. A famous French physician he consulted would ascribe Hay's symptoms to *neurasthénie céphalique*, but being told that he had weak nerves hardly seemed an adequate answer. Finally, an editor friend offered a more plausible diagnosis. The cause, Whitelaw Reid suggested, was Cleveland itself. Hay always miraculously recovered when away from Ohio, the editor of the *New York Tribune* pointed out, but consistently fell ill on returning to Euclid Avenue.[13]

Not so many weeks later, the ailing and depressed Amasa Stone shot himself in his bathtub. Stone's death meant that the pressure he exerted to keep Clara, John, and their children near at hand was gone, and the Hays went from being merely rich to what the well-informed Clover Adams termed "tri-millionaires."[14] Hay's illness and Clara's inheritance provided the impetus for leaving Ohio.

During an earlier eighteen-month stint John Hay spent in Washington as assistant secretary of state in the administration of Rutherford B. Hayes, the Adams-Hay foursome had gotten in the habit of taking daily tea together on H Street. They were all short of stature (at five feet four, Henry was the tallest) but otherwise quite unalike. John and Henry held strong political opinions that often conflicted. Clara was the antithesis of the frank and outspoken Clover, and on first meeting, the latter had remarked: "Mrs. Hay is a handsome woman—very—but never speaks." (She also observed that Clara's

---

* Coauthored with fellow Lincoln aide John George Nicolay, the ten-volume *Abraham Lincoln: A History* would not be published until 1890. It remains a starting point for Lincoln scholars, while Hay's only novel, *The Bread-Winners* (1883), is largely forgotten.

silence mattered little since John "chats for two.")[15] The Hays had a houseful of children, while Henry and Clover, to their disappointment, had none. But the Adamses enthusiastically embraced the idea that their friends might return to Washington. When a rumor circulated in autumn 1883 that a large parcel of land adjacent to their rented house might be for sale, Henry immediately dispatched a letter to Cleveland.

The Hays came to Washington in November to see the property for themselves. They liked what they saw, and at their request, Adams quietly negotiated a deal on their behalf. For the sum of $73,800, Hay acquired a tract consisting of three lots with a combined 99 feet of frontage on H Street and 131 feet on Sixteenth Street.

A second transaction soon followed. Clover, to her surprise, had experienced a change of heart. "I who have always been utterly opposed to building am the one who jumped first," she told a friend. "I like to change my mind all of a sudden."[16] Not only had she come to like the house Richardson had built on K Street—"it does Richardson great credit," she told her father—but she also admitted, "It would suit us a to a T."[17] Henry, too, had come around and described the house to Hay as "the handsomest and most ultimate house in America in my opinion, and the only one I would like to own."[18]

Though well-do-do, Henry and Clover were people of lesser means than the Hays. Family legacies made them comfortable enough to take extended trips to Europe, but they brought back drawings rather than more costly works on canvas. With their wealthier friends planning to build themselves a large mansion, Adams thought it proportionate for him and Clover to construct a more modest house next door. John Hay readily agreed, and in early January 1884, Henry Adams purchased one-third of Hay's new property from his friend.

The "whispering gallery," as Clover called the men and women of Washington's newspapers, soon spread word of the Hay-Adams plan.[19] The press also offered a reasonable conjecture. "The Sunday papers," Clover noted, "tell us Richardson is to be our architect."[20]

Though delayed a few days by a blizzard, Richardson arrived in Washington on January 16, 1884. He understood this new job was unusual, since the two client couples, despite very different needs, budgets, and personalities, wanted abutting houses that looked like they belonged together. But two days later, as he made his way back to the train station after nearly nonstop conversations with the Adamses, he understood he faced a much bigger challenge than merely designing and overseeing construction of dissimilar houses.

His dear friends Henry and Clover Adams would be tenacious, insistent, and opinionated clients, always a challenge for an architect when working for individuals rather than institutions. John Hay had sent a plan drafted by the builder of his Cleveland house, which was bad enough, but Henry Adams had handed over his own drawn-to-scale floor plan and a front elevation. The well-traveled Adams demanded his house be organized like a Venetian palazzo, with the kitchen and the servants' quarters on the ground floor. According to Adams's scheme, a hall and stair would then lead to the main public spaces on the floor above, the *piano nobile* (grand floor), with the bedrooms on the third and top floor. Clover and Henry wanted a large room (they specified twenty-two by twenty-seven feet) that would double as a parlor and library, along with an adjacent study and a north-facing dining room with steps that descended to a garden. Clover needed a north-facing photography studio on the third floor and a well-ventilated darkroom. They envisioned eleven-foot ceilings, and perhaps most shocking of all for Richardson, a man who cherished his embellishments, Clover imagined an interior that was as "plain as a pike staff."[21] Henry termed it a "Spartan little box."[22] The many and specific directives would be a test of Richardson's ingenuity.

On the morning of his departure from Washington, he posed for Clover. Seated at Henry's desk, Richardson sat for an interminable, ten-second exposure. He held a T square in his hand, with plans for the houses spread before him. Despite the difficult discussions he had just had with his clients, the result was a surprisingly companionable picture, with a slight smile on Richardson's face that suggested something of his affection for the photographer.

Like Richardson and Olmsted, Henry Adams was in the vanguard of his profession. After 1825, German scholars at Göttingen and Berlin had introduced fresh intellectual rigor into the study of history, a pursuit that previously had been, in effect, a branch of literature. They put a new emphasis on the examination and analysis of historic documents. Taking a page from the lab books of their scientific colleagues, the new historians established standards for research and training. This new approach, with its reliance on primary sources and international politics, spread to England and the United States, and Adams had come to share the changed perspective. He believed that history shouldn't be a matter of "mere narrative, made up of disconnected episodes having little or no bearing on each other."[23]

Members of this new profession maintained that the stories of the past

Clover Adams's portrait of her architect friend. In her photo album, she captioned the image simply: "H. H. Richardson, 1884."

should incorporate a broad view of cultural factors such as economics, sociology, aesthetics, and psychology. Such an analytical approach made history a fit subject for the academy, and Adams himself had been among America's first history professors when Harvard president Charles W. Eliot granted him a professorship of medieval history at the college in 1870. In his history seminars, the first conducted at an American college, Adams looked to apply logic, accuracy, and objectivity to the laborious study of documents and data in order to distinguish patterns. Unlike his Washington neighbor George Bancroft, whose histories presumed that divine providence guided events, Adams saw the past and his country in evolutionary terms. He regarded the writing of history not as an art but as fundamentally scientific.

By the time he and Clover sat down with Richardson to talk about the design of their proposed house, Henry had written a number of books about such long-dead historical figures as Albert Gallatin, Jefferson's secretary of the treasury, a man Adams admired; Virginian John Randolph, whom Henry hated as a bitter opponent of both President Adamses; and Aaron Burr, the depraved "scamp" he could not help but like.*

Adams had also exhibited his own mischievous side, having written a novel about contemporary political mores, *Democracy*, which, at his insistence, had been published anonymously on April Fool's Day, 1880. His was admittedly a smirking anonymity. "My ideal of authorship," he told Hay, "would be to have a famous *double* with another name, to wear what honors I could win."[24] The book had been much talked about, especially in Washington, with close readers speculating on the resemblance between the fictional characters and current actors on the political scene, among them past presidents and sitting senators. The book sold out several printings, as guessing the author's identity became something of a Washington pastime. The names Adams and Hay were bandied about, and Clover's father actually thought she had written it. But the secret of the book's authorship held.[†]

Henry had shifted his literary energies back to the history of the Madison and Jefferson administrations. By the summer of 1883, he completed the first part of his presidential history and arranged for a few copies to be printed privately for review by trusted friends.

Clover kept herself otherwise occupied, pursuing her amateur photography with fresh vigor after acquiring a "new machine."[25] The camera, made of mahogany with brass fittings, used five-by-eight-inch glass plates. Taking pictures had gotten a little easier since Carleton Watkins had needed a mule train of equipment to capture his Yosemite images in 1861. Dry-plate negatives were now

---

* Adams's take on Burr would never be published. His publisher turned down the book, Adams moved on, and his manuscript was destroyed or lost.

† The task of publicly revealing the identity of the author of *Democracy* was left to Henry Holt and Company, which republished the book as the work of Henry Adams after his death in 1918.

sold pretreated with a light-sensitive gelatin-bromide coating. Regardless of the negatives used, however, the entire process remained cumbersome, requiring Clover and a servant to wrestle with the large camera and the wooden boxes of fragile glass plates. The exposed plates still required development and printing in her H Street darkroom, separate processes that involved multiple chemical baths and the use of potassium cyanide.

Over a period of months, she posed her husband and some of their friends in Henry's study. In one image, John Hay holds a copy of *Démocratie*, a French edition of the book that some believed he had written. In another, the book's real author sits at his desk, pen in hand. Clover took pictures of family—her father, her nieces, Henry's dour parents—and of historians Francis Parkman and Bancroft. Even her much-adored dogs sat still for long enough to be recorded on chairs around a tea table as if waiting for their mistress to fill their cups. Whatever her subject, Clover took a thoroughly professional approach to the photographic process, noting exposures, dates, places, and other details for each plate in a small notebook.

Only Clover knew that Henry had set aside his nonfiction labors and was quietly writing a second novel that was much more personal than *Democracy*, one rooted in their lives together. They had married in 1872 despite his father's objections, which were based on her family's past. In the small world that was Boston, everyone knew one of Clover's aunts had killed both herself and her unborn child by swallowing arsenic. On becoming engaged, Henry had confided in an English friend, "She is certainly not handsome. . . . She knows her own mind uncommon well. . . . She dresses badly. . . . She rules me as only American women rule men, and I cower before her."[26] They had lived in Boston during the four-year construction of Trinity Church, watching their close friend's masterpiece rise; when he contemplated taking another foray into writing fiction, Adams later admitted, he "took the building of Trinity church as the inspiration . . . and worked [my] plot about it," incorporating such details as the red walls of Richardson's "color church."[27]

With his second novel, Adams again chose to keep the writer's identity a secret: *Esther* appeared in 1884 under the nom de plume Frances Snow Compton. Rather than politics, this time he opted for

Henry Adams, historian and sometime novelist, at work, in a photograph taken by his wife.

religious faith and artistic collaboration as the book's themes. He based his title character on Clover.

Real-life events provided the milieu. The Trinity project had cemented the couple's friendship with John La Farge, and Adams based a key character in the book, an artist named Wharton, on the painter. The Reverend Stephen Hazard, a thinly veiled version of Phillips Brooks, would be pivotal to the book's events. As the novel opens, Wharton and Hazard are both fascinated by the independent-minded Esther Dudley. When she exhibits drawing skill, Wharton invites her to help decorate a new church in New York called Saint John's.

Esther paints the figure of Saint Cecilia, the blind patroness of music, in the north transept, working "high up toward the vault of the roof [which] was still occupied by a wide scaffold."[28] On completing the work, Esther feels "a little depressed." She misses "the space, the echoes, the company, and above all, the sense of purpose, which she felt on the scaffolding."[29] Adams employed the setting of his friend's church, along with the artistic collaboration of artist friends, as the backdrop for a consideration of the artistic process and an exploration of faith ("Is religion true?" Esther wonders as she paints the church). From a discrete fictional distance, he considered his wife's religious skepticism and the dangers of artistic ambition. He also employed the death of a fictional doctor, a man unmistakably modeled on Clover's father, Robert Hooper, as a test of her faith.

By the time their collaboration with Richardson began in Washington, Henry had before him the proofs for his finished novel. In his portrait of a lady, plainly a shadowy version of his wife, Henry seemed to be pondering, consciously or unconsciously, how his world—and Clover's—would change when she confronted, as Esther did in the pages of the book, the death of her father. That question would be answered all too soon, since Henry Adams's *Esther* tragically anticipated the terrible personal drama that was about to unfold.

Before departing Washington in January, Richardson agreed to follow the Adams's wishes for their house. "He was quite angelic," Henry told Hay, "and goes in with enthusiasm for all my peculiar idiocies." Ever the self-effacing wordsmith, he added: "In my humble opinion I shall have a house which will be the laughing-stock of the American people for generations to come. Quite unutterably unutterable."[30]

The architect was less keen for the plan that Hay sent for his property, but he soon persuaded his Ohio client that the entrance to his home should be shifted around the corner. Richardson argued the façade should overlook Sixteenth Street in order to take in the view of Saint John's, a columned, classical church designed by the nation's first professional architect, Benjamin Henry Latrobe. That necessitated a complete rethinking, and as Richardson sketched, he added a hip roof, a central gable, and a pair of towers (one cylindrical, the other semi-octagonal), all elements common to many Victorian houses of the day but none of which he would use next door at the Adams house. The Hay home would be large, extending ninety-nine feet along Sixteenth Street and fifty-four feet on H Street; the Adams house would be smaller, its façade forty-four feet wide. Richardson's plan called for both to be unornamented and clad in yellow sandstone with brownstone trim.

After much prompting from Clover and Henry via both post and telegraph, the draft plans arrived from Richardson's office. Hay was in town and joined his friends to examine Richardson's design shoulder to shoulder. When Adams compared his and Hay's houses, he preferred his friend's.

The Adamses' floor plan, particularly for the main floor, had an easy simplicity, an openness, with sets of double pocket doors, which slid into the wall cavity when open, connecting the library, study, and dining room, whereas the Hay house, designed for formal entertaining (it was said that evening never caught Hay in day dress), had a more traditional room sequence with a grand entry stair hall, a reception room for filtering guests, and a much larger dining room and library. Adams wrote to Richardson to complain.

In his response Richardson placed the blame clearly on Adams. "Your liking Hay's house better than your own is accounted for easily I think by the fact that in designing the former I was left entirely untrammeled by restrictions wise or otherwise"—in short, it was Adam's own fault for interfering. But Richardson then softened his words with an aside ("How's that old boy—couldn't help it—too good to pass") and swore he would try to make the Adams house "*at least* as attractive as Hay's and saving *all* your pet notions also."[31]

In early July, just before their summer vacations, Hay and the Adamses went together to Brookline, where they approved the final plans, which incorporated only minor changes. The digging of the cellars began, and by the time Henry and Clover returned to H Street in October 1884, there was much to see. Henry had wanted a brick exterior from the start, but Richardson favored a mixture of stone. The pivotal moment in their ensuing discussions occurred when Adams visited the Ames Gate House in September and saw its rude stonework. He told a friend, it "looks like the cave of Polyphemus," an unflattering reference to the monstrous cyclops in Homer's *Odyssey*.[32] Only then had Richardson agreed to compromise. "I have suppressed the light stone in the upper stories," he wrote to Hay.[33] Above the first level, both houses would be entirely of brick.

After a winter hiatus, construction work resumed in early 1885. The Adams house was finally getting a roof, but that good news was far outweighed by word of illness in Clover's family. On learning that her father's angina had worsened, she immediately headed for Boston.[34]

The patient had been relocated to Cambridge and the care of her sister and brother, but Clover soon wrote that Dr. Hooper lay dying. The old man wanted to be nursed by his children, she confided, so she intended to remain in Boston for the duration. Henry was left alone to deal with a lingering tooth ailment and the constant racket of carpenters pounding away next door.

Clover Adams recorded moments in the construction of her new home. In this photograph, taken in late 1884, the pair of arched openings to the Adams house are in the foreground. The Hay house is partly obscured by scaffolding beyond.

Richardson arrived, surprising Henry, and they met with the local contractor. Adams wrangled an invitation for them to dine at the White House, where they ate with the new president, Grover Cleveland, but after receiving an ominous summons from Clover on Monday, March 23, the two Henrys caught a northbound train.

Adams remained in Massachusetts four days before returning to Washington, where he found Hay's roof nearly complete. Though Dr. Hooper no longer took nourishment, he lingered, and Adams worried about Clover. The loss of her father would be a terrible blow, and the long nights of nursing exhausting. These weeks were the first sustained parting of their marriage; though he regretted that, he felt he needed to be in Washington to make the many day-by-day decisions to keep the work on track.

On April 9, he went shopping for marble at Washington's new museum, the Smithsonian, of all places.* In his daily letter to Clover,

---

* Adams happened to have a strong family connection to the place. In 1842, Congressman John Quincy Adams had shepherded a bill through Congress that earmarked a generous bequest from one James Smithson for the creation of the Smithsonian Institution.

he told her he found a Mexican onyx he liked, its "sea-green translucency so exquisite as to make my soul yearn."[35] He wanted it for their drawing-room mantelpiece. The carpenters were putting down Hay's floor. "[Hay's] house looks vast," Henry told Clover, "and dwarfs ours to a wood-shed."[36]

Then, on April 13, Dr. Hooper's heart stopped. Henry hurried to Cambridge for the funeral, but within a week, he and Clover arrived back in Washington. At age forty-one, Clover lost the father who had raised her since her mother's death when she was five. She had run his household and been his companion until she married Henry at age twenty-eight. Now, feeling very much an orphan, she resumed supervision of the dual house project. To Henry, Clover seemed to deal with her loss with a surprising equilibrium. As he confided in Hay, "[She] has come back in better condition than I feared."[37]

The costs of each house exceeded early estimates, as so often happened when Richardson enriched his designs, but both Hay and Adams, despite earlier resolutions to control costs, had agreed to many of their architect's "ravishing designs" for carving and woodwork. For the Adamses, $30,000 rose to $40,000, then $50,000; Hay's $50,000 would eventually reach $80,000.

Richardson himself came and went. Seeing him left his friends newly conscious of how bloated he had become. He could no longer walk a full city block and required a carriage to transport him any distance; given his bulk, not just any carriage would do. Hay and Adams took to conflating Richardson's profligate spending with his obesity. In jest, Adams called him an "ogre [who] devours men crude, and shows the effects of inevitable indigestion in his size."[38] He was "Richelaisian," Adams quipped, alluding to Rabelais.[39]

Always a man of voracious appetite, Richardson's intake seemed greater than ever despite continued warnings from his doctors. The insatiable thirst born of Bright's disease now seemed unquenchable. July 1885 brought a "a sharp attack of bleeding at the nose," and he was ordered to stop work for a month of vacation.[40] His joy in food and drink, in laughter, the ebullience with which he told stories, and the pleasure he found in the company of others were all intoxicating. He bought objects he loved, even when he could ill afford them. He was larger than life, his newer friend John Hay saw. They all knew that. But his appetites, and his disease, were taking a toll.

For the most part, the Hay and Adams houses rose as Richardson designed them. Hay tended to go along with the architect's suggestions, and Richardson became adept at defusing Adams's occasional pique. "Great God you can growl!!" he wrote to Adams on one occasion.[41] Their biggest disagreement surfaced over a decorative carving above the Adams's main entrance, but ultimately, Adams let the Christian emblem happen.

Hay met Richardson in New York in October to select furnishings. Carver John Evans was at work in Washington. The rare marbles Adams specified caused some delays, and there was further debate about the carvings since the Adamses wanted dogs on the corbels and Richardson gave them lions. But by mid-November 1885, the floors were oiled, the fireplaces nearly finished. The furnaces had been fired.

But Clover was not well.

On December 6, 1885, eight months after the death of her father, Clover and Henry shared a quiet breakfast. Afterward, although it was Sunday, Henry departed to consult his dentist, who had agreed to see him yet again about the pain in his jaw.

Clover remained at home. With the autumnal shortening of daylight hours, her days, too, had gotten darker. Henry had noticed, but he shielded her from well-intentioned friends, describing her as "out of sorts." Other than her husband, she saw no one.

For Clover, Sundays in particular brought a burden of sadness. Her letters to her father, always written on the sabbath, had been one of the great constants of her married life. She had written the first aboard the SS *Siberia*, in 1872, on her wedding trip. That one closed with the words "much love from Henry and me," but thereafter Clover had dispensed with the pretense. The letters came from her alone, for his eyes only.

With the inevitability of the homing pigeon that always finds its way, Clover's voluminous letters sped weekly to Boston. Addressed to "Pater," they reported on her and Henry's public life, the people they had seen, the parties, the plays, the teas, her insights and intimate conversations. She displayed a writerly gift, a sharp mind, and a daughter's love. But her detailed missives represented even more to her. They were the means by which Clover reckoned with her position in Washington, as a wife and a hostess, as an exceptional and forthright woman with opinions, intelligence, and artistic sensibilities that Victorian society forbade her to put to practical use. Understanding their importance, her father had gone to pains to save every letter. With his death, the ritual of explaining herself to her father—and herself to herself—came to an end.

Richardson had recently visited the Adamses at their H Street rental. "Just before Thanksgiving [I] was with her two days," he wrote to John Hay. He was aware of her sadness but thought "she was much improved." The house was nearly done, and, Richardson thought, she was "decidedly interested."[42] But he had read her wrong.

On that first Sunday in December, with the view of Lafayette Square before her, Clover sat at her writing desk to pen a note. In it, she absolved Henry of blame for what she was about to do, describing him as having been "more patient and loving than words can express."[43] She would neither mail the letter nor hand it over. Her husband was destined to find it for himself.

Clover found the means of her release on a shelf in her darkroom. No more than one swallow of the potassium cyanide salts was needed, and in a matter of moments, her lungs no longer able to function, her mouth and throat afire, her heart racing, she slumped to the floor. Minutes later she was dead.

When Henry returned, he found her on a carpet in front of an upstairs fireplace, the air perfumed with the odor of bitter almonds. The horrified husband carried his wife to a sofa as if for comfort. Though her body remained warm, he knew she was gone. He sent telegrams to Boston family members, but until they arrived the following day, he refused to see anyone. The body that had once housed Clover's remarkable spirit lay on the bed he had shared with her.

The funeral was on a rainy Wednesday, and to the surprise of her siblings, she was interred at Rock Creek Cemetery in Washington, her adopted city. Friends and family bemoaned her loss. "What a different end to what we all looked forward to," Richardson wrote in a condolence letter to the widower.[44] John Hay was more voluble, describing her "high intrepid spirit, that keen fine intellect, that lofty scorn of all that was mean, that social charm which made your house such a one as Washington never knew before."[45]

The benumbed widower carried on. He read Shakespeare aloud to family members before they returned to Massachusetts. He wrote notes of acknowledgment to friends who sent condolences. He moved his books into the new house. Surrounded by the furniture, wallpapers, and mantels they had chosen together, he hung the pictures according to the plan he and Clover had agreed upon. Instead of talking about his grief, he wrote to John Hay about carpets. "I did want a carpet and had a good one in mind [for the dining room], such a one as would key up the whole thing."[46]

He packed a trunk with the clothes Clover liked best, locked it, and placed it permanently in the cedar closet. In late December, just three weeks after his wife's death, he took up residence in the new house. Richardson urged Hay to move from Cleveland as soon as possible to be with the widower, "even if it does necessitate some little picnicking and even discomfort in the beginning."[47] Hay obliged, moving his family into the unfinished house in late January.

Henry Adams had once described Clover as "far superior to any woman I had ever met."[48] Although he lived another thirty-six years, he never recovered from her loss; in the book by which posterity would best remember him, *The Education of Henry Adams*, privately published in 1907, his wife of thirteen years was not mentioned.* On the other hand, the then-dead Richardson appeared often in its pages. Adams's *Mont-Saint-Michel and Chartres* (1904) became an instant classic too, with Adams crediting the inspiration to his old friend. "I am now all eleventh and twelfth century," he admitted in a letter to a close confidante. "I caught the idea from dear old Richardson who was the only really big man I ever knew."[49]

Despite his frequent travels—he often wintered in Paris—Henry Adams would always return to his memory place, the house

---

* *Education*, released to the public only after Henry's death in 1918, won the Pulitzer Prize for biography the following year.

on H Street. His "breakfasts" (more accurately, luncheons) would become a Washington institution, to which he welcomed old friends like La Farge and Saint-Gaudens, and even President Theodore Roosevelt. John and Clara Hay, too, would live out their days in their Sixteenth Street house, and neither Adams nor the Hays would make major changes. But Richardson's twin project survived only until 1927, when both residences were razed to make way for today's Hay-Adams Hotel.

The disappearance of the two monumental houses would be among the many reasons that Richardson's fame, nearly universal when Henry Adams and John and Clara Hay moved into their new domiciles, would be fading like a sunned photo graph just a few decades later.

Chapter Sixteen

CHICAGO STYLE

[Richardson's] work appeared to be not so much complete as newly begun.

—EDWARD HALE

John J. Glessner had been told not to waste his time asking Richardson to design his new Chicago home; word was out that the architect "would undertake only monumental buildings."[1] Thus deflected, Glessner sought out both Stanford White and William Potter at their respective offices on a business trip to New York in the spring of 1885. He even asked Potter to draw up a plan. Only on his return to Chicago did Glessner resolve, despite what others said, to consult the man people claimed was the finest architect in the country.

To John and Frances Glessner's delight, Richardson responded enthusiastically to their letter of inquiry. In four days he would be on his way to Chicago, he wrote back, where the city's greatest merchant, Marshall Field, wanted a new wholesale store. In fact, Richardson was keen to do smaller jobs too. "I'll plan anything a man wants," the architect told the Glessners, "from a cathedral to a chicken coop. That's the way I make my living."

When Richardson lumbered into their home on Washington Street, on May 15, 1885, the sedate Glessners were taken aback. "He is largest man I have ever seen," Frances Glessner noted in her diary. "He stutters and sputters—breathes very heavily." Her husband observed the bold colors of Richardson's clothes and the outlandish size of his spectacles. He also thought their guest looked like a man who needed to sit down. Richardson had slept little, his girth making it impossible for him to lie down in a train's sleeping car.[2]

Glessner gestured to a comfortable seat, but Richardson declined. "I can't get up easily from one of those easy chairs," he explained. He chose instead the sturdy piano bench as he listened to his new clients describe their desire for a house in a new neighborhood. John's farm machinery business, Warder, Bushnell & Glessner, had made him wealthy, and he could now afford to live among Chicago's elite on Millionaire's Row, the most exclusive section of Prairie Avenue. After purchasing three adjacent lots on the corner of Eighteenth Street, he wanted to live down the street from Marshall Field and the king of meatpacking, Philip Armour.

The more they talked, the more Richardson became convinced that this might be an important and highly visible assignment. He asked what rooms they required on the first and second floors, and learned the Glessners had two young children, whom they planned to educate at home for health reasons and who needed a schoolroom. Mrs. Glessner said she liked the "cosy effect" of their present house, and Mr. Glessner wanted a library. They needed a large space for her musical evenings and to entertain fellow members of the Society of Decorative Art.

"How will you have them placed?" Richardson asked of the room arrangement.

"Oh, no, Mr. Richardson," John Glessner deflected, "that would be me planning the house. I want you to plan it." The Glessners—avid, curious, open, and secure—were the sort of client Richardson liked best.

Glancing around the room, he noticed a small, framed photograph. It depicted an early medieval stable at Abingdon Abbey, a largely unrestored ruin in Oxfordshire. It had a stern stone façade, one broken by few windows. "Do you like that?" Richardson asked.

They said they did.

"Well, give it to me. I'll make that the keynote of the house."

Richardson had long ceased designing according to the conventions of a given style, and he had just been handed the first piece of the design puzzle. He would imagine something altogether new for the Glessners.

The conversation continued when the men drove to the proposed building site two miles away. Having climbed laboriously into Glessner's carriage, Richardson chose to remain seated and, during their twenty-minute visit, spoke little. After scanning the property carefully for some minutes, he blurted out, "Have you the courage to build the house without windows on the street front?"

The very idea ran counter to the most basic notions of suburban architecture. Indeed, across the intersection the immense Second Empire mansion of George Pullman, the industrialist who manufactured the railroad sleeping cars that bore his name, overlooked the streetscape, its grand three-story façade lined with windows, many of them floor-to-ceiling.

But Glessner was not particularly fazed by the question. "Certainly," he replied, thinking to himself that, if he didn't like the plan, he could insist upon changing it.

"I wish I didn't have to go to dinner this evening," said Richardson, pleased at Glessner's apparent agreement. "I'd give you the plan of your house in the morning."

He nearly did. After dining with Marshall Field that night, he returned to the Glessners' house for dinner the following evening. While the dessert course was being prepared, he asked that pencil and paper be brought to him, remarking, "If you don't ask me how I get into it, I will draw the plan for your house." Without further discussion, he completed a rough sketch of the floor plan before the strawberry shortcake arrived.

The friar in his cell? Richardson cultivated the notion that he was a medieval artisan in the modern age, and he sent the Glessners this posed studio photograph of himself in monk's hood and robes. The photographer, George Collins Cox, was a friend of Augustus Saint-Gaudens.

After expressing his admiration for the dinner—"Mrs. Glessner, that's the best pie I ever put in my mouth"—Richardson departed for the station in time to catch the night train for Boston. The Glessners reserved judgment about their first glimpse of his proposed design, but Richardson, with his promise to build them "an ideal house," had certainly left his new clients with much to think about.

"I have been carefully considering your scheme," Richardson wrote four months later, "and would like very much to have an opportunity to talk it over with you here in my office."[3] The Glessners agreed to come. On Sunday, September 27, 1885, they emerged from Boston's Tremont Hotel and stepped into the Richardsons' waiting brougham for the picturesque ride through several of Olmsted's parklands to the house on Cottage Street.

There they first glimpsed "an old rambling house of frame."[4] Eighteen-year-old Julia Richardson, known affectionately as Lulu, answered the door, and she and her younger sister Mary welcomed the out-of-towners. The man of the house was not yet dressed, and wife Julia was still at church, but their girls were accustomed to taking part in the wooing process.

When Richardson appeared, he ushered his guests through the house. The visitors were given a glimpse of the parlor. Mr. Glessner thought the dining room "brilliantly sunny" despite just a single window. He noted with interest a narrow plate shelf lining the walls just beneath the cornice that displayed Arts and Crafts ceramics and tiles, objects much like those Mrs. Glessner collected. He liked the library too, thinking it "a dream—open-fired, low ceiling, small windowed, comfortably chaired."

Richardson walked his guests through the labyrinth of drafting tables that was the Coops. Even on Sunday, draftsmen were at work. Skylights and large windows lit the space, and drawings and photographs from the firm's portfolios decorated the walls. The higgledy-piggledy Coops led to a short hall and the entrance to a sturdy structure of fireproof masonry.

If architects aspire to create the world as they would have it, then Richardson surely accomplished that in building his inner

The Richardson brood, pictured in 1882, included two daughters, Mary and Julia (second and third from left), and sons Philip, Hayden, Henry, and Olmsted's namesake, Frederick.

sanctum in Brookline.* Besides the fact that his size and worsening health made travel difficult, he sought to lure potential clients into his lair, which exhibited his design philosophy. The Glessners had taken the bait willingly.

The rectangular room they entered was large, roughly twenty-five feet by thirty. Richardson had tended to its every detail. Like a painter preparing a canvas, he had decorated the room first with fields of color, painting the walls maroon and installing a wall-to-wall floor covering of blue carpet. Gilding covered the ceiling panels between the heavy cherry beams. A large central skylight gave the space a rosy hue, the natural light suffused by a curtain of pale India

---

* Credit Geoffrey Scott, in his *Architecture of Humanism* (London: Constable and Company Ltd, 1914), for the useful coinage "the world as he would have it."

*Richardson's End Room, chockablock with his books, artifacts,
and enormous desk.*

silk. Intricately worked lamps hung from the ceiling to provide illu-
mination after sunset.[5]

Glessner was impressed: "[Richardson's] private office was a
large & beautiful room, with just enough disorder always to be pleasing." Photographs of medieval and ancient architecture covered the
room's walls. One end was dominated by a large recess before the
fireplace, an inglenook, which was a step higher and almost a room
by itself, with bench seats on either side of the tall mantel, a huge firebox, and a set of heavy William Morris curtains. A "pleasant pungency
of wood smoke" permeated the room.[6]

The room's centerpiece was an enormous table, its top
mounted on a podium of wide drawers packed with the firm's finest
architectural drawings. Glessner thought it "the largest table I ever
saw, so long and so wide that the maid could dust it only by getting
on & sweeping the top with a broom." An assortment of "objects of

beauty and use" covered its surface.[7] Bookcases lined one long wall, the shelves overflowing with rare architectural folios bound in leather. Every horizontal surface in the room held vases, architectural artifacts, natural history specimens, and other objects that Richardson had spied on his travels and brought home for display. The room was both an indulgent reflection of his tastes and a teaching collection that amounted to "the tools of its owner."[8]

Window seats and divans offered comfortable seating, including a Richardson-size couch that backed against the central table, facing the fire. The chairs were unusually large too, and patterned oriental area rugs covered much of the carpet. This was a room, in the eyes of apprentice Charles Coolidge, "where everything had a place and reason for being there, and Richardson himself sitting in his big chair made it complete."[9]

If the room helped cast a spell, the more time the Glessners spent with Richardson, the deeper the impression the man himself made. "When he spoke you instinctively felt that he knew the subject he spoke about," Glessner wrote. Richardson was, in the Chicagoan's view, "a great big whole-souled, hearty, broadminded, vigorous, forceful man, courteous & affable & with all human & manly qualities." This visit confirmed that he was the perfect man to design the couple's new home.

The Glessners returned to the dining room and its oval table for Sunday dinner, with all eight Richardsons and two draftsmen, including Coolidge, who would soon be designing the chairs for the Glessners' dining room, based on the comfortable library chairs found in Richardson's public libraries. After their repast, Richardson resumed his role as tour guide, this time taking his guests on a tour of Brookline. He made a point of stopping at Fairsted, where the Glessners were personally introduced to Olmsted. With the pleasantries completed, Olmsted engaged Richardson in a brief discussion of a proposed trip to Newport concerning a lighthouse project. Glessner watched the two friends with interest. "They were very dissimilar men," Glessner recalled, "one big of bulk, the other small." But he recognized their bond. "Each [knew] the other[']s peculiarities thoroughly, warmest friends."[10]

Olmsted himself was no stranger to the city the Glessners called home. Twenty years before, he observed of Chicago that it needed a "great public improvement" akin to Central Park.[11] His park work in the city itself would come soon after, but his first assignment had been a suburban community called Riverside, located on undeveloped prairie nine miles west of Lake Michigan, which he and Calvert Vaux designed in 1868.

The Des Plaines River flowed through the neighborhood's 1,560 acres, inspiring its name. Although commissioned by a real estate developer, Riverside had been Olmsted's first opportunity to design an ideal suburb, and he laid out a community of broad streets "of gracefully curved lines." Disliking as he did the right-angle grids of cities like New York, he mimed the lazy curves of the river to avoid all "sharp corners," hoping to convey to future inhabitants a sense of "leisure, contemplativeness and happy tranquility."[12] That sense of ease would be enhanced by the common spaces, amounting to nearly half of the total acreage, open areas where inhabitants could absorb "the scenic."[13] Intended for people of some means, this would be no cheek-by-jowl housing development.

Olmsted's involvement at Riverside had led to an invitation, in 1870, from the Chicago South Park Commission for a greenspace like Central and Prospect Parks. Two of the commission members had served on the Sanitary Commission with Olmsted during the Civil War and knew him as a man of vision who could get things done. Olmsted and Vaux conducted their usual close survey, enumerating in their report the future parklands, cumulatively totaling a thousand acres, located six miles south of Chicago's center. The Lower Division—effectively, a separate park—would occupy a shoreline site, an expanse of dunes and swamps. The flat prairie land of the rectangular Upper Division lay a short distance inland. Connecting the two would be the Midway Plaisance, a parkway roughly a mile long and six hundred feet wide. Yet Olmsted and Vaux recognized the biggest challenge: none of the acreage was desirable land. "No part of any one of the sites," they noted, ". . . would generally elsewhere be recognized as well adapted to the purpose."[14]

The lake winds and a high water table made tall trees difficult to grow in the Lower Division. Despite being "a swamp without beauty," it did have one signal asset, the expansive blue waters of Lake Michigan, which could, Olmsted argued, "fully compensate for the absence of the sublime or picturesque elevations of land." He proposed dredging the swamp, then using the sand and silt collected to build up the shoreline of a man-made lagoon of 165 acres. Water would unify the entire plan, with the Midway Basin running the length of the Plaisance to the Upper Division and a small lake they called the Mere. A thousand-foot pier would extend into Lake Michigan for easy and inexpensive transport of Chicagoans by ferry from the city. Islands in the lagoon would provide habitat for wild birds. In the Upper Division, Olmsted and Vaux envisioned a deer paddock, a stable, a rugged ramble, and the Southopen Ground, a hundred-acre open meadow for parades and games. A pavilion would stand nearby for use as a refectory. Olmsted imagined fourteen miles of roadways and thirty miles of paths within the park.

The varied plan was admired by many Chicagoans, but the Great Chicago Fire in 1871 had interrupted construction; with virtually an entire city to rebuild, resources were immediately reallocated. By the time the Upper Division gained the name Washington Park in 1880, honoring the nation's first president, a portion of Olmsted's original concept had been executed by another designer, while the Lower Division of South Park, renamed Jackson Park for the nation's seventh president, would remain little improved until it was chosen as the site for the World's Columbian Exposition in the next decade.

Construction at Riverside had also slowed due to the developer's 1873 bankruptcy and the national economic downturn. But Olmsted's vision hadn't been entirely lost. Riverside represented the nation's first planned suburban community, a place of such evident livability that its sound principles—the houses were set well back from the streets; walks and wheel ways were separated; it had generous common grounds—had already had an impact on other proposed or emerging suburbs. Even today, Olmsted's visionary thinking about suburbs, as expressed in Riverside and later designs in Buffalo, Atlanta, and elsewhere, represent received knowledge for those laying out virtually every suburb constructed since.

On first acquaintance, the Glessners had been a bit baffled by Richardson. Yet what soon became evident was that the seeming opacity of Richardson's words was far from accidental. He was "a master of men as well as of his art," one of his draftsmen, H. Langford Warren, remarked. Warren, who would later become founding director of Harvard's architecture school, watched Richardson "read men as he would a book." He "moved [his clients] almost as he willed . . . [and] exercised such rare tact in dealing with people that it was more of a pleasure to yield to him than it was to triumph over most men."[15]

For the Glessners, their moment of revelation arrived when the post brought them a sheaf of drawings that Richardson and his draftsmen worked up. The "ideal house" that Richardson promised broke defiantly with tradition. The mansion would not face the outside world in the traditional sense. Instead, the longest façade, which lined Eighteenth Street, looked more like an arsenal than a domicile. Built with no setback from the street, the granite wall rose hard by the sidewalk, most of its few windows little more than slits. On the inside, those openings would illuminate not family spaces but hallways and service quarters. Even on the narrow entrance elevation, facing Prairie Avenue to the east, the family quarters were well above the street, aloof and apart, the basement windows half-hidden behind forbidding grills of stone.

In designing this urban house, Richardson chose to separate the Glessners from the noise, dust, and north wind of the city. The idea of turning away from the street was a novel one, and it ran counter to the American tradition of building big houses as an open display of wealth. His recent collaborations with Olmsted in and around Boston had served him well, enabling him to look and listen to a city and, in the way that Olmsted did better than anyone, to anticipate. This was an increasingly congested neighborhood in busy Chicago. Large lawns were disappearing, and the avenues grew crowded. With unrest on the streets, thievery was commonplace, and the Glessners were anxious about security. Recently John Glessner himself, revolver in hand, had confronted an intruder in his home.

Although this would be a house in which the family could feel secure, Richardson's design was not a sentence to a prison-like existence. In another Olmstedian turn, the L-shaped footprint would

An escape from the cityscape: the perspective presentation drawing (below) conveys clearly the contrast between the almost country-house character of the Glessner courtyard and the fortress-like street elevation.

create a sheltered space away from the streetscape. Facing south and west, a cloistered private garden promised to be bright as well as private, in effect a small parkland dotted with shrubs and trees, a livable but contained space with walks, a carriage loop, and a lawn. Furthermore, the character of the house that faced the courtyard differed from the street façade, lined as it was with large windows and picturesque bays. The backyard would be altogether more welcoming and playful than the house appeared from the street.

Seeing the drawings would have been a shock to anyone with a Victorian sensibility. The public side had few of the usual elements, lacking porches, bays, or large windows. But the Glessners had come willingly under the influence of the man they called the "most dominating person" they ever met, and they experienced no regret at hiring him. As John Glessner remembered the moment, "One glance at Richardson's [design] made up my mind."[16]

Marshall Field already lived on Millionaire's Row. Richard Morris Hunt had designed his three-story mansion the previous decade, the first Chicago home with electric lights, and a then au courant mansard roof. Although the reported cost had been a stunning $2 million, Field could afford it.

The rise of the Yankee farm boy to the status of mogul paralleled that of his adopted city. Born in the rural western Massachusetts village of Conway in 1834, a year after the town of Chicago had been incorporated, Marshall Field went west at twenty-one. By then, what had initially been little more than a portage between Lake Michigan and the Mississippi River watershed was booming, powered by the Illinois and Michigan Canal, which had opened in 1848 to link the Mississippi and the Great Lakes.

Field first worked as a clerk and traveling salesman before gaining a junior partnership in a dry-goods firm. Chicago was emerging as the Midwest's principal rail hub, the transit point for eastbound foodstuffs from the surrounding prairie states and for goods heading to the West from the industrial cities of the Northeast. By the time he summoned Richardson to Chicago in 1885, Field had parleyed his stakes in a series of partnerships into full ownership of the firm, which he renamed Marshall Field & Company. Adopting the innovative notion that "the customer is always right," he had created an elegant and welcoming retail setting at his flagship store on State Street, which catered to fashionable Chicago women. But his fortune had been built on wholesale. The traveling men who came to town to stock their own stores accounted for more than 80 percent of the company's sales.

The wholesale division had long since outgrown its existing headquarters. A nonstop flow of buyers arrived to make purchases each morning, typically by train. The travelers would walk from department to department, select the wares they wanted, make credit and shipping arrangements, and catch the evening train home. The emphasis at Field's wholesale market had never been on stylish presentation or personal service, unlike at his State Street store, but the wholesale buyers had begun to complain of a lack of space. Field wanted a new building where an ever-growing array of goods could be laid out in an uncluttered and orderly way to serve the region's rapidly growing population. Chicago itself would see a doubling of its citizens in the 1880s to more than a million people.

He owned the ideal site in the midst of Chicago's bustling wholesale district, just north of the city's center. Over the years he had acquired fifty-one separate parcels that filled the city block bounded by Fifth Avenue and Adams, Franklin, and Quincy Streets, and in April 1885, the city's merchant king went shopping for a design. He wanted a man to devise a wholesale store of great size and practicality but also of distinction.

The *Chicago Tribune* went public first with word of Field's new building on September 30, 1885. Citing an unnamed contractor as his source, the paper's real estate reporter got the address right but not much else. He exaggerated the proposed building's height (to ten stories rather than seven) and credited its design to "S. S. Beaman" (referring to Solon Spencer Beman). But an immediate complaint from the client led to a next-day correction: "Mr. Field said that the plans for [his new building] have been prepared by Architect Richardson."[17]

When Richardson came to town the next month, the reporter got the benefit of an audience with him at the Grand Pacific Hotel, just a block from the building site. *Tribune* readers then learned that

Field's store would "be one of the largest and most imposing structures devoted to business uses in the world." Richardson explained
to the newspaperman that he aimed for beauty, "but it will be the
beauty of material and symmetry rather than of mere superficial ornamentation." The article concluded that the Field store "will be a
distinct advance in the architecture of buildings devoted to commercial purposes."[18]

Marshall Field's was not the first commercial building Richardson had designed, but it was by far the most important. In imagining
it, the architect did as he had with train stations, public libraries,
and other fresh building types: he thought less about precedent
than purpose. The workmanlike interior of the structure, which was
as much a warehouse as a store, would be an expansive selling space,
divided only by a forest of columns and a pair of heavy fire walls—
Field had already lost two retail stores to fire—that divided the interior into three parts. The challenge would be to build a dauntingly
large building that both welcomed the customer and looked like it
belonged on the existing streetscape.

Richardson's first commercial structure had been constructed
for his wife's siblings in Boston in 1875, but the Hayden Building
was tiny in comparison to Field's. The 1876 Cheney Building in
Hartford and an 1882 store for F. L. Ames in Boston both had larger
footprints, but in all three earlier commercial designs, Richardson's
exteriors looked quietly elegant and much simpler than they actually were. At each of the buildings, a sequence of arched openings
grew smaller from the lower to upper stories, which disguised floor
levels and the buildings' overall height. In Richardson's hands, the
meticulous patterning of fenestration and stonework looked neither
plain nor overstated. These were buildings Richardson suited to
their settings by manipulating shapes and materials.

Field's Chicago commission raised the challenge a full order of
magnitude. The footprint was much larger, at 325 feet long and
190 feet deep, amounting to nearly an acre and a half of space per
floor. The seven tall stories would top out at a cornice 130 feet above
the street, and since the store commanded an entire block, it would
have four distinct public faces. This would be a monster of a building, but it could not look monstrous.

In conceiving his design, Richardson once again reached into his architectural memory. One prototype dated from childhood: his father's house on Julia Row, a major set of row houses constructed in New Orleans in 1833. The façades of the thirteen homes filled a city block, with service wings extending to the back. Richardson would adopt just such a public-face, private-business division in Chicago.

Field's would be a palatial building, and another source of inspiration was the in-town Renaissance palazzo, a building type both Richardson and Field knew from visits to Florence, with its sequences of arched window openings and overhanging rooflines. The architect found inspiration closer to home too. As he had remarked to a friend during the rebuilding of Boston after the November 1872 fire, "there was more character in the plain and solid warehouses that had been destroyed than in the florid edifices by which they had been replaced."[19] He had in mind the great granite boxes that, though largely undecorated, had a plainspoken power.

Richardson specified little ornamentation for the Marshall Field Wholesale Store. As he told the *Tribune*, he wanted it to be "as plain as it can be made." Rather than relying on carved decorations, columns and pilasters, or other traditional architectural elements to elaborate its surface, he would manipulate "'voids and solids' . . . [and] the proportions of the parts."[20] He opted for symmetry, with evenly spaced windows—thirteen sets across the front, seven on the sides—set deeply into the walls to emphasize the stone, which would be Missouri red granite to the second-floor windowsills, Longmeadow red sandstone from there up. He specified mammoth slabs at ground level, some of them eighteen-feet long, with alternating narrow and broad courses of sandstone above. One set of tall arches enclosed stories two, three, and four, the next set, floors five and six, with an attic story above.

Richardson heeded Field's mercantile needs too. Breaking the line of the rectangular footprint, the building's rear elevation had an indentation for a glass-covered court containing a loading dock. Inside the building, a broad stair stood near the center, along with secondary stairs, freight elevators, and a pair of passenger elevators. The store's organizing logic called for ground-level offices and five floors of merchandise display, with packing and shipping largely out of sight on the seventh.

This would be an eminently practical building but one that would command attention from the street. Although the Field warehouse was completed after Richardson's death, his manipulation of shapes, surfaces, and rhythms and his avoidance of architectural symbolism spoke to many. One in particular who recognized its beauty was an early admirer of Richardson's Boston work, Louis Sullivan. He had left MIT after just a year, worked briefly in Philadelphia, then moved to Chicago and become a noted architect in his own right. Although the building was not yet completed when he saw it in 1886, he was so struck by the Marshall Field Wholesale Store that he returned to his drawing board and revised the plans for the soon-to-be famous Auditorium Building. He replaced his own picturesque elements with Richardsonian broad stone arches.

In December 1885, Richardson's eldest son, John Cole Hayden Richardson, then sixteen and known as "Hayd," had the honor of accepting an invitation from Marshall Field and his wife. Accompanied by George Shepley, one of Richardson's MIT-trained draftsmen, he took the train to Chicago, where, as a houseguest, Hayd would attend the Fields' New Year's Day Mikado ball, along with some four hundred other youthful acquaintances of Marshall Field II, seventeen, and his younger sister, Ethel. The party theme came from Gilbert and Sullivan's comic opera of the same name, which had taken the English-speaking world by storm earlier in the year. The extravagant affair would cost $75,000, including payment to Louis Sherry for bringing two railcars packed with china, silver, linens, and food from the famed New York restaurant that bore his name.*

From Brookline, the elder Richardson offered his son fatherly guidance in a letter. Always mindful of sartorial matters and undoubtedly worried about the loose and flowing Far Eastern costumes that guests were expected to wear, he instructed, "Be sure and wear a pair of drawers the night of the party rather tight than otherwise and cut off above the knee."[21] He recommended sights for his son to

---

* Sherry (1855–1926) operated a series of restaurants in various locations around Manhattan; his name survives today in the city's landmark Sherry-Netherland hotel and apartments.

see in Chicago, among them "the cattle yards [and] the system of parks which is very fine . . . originally laid out by Mr. Olmsted." Although work had begun earlier in the month, only the foundation of his new building for Mr. Field could be seen, still below street level. Dismissing all further architecture, he observed that "there is no public building in Chicago worth seeing."

His advice was scattershot, the stream-of-consciousness thoughts of a man worried about his son's entrance into a nuanced social world. "Don't leave family letters lying around loose[,] servants are fond of prying," he wrote, "and don't laugh too loud nor immoderately." His correspondence also conveyed a consciousness of the father's place in—and absence from—the society his son was encountering. Richardson asked that his regards be extended to Mrs. Field. He requested most particularly: "If you see Mrs. Glessner be very polite to her. You know I am designing a house for her."

Confined by poor health and doctor's orders, Richardson now rarely left his home and studio. He had developed another hernia, this one umbilical, necessitating a second truss. "I am really now . . . so covered and held together with pads, buckles, straps etc.," Richardson complained to John Hay, "that when I stretch real hard, I'm not quite certain that I'll come together in the same place again."[22] Yet, despite continuing ill health, he welcomed multiple new assignments, including a chamber of commerce building in Cincinnati, a courthouse and jail complex in Pittsburgh, and houses in Saint Louis and Chicago.

Compelled to rely upon go-betweens, he deployed draftsmen into the field. He had a clerk-of-the-works in charge of construction projects in Chicago, Edward Cameron, and another in Washington, Alexander Wadsworth Longfellow, nephew of the poet. He peppered each with questions by mail and telegraph. He felt the distance acutely, never doubting he was his own best representative in selling and honing a design, and urged his young men to write frequently with progress reports.

Richardson trusted one member of his staff above all the others. Among his draftsmen, George Foster Shepley hadn't the longest tenure, having joined the firm in 1882, but Richardson assigned him much more than the task of getting Hayden to the ball and back. From Chicago Shepley had gone on to his hometown, Saint Louis, where several local house commissions were pending, including a sprawling variation on Mrs. Stoughton's shingle-clad Cambridge home. Before returning to Chicago to escort Hayd home after the ball, Shepley also detoured to Cincinnati. "Don't forget to bring with you an accurate survey of [the] Chamber of Commerce," Richardson instructed from Brookline.[23] A year earlier, Richardson himself had visited the Queen City with Shepley in tow, looking to woo the building committee and collect inside knowledge regarding the chamber's specific desires for a new headquarters. He had bested a strong field of architects to win the chamber of commerce competition, but he wanted Shepley to smooth the process.* The job was just out to bid, and there were worries the cost estimates might run high. His winning design featured a pair of turrets on the corners of the main façade, with a cleverly layered interior featuring a grand exchange hall with a forty-eight-foot-tall ceiling.

Richardson so wished to be on the road that, when his wife went to Washington, D.C., in February 1886 for a respite from the Boston winter, he asked her, too, for a report from the front. "Write me about the Hay house," he insisted in a letter. The next day he scrawled at the bottom of another sheet, "Why dont somebody write me about the Hay house & the Anderson house. I am longing to hear what you think of them."[24]

During their days away, he felt acutely the absence of his wife and eldest daughter, Lulu. He put the best face he could on his health, but he was suffering. He resisted telling Julia for several days before finally confessing to his latest ailment. "While I did not wish to worry you with my trouble while you were away now that I am I hope over the crisis I might as [well] tell you that I have been quite ill . . . with the most terrible earaches." A pair of abscesses in his right ear had required visits from a "constellation of doctors." They were so painful that chewing was excruciating. "I have not been able to eat anything," he wrote to Julia. He had been limited to gruel and milk for four days because he could not even chew bread.[25] His

---

* The other entrants included George B. Post and Bruce Price, both of New York, and Chicagoans Daniel Hudson Burnham and John Wellborn Root.

body, unable to cleanse itself from within due to his failing kidneys, was breaking down.

News of his confinement got around, and friends came calling to lift his spirits. But the best tonic of all was architecture, and Shepley, alternately in Brookline and on the road in those weeks, was Richardson's eyes and ears. Ill as he was, he turned to work rather than rest. He and his office were as busy as they had ever been, his draftsmen racing to complete new plans, as well as details, specifications, and revisions for ongoing jobs.

In one note to Shepley, completed in haste after the dinner gong had rung and a messenger waited to post the letter, Richardson ran down a partial list of the work that preoccupied him. Among the jobs were the chamber of commerce building, a railroad station in Springfield, Massachusetts, a mansion for British portraitist Hubert von Herkomer to be built outside London, and a house in Buffalo. Fred Ames wanted another Boston store, and construction continued on the yet-to-be-completed Billings Library in Burlington, Vermont. Richardson wanted news of another Chicago house, this one for wholesale grocer and attorney Franklin MacVeagh. There were meetings to be had with O. W. Norcross in Chicago and discussions with Field regarding window arrangements. The Glessner job needed estimating. Though many commissions were far afield, others were as close to home as a house for a Harvard doctor, Henry Bigelow, in adjacent Newton.

At some level, conscious or not, Richardson was aware mortality loomed. As he observed to one office visitor, "There is lots of work to do, isn't there? And *such* work! And then to think that I may die here in this office at any moment. Well, there is no man in the whole world that enjoys life while it lasts as I do."[26]

One job in particular stood out in Richardson's mind. The Allegheny County Buildings, a tandem of structures in Pittsburgh, would be every bit as bold as Trinity Church. The city had lost its domed Greek Revival courthouse to fire in 1882, and the following year Richardson had been one of five architects invited to submit a design to replace it. Just as Olmsted often did, Richardson accompanied the submission drawings with a fulsome description of the building, typeset and privately printed. His design, which won him the commission in January 1884, would put a proud public face on the courthouse, with the county jail rising directly behind it. The buildings were as unlike as cousins can be, yet both possessed an undeniable majesty. The courthouse was a symbol of the law's power with its three-hundred-foot-tall clock tower overlooking the city. An interior courtyard meant that the two-story courtrooms, Richardson promised, would "receive floods of light from *two sides*."[27]

In contrast, the forbidding jail had few exterior windows and an enclosing wall. Not for a moment would its inmates imagine they were free men. The sense of incarceration was emphasized by the mode of access to the courtrooms. Prisoners would be marched across an enclosed stone bridge—a "bridge of sighs," some called it, referencing the name of the famed bridge in Venice—to keep them apart from the public. Yet the two buildings were of a piece. As Richardson put it, "A free treatment of Romanesque has been followed, throughout, as a style especially adapted to the requirements of a large civic building."[28]

Given his health, Richardson was aware how central this commission might be to his legacy. Construction had been put in the reliable hands of O. W. Norcross. The crew was testing out some new building techniques too, using exposed metal framing in the courtrooms, and a sophisticated heating and ventilation system carefully obscured within the fabric of the great granite edifice.

Despite Shepley's frequent absences, Richardson's most valued lieutenant had won the esteem of another denizen at 25 Cottage Street, further cementing his bond with Richardson: Shepley had asked for his daughter Julia's hand in marriage. Having turned nineteen in November 1885, Lulu would be coming out in Boston society, a rite of passage that Richardson planned to celebrate with a dancing party. He heartily approved of the match and, after some consideration, gave Shepley a raise in pay to $3,000 a year. He recognized how valuable Shepley had become, "visiting my clients & watching interests and work at a distance—saving me great discomfort and time & thereby allowing me to devote myself much more profitably— (in every way)—to the work in the office." He confided in the young man, "Until now I had never found one to whom I could heartily entrust this delicate & peculiar kind of work."[29] But he also asked

A rendering of the Allegheny County Courthouse with its attached jail just visible behind. The design for Pittsburgh was as clever as it was spectacular, with a ventilation and heating system borrowed from Britain's Parliament, which Richardson visited. It used the "nostrils" at the top of the tower as an intake in combination with "fan chambers and engine rooms" in the basement.

that the public announcement of the engagement be postponed to June 1886, permitting Julia her solo moment in the social spotlight.

In early April, the Glessners returned to Brookline to check on Richardson's plans. Given his multiple discomforts—stricken with a case of tonsillitis, he had again been forbidden by his doctors to leave the house—he might have avoided such a meeting. But Richardson continued to relish an audience, and he clearly liked the Glessners. He welcomed them in his bedroom, where they remarked upon the cork walls, which were both pleasing to the eye and useful for tacking up fresh sketches or photographs of subjects of current interest, like doorways or towers or bridges. But signs of Richardson's growing disability were everywhere.[30] He required a pair of large rings, hung by straps from the ceiling, to maneuver his immense bulk in and out of bed. The Glessners also noted that his unusually large bathtub was equipped with steps, inside and out, to ease his access.[31]

That day Richardson and the Glessners reviewed the final plans for the house on Prairie Avenue. They made a few changes, but when Richardson put down his pencil, he sounded a note of finality. "There, Mr. Glessner," he said, having just located the light fixtures. "If I were to live five years longer, that is the last thing I would do on your house, my part is finished."[32]

The weeks of confinement began to weigh heavily, and some days later, restless and impatient, Richardson gave in to the old impulse to embark on an inspection trip. Traveling as an invalid, he boarded a train for the long journey to Washington, D.C.

In the capital on business of his own, Olmsted got wind of Richardson's arrival. When he went to visit his friend, he found Richardson in his hotel room, his face noticeably flushed, his eyes bloodshot. He seemed to be hovering on the verge of unconsciousness, slumped in a reclining chair, breathing with difficulty. Beads of sweat glistened on his forehead. According to Olmsted, "He spoke feebly, hesitatingly, and with a scarcely intelligible husky utterance."[33]

As they sat together in Richardson's room, Olmsted urged his friend to return home. He hoped that a doctor's care and Julia's ministrations might restore him to health. Then a Richardson client arrived, interrupting the conversation. Richardson had designed a house for the man, and the talk shifted to the drawings of the structure. After a time, the conversation took a philosophical turn, and Richardson mused on the creative process, how the first mind's-eye glimpse gave way to detailed renderings. One change in plan would beget a second, "the design always gaining as a turn of one detail led to the reconsideration of another . . . steadily in the direction of simplification." Olmsted listened, recognizing his friend's method, so often rethinking and redrawing, aiming for an essence that only he could see.

As they talked, Richardson rallied, and he soon dominated the conversation as he so often had in the past. No longer slouching, he sat erect. Olmsted was reminded of all-night discussions a decade earlier when they shared the New York State Capitol project, "when he was," Olmsted remembered, "yet a lithe, active, healthy fellow."

Richardson's discourse that evening encompassed the art of architecture. The most valuable of the architect's tools, he told Olmsted, were tracing paper and India-rubber erasers. "There was no virtue in an architect more to be cultivated and cherished than a willing spirit to waste drawings." His voice clear and emphatic, Richardson elaborated: "Never, never, till the thing [is] in stone beyond recovery, should the slightest indisposition be indulged to review, reconsider, and revise every particle of his work, to throw away his most enjoyed drawing the moment he felt it in him to better its design."

His eyes flashed. The exhausted and dangerously ill Richardson seemed to have vanished. In his place, the invigorated and impassioned enthusiast rose to old heights, seemingly healthy, smiling as he "laughed like a boy, really hilarious."[34]

An hour into his visit, Olmsted rose to take his leave. As they parted, he promised to pass on news of Richardson to a mutual friend. "I shall have to report that I never saw you in better condition than you have been this evening," said Olmsted. Both men knew it wasn't true, but Richardson laughed in agreement.[35]

In the days that followed, both men returned to Brookline. Richardson would spend most of the next fortnight sleeping. The doctor predicted the patient would pull through, and in his wakeful moments, Richardson talked about a recuperative trip to the island of Nantucket. But on April 27, 1886, the sick man's body finally failed him, at age forty-seven. As Olmsted reported, "The sleep came in which he passed so quietly and softly that no one present knew when death occurred."[36]

The death of Olmsted's brother, John, had left a hole in his life that had not been filled until he met Richardson a decade later. He and Richardson were soul mates who lived their art, and there was no denying that, again, with the death of Richardson, Olmsted had lost a brother. He would keep a photograph of his friend's visage on the wall of his office for the rest of his life.

Chapter Seventeen

THE RICHARDSON MEMORIAL

No two careers could interweave more.

—JAMES O'GORMAN

Trinity Church was the inevitable choice for the funeral. Richardson was famous, his obituary widely published, and the crowd that wished to remember this "notable public character" grew large.[1] As they entered the great "color church," those who assembled found that the chromatic volume of the building swelled with dramatic lighting effects, the immense murals and richly carved sculptural details illuminated by stained-glass windows. The man who imagined this place had died, but as he had done in life, his building inspired people to regard the world in a new way.

Many of those seated in the pews knew the church well. Henry Adams had made haste to Boston for the service though still in mourning after Clover's death a few months before. Many of Richardson's collaborators were present too, including sculptor Augustus Saint-Gaudens, who could look up to see the prophets and angels looking down, the painted murals that, as a recently arrived Irish immigrant struggling to make his name, he had helped John La Farge execute.

Virtually the entire architectural profession of Boston, some fifty men, came to pay their respects. Other practitioners made the trip from Manhattan, among them Stanford White and Leopold Eidlitz, with whom Richardson had redesigned the New York State Capitol.

The crowd that packed the pews and the elevated galleries listened to another friend of the dead man. Like many of those in attendance, Phillips Brooks had experienced a deep personal loss. He had not only hired Richardson to design this church, but as a confidant and occasional traveling companion, Richardson had become a true friend whom Brooks loved dearly. Perhaps more than anyone he saw the symmetry in his delivering the eulogy in the Protestant cathedral on which they had collaborated.

Right Reverend Brooks extolled the deceased as both an architect and a vital presence in the lives of those who knew him. "The fire of distinct genius, indefinable and unmistakable, [burned] brightly," he told his listeners. "His buildings opened like flowers out of his life . . . [which] was like a great picture full of glowing color. The canvas on which it was painted is immense. It lighted all the rooms in which it hung. It warmed the chilliest air."

Bringing his words to a close, Brooks observed, "When some men die it is as if you had lost your penknife and were subject to perpetual inconvenience until you get another. [Richardson's] going is like the vanishing of a great mountain from the landscape, and the outlook of life is changed forever."[2]

No one in the cavernous church could better appreciate Brooks's scenic simile than Olmsted, who fittingly stood by as one of the pallbearers. He possessed a rare capacity for taking an eagle-eye view, not only of his immediate surroundings, of natural wonders, and of cities, but even the tides of time. Reading the future was requisite for a man who planted saplings that would over many decades grow into trees of vastly greater height and breadth.

Olmsted sensed how long a shadow Richardson would cast, and an idea simmered in his brain. Whatever the merits of Brooks's eulogy, Olmsted wanted to memorialize their friend in a more permanent way. Richardson's career had been abbreviated, but his reputation and his genius, Olmsted believed, needed to be recognized, recorded, and remembered. Olmsted resolved to set in motion an enterprise to honor his prematurely dead friend.

On Monday, May 3, 1886, George Shepley climbed aboard a train, departing Boston for points west. The father of his betrothed was only six days dead, his remains interred in Brookline's Walnut Hills Cemetery, but Shepley could wait no longer. Sporting a thick mustache that made him look older than twenty-six, he embarked on a mission to secure Richardson's professional practice. Two dozen pending projects had been orphaned, and Shepley needed to win the allegiance of the clients if the business in Brookline was to survive.

Only in his last hours had Richardson grappled with the inevitable. His body more bloated than ever, his kidneys in shutdown, he neared death. Unable to leave his bed, he dictated just eighty words as notes toward a plan of succession for his architectural heirs:

> While I am unable to attend personally to the affairs of my office, it is my wish that all my professional business shall be carried on by my assistants Messrs Shepley, Coolidge and Rutan in all of whom I have full confidence. In case of any question as to the control of my affairs or as to the execution of my designs the final decision must rest with Mr. George F. Shepley whom I hereby appoint as my personal representative.

This rudimentary statement of intent was hardly a legal instrument, but Richardson left no will at all for his family. No doubt he knew that he bequeathed little—architecture had never been a profession that led to great wealth—and as a profligate man in almost every way, he lived beyond his means, indulging himself, his family, friends, and large staff. As a man at the pinnacle of his profession, he might have been expected to leave an estate that would provide for his wife and children, but Julia Hayden Richardson discovered after her husband's demise that he died not only intestate but in debt. When probated, his personal holdings (including the dining room table, the family silver, and his collection of bric-a-brac), plus the entirety of his professional assets (primarily design fees due and the book and photograph collections), amounted to $28,425.90, a sum roughly $5,000 less than his liabilities.[3] Among the itemized creditors were Norcross Brothers, London tailor Henry Poole, and F. L. Olmsted.

To the good fortune of his heirs, the deceased did leave an abundance of goodwill. Old friend and landlord Ned Hooper immediately promised Richardson's widow five years of rent-free tenancy in her rented home. The future of the atelier and the twenty-one draftsmen on the payroll was another matter altogether, but there too, Hooper had a plan. He reached out to Frederick Ames, Richardson's devoted client and one of Boston's richest men. Ames agreed to help underwrite the founding of a new firm in order that existing plans might be purchased, thereby providing Mrs. Richardson with some money and enabling the work of her late husband to be carried forward.

Aided by the warmth with which the dead man was regarded, Shepley returned from his trip to the Midwest with promises from the major Richardson clients. A new partnership rapidly took shape, with Shepley, a young man of "much sense and pluck," becoming the senior partner.[4] With seventeen years of experience at Richardson's elbow, Charles Rutan, thirty-six, would continue to tend to matters of engineering, construction, and the back office. Charles Coolidge, age twenty-seven and Richardson's favorite among the Coop's draftsmen, would become chief designer. Formally known as Shepley, Rutan and Coolidge, theirs would be a partnership of equals and equal pay, at $3,000 a year each.

Like one of his crude sketches, the uncomplicated partnership plan had been of Richardson's own devising, and four weeks and one day after his death, on May 26, 1886, the legal particulars were memorialized in a memorandum of agreement.[5] But the firm's future was hardly assured, since American architectural practices, dependent upon the fame and imaginations of their founders, rarely survived into the next generation.

Under the supervision of Shepley, Rutan and Coolidge, Norcross Brothers built the Glessners their dream house. Plate rails were specified for Frances Glessner's collection of fine ceramics, tiles, and vases. John Glessner's library become an homage to what he called Richardson's End Room.

The Glessners loved their house, but it would annoy some people who didn't appreciate its quiet originality. While Marshall Field thought "that house is coming out all right," George Pullman complained about having to look at it every morning as he departed his own house. "I don't like it, and wish it was not there," he said. One woman remarked, "It looks like an old jail." She was politely upbraided by her companion, who said, "I only hope I shall be arrested and put in it, when it is finished." Others found it confusing, wondering where the entrance was.

Richardson's idea had been to build a house that fit its context, an original design for a changing neighborhood. Regardless of the curbside criticism, the Glessner House became an unavoidable reference point for future architects. When Charles McKim arrived for a tour, he emerged saying, "in the most emphatic terms it was the best thing in every respect" that he had ever seen. Olmsted considered it "the most beautiful house that had ever been put upon paper."[6]

Richardson did get to see his vision fulfilled in one sense. The Glessners positioned his likeness, a print of a posthumously completed portrait, in the downstairs entry hall. From there the architect oversaw the life of the house, his direct gaze seeming to look every visitor in the eye.

Although his successor firm supervised its construction, Richardson never saw the completed Marshall Field Wholesale Store. When the new establishment opened for business more than a year after Richardson's death, Field launched an ad campaign in which he pictured not his wares—which he listed as "wholesale dry goods, carpets, & upholstery"—but his new seven-story building. In an atmospheric perspective drawing, carriages rolling past on Adams Street were dwarfed by "the finest and largest structure in this country designed for commercial use."

Richardson had imagined a large building for Marshall Field, but its impact would be bigger still. The Marshall Field warehouse would become an essential reference point that anticipated much that would follow. Richardson had looked respectfully back in time, reproportioning familiar forms, particularly the arch, to impose a structural logic; this rescaling meant the huge building didn't overwhelm the streetscape. He stripped away ornament, surfacing the building with plain though textured stone. Both notions were imaginative leaps that would be widely imitated. Unlike Olmsted, Richardson rarely explained his thinking, but at the end of his life, he

The Marshall Field Wholesale Store as pictured in an advertisement, which claimed "twelves acres ... [of] the best selected stock of dry goods in the world."

did use the same phrase several times to identify buildings, labeling them "dignified, monumental work." A key characteristic, he wrote, was "a perfectly quiet and massive treatment of the wall surfaces."[7] No building conveyed that better than Field's.

In constructing the store, Richardson had taken a conservative approach, relying as he usually did primarily on old-fashioned weight-bearing masonry. But he also took a step toward the future: his brick and stone masked I beams, an early symptom of the coming shift to steel skeletons that would soon dominate high-rise construction with completion of the twelve-story Rookery and the sixteen-story Monadnock, in 1888 and 1891, respectively, both in Chicago.

With his work for Field and Glessner, along with his jobs in Cincinnati, Pittsburgh, and Saint Louis, Richardson's architectural practice had gone national, and when his organs failed him, he had been at the threshold of a much larger career. He had recognized that the Midwest was fertile ground, regarding Cincinnati in particular as a cultured place. As a writer in the *Century* reported that year, Cincinnati was "the first of the Western cities to be known as a home of picture collectors and it holds the first place at the present time in the amount of its recent gifts to art."[8] Chicago, meanwhile, was on the verge of becoming America's capital of architecture, with a series of trendsetting buildings.

On the day he died, Richardson told his doctor that he wished "to live two years to see the Pittsburgh court-house and the Chicago store complete." He felt certain these works were his best ever: "If they honor me for the pigmy things I have already done, what will they say when they see Pittsburgh finished."[9] Indeed, his influence on the cityscape became more profound in the years immediately after his death; in Chicago alone, landmarks like Louis Sullivan's Auditorium Building, Daniel Burnham's and John Wellborn Root's Rookery, and Frank Lloyd Wright's Prairie-style homes would all be indebted to Richardson's designs.

Thanks to Richardson, the architecture profession had begun to think in a new way. His early training in Paris had been to apply the rules of classical architecture, but he had shifted priorities to favor needs and functions. In his most essential works, his peers could see how an architectural program—the client's list of requirements for a building—would first beget a two-dimensional floor plan, for which Richardson would then imagine a three-dimensional container in which the idea would dwell. His orderly thinking produced new forms for commercial, private, academic, and transportation buildings, which emerged in his little drawings. He was alive to the changing needs of a nation that was shifting its focus from the country to the city. His admirers saw in Richardson both a fearless originality and a facility for applying the lessons of the past.

In the days after Richardson's funeral, Olmsted dispatched a letter to M. G. Van Rensselaer, an art and architecture writer whom both he and Richardson had known for several years. It was a note of shared loss and consolation.

Mrs. Mariana Griswold Van Rensselaer had taken the train from New York three years earlier, arriving in Brookline to interview both Olmsted and Richardson. On visiting Richardson's house and studio in Brookline, she was immediately struck by the energy of the place, describing it as "the busiest home I ever saw."[10] Her engaging articles were still running in the prestigious *Century Magazine* when

Richardson was interred, published in a series under the rubric "Recent Architecture in America." Olmsted read them with great interest, not least since they revealed a keen appreciation of Richardson. One described the Crane Library in Quincy, Massachusetts, calling it "one of the most perfect of Mr. Richardson's buildings."[11] Another considered the Copley Square church at great length. It concluded with a sweeping claim. "In building Trinity," Van Rensselaer wrote, "Mr. Richardson gave us the most beautiful structure that yet stands on our side of the ocean."[12]

Commenting on the public buildings in North Easton, Massachusetts, Van Rensselaer wrote that Richardson had been "fortunate in having the assistance of Mr. Frederick Law Olmstead in the arrangement of connecting grounds and terraces, and the result is one of the most delightful groups of harmonious yet contrasting works of which we can yet boast."[13] Even if the author misspelled his surname, Olmsted sensed she was a rarity among writers and critics, understanding in a way that the general public and even architects rarely did, the importance of connecting a building to its place.

Van Rensselaer replied to Olmsted's May 2, 1886, letter and echoed his sense of bereavement. Thus prompted, Olmsted wrote again, this time confiding that he found it "particularly hard to become accustomed to think of [Richardson] as gone."[14] After speaking with his neighbor Charles Sargent, a man with deeper pockets than his own, he wrote Mrs. Van Rensselaer a third letter later that day. This time he confided that he had a publishing enterprise in mind. His notion was a "memorial book." He hoped that such a volume would give "some account of [Richardson] and his works with illustrations . . . [and] that it should be set about at once, before his office is dismantled, his friends dispersed and while memories of him are fresh."

To Mrs. Van Rensselaer's surprise, Olmsted concluded, "You would be much the best person to undertake it."[15] Sargent would negotiate a deal with a publisher. A Richardson partisan and heir to a substantial railroad fortune, he knew a good investment when he saw one, and was willing to put some of his own money into the project.

Olmsted seemed convinced she could do the job, but Van Rensselaer had her doubts. She had published many articles, including more than a few about buildings, but she had never written a book. With no training in architecture, she wondered whether she possessed the vocabulary and sophisticated knowledge to take on the technical aspects in a book-length treatise. While Olmsted promptly offered his assurances that even architects wouldn't want an overly technical book, she also worried that she didn't know the deceased well enough. Again, Olmsted saw no obstacle, telling her that "it is not desirable that you should have been nearer to Mr Richardson." What was needed, he believed, was "a thoroughly discriminating, candid historical view." Her mix of knowledge and distance meant "no one could be better placed than you to think out the true instructiveness of his life."[16]

Given Olmsted's insistence, she could hardly say no, especially since her own circumstances argued for taking on the project. In March 1884, her husband had died of acute bronchitis, leaving her to raise their nine-year-old son alone. Now thirty-five, she remained a well-to-do woman. Her own family, the Griswolds, had been important New York merchants for generations, and her late husband, Schuyler Van Rensselaer, was a scion of one of wealthiest and most powerful families in the Empire State, having once controlled much of the land around Albany on both sides of the river. But she valued the income from her writings and was willing to say so. As she wrote that year to her editor at the *Century*, "I hope you have thought about the suggestion I made . . . about raising my wages. . . . I am, of course, anxious to have all the farthings I have any right to wish for."[17]

Van Rensselaer wanted to establish herself as a strong and independent critical voice. Her articles had already run not only in the *Century* but also in *Harper's, Lippincott's,* and many issues of *American Architect and Building News,* starting with its first. She wrote about music and fiction as well as art and architecture. As her first book, a biography of the nation's most essential architect could only enhance her standing.*

Mariana Griswold Van Rensselaer was a keen and worldly observer. Raised in a Fifth Avenue mansion a few blocks north of Wash-

---

* There are those who would argue that Richard Morris Hunt occupied—or at least shared— the top spot. However, Richardson took on a greater diversity of commissions and executed them with more originality than Hunt, a man best known for his Gilded Age mansions and a reliance on the French classical manner he learned at the Ecole des Beaux-Arts.

ington Square Park, her life's horizon line had changed abruptly when she was seventeen. Mariana's mother, after discovering her husband had been unfaithful, packed up her daughter and son and sailed for Europe.[18] The five years Mariana spent there had been an immersion in European art and culture, a sequence of museums, opera houses and concert halls, theaters, parks, and churches. She learned French and German and gained fluency with influential thinkers like Johann Joachim Winckelmann, the German who had almost single-handedly invented archaeology, the great French medievalist Eugène Viollet-le-Duc, and English critics John Ruskin and Matthew Arnold.

After her marriage, she returned to America in 1873, four years after the completion of the transcontinental railroad. Settlers were swarming into the great spaces in between the coasts under the terms of the Homestead Act. Wartime industrialization and territorial expansion meant the United States could claim to be the wealthiest nation on earth, but the still-young country had yet to earn the respect of the Old World. Fresh from abroad, Van Rensselaer was acutely aware of the condescension that cultured Europeans had for her up-and-coming native land.

For Van Rensselaer, America was a land of immense possibility, and she had been drawn to artists on the American scene. In Richardson she saw a case in point. Despite the brevity of his life, he had demonstrated a capacity to make buildings that were original and native to her land. Determined to make this argument for posterity, she agreed to write the book. When published two years later in the spring of 1888, *Henry Hobson Richardson and His Works* became the first book devoted to an American architect.

Luxuriously printed by Boston's Riverside Press, an imprint of Houghton Mifflin Company, the volume sold for twenty dollars, a sum roughly equal to two months' wages for a laborer or a soldier. Such a premium price meant a small run of five hundred hand-numbered copies, but the book still proved popular, selling 438 copies in the first year after publication. The venture generated a tidy profit for the publisher and Sargent, each netting $1,304.21. Van Rensselaer's 10 percent royalty earned her just under $1,000 dollars, half of which she was paid prior to publication.[19]

The reception of the handsome folio was largely positive. In the building business, the book's photographic reproductions were widely admired. That the author was a rare female in the overwhelmingly male world of architecture did not go unacknowledged, and

the *Nation* condescended to call Van Rensselaer's approach "sisterly rather than judicial."[20] One reviewer complained there were too few details of Richardson's personal life, though admiring critics described Van Rensselaer's writing as "clear, discriminating, and agreeable," and the project was lauded as a "big book about a big man."[21] Olmsted and Sargent were both pleased too, as was Richardson's widow. As Julia told Olmsted, "I think it is perfectly wonderful, perfectly wonderful! How she has brought things together."[22]

Mariana Griswold Van Rensselaer, as painted by William A. Coffin, probably in New York, about 1890.

Van Rensselaer's monograph served one of Olmsted's goals by keeping Richardson's work alive in the public mind. Richardson left a mere eighty-odd buildings. In contrast, the younger Frank Lloyd Wright, who lived to age ninety-one, would build more than five hundred. Yet, thanks to the book, Richardson's architectural heirs, and the appetite of clients eager to have buildings like those he had designed, the Richardsonian diaspora would continue to grow.

As the nation's first architectural celebrity, Richardson would prove a hard act to follow. An expansive persona had made him vastly popular among his peers, the well-to-do movers and shakers with the means to hire him to make great buildings.

His work had gained fame partly due to his promotional savvy. At a time of rapid advances in printing technology, he had allied himself with the *New-York Sketch-Book of Architecture*, established in 1874, and its successor, the weekly *American Architect*. These publications, intended for a general audience, pioneered the use of heliotype, a photomechanical process that produced crisp and detailed photographic images, which served his buildings particularly well, emphasizing the play of light and dark, drawing attention to the stonework and its relation to the surrounding landscape.[23] Richardson had overseen the publication *Monographs of American Architecture*, which further documented his works in book form. His buildings had appeared more frequently than anyone else's in the pages of the building business organ *American Architect and Building News*.

Striving to fill the vacuum Richardson left behind, George Shepley and Charles Rutan focused much of their energy on completing ongoing, unfinished projects, while Charles Coolidge volunteered to be the firm's front man and traveled widely. He would return with a mix of new educational, commercial, civic, and residential commissions, among them two major California jobs. One was the Wells Fargo Building in San Francisco, the other a new university in Palo Alto.

Leland Stanford, an immensely wealthy merchant and railroad man, had lost a son at age fifteen to typhoid. He wanted to honor the boy by establishing a fine college in his adopted state, one as good as the finest universities back East. He was impatient to get Leland Stanford Junior University built and, favoring East Coast designers and finding Coolidge eager and at hand, put the firm to work immediately. "I made the drawings during the night," Coolidge remembered, "and they dug the foundations in the day; and that is the way the thing started."[24] A bonus came with the big California job: Stanford chose Olmsted and his team as Shepley, Rutan and Coolidge's collaborator in laying out his university. Coolidge would design buildings and arcades with short Richardsonian columns and low arches, while Olmsted designed a campus that took advantage of its dry Mediterranean climate, employing ornamental palms and paving rather than the meadows and glades typical of his East Coast parks. The result would fulfill the client's every expectation.

Shepley reeled in jobs in his native Saint Louis. There would be a Shepley, Rutan and Coolidge church in Pittsburgh and a library in New Orleans. Although the firm relocated to downtown Boston, it continued to collaborate regularly with the Olmsted firm, and in Brookline alone they would share roughly a dozen projects.[25]

In their work for the Boston and Albany Railroad, Richardson and Olmsted had helped persuade city dwellers to depart the cityscape for developing suburbs, and in the years leading up to World War I, their ideas reached a national audience in the pages of *Architectural Record, House and Garden,* and *Suburban Life.* Richardson apprentice Edward Cameron, sent to supervise the Glessner and the Marshall Field projects, moved on to establish his own architectural practice, which produced the largest rail depot in the world in Saint Louis, completed in 1894 and thought by some to be more Richardson than Richardson.[26] Richardsonian rail stations with characteristic expansive roofs over low stone structures, some of them built by Shepley, Rutan and Coolidge, many more by other firms, would appear in Georgia, Texas, Chicago (Bradford Gilbert's Illinois Central Station), and Nashville, where Union Station was an homage to Pittsburgh's Allegheny Courthouse.

Alexander Wadsworth Longfellow and Frank Ellis Alden, two Richardson protégés who worked on the New York State Capitol, helped launch Andrew Carnegie's great library initiative; dedicating much of his vast fortune to the diffusion of knowledge, Carnegie aimed to establish public collections across the country. The first of more than twenty-five hundred libraries that truly made the public library a national phenomenon in the coming decades, the 1890 Allegheny Carnegie Library on Pittsburgh's North Side, was based on Richardson's Woburn Public Library, and a series of other Carnegie-related works were designed by Alden and his partner, Alfred Branch Harlow, in the Richardson manner.[27]

Countless other architects adopted his mode too. In the twenty-five years between 1882 and 1907, no fewer than forty-seven courthouses were built in the Romanesque style in Georgia alone. Among the many others, a Richardsonian courthouse graces Sulphur Springs, Texas, and the tower at the San Antonio Post Office and Courthouse is a direct lift from the Brattle Square Church. A Minnesota courthouse is the unmistakable progeny of Pittsburgh's own. Other replicas appeared in Oklahoma, Iowa, Texas, and Sioux Falls. Chicago had a Richardsonian interlude that saw a mix of Romanesque structures; a library, numerous houses, and several important downtown commercial buildings emerged from the drafting rooms of Adler and Sullivan, Burnham and Root, and others.[28] The brothers Charles Sumner Greene and Henry Mather Greene in California were also strongly influenced by Richardson.

The appearance of Van Rensselaer's biography of Richardson in 1888 had added to the national taste for Richardsonian design. Houses indebted to him appeared in many prosperous cities, including Richmond and Savannah, Louisville and Cleveland, Saint Paul, Saint Louis, and Provo, Utah. Richardson-inspired works were constructed in Europe too, among them a monument in Westphalia, a Dresden church that was an unmistakable variation of Trinity, a Berlin store, and the Finnish pavilion at the Paris international exhibition in 1900. Architects also designed Richardsonian buildings in Holland, Scandinavia, Australia, and Great Britain, where Richardson posthumously was made an honorary member of the Royal Academy of British Architects.[29]

While the taste for the Richardsonian Romanesque had its vogue, it would not endure. A towering commercial project at 1 Court Street in Boston from Shepley, Rutan and Coolidge itself signaled the beginning of the end. When completed in 1893, the thirteen-story Ames Building, commissioned by Fred Ames, was the tallest masonry structure in the world and Boston's first skyscraper. On the building's completion, the firm set up offices in the attic story, where it would remain for nearly a century. However, the broad overhang of the building's "hat brim" cornice, a distinct departure from the Romanesque manner, demonstrated that, in the absence of Richardson's leadership, Ames and the firm had moved on. This early harbinger of change would be rapidly adapted as the norm.

By the time the last remaining copy of Mrs. Van Rensselaer's biography left Houghton Mifflin's warehouse in 1893, Richardson's manner of building was no longer at architecture's cutting edge, though its popularity would endure in many parts of the country. Shepley, Rutan and Coolidge's last project in the pure Richardsonian tradition was the West Porch of Trinity Church, added in 1894–95. The firm continued to prosper and survives today as Shepley, Bulfinch, Richardson and Abbott, but Richardson's old draftsmen, like almost everyone else in the architecture business, would abandon the twelfth century. Charles McKim and Stanford White had been carried by the changing tide of public taste. They joined Richard Morris Hunt, reverting to classically inspired buildings, reproducing columns, pediments, domes, and a multitude of Roman motifs, as Thomas Jefferson had done a century before. Richardson's inclination to draw from medieval models—as well as his sense of originality—had lost its luster. In winning such important commissions as the Art Institute of Chicago, Langdell Hall at Harvard Law School, and the Chicago Public Library, Shepley, Rutan and Coolidge would shift to giving their clients buildings in the newly dominant classical taste.

Even as Olmsted saw Richardson fading from public memory, his own ever-growing list of accomplishments left him feeling optimistic about his labors. Taken collectively, he told an old friend, the landscapes he shaped and conserved "are having an educative effect, . . . a manifestly civilizing effect" on the land.[30]

Nevertheless, he remained deeply worried about the future. He constantly fought off encroachments on his scenic spaces, including a proposed racetrack for Central Park that was authorized by a bill signed in March 1892. He struggled to imprint upon the public mind that his was a legitimate profession. He resisted the label *landscape gardener*, arguing that the task of gardener amounted to a "service corresponding to that of carpenter and mason." He contrasted that to the higher calling of the *landscape architect*, which was "more discriminating, and prepares the minds of clients for dealing with [one] on professional principles."[31] But he regarded his legacy as far from assured.

Despite adding partners to his firm, which had become F. L. Olmsted & Company in 1889, the founder as he neared age seventy remained a driven man, committed to his practice and his profession. He was keenly aware that no systematic book on landscape design existed to help ensure his legacy. He routinely wrote voluminous reports on his projects, but he lacked confidence in his own writing skills, saying to Van Rensselaer, "I have always been a bad writer."[32] From his own venture into journalism in his twenties, when he wrote for the *New-York Daily Times* and published several books, he understood the power of the printed word, which made him doubly receptive to Charles Sprague Sargent's notion of a magazine to advance their shared mission to raise the American consciousness regarding the nation's landscape. Without hesitation, Olmsted agreed to be an adviser to Sargent's venture, a weekly to be called *Garden and Forest*. He even reached into his own pocket and made a modest contribution to help launch the first issue, which appeared in 1888.

Once again, he and Sargent turned to Mariana Van Rensselaer, who had become a public conduit for Olmsted's ideas. Olmsted put it to her directly: "I am in wondering and grateful admiration of all you have written that I have seen upon Landscape Gardening. I want to see more."[33] As she had done for American buildings in the *Century*, she wrote a series of insightful articles for *Garden and Forest* that focused on landscape architecture. She maintained a vigorous correspondence with Olmsted, by now a trusted intellectual confidant, and he tutored, trusted, and encouraged her. As he had written to her a few years earlier, "The interpretation of artists to the public is your public mission."[34]

Van Rensselaer argued that landscape architecture should have high status as the fourth art, along with architecture, painting, and sculpture. She defined it for readers of *Garden and Forest* as "the art whose purpose is to create beautiful compositions upon the surface of the ground."[35] She defended the uniqueness of her native land, advising readers, "Nature speaks to us more variously and naturally in America than in Europe."[36] As a body of work, her writings amounted to a thorough overview of the status of the American landscape and those who were shaping it. An optimistic Olmsted thought her work and that of the magazine represented "the dawn of a new day." He continued, "It gives me satisfaction to think that though I . . . have been all my life swimming against the tide I shall not sink before I die."[37]

Van Rensselaer's friendship and writings buoyed him, and his confidence in her was rewarded. When her book *Art Out-of-Doors* appeared in 1893, it quickly became the most essential reference on the new discipline's theory. The voice of Olmsted was a strong undercurrent throughout, and one she openly acknowledged, describing her mentor as "the most remarkable artist yet born in America."[38]

That year, Van Rensselaer would again employ her biographical skills. At the behest of the editor of the *Century*, she wrote a profile of Olmsted. Although he was initially reluctant, she gained his cooperation; after a visit to Brookline to interview him, she left weighted down with material for her article. He followed up on the visit with a series of letters. "I don't like talking so much of myself," he admitted, but he embraced the larger purpose, which he saw as another attempt "to educate the public to a better understanding of what the art is in its essence, . . . a love for intelligent cultivated regard for scenery."[39] One of his letters ran ten pages in length.

Olmsted saw an opportunity to leverage his story to convert more people to his cause. Van Rensselaer carefully recounted the events of his life, starting with his Connecticut childhood; despite Olmsted's national notoriety and long career, the article was the first biographical profile of the man. In one sense, Van Rensselaer's article, titled simply "Frederick Law Olmsted," planted Olmsted's flag, laying claim to his status as the first American landscape architect. But in retrospect, its publication in the *Century* possessed a certain irony as a premature epitaph.

Chapter Eighteen

SUNSET AT BILTMORE

I have all my life been considering distant effects and always sacrificing
immediate success and applause to that of the future.

——FREDERICK LAW OLMSTED

At twenty-five, George Washington Vanderbilt had yet to leave the
nest. His three older brothers each ran one or more of the railroad
companies that made the Vanderbilts America's richest clan. But his
father's favorite and the youngest by six years, George had remained
at home with his aging parents. Private tutoring and regular European travels had permitted him to become "a delicate, refined and
bookish man." He was a student of literature and a connoisseur of
the paintings by J. M. W. Turner, Ernest Meissonier, and Jean-Léon
Gérôme that lined the two-story gallery of his father's palatial mansion on New York's Fifth Avenue.[1]

After his father died in December 1885, George and his mother
traveled to North Carolina seeking a milder winter climate. In Asheville they found a unique natural beauty in the shadows of the Blue
Ridge and the Great Smoky Mountains. With its resort hotels, the
so-called Land of the Sky had for decades been a destination for
wealthy planters from the Carolina coast, and with the recent arrival
of the railroad, made possible by a newly dug tunnel, the seasonal
visitors now included a growing number of northerners.

While Maria Vanderbilt found treatment at a local sanatorium
for a recurring case of malaria, her son took contemplative rides in the
woods. He found the climate mild and invigorating and the vistas to
his taste. At the crest of a hill on one ramble he glimpsed a "prospect

finer than any other I had seen." In that moment, an idea blossomed: "It occurred to me that I would like to have a house here."

George Vanderbilt could do as he wished. As a fourteen-year-old, he had inherited $1 million from his grandfather, Cornelius "Commodore" Vanderbilt. At twenty-one, he received another $1 million, which had been followed, on his father's demise, by an inheritance of $5 million in cash and $5 million in trust. In Asheville, he worked anonymously through agents and attorneys, and by June 1888, he owned 661 parcels of land, mostly small farms, totaling some two thousand acres, all part of the viewscape that had captured his fancy.

Had his father still lived, George might have sought his counsel regarding a persistent question that dogged him. His brothers had chosen to build mansions in New York and immense "cottages" in warm-weather escapes around the Northeast, primarily in Newport, Rhode Island. Making a shift in allegiance to western North Carolina would break the tradition of vacationing in New England, but as he contemplated his Asheville acreage, George instead consulted Olmsted, one of his father's contemporaries and a family friend.

Working as a farmer and nurseryman on Staten Island many years before, Olmsted had been a neighbor to the Vanderbilts. More recently, he had landscaped the grounds around the Vanderbilt mausoleum in a Staten Island cemetery, a fine Romanesque building designed by Richard Morris Hunt, and had done some landscaping around George's existing summer home in Maine. Olmsted was thus invited to come to Asheville in August 1888, where young Vanderbilt wanted Olmsted to tell him whether he had been "doing anything very foolish."[2]

Rail thin, handsome, and impeccably dressed, George Vanderbilt looked the part of a city boy, a scholar fluent in eight languages, and a bibliophile more comfortable in the quiet of his library than in the woods. In contrast, Olmsted looked his age. Now sixty-six and nearly bald, he had grown a flowing gray beard as a sort of disguise after one person too many mistook him for Governor Benjamin Butler of Massachusetts, whom he despised.[3] Though he felt acutely the toll taken by a life of hard work, Olmsted was still stirred by a new challenge.

As they gazed together that August across the valley of the French Broad River toward Mount Pisgah, the tallest peak in the vicinity, Olmsted asked the obvious question.

"What do you imagine you will do with all this land?"

"Make a park of it, I suppose," Vanderbilt replied.

"You bought the place then simply because you thought it had good air," Olmsted offered, "and because from this point, it had a good distant outlook. If that was what you wanted you have made no mistake. There is no question about the air and none about the prospect."

By nature, however, Olmsted was no flatterer. He felt honor bound to add his unvarnished opinion of whether Vanderbilt's new holdings might become a parkland, and the answer was no. "The woods are miserable," he told Vanderbilt, "all the good trees having again & again been culled out and only runts left. The topography is most unsuitable." He concluded, bluntly, "It's no place for a park."

When Olmsted reconstructed the story a few years later, he did not report whether Vanderbilt reacted with either disappointment or shock. Instead, knowing and trusting the older man, Vanderbilt asked what might then be done with the expanse of acres. To that question, Olmsted was able to provide a more encouraging answer. He advised that "such land in Europe would be made a forest."

As Richardson had been wont to do—he had demonstrated the same legerdemain in designing Trinity Church, the Glessner House, and dozens of other buildings—Olmsted divined in that moment a vision that was destined to be fulfilled. He told Vanderbilt that "a preserve for game" could be created, one that would be compatible with timberland for harvest, which, in turn, would likely mean a fair return on the capital invested. Looking to satisfy his client's desire for park scenery, he ventured that the immediate environs of his proposed house might become "a small pleasure ground & garden." As Olmsted talked, the proposal gained detail. The bottomland could be farmed, he suggested. Pastures would fatten livestock, producing both foodstuffs and manure that could be used to improve the tired soil.

Ever conscious that "the art of the landscape architect is a specialty which, in its exercise, peculiarly demands a forecast of the future," Olmsted thus described a new kind of project.[4] Forty years before, he had read the future of city life, concluding it required parks to serve as the "lungs of the metropolis." In his more recent travels to the West he had been struck by the degradation of a once densely forested landscape as he clattered past immense former forests that had been clear-cut. He recognized that the epic and seemingly limitless primeval timberland that had drawn early settlers to the New World was rapidly disappearing.

Here on Vanderbilt's mountaintop, Olmsted saw another kind of opportunity, one that brought him full circle. He had been a tree man before he had become a park man. On his Staten Island farm, he had nurtured an existing orchard and planted a wide variety of ornamental and forest trees. He had subsequently helped preserve the sequoia at Yosemite and Mariposa, and later his work with Sargent had resulted in the Arnold Arboretum. Just months before, he had helped found *Garden and Forest.*

In Asheville, Olmsted thought, Vanderbilt could lay the groundwork for a new and necessary American discipline. Though many in Europe managed their woodlands in a sustainable way, forestry—the work of scientifically planting and managing a healthy wooded area while harvesting timber—was virtually unknown in the United States. Olmsted drew a clear conclusion for Vanderbilt: "It would be of great value to the country to have a thoroughly well organized and systematically conducted attempt in forestry made on a large scale."

Vanderbilt took these words seriously. In a matter of months, Olmsted delivered a preliminary plan and Vanderbilt approved it.[5] Together, they were about to embark upon what Olmsted called "a private work of very rare public interest."[6]

Olmsted's North Carolina design partner would be Richard Morris Hunt. With Richardson gone, Hunt stood out indisputably not only as America's most prestigious designer but as the Vanderbilt architect of choice. Over the years, he had designed homes for Vanderbilt family members in New York and Newport, including the mansion on Fifth Avenue where George had grown up.

But Hunt and Olmsted hadn't always seen eye to eye. Their adversarial history went back twenty-five years. Olmsted and Calvert Vaux had fought off Hunt's proposed grand entrances to Central Park, arguing that the architect was wrong to make "natural eloquence" play second fiddle to "architectural grandiloquence."[7] The skirmish had been a rare defeat for Hunt, whose park gateway had not been executed, and Olmsted's arguments had bested his again when they later clashed over the redesign at the Albany capitol and a proposed building for the New-York Historical Society within Central Park's boundaries.

In North Carolina, too, they found themselves at odds. On reviewing some preliminary house plans, Olmsted objected. "The house should have had a broad terrace from which the outlook can be enjoyed by a large party," he told Hunt. Affronted by the suggestion, Hunt replied in what one observer remembered as very "lurid language." He defended his design, pointing out that a terrace would not be in keeping with the style of the house. "Then you have made an error," Olmsted shot back, "in your selection of the house type."[8]

Olmsted went to extraordinary lengths to make his case. He ordered the construction of two temporary observation towers, complete with handrails and stairs, to demonstrate where best to capture the view that had inspired George Vanderbilt to embark on the project.[9] While he won this battle, he did meet Hunt halfway when he proposed a formal pleasure garden near the house. Though symmetry and geometric plantings were never Olmsted's first choice, he agreed to play the role of André Le Nôtre, Louis XIV's principal gardener, around what was an American Versailles in the making. This clearly would be a grand palace, since Vanderbilt's original notion of a modest frame house was discarded after a trip with Hunt to France and the Loire region. On returning, Hunt produced plans for a château with 255 rooms, making it the largest private house in the country.

At the same time, Olmsted found a way to remain true to the capabilities of the picturesque surroundings. He devised a three-mile approach road that meandered through a naturalized landscape, with "incidents" along the route "consistent with the sensation of passing through the remote depths of a natural forest." As if rising from its surroundings, the towered mansion in all its Gothic glory would, as he wrote to George Vanderbilt, eventually loom up within a "trim, level, open, airy, spacious, thoroughly artificial Court."[10]

Once within this four-acre Esplanade, as Olmsted called the house's immediate setting, all eyes would be drawn to the house's tall façade of Ohio limestone. But that, too, would serve Olmsted's purpose, since the great château screened the panoramic mountain view on the opposite side. Only after passing through the interior to the major public rooms would a visitor lay eyes upon the vast and mountainous western overlook. Thus, Hunt's house would take possession of the immediate site while Olmsted enabled Vanderbilt to display the vast viewscape he now owned. The terrace, an area south of the mansion and as large as its footprint, he called "a great out of door general apartment."

Olmsted genuinely liked George Vanderbilt and his "frank, trustful, confiding and cordially friendly disposition."[11] Vanderbilt more than embraced the forestry plan, and by the time he had acquired his last parcel of land, the estate's forests encompassed 120,000 acres, extending all the way to and including Mount Pisgah. In comparison to Central Park's 840 acres, the area was almost unfathomably large, but after decades spent waiting for legislative appropriations and wrestling with public personalities, Olmsted reveled in working with a client who possessed the means and the inclination to see the job done properly and promptly.

Olmsted suggested the house be christened "Broadwood," after the nearby French Broad River. Vanderbilt liked the sound of "Bilton" better but changed the name when local postal authorities expressed concern it might be confused with Bolton, North Carolina. A compromise choice was soon agreed upon. *Biltmore* it would be.

The Olmsted firm was busier than ever. Three enormous projects were on the drawing board, all far from Brookline. In addition to the commission to design the campus for Leland Stanford Junior University in 1886 and Biltmore in 1888, the assignment came in 1890 to remake Chicago's Jackson Park into the grounds for the 1893 World's Columbian Exposition—and to do so on a nearly impossible schedule. Other jobs, too, were launched in Richmond,

Virginia, in Atlanta and Louisville, in New Jersey, Massachusetts, and elsewhere.

With the arrival of the new decade, Olmsted often felt the inexorable advance of his own mortality. In 1890, on a trip to Biltmore, he fell very ill. According to the "Confederate surgeon" he consulted, his ailments included "lumbago, sciatica, intercostal rheumatism, facial neuralgia . . . some danger of pneumonia [and] a case of the true Grip."[12] A year later, Olmsted experienced an episode of arsenic poisoning. Copper arsenite was a common pigment used to dye hats and fabrics, and even to paint children's toys; Olmsted's exposure came via the Turkey red dye of the new wallpaper in his bedroom.[13] Another new symptom, a persistent ringing in the ears, interfered with his ability to converse. "If I live another year" became a refrain in his correspondence.

Though reluctant to cede control, Olmsted did contemplate how to hand over the reins to other men he had trained, in particular to his stepson John and apprentices Charles Eliot and Henry Codman. But Codman's sudden death in January 1893 at just twenty-nine, after an appendectomy, came as a fresh reminder of how fragile the infrastructure of the profession was.

In March 1893, Olmsted chose to be in North Carolina rather than at a celebratory dinner preceding the opening of the World's Columbian Exposition he had helped plan. Had he been in Chicago, he would have heard himself extolled as the chief designer of the 690-acre grounds. "Each of you knows the name and genius of him who stands first in the heart and confidence of American artists, the creator of your own parks," said Daniel Burnham, one of the directors of the world's fair. "As an artist, [Olmsted] paints with lakes and wooded slopes; with lawns and banks and forest-covered hills; with mountainsides and ocean views. He should stand where I do tonight . . . for what his brain has wrought and his pen has taught for half a century."[14]

Olmsted's daunting workload and poor health were taking a growing toll. His insomnia was especially acute when traveling, as his inability to sleep on overnight train trips often left him ill on arrival, requiring him to take to bed to recover. Just as worrisome were his memory lapses. Even before Richardson's death, he had acknowledged to his stepson his unnerving inability to keep track of names.[15]

For many years Olmsted had planned to draw Frederick Olmsted Jr. into the business. In September of 1890, he told twenty-year-old Rick, who had just enrolled at Harvard, that he expected him to spend at least five hours a week thinking about landscape architecture.[16] By 1894 the freshly graduated Rick was apprenticing at Biltmore, working on a project that, Olmsted hoped, "will, twenty years hence, be what Central Park has been to me." He wanted Biltmore to be the next generation's calling card, "the first great *private* work of our profession in the country."[17]

Olmsted's seven-year labor at Biltmore amounted to a coda to his remarkable career and a closing recapitulation of his life's work. After the long carriage ride along the approach road, the siting of the immense house on Vanderbilt's chosen hilltop brought to mind his work at the U.S. Capitol. The house both dominated the immediate view and embraced and integrated with the larger landscape. Nearby stood the Walled Garden. Vanderbilt and his guests could walk a "scenic progression" into the Ramble, a favorite conceit of Olmsted's that dated to Central Park. Olmsted imagined a nine-mile arboretum, a "Museum of Trees" far larger that Sargent's, though it would ultimately not be realized. He oversaw the creation of water features, including a lake with man-made islands for aquatic plants and wild birds. The immense forest surrounded it all.

In the end, the collaboration with Hunt went surprisingly well. Yet, in March 1895, when Olmsted and his wife, Mary, arrived at Biltmore together, a vast amount of work still remained to be completed, on both the house and the landscape—and George Vanderbilt wanted it done by Christmas so that he could welcome his siblings and their families to Asheville. The logistics throughout had been immense, with a rail spur constructed to bring in Indiana limestone, crushed stone, brick, steel, cement, and other building supplies. The mountaintop site had been flattened for the house. Olmsted created a nursery for maturing plant materials and later laid out a village at the mouth of the approach road, revising Hunt's plan for a French-style village, opting instead for a New England–inspired hamlet.[18] A waterworks, herbarium, and quarries were established on the property.

Hunt and Olmsted, along with a platoon of on-site managers and a thousand-man army of workers, were creating a latter-day Chatsworth.

In mid-May, Hunt and his wife, Catherine, arrived on Vanderbilt's private railway car. Another guest also stepped off the train at Biltmore's rail station that day, the eminent portraitist John Singer Sargent. Vanderbilt had commissioned him to memorialize the two men most responsible for the magnificent estate in pendant portraits. If they were painted from life, Vanderbilt believed, the artist would "feel en rapport with his sitters" and might produce "two masterpieces."[19]

Whatever their artistic merits, the two life-size canvases (each stood eight feet high) would capture moments in the lives of both subjects in ways that no one anticipated. Sargent posed Hunt in Biltmore's courtyard, framed by the lines of his architecture. He positioned Olmsted just off the approach road, with a woodland backdrop of native flora, a mix of rhododendron, mountain laurel, and dogwood. Both men looked old, with Hunt bracing himself on a wellhead, and Olmsted leaning on his cane.

The finished Hunt painting proved particularly prescient. Mrs. Hunt did not like it, observing that "the portrait represents a man thin and worn from suffering, and, though it has a certain likeness, the fire, the vigor and the personality are all wanting."[20] Sargent had clearly seen something she did not wish to acknowledge. The wan Hunt he recorded on canvas was sicker than anyone realized, and a few weeks later, he fell deathly ill back home in Newport. Suffering from a mix of ailments, he died on July 31, 1895.

The truth in the other portrait is harder to fathom. Olmsted was not dying—then seventy-three, he would live another eight years—but the likeness Sargent recorded is of a remote figure, who engages neither artist nor viewer. Olmsted, who was known to speak of himself in the third person, has a distant, even vacant expression. He, too, was clearly in decline.

His sons had also begun to wonder at his ability to carry on. In the days before Sargent's arrival, the elder Olmsted had confided in John, "It has today for the first time, become evident to me that my memory as to recent occurrences is no longer to be trusted. . . . It follows, simply, for the present, that it will be prudent for you . . . to trust a little less to my presence of mind."[21]

Sargent completed Olmsted's head indoors at Biltmore, working in a makeshift studio inside the unfinished house. Ironically, all the windows with the grand western view of the mountains were blacked out, with a single window providing the artist's preferred northern light.

Vanderbilt, too, had become aware of the man's forgetfulness when, disregarding the agreed-upon plan, Olmsted had ordered tulip trees planted that would block the view of the house's entrance façade. After Vanderbilt pointed out the unaccountably large mistake to young Rick Olmsted, John Olmsted instituted a search of the files in Brookline and uncovered the drawing Vanderbilt had signed off on long before. "I am inclined to think that Father had better come home," John wrote to Rick from Brookline, ". . . as soon as Mr. Sargent can let him off from the [portrait] sittings."[22] They would need "someone with a clearer head than Father now has to keep affairs well in hand."[23]

Olmsted departed in early June, though Sargent had yet to complete work on his portrait. A series of sunny days had interfered—the artist wanted diffused light to dapple the sylvan setting—and after his father's departure, as Rick remembered years later, "Sargent had me pose in father's clothes, at the point originally chosen and in overcast weather."[24]

Once back in Brookline, Olmsted wrote to Rick, who remained to supervise at Asheville, "I have rarely felt so little master of myself."[25] The look that Hunt captured on canvas wasn't that of the visionary landscaper. Unfortunately, as his family now understood, Olmsted was a man fading into a permanent bewilderment. John and Rick saw no alternative, and in August 1895, Frederick Law Olmsted retired from the firm, withdrawing from active work in the field of landscape architecture. Having been drafted into donning his father's clothes for John Singer Sargent, Frederick Law Olmsted Jr.

was about to become a partner in Olmsted Brothers, embarking on a career in landscape that would last more than a half century.

His family took Olmsted Sr. to England and then to the Maine coast, but neither place enabled him to find the quiet equilibrium hoped for, away from the business that was still being conducted out of Fairsted's domicile-office. Despite Mary's efforts, home care for her husband proved impossible, and he was confined at McLean Hospital (formerly McLean Asylum) in Belmont, Massachusetts. He made little sense in his last years, though he had moments of lucidity. Once, in 1900, he wrote to his wife and sons, irritated by the landscape at McLean. The bane of his professional life, the bureaucracy, had dealt him one last blow. "They didn't carry out my plan," he complained.[26] Frederick Law Olmsted would die on August 28, 1903, with Rick at his side. At the insistence of the deceased, his body was cremated.

None of Olmsted's contemporaries did for him what he had done for Richardson. Some years before, Van Rensselaer had considered a full-scale biography of Olmsted and even began writing of his early years.[27] Though the book would likely have found an honored place on the shelf beside her life of Richardson, Van Rensselaer's time with Olmsted while writing the 1893 *Century* profile had shown her how fretful and forgetful Olmsted could be, and she abandoned the idea of a biography. In 1922 and 1928, two volumes with Olmsted's name on the covers, titled *Forty Years of Landscape Architecture*, went to press; edited by Rick, they amounted to little more than excerpts from his father's voluminous writings and reports. Another half century would pass before an authoritative life was published, in 1973, a two-decade labor of love by Laura Wood Roper, published as *FLO: A Biography of Frederick Law Olmsted* and written with Rick's extensive cooperation, prior to his own death in 1957. Yet, unlike the built works of his friend Richardson, many of which would be demolished in the course of the twentieth century, Olmsted's parks in particular seemed to gain luster over time. Many is the American metropolis today where citizens know—and are quick to point out—that their city park is the work of Frederick Law Olmsted.

Epilogue

LEGACIES

It sure must be / Almost the highest bliss of human-kind /
When to thy haunts two kindred spirits flee.

—JOHN KEATS

Near the end of Olmsted's working life, a bicyclist turned into Fairsted's driveway. The young man had been told that he might come to call so that Mr. Olmsted could advise him on becoming a landscape architect.[1]

Although his MIT engineering degree positioned him perfectly to join the family business of making fine surgical instruments, Arthur Shurtleff had other ideas. An outdoorsman at heart, he wanted to engage in the "planning and construction for scenes of daily life."[2] Always on the lookout for young converts essential to the survival of the profession he had pioneered, Olmsted craved this sort of conversation.

Casually dressed in homespun, the older man was cordial and unhurried. He questioned Shurtleff at length, listening attentively to the twenty-four-year-old's answers. As Shurtleff later recalled, Olmsted then discoursed about his profession, speaking of the arduous work involved and the challenges of getting architects, engineers, politicians, owners, sculptors, and other designers to cooperate with one another. He talked about soils, climate, marginal walls, vegetation, trees, uplands and lowlands, roadways, and "recreative quietude." He described his labors at Yosemite, in city parks, and at the Chicago exposition.

After more than two hours spent with the "dignified" and "kindly" Olmsted, Shurtleff was no less keen than on arrival. He climbed back on his bicycle and retraced his three-mile route to

Richardson and noted British portraitist Hubert von Herkomer reached an understanding. "If you will sketch an elevation for my house," the artist proposed, "I'll paint your portrait." No money changed hands, but Lululand, Herkomer's mansion outside London, would be the architect's only British work. This vivid portrait, based on a charcoal sketch Herkomer made from life in Richardson's last months, was regarded by clients, draftsmen, and family members as a very good likeness.

Boston's Beacon Hill, only to return, two years later, with another degree, this one cobbled together at Harvard, where no one yet offered coursework specifically in landscape architecture. He spent the next eight years apprenticing at the Olmsted offices before departing to establish his own practice. In the ensuing fifty years, he would do important work as a park consultant, city planner, and as chief landscape architect for Colonial Williamsburg.*

---

* As a man of sixty Arthur *Shurtleff* would change his name to Arthur *Shurcliff*, reverting to an earlier spelling of the family surname.

He would be one of many men who spread the gospel according to Olmsted, among the most important of whom would be Olmsted's stepson and son. In 1899, Rick and John helped found the American Society of Landscape Architects, the field's first professional membership association. In 1900, Rick accepted an appointment at Harvard as an instructor, a role that led to the establishment of the country's first university curriculum of professional training in landscape architecture. He later became the first president of the American City Planning Institute, established in 1917. Rick would also help draft the Organic Act of 1916, establishing the National Park Service. He wrote its statement of purpose, which might well have been written by his father: "To conserve the scenery and the natural and historic objects and the wild life therein and to provide for the enjoyment of the same in such manner and by such means as will leave them unimpaired for the enjoyment of future generations." Together the brothers would play a major role in the shaping the National Park Service, a bureau under the aegis of the Department of the Interior charged with managing and protecting national parks and monuments.

As Olmsted Brothers, the firm carried on the work of the founder almost seamlessly, operating the largest landscape architecture firm in the country. When John died, in 1920, his pet projects included park systems for Portland, Maine, and Portland, Oregon, Charleston, Seattle, Dayton, Spokane, and New Orleans, and college campuses for Smith, Mount Holyoke, the University of Chicago, and the University of Washington. Rick carried on until his retirement in 1949, accepting commissions for the cities of Detroit, Utica, Boulder, Pittsburgh, New Haven, and Newport. His work included the commuter suburb Forest Hills Gardens in Queens, New York, and the expansive Rock Creek Park in the District of Columbia. Among the roughly four thousand commissions that entered the Olmsted offices was a design for Fort Tryon Park, which took Rick back to his father's old Manhattan territory, and conservation efforts including Acadia National Park in Maine, Point Lobos near Monterey, California, and the Florida Everglades. The sons carried on the founder's vision so well that today the nineteenth-century works of Frederick Law Olmsted are regularly conflated with the twentieth-century designs of Rick and John.

Over the course of the centuries, American architecture has seen three great avatars. As a tastemaker and amateur architect, Thomas Jefferson made classicism our default national style for public buildings. As the country's best remembered architect, Frank Lloyd Wright was a self-referential romantic who shaped an "organic architecture" as he made his own idiosyncrasy a much-loved art form. Located chronologically between the other two, Richardson completes the triumvirate, a man widely regarded by architectural historians as America's most important architectural form-giver.

He lived in an era of extraordinary change. When people wanted public libraries, he provided an archetype. As labor, capital, railroads, and industry drove people to the cities, Richardson designed buildings and stores to serve office and mercantile needs on

Olmsted at leisure, in England, in 1894.

new urban streetscapes. Countless residents escaping the cities, for whom Olmsted provided prototype suburban plans, found themselves frequenting suburban rail stations that were Richardsonian in style. He designed unique homes adapted to the countryside, others suited to frenzied downtown streets.

Unlike the designs of his contemporary Richard Morris Hunt, however, whose career spanned four decades, Richardson's iterations of a given building type typically were few. He built a handful of large and small Shingle-style homes; those who followed him built many thousands. Some of his most striking buildings were, in effect, one-offs, yet widely imitated. It is notable that after Seattle was leveled by a disastrous fire in 1889, the rebuilt downtown emerged as a truly Richardsonian city, in which the majority of the reconstructed office, warehouse, and residential buildings were built in his unmistakable Romanesque manner.

Given the finite number of his buildings, perhaps it is not surprising that despite Richardson's status in the eyes of his profession, his name fell from most people's mental *Who's Who* after his premature death. Inevitably that prompts head-scratching as to what he might have accomplished had he lived longer. In his last months he designed the universally admired Marshall Field Wholesale Store. At the Glessner House, another end-of-career design, Richardson rejected the then-fixed expectation of how a house ought to relate to the street. Barely a decade separated all his major works, and in his last days he produced two more extraordinary buildings, one in Pittsburgh and another in Cincinnati. One can only speculate where his imagination might have taken him.

One thing known for certain is that in the decade after his death, Richardson assumed the role of architect's architect for his profession. Late in Louis Sullivan's life, long after he had become one of the leading designers of his generation, he wrote that Richardson's work "stands as an oration of one who knows well how to choose his words, who has some[thing] to say and says it—and says it as the outpouring of a copious, direct, large and simple mind."[3] Sullivan for one had paid homage in his own work to Richardson as he played a key role in making the city of Chicago a place that took pride in its architecture.

Sullivan's sometime lieutenant Frank Lloyd Wright owed an immense debt to Richardson. When he designed a home for his young family in Oak Park, Illinois, he had just read Van Rensselaer's life of Richardson; he chose to build the house in the Shingle style. The Winslow House, among the most admired of Wright's Oak Park designs, borrowed from Richardson, using the horizontal organization of its elevation, an echo of the Marshall Field warehouse, and a Glessner House–like arrangement with restrained rectangular lines on its front façade contrasting sharply with the free-form curves of the conservatory to the rear. Throughout his long career, Wright would frequently use arches, stone piers, and rooflines that were unmistakably Richardsonian. To visit the libraries where Richardson created drama with varying ceiling heights is to anticipate the sense of spatial play that characterizes many works of Wright and his successors. His indebtedness was undeniable, though given his egotism, Wright rarely and reluctantly acknowledged it, more often maintaining what he called a "secret respect, learning a little toward envy . . . for H.H. Richardson."[4]

The works of Wright and Sullivan would have been different if Richardson had not been a part of the genetic code of American architecture. Absent Richardson's tutelage and their years as his draftsmen, McKim and White, gifted though they were, would have produced different designs. Many calendar pages down the road, architectural historians like Henry-Russell Hitchcock and Philip Johnson extolled Richardson as a proto-modernist, acknowledging him as an essential progenitor to many European and American designers. Even if Richardson's renown among the general public is low, architecture students today know and speak reverently of his work.

Richardson's greatest legacy may well be more than a matter of style, memorable as his Romanesque experiments are. He approached design in a way that broke boundaries. At the Ecole des Beaux-Arts, he had been trained to think in shorthand by producing *esquisses*, the little epiphanies that neatly encapsulated the schema of a building to come. Beginning with a configuration of rooms, he and his fellow *élèves* would then apply the classical dress that was de rigueur at the Beaux-Arts. But Richardson would abandon the Beaux-Arts strictures, and over the course of his career, he not only left behind the Roman raiment but also altered the way he thought about building. He considered the mass of a building from the outside in; he thought in volumes from the inside out. Buildings in his imagination became open, shared spaces that flowed into one another, unrestricted by traditional thinking. The skin he applied was, Mariana Van Rensselaer pointed out, "organic" to the forms he shaped, often involving native materials that bound structure to setting.

His multiple porches and rows of windows welcomed the contours of the land. Thanks to the influence of Olmsted, many of Richardson's best buildings were linked to the natural world in new ways. If his work was as prelude to the openness of modern architecture, he equally thought of interiors in terms of continuity of space. Some of those interiors flowed into outdoor "rooms," with the effect of making buildings belong to their sites as the designs of others did not. Today such thinking is common, but in Richardson and Olmsted's time, it was a revelation to a clientele acquainted with an architecture of enclosed boxes.

Richardson left an indelible imprint on the designs of homes, libraries, hospitals, transportation hubs, stores, offices, academic buildings, and churches that enlivened and defined the taste of his era. "For a space of time," remembered an architect whose career launched just as Richardson's ended, "we were all Richardsonians. . . . How could we do otherwise? Here was a real *man* at last."[5]

Nature had been the enemy when Olmsted's seventeenth-century ancestors made landfall in North America, but by the nineteenth century, simple survival in the face of a dangerous and intimidating wilderness had long ceased being the primary concern. In his time, Olmsted looked into a different problem: he worried about the loss of natural wildness and, more than anyone else, went about making it part of the future.

Olmsted and Richardson watched as a largely rural nation became increasingly urban and suburban, bound together by iron rails. The millennia-old notion that agriculture held primacy in the wealth of nations ceased to be true. The tallest things in sight had long been church spires and ships' masts, but developing cities gained new buildings a dozen or more stories tall for which the name *skyscraper* was coined. The population of the United States increased eightfold in Olmsted's lifetime; the city of Chicago was transformed from frontier trading post to the nation's second-largest city. A country once without urban parks gained dozens, most of them from the brain of Olmsted.

Few people think a generation into the future, and only a tiny minority of those may glimpse two or more generations down the road. Olmsted's ability to do so made him one of the great visionaries of the nineteenth century. Charles Eliot Norton put it well in a condolence note to Rick. "Few men have done better service than he," he wrote, "service beneficent not only to his own generation, but to generation after generation in the long future."[6]

Olmsted was a sentinel warning of a future deprived of the scenic, and he elevated preservation to priority status by inspiring efforts to conserve Yosemite, Niagara Falls, and other unspoiled and dramatic natural scenes. Ralph Waldo Emerson sensed the transcendence of the American landscape, but Olmsted offered a means of making it a part of the city dweller's daily life. He was a democratic designer of places that belonged to everyone, seeking to employ the "profuse careless utterance of Nature" across a full spectrum of parks and preserves.[7] Many decades after his death, Olmsted's writings gained new readers and currency in the late twentieth century. As an environmental planner, a label he would not have known but would likely have embraced, he became godfather to an ecological consciousness that came well after he died.

Olmsted was a pragmatic utopian; as one contemporary put it more simply, he was "long-headed."[8] Together with Richardson, he pioneered the planting of buildings on their sites in ways that are aptly termed Olmstedian. To look at the spreading roofs on Richardson's train stations and the way they were settled into the landscape by Olmsted is to glimpse the future. To consider the Gate Lodge, Ames Memorial Hall, or Stonehurst is to ponder where the ground ends and structure begins, to wonder where precisely the building becomes the landscape.

Whatever their era, the best buildings and constructed landscapes exist not merely in the moment; rather, they defy time. How else to explain, a century after its completion, how Trinity Church compelled I. M. Pei to clad his John Hancock Building in mirrored glass, the better to reflect the neighboring church? How else to account for the survival of Central Park, largely unchanged and cherished for all the virtues Olmsted designed into it sixteen decades ago?

Richardson imposed his personality on his buildings, creating an architectural manner that was original and individualistic. Olmsted left an imprint on the American landscape more expansive than anyone before or since. These two unlike men—the pragmatist Olmsted, a manager, futurist, park man, and environmentalist, and the artist Richardson, right-brained, frequently impractical, and instinctive—became great friends. Together they improved the world in which their fellow citizens, then and since, live, work, learn, and play. Their shared understanding of the unfolding panorama of American life in their time informs ours.

ACKNOWLEDGMENTS

This book began with the desire to right an injustice. Henry Hobson Richardson has been pincered by a historic irony. Little known to most people, he is esteemed by many architectural historians as America's most important architect. He dominated his era, inspired the next generation of designers, and exerted an influence on American building rivaled only by that of Frank Lloyd Wright (who quietly revered him) and Thomas Jefferson. Having written about both Wright and Jefferson, my desire was to help bring Richardson back into the mainstream conversation.

I said as much to my valued friend and editor George Gibson. After a respectful silence, George inquired, "If so few know him, who will buy your book?" The question initiated a process, and with George's good guidance, *Architects of an American Landscape* has emerged over the course of the ensuing six years. Frederick Law Olmsted came aboard as a co-protagonist, enlarging the book's subject, focusing as this volume does on the lives of both men, their creative friendship, and the radical transformation of American cities, landscape, culture, and life in the late nineteenth century. My particular appreciation, then, to George, for consistently challenging me to write a more ambitious book.

My indebtedness extends to many others, first among them Gail Hochman, agent and friend of more than forty years' duration, who also played a role in the evolution of my small notion. To research Richardson is to encounter James O'Gorman, whose ongoing Richardson scholarship has enriched the literature for a half century and whose direct counsel has informed my thinking. If Jim is the admiral, others who captained ships in the Richardson flotilla include Kenneth Breisch on libraries; Margaret Henderson Floyd and Ann Clifford at Stonehurst; Marc Friedlaender at the Hay-Adams houses; Larry Homolka at North Easton; Frank Kowsky in Buffalo; Mark Wright on the Reverend Browne House; and Jeffrey Karl Ochsner for that foundation stone, the catalogue raisonné *H. H. Richardson: Complete Architectural Works* (1982). This is hardly a complete list, given how many fine scholars have invested their time in Richardson, but all of those I consulted are cited in the notes and bibliography. To them I extend my thanks.

In the land of Olmsted, the tour guides are many. Laura Wood Roper's *FLO: A Biography of Frederick Law Olmsted* (1973) remains the bible, not least because of the extensive cooperation she received in its preparation from Rick Olmsted. Rick and coeditor Theodora Kimball also made a signal contribution with their two-volume *Forty Years of Landscape Architecture* (1922, 1928). Justin Martin's *Genius of Place* (2011) is sound and highly readable. Other writers and scholars—among them Ethan Carr, Charles Beveridge, David Schuyler, and Cynthia Zaitzevsky—have cast invaluable light on Mr. Olmsted's life and works.

Writing this book has meant much travel. My policy as a writer about places is, if possible, to visit the sites I wish to describe. My quest has taken me to Boston and more than a dozen of its suburbs. To Manhattan and Brooklyn and Albany. To Hartford and New London, Washington, D.C., New Orleans, Saint Louis, Buffalo, Chicago, and Asheville, North Carolina. To Leland Stanford Junior University and Yosemite National Park.

Those journeys have benefited from the goodwill of people like Joe, who greeted me at the Marriott Residence Inn in Hartford, Connecticut, and upgraded me to a fifth-floor room behind the Richardsonian arches overlooking Main Street in what was known to its designer as the Cheney Building. William B. Ames opened multiple doors to me in North Easton; his brother Frederick L. Ames taught me much about Ames Memorial Hall; and Oliver Ames Jr. invested a Saturday morning in March to showing me the remarkable Gate Lodge.

John I Mesick gave me access to his architectural library and an extraordinary tour of the Albany capitol, which he knows as perhaps no one else. I extend large thanks to Ann Clifford at Stonehurst for her help and scholarship; to Father Jack Butler, Laura Romeo, and especially Fran McMillen, who gave me the tour of Bryant House, in Cohasset, Massachusetts, a property owned by Boston College; to Michele Clark at the Frederick Law Olmsted Historic Site in Brookline, Massachusetts; and William Tyre, director of the Glessner House in Chicago. Bradley Sumrail gave me a look at the Richardsonian wing of the Ogden Museum of Southern Art, New Orleans; Susan Hall did the honors at Project Adventure, which owns many acres of the onetime Phillips Estate in Beverly, Massachusetts. I got a thorough tour of the Malden Public Library courtesy of Dora St. Martin, John Tramondozzi, and Caron Guigli. One of my favorite stops was at Stoughton House, Cambridge, Massachusetts, now the home of the gracious Susan W. Paine.

My research has been aided by many librarians and archivists. In institutional order, I must thank Catharina Slautterback and Carolle Morini, Boston Athenaeum; Christopher Glass, Boston Public Library; Timothy J. DeWerff, Century Association; Karen Bucky, Clark Art Institute; Lana Newman at Avery Library, Columbia University; and Sue Mehrer, Dennis Brown, Lili Hanft, Loey Crooks, Eileen Potts, Laura Graveline, Emily Wiedrick, and Lucinda Hall at Dartmouth's Baker-Berry Library, my library of first resort, and the conjoined Sherman Art Library. Thanks, too, to Morgan Swan and Jay Satterfield at Rauner Special Collections, Dartmouth College. Access to the numerous holdings of Richardsoniana and Olmsted papers at Harvard University was provided by Jessica Evans Brady and Nanni Deng, Fine Arts Library; the ever-patient Susan Halpert and Emily Walhout at Houghton Library; Mark Johnson at the Harvard Film Archive; and Ines Zalduendo and Ardys Kozbial, Loeb Special Collections. Though officially retired, Hope Mayo remains an expert presence when it comes to the Richardson drawing collection. I thank, as well, Lorna Condon, at Historic New England. My valued colleague Kathy Woodrell opened doors at the Library of Congress, directing me to Barbara Bair and Jeffrey Flannery. At the Massachusetts Historical Society, Daniel Hinchen and Anna

Clutterbuck-Cook were most helpful, as was Richard Potter at the Royal Academy Library, London.

My appreciation to Rob Roche, archivist at Shepley, Bulfinch, Richardson and Abbott, as well as Gerrit Zwart, long of Shepley Bulfinch, for their guidance and deep institutional knowledge of the successor firms to H. H. Richardson's practice. My thanks to Nicole Casper at Stonehill College Archives; to Sandra E. Marxon, archivist at Trinity Church, Boston; Dorothy Meaney and Harriet Chenkin, Tisch Library, Tufts University; Jeffrey Marshall and Prudence Doherty, Silver Special Collections Library and Billings Library, University of Vermont; and, finally, at Williams College, to Christine Menard and Alison O'Grady, as well as the now retired Rebecca Ohm and emeritus director David Pilachowski.

At Grove Atlantic, my thanks to Emily Burns, whose editorial instincts, interlinear jottings, and attendance to a multitude of details made this a much better book. My appreciation as well to copyeditor Amy Hughes, proofreader Maureen Klier, and managing editor Julia Berner-Tobin for their close attentions and for identifying many a misstep and omission, and Gretchen Mergenthaler for her imagining a way to combine too many elements into an elegant jacket design.

Lastly, there are the kith and kin. They are too many to enumerate here, but the short list must include such varied folks as the late Don Carpentier and Ann Dobie Howard, Fiske Kimball, Bruce Boucher, Roger Straus, Jerry Grant, and a host of others who, in ways small and large, opened my eyes to how buildings and artifacts speak to us of our past.

NOTES

PROLOGUE

1 Bowles, *Our New West* (1869), p. 68.

2 FLO to Mariana Griswold Van Rensselaer, February 6, 1887.

3 Adams, *The Education of Henry Adams* (1918), p. 5.

4 Henry David Thoreau, *Walden* (Boston: Ticknor and Fields, 1854).

5 Olmsted, "The Yosemite Valley and the Mariposa Big Trees: A Preliminary Report" (1865).

6 Charles Nordhoff, "California." *Harper's New Monthly Magazine* 44, no. 264 (May 1872), p. 877.

7 FLO to Mariana Griswold Van Rensselaer, February 6, 1887.

8 "The Ten Best Buildings in the United States," *American Architect and Building News,* June 13, 1885. The Richardson works cited, in addition to Trinity Church, were Sever Hall at Harvard, the New York State Capitol, Albany (NY) City Hall, and the North Easton Town Hall.

9 "Some Incidents in the Life of H. H. Richardson" (1886), p. 199.

10 Cram, *My Life in Architecture* (1936), p. 31.

11 *Scientific American*, October 21, 1882, p. 259. In 1936, Henry-Russell Hitchcock claimed that Richardson visited Sherman, in 1879, in the company of Frederick Ames and Saint-Gaudens but cited no source. More recently, Ethan Carr spotted a passing reference, by Frederick Ames, to a trip in the Ames railroad car, in September 1883, that may have provided Richardson a chance to see his design as executed. See Hitchcock, *The Architecture of H. H. Richardson and His Times* (1936), p. 204; and Carr, "Eastern Design in a Western Landscape" (2015). See also Susan Danly, "Andrew Joseph Russell's *The Great West Illustrated*," in Danly and Marx, *The Railroad in American Art* (1988), pp. 93–112.

12 Carr, "Eastern Design in a Western Landscape" (2015); FLO to Frederick Lathorp Ames, January 29, 1887.

13 FLO to Mariana Griswold Van Rensselaer, February 6, 1887.

14 Van Rensselaer, *Henry Hobson Richardson and His Works* [hereafter *HHR and His Works*] (1888), p. 72.

15 FLO to Mariana Griswold Van Rensselaer, February 6, 1887.

CHAPTER 1

1 *Savannah Republican*, February 22, 1853.

2 FLO to Samuel Cabot Jr., August 18, 1857.

3 George William Curtis to FLO, August 8, 1857.

4 FLO to Edward Everett Hale, January 10, 1857.

5 John Olmsted to FLO, November 28, 1857.

6 FLO to Mrs. William Dwight Whitney, December 16, 1890.

7 FLO, "Passages in the Life of an Unpractical Man," in Olmsted and Kimball, *Forty Years of Landscape Architecture*, vol. 1 (1922), p. 46.

8 Olmsted, "Autobiographical Passages," in Olmsted and Kimball, *Forty Years of Landscape Architecture*, vol. 1 (1922), p. 46.

9 John Olmsted, quoted in Olmsted and Kimball, *Forty Years of Landscape Architecture*, vol. 1 (1922), p. 4.

10 FLO to Mrs. William Dwight Whitney, December 16, 1890.

11 Van Rensselaer, "Frederick Law Olmsted" (1893), p. 860.

12 Olmsted, "Autobiographical Passages," in Olmsted and Kimball, *Forty Years of Landscape Architecture*, vol. 1 (1922), p. 61.

13 Downing, *Cottage Residences* (1842), pp. ii, 22.

14 FLO to Charles Loring Brace, July 30, 1846.

15 FLO, "Autobiographical Passages," in Olmsted and Kimball, *Forty Years of Landscape Architecture*, vol. 1 (1922), p. 61–62.

16 William Bradford, *Of Plymouth Plantation, 1620–1647* New York: Knopf (1952), p. 62.

17 See Alan Stewart, "The Fight for Central Park," in Bruce Kelly et al., *Art of the Olmsted Landscape* (1981), p. 87.

18 William Cullen Bryant, "A Forest Hymn" (1825); and Bryant, quoted in Olmsted and Kimball, *Forty Years of Landscape Architecture*, vol. 2 (1928), p. 23.

19 Olmsted and Kimball, *Forty Years of Landscape Architecture*, vol. 2 (1928), p. 35.

20 FLO, *Walks and Talks of an American Farmer in England*, vol. 1 (1852), p. 79.

21 Ibid., p. 133.

22 Olmsted and Kimball, *Forty Years of Landscape Architecture*, vol. 2 (1928), p. 35.

23 FLO to John Hull Olmsted, September 11, 1857.

24 FLO to the president of the Commissioners of the Central Park, August 12, 1857.

25 Asa Gray to the commissioners, August 24, 1857, quoted in Olmsted, *The Papers of Frederick Law Olmsted* [hereafter *FLO Papers*], vol. 2 (1981), p. 78, n1.

26 FLO, "Autobiographical Passages," in Olmsted and Kimball, *Forty Years of Landscape Architecture*, vol. 1 (1922), p. 63.

CHAPTER 2

1 G[eorge]. Blackman to Jefferson Davis, May 9, 1854; Coolidge, "H. H. Richardson's Youth: Some Unpublished Documents" (1982), p. 166.

2 Van Rensselaer, *HHR and His Works* (1888), p. 4. Richardson's first biographer, Mariana Griswold Van Rensselaer, stated with apparent certainty—her primary sources being Richardson's friends and family—that the halt in Richardson's speech was the reason for his rejection at West Point. No confirming documentation survives.

3 Van Rensselaer, *HHR and His Works* (1888), p. 4.

4 William Priestley Richardson, quoted in Van Rensselaer, *HHR and His Works* (1888), p. 4.

5 Benjamin Henry Latrobe, quoted in Floyd, *Henry Hobson Richardson* (1997), p. 16.

6 Van Rensselaer, *HHR and His Works* (1888), p. 5.

7 Brooks, "Henry Hobson Richardson" (1886), p. 2.

8 Coolidge, "H. H. Richardson's Youth: Some Unpublished Documents" (1982), p. 167.

9 Crowninshield, *A Private Journal: 1856–1858* (1941), pp. 8, 13, 59, 77, passim.

10 John D. Bein to James Walker, May 5, 1857; reprinted in Coolidge, "H. H. Richardson's Youth: Some Unpublished Documents" (1982), pp. 168–69.

11 Charles Francis Adams Jr., "Commencement Address" (1886).

12 Quoted in O'Gorman, *Living Architecture* (1997), p. 24.

13 Adams, *The Education of Henry Adams* (1918), p. 55.

14 Ibid., pp. 64–65.

15 James Rumrill, quoted in O'Gorman, *Living Architecture* (1997), p. 51.

16 Van Rensselaer, *HHR and His Works* (1888), p. 5.

17 John D. Bein to HHR, February 5, 1859; reprinted in Coolidge, "H. H. Richardson's Youth: Some Unpublished Documents" (1982), p. 169. Spelling as in original.

CHAPTER 3

1 Here and after, Olmsted and Kimball, *Forty Years of Landscape Architecture*, vol. 2 (1928), pp. 38–40.

2 FLO to Asa Gray, October 8, 1857.

3 Stevenson, *Park Maker* (1977), p. 158.

4   Calvert Vaux to Clarence Cook, June 6, 1865; quoted in Kowsky, *Country, Park, and City* (1998), p. 120.

5   Frederick Kingsbury, quoted in Olmsted and Kimball, *Forty Years of Landscape Architecture*, vol. 1 (1922), pp. 85–86.

6   "Historical Notes," *Transactions of the American Society of Landscape Architects* (Harrisburg, PA: J. Horace McFarland Company, 1899–1908), p. 81.

7   FLO, "Public Parks and the Enlargement of Towns" (1870), reprinted in *FLO Papers*, supplementary series, vol. 1, pp. 192–93.

8   "The Conception of the Winning Plan Explained by Its Authors," in Olmsted and Kimball, *Forty Years of Landscape Architecture*, vol. 2 (1928), pp. 45–46.

9   See Heckscher, "Creating Central Park" (2008), for a thoughtful and well-illustrated discussion of the competing plans, pp. 21ff.

10 FLO to John Olmsted, January 14, 1858.

11 FLO, "Description of the Central Park" (1859), in *FLO Papers*, vol. 3 (1983), p. 213.

12 FLO to Charles Loring Brace, December 1, 1853.

13 Rosenzweig and Blackmar, *The Park and the People* (1992), p. 166.

14 See Francis R. Kowsky's biography of Vaux, *Country, Park, and City* (1998), pp. 104ff, for a thoughtful and detailed summary history of Vaux's Central Park bridges.

15 *New York Times*, June 7 and 10, 1858.

16 John Hull Olmsted to FLO, November 13, 1857.

17 Frederick John Kingsbury to John Hull Olmsted, February 16, 1847.

18 FLO to Parke Godwin, August 1, 1858.

19 John Hull Olmsted to FLO, November 13, 1857.

20 John Olmsted to John Hull Olmsted, February 3, 1846; FLO to Charles Loring Brace, February 5, 1846.

21 FLO, "Instructions for the Keepers," March 12, 1859.

22 FLO to John Olmsted, September 23, 1859.

23 FLO to John Olmsted, June 14, 1860.

24 FLO to John Olmsted, July 22, 1860; FLO, *Preliminary Report in Regard to a Plan of Public Pleasure Grounds for the City of San Francisco*, March 31, 1866 New York: W. C. Bryant, 1866).

25 The several versions of this story differ in some particulars, recollected as they were years later. See FLO to Mrs. William Dwight Whitney, December 1, 1890; Roper, *FLO: A Biography of Frederick Law Olmsted* [hereafter, *FLO*] (1973), p. 150, an account based in part on interviews with FLO Jr.; and Mary Perkins Olmsted's late-in-life recollections, rendered on July 16, 1920.

26 FLO to Mrs. William Dwight Whitney, December 1, 1890.

27 Ibid.

28 He likely refers to a toilet "seat." FLO to John Olmsted, October 1, 1860.

29 FLO to John Olmsted, March 22, 1861.

30 FLO to John Bigelow, February 9, 1861.

31 FLO draft of presentation to commissioners for meeting of January 22, 1861.

32 FLO to Calvert Vaux, March 25, 1864.

33 FLO to Charles Loring Brace, December 8, 1860.

34 Alfred Field to Lottie Field, May 14, 1861; quoted in Roper, *FLO* (1973), p. 158.

35 Henry Bellows to FLO, June 1861.

36 FLO to Philip Bissinger, July 15, 1873.

CHAPTER 4

1 Joseph [Josiah] Bradlee, quoted in Van Rensselaer, *HHR and His Works* (1888), pp. 6–7.

2 The summary here of instruction at the Ecole des Beaux-Arts is drawn largely from Richard Chafee's "Richardson's Record at the Ecole des Beaux-Arts" (1977), and his "The Teaching of Architecture at the Ecole des Beaux-Arts" (1977).

3 Joseph [Josiah] Bradlee, quoted in Van Rensselaer, *HHR and His Works* (1888), pp. 6–7.

4 Henry Adams to Charles Francis Adams Jr., October 5, 1861.

5 HHR to Julia Hayden, April 25, 1862.

6 HHR to Julia Hayden, April 17, 1862.

7 Ibid.

8 HHR to Julia Hayden, May 16, 1862.

9 HHR to Julia Hayden, May 29, 1862.

10 Joseph [Josiah] Bradlee, quoted in Van Rensselaer, *HHR and His Works* (1888), p. 7.

11 HHR to Julia Hayden, May 29, 1862.

12 HHR to Julia Hayden, May 23, 1862.

13 HHR to Julia Hayden, August 29, 1862.

14 Chafee, "Richardson's Record at the Ecole des Beaux-Arts" (1977), p. 184, n.33.

15 Quoted in O'Gorman, *Living Architecture* (1997), p. 65

16 Adams, *The Education of Henry Adams* (1918), pp. 213–14.

17 Henry Adams to Elizabeth Cameron, June 4, 1891.

18 Emmanuel Pontremoli, quoted in Chaffee, "The Teaching of Architecture at the Ecole des Beaux-Arts" (1977), p. 94.

19 Clark, "H. H. Richardson" (1888), p. 151.

20 In tables appended to Chafee, "Richardson's Record at the Ecole des Beaux-Arts" (1977), the author recounts in detail Richardson's *concours* successes and failures.

21 Phené Spiers, quoted in Van Rensselaer, *HHR and His Works* (1888), p. 9.

22 Gustave-Adolphe Gerhardt, quoted in Van Rensselaer, *HHR and His Works* (1888), p. 9.

23 William Priestley Richardson to HHR, July 5, 1865, in Coolidge, "H. H. Richardson's Youth: Some Unpublished Documents" (1982), p. 171.

CHAPTER 5

1 Strong, *The Diary of George Templeton Strong* (1952), vol. 3, p. 276.

2 FLO to John Murray Forbes, December 5, 1861.

3 FLO to John Charles Olmsted, October 17, 1861.

4 Strong, *The Diary of George Templeton Strong* (1952), vol. 3, p. 221.

5 Cornelius Rea Agnew's description, according to ibid., vol. 3, p. 291.

6 Henry Whitney Bellows to FLO, August 13, 1863.

7 FLO to Mary Olmsted, August 12, 1863.

8 FLO to Mary Olmsted, September 25, 1863.

9 The story of the battalion's arrival in the Yosemite Valley was reported variously in the years after. The most detailed version appears in Lafayette Bunnell's *Discovery of the Yosemite and the Indian War Which Led to That Event* (1880). Bunnell himself offered at least one variation ("How the Yo-Semite Valley Was Discovered and Named," in *Hutchings' California Magazine*, 1859), as did the anonymous "M," in "Savage's Entry into Yosemite Valley: A Letter from 'M,' Published April 23, 1851," reprinted in Russell, *One Hundred Years in Yosemite* (1992).

10 Bunnell, "How the Yo-Semite Valley Was Discovered and Named" (1859), p. 500.

11 "Savage's Entry into Yosemite Valley: A Letter from 'M,' Published April 23, 1851," reprinted in Russell, *One Hundred Years in Yosemite* (1992), p. 203.

12 Bunnell, *Discovery of the Yosemite* (1880), p. 54.

13 Huntley, *The Making of Yosemite* (2011), p. 76.

14 Quoted in Huth, "Yosemite: The Story of an Idea" (1948).

15 FLO to Mary Olmsted, November 20, 1863.

16 FLO to Mary Olmsted, October 15, 1863.

17 FLO to Mary Olmsted, November 20, 1863.

18 FLO to John Olmsted, March 11, 1864.

19 FLO to Edwin Lawrence Godkin, July 24, 1864.

20 Mary Olmsted to Calvert Vaux, [August] 1864. John Charles Olmsted Papers, Harvard University.

21 John Charles Olmsted, [*Mariposa*] *Journal of John C. Olmsted* [hereafter Olmsted, *Mariposa Journal*] (1864–65), p. 8.

22 "Harriet Errington's Letters and Journal from California," July 16, 1864, John Charles Olmsted Papers, Harvard University.

23 FLO to unknown correspondent (letter fragment), July 20, 1864.

24 FLO to Henry Whitney Bellows, August 8, 1864.

25 FLO to John Olmsted, June 25, 1864.

26 Greeley, *An Overland Visit from New York to San Francisco in the Summer of 1859* (1860), chap. 28.

27 Watkins, *In Focus: Carleton Watkins* (1997), p. 138.

28 Grenbeaux. "Before Yosemite Art Gallery: Watkins' Early Career" (1978), p. 225.

29 Oliver Wendell Holmes, "Doings of the Sunbeam," in *Atlantic Monthly* 12 (July 1863), p. 8.

30 *New-York Times*, October 20, 1862.

31 Runte, *Yosemite: The Embattled Wilderness* (1990), p. 38.

32 Olmsted, *Mariposa Journal* (1864–65), p. 11. Despite John Charles's youth, his journal is lucid, carefully observed, and remarkably readable.

33 FLO to John Olmsted, August 17, 1864.

34 Huth, "Yosemite: The Story of an Idea" (1948).

35 An Act Authorizing a Grant to the State of California of "the Yo-semite Valley," and the land Embracing "the Mariposa Big Tree Grove," approved June 30, 1864 (13 Stat. 325).

36 Olmsted, *Mariposa Journal* (1864–65), p. 9.

37 FLO to John Olmsted, July 5, 1865.

38 Bowles, *Across the Continent* (1866), p. 231.

39 Richardson, *Beyond the Mississippi* (1867), pp. 422–25.

40 Here and after, see Olmsted, "Preliminary Report upon the Yosemite and Big Tree Grove" (1865).

41 Henry Whitney Bellows to James Miller McKim, August 18, 1865. Bellows Papers, Massachusetts Historical Society.

42 FLO to Carleton Watkins, August 9, 1865.

43 Martin, *The Life and Public Services of Schuyler Colfax* (1868), p. 222.

44 Bowles, *Across the Continent* (1866), p. 233.

45 Richardson, *Beyond the Mississippi* (1867), pp. 420, 426, 429, 435. See chap. 35, pp. 420ff., at the University of Michigan's Making of America digital books collection, https://quod.lib.umich.edu/m/moa/aja5162.0001.001/454?page =root;size=100;view=image;q1=olmsted.

46 FLO to John Olmsted, August 17, 1864.

47 Miss Errington's letters home to England provided a number of the details concerning the Olmsteds' stay in Yosemite. "Harriet Errington's Letters and Journal from California," John Charles Olmsted Papers, Harvard University.

48 FLO to John Olmsted, September 14, 1864.

49 FLO to Calvert Vaux, June 8, 1865.

CHAPTER 6

1   FLO to William Butler Duncan, September 22, 1870.

2   Van Rensselaer, *HHR and His Works* (1888), p. 17; HHR to Billy [William Richardson], April 25, 1866.

3   Here and after, the details of Richardson's boardinghouse life are drawn from "Some Incidents in the Life of H. H. Richardson" (1886), pp. 198–99.

4   HHR to Billy [William Richardson], April 25, 1866.

5   Calvin Vaux to FLO, January 9, 1865.

6   *Brooklyn Eagle*, February 6, 1874.

7   Calvert Vaux to FLO, January 9, 1865.

8   Ibid.

9   Ibid.

10 FLO to Calvert Vaux, March 12, 1865.

11 Calvert Vaux to FLO, May 10, 1865.

12 FLO to Mariana Griswold Van Rensselaer, May 22, 1893.

13 "Century Association Constitution," in Century Association, *The Century 1847–1946* (1947), p. 5.

14 Ibid.

15 "Some Incidents in the Life of H. H. Richardson" (1886), pp. 198–99.

16 Wight, "H. H. Richardson" (1886), p. 59.

17 Ibid.

18 Van Rensselaer, *HHR and His Works* (1888), p. 18.

19 "Some Incidents in the Life of H. H. Richardson" (1886), p. 199.

20 Van Rensselaer, *HHR and His Works* (1888), p. 18.

21 Calvin Vaux to James Stranahan, January 10, 1865.

22 FLO, *Preservation of Natural Scenery* (1890). Reprinted in *FLO Papers*, supplementary series, vol. 1 (1997), pp. 535–75.

23 Olmsted, Vaux & Co, "Preliminary Report to the Commissioners for Laying Out a Park in Brooklyn, New York: Being a Consideration of Circumstances of Site and Other Conditions Affecting the Design of Public Pleasure Grounds" (1866). Emphasis found in the original. Reprinted in *FLO Papers*, supplementary series, vol. 1 (1997), pp. 81, 83.

24 *Æsopus, The Fables of Æsop, and Others, With Designs on Wood, by Thomas Bewick* (1818), cited in *PFO,* supplementary series, vol. 1, pp. 107–8.

25 Olmsted, Vaux & Co, "Preliminary Report" (1866), in *FLO Papers,* supplementary series, vol. 1 (1997), pp. 86–87.

26 Ibid., p. 101.

27 Ibid., p. 91.

28 Ibid., p. 88.

29 Mrs. John Cole Hayden to Julia Richardson, January 13, 1867.

30 The roof type got its name from Jules Hardouin Mansart, who built many elaborate Baroque buildings during the reign of Louis XIV of France.

31 O'Gorman, "Documentation: An 1886 Inventory of H. H. Richardson's Library, and Other Gleanings from Probate" (1982), p. 153; Hitchcock, *The Architecture of H. H. Richardson and His Times* (1936), p. 72.

32 Julia Richardson to Mrs. John C. Hayden, March [15?] 1867.

33 Crowninshield, *A Private Journal: 1856–1858* (1941), pp. 114, 124, passim.

34 Charles H. Learoyd to HHR, March 21, 1867, quoted in Guiffre, *A Documentation of Grace Episcopal Church* (1975), p. 70.

35 P. C. Brooks to Charles L. Hutchins, quoted in Guiffre, "A Documentation of Grace Episcopal Church" (1975), pp. 120–21; Van Rensselaer, *HHR and His Works* (1888), p. 50.

36 Longfellow, "Gaspar Becerra" (1850), ll. 27–28.

37 Mrs. John C. Hayden to Julia Richardson, April 30, 1867.

38 Van Rensselaer, *HHR and His Works* (1888), p. 19.

CHAPTER 7

1 William Dorsheimer to FLO, August 12, 1868.

2 "Local Department: The New Park," *Courier & Republic* (Buffalo), November 26, 1869.

3 Anthony Trollope, *North America,* vol. 1 (Philadelphia, PA: J. B. Lippincott and Co., 1863), p. 180.

4 "S. S. Jewett Dead," *Commercial Advertiser* (Buffalo), March 1, 1897.

5 "Local Department: The New Park," *Courier & Republic* (Buffalo), November 26, 1869.

6 See Chafee, "Richardson's Record at the Ecole des Beaux-Arts" (1977), p. 187.

7 The story of the Codman residence and Codman's words here and after are found in from Codman, *Reminiscences of Richard Codman* (1923), pp. 29–31.

8 See Scully, *The Shingle Style and the Stick Style* (1955), for a detailed analysis of Richardson's Codman design.

9 FLO to Mary Olmsted, August 25, 1868.

10 Ibid.

11 Here and after, from "The Buffalo Park Project," *Courier & Republic* (Buffalo), August 26, 1868.

12 FLO to Mary Olmsted, August 26, 1868.

13 Ibid.

14 "Alexander Dallas Bache," in *FLO Papers,* vol 4. (1986), pp. 81–82.

15 HHR to FLO, October 12, 1868.

16 C. P. Patterson to FLO, July 13, 1868.

17 Dorsheimer, "Address at the Brooklyn Academy of Music," November 28, 1880; quoted in Kowsky, "The William Dorsheimer House" (1980), p. 141.

18 HHR, Henry Hobson Richardson Sketchbook, 1869–[1875]; transcription in O'Gorman, *Selected Drawings* (1974), appendix 44, p. 211.

19 Christ Church, Minutes of the Vestry, July 12, 1869; cited in Kowsky, *Buffalo Projects* (1980), p. 8.

20 Edward Jarvis, quoted in Grob, *Mental Institutions in America* (1973), p. 117.

21 Yanni, *The Architecture of Madness* (2007), p. 38.

22 See Grob, *Mental Institutions in America* (1973), pp. 98ff.

23 "State Provision for the Insane," *American Journal of Insanity* 29 (July 1872), p. 3.

24 HHR to Julia Hayden, July 18, 1862.

25 FLO to Henry Bromfield Roberts, December 13, 1872.

26 Julia Hayden to Mrs. John C. Hayden, December 12, 1869.

27 FLO to Henry Bromfield Rogers, December 18, 1872.

28 HHR, Henry Hobson Richardson Sketchbook, 1869–[1875]; transcription in O'Gorman, *Selected Drawings* (1974), appendix 44, p. 212.

29 Coolidge, John, "The Architectural Importance of H. H. Richardson's Buffalo State Hospital," in Schneekloth et al., *Changing Places: Remaking Institutional Buildings* (1992), p. 97.

30 FLO to J. P. White, March 9, 1877 [draft].

31 Stevenson, *Park Maker* (1977), p. 301.

32 "Preliminary Suggestions for the Grounds of the Buffalo State Hospital for the Insane," July 7, 1871, in *FLO Papers*, vol. 6 (1997), p. 452.

33 FLO to J. P. White, March 9, 1877 [draft]. Emphasis added.

34 Hitchcock, *The Architecture of H. H. Richardson and His Times* (1936), p. 119.

35 Priestley, *Familiar Introduction to the Theory and Practice of Perspective* (London, 1770).

36 HHR quoted in Van Rensselaer, *HHR and His Works* (1888), p. 57.

37 HHR, Sketchbook, 1869–[1875], transcription in O'Gorman, *Selected Drawings* (1974), appendix 44, p. 211.

CHAPTER 8

1 McKinsey, *Niagara Falls* (1985), pp. 7–8.

2 Quoted in ibid., p. 55.

3 Isabella Lucy Bird, quoted in McGreevy, *Imagining Niagara* (1994), p. 85.

4 Thomas Cole quoted in Nash, *Wilderness and the American Mind* (1967), p. 78.

5 French, *Art and Artists in Connecticut* (1879), p. 129.

6 Howat, *Frederic Church* (2005), p. 11.

7 The critic, William James Stillman, was a somewhat disgruntled former student of Church's; see Stillman, *Autobiography of a Journalist* (Boston, MA: Houghton, Mifflin, 1901), vol. 1, pp. 114–15.

8 Amelia Sturges, July 17, 1856, quoted in Howat, *Frederic Church* (2005), p. 69.

9 [John Durand], "Domestic Art Gossip," *Crayon* 4, no. 2 (February 1857), p. 54.

10 M[ary]. E[lizabeth]. W[ilson]. Sherwood, "Studio Gathers Thirty Years Ago—New York's Former Bohemia," *New York Times*, April 21, 1900.

11 French, *Art and Artists in Connecticut* (1879), p. 129.

12 Reprinted in Dow, *Anthology and Bibliography of Niagara Falls* (1921), vol. 2, p. 907.

13 Adam Badeau, "The Vagabond" (1859), quoted in Huntington, "Church's Niagara" (1983), p. 101.

14 M[ary]. E[lizabeth]. W[ilson]. Sherwood, "Studio Gathers Thirty Years Ago—New York's Former Bohemia," *New York Times*, April 21, 1900. The painting was Turner's *The Slave Ship*.

15 Ibid.

16 "Notes by Mr. Olmsted," in *Special Report of New York State Survey* (1880), p. 27.

17 "Editor's Easy Chair," *Harper's New Monthly Magazine* 71, no. 425 (October 1885), p. 802.

18 Henry James, *Portraits of Places* (Boston, MA: J. R. Osgood, 1884), p. 372. His Niagara notes originally appeared in 1871 in the *Nation*.

19 Olmsted and Vaux, "General Plan for Improvement of the Niagara Reservation" (1887), in *FLO Papers*, supplementary series, vol. 1 (1997), pp. 535–75.

20 Van Rensselaer, *HHR and His Works* (1888), p. 27.

21 FLO to William Butler Duncan, September 22, 1870.

22 HHR to FLO, December 6, 1874.

23 FLO to A. J. Bloor, August 4, 1882. See also Kowsky, *Country, Park, and City* (1998), pp. 226–27.

24 Here and after, the account of the wedding journey is drawn from a letter Olmsted wrote to Mrs. Van Rensselaer. See Van Rensselaer, *HHR and His Works* (1888), p. 27.

CHAPTER 9

1 James McKim had invested $1,000 some years before in the founding of the *Nation* magazine.

2 Wickersham and Milford, "Richardson's Death, Ames's Money, and the Birth of the Modern Architectural Firm" (2014), p. 115.

3 Baldwin, *Stanford White* (1931), p. 45. Although his biography of White has evident imperfections (for example, the author places Richardson's office in Boston years before he relocated it there), Charles Baldwin, a New Yorker and a contemporary of White's, collected valuable anecdotes from many who had known Richardson.

4 Van Rensselaer, *HHR and His Works* (1888), p. 20.

5 Sullivan, *Autobiography of an Idea* (1924), p. 187.

6 Ibid., p. 188.

7 Here and after, Trinity Church Building Committee to HHR, March 12, 1872.

8 Probably Herbert Langford Warren, in the anonymous "Mourned by Lovers of Art" (1886).

9 Allen, *Life and Letters of Phillips Brooks,* vol. 1 (1900), p. 115.

10 Paine and Pope, *Paine Ancestry* (1912), p. 282.

11 Ibid., p. 281; and "Trinity Church: Report of Committee," January 12, 1871.

12 Phillips Brooks, Diary, 1872, Phillips Brooks Papers, Houghton Library, Harvard University.

13 Quoted in O'Gorman, *The Makers of Trinity Church* (2004), p. 26.

14 In Adams, "The Birth of a Style" (1980), p. 409, n1; see also "H. H. Richardson's Men" (n.d.), p. 3.

15 Paine and Pope, *Paine Ancestry* (1912), p. 281.

16 Sullivan, *Autobiography of an Idea* (1924), p. 181.

17 Paine, "Report on the Activities of the Trinity Church Building Committee, 1872–1877."

18 Ibid.

19 Richardson, "A Description of the Church," in *Consecration Services* (1877), p. 56.

20 Stebbins, "Richardson and Trinity Church: The Evolution of a Building" (1968), p. 285.

21 Paine, "Report," 1877.

22 Much of the Norcross biographical material is drawn from Girr, "Mastery in Masonry" (1996), and O'Gorman, "O. W. Norcross, Richardson's 'Master Builder'" (1973).

23 The predecessor of Dun and Bradstreet, R. G. Dun & Co., quoted in Wermiel, "Norcross, Fuller, and the Rise of the General Contractor in the United States in the Nineteenth Century" (2006), p. 3301.

24 Edith Norcross Morgan (O. W.'s daughter), quoted in O'Gorman, "O. W. Norcross, Richardson's 'Master Builder'" (1973), p. 106.

25 Stebbins, "Richardson and Trinity Church" (1968), p. 290.

26 Phillips Brooks to HHR, April 17, 1874.

27 Van Rensselaer, *HHR and His Works* (1888), p. 64. There is scholarly debate regarding this story. Michael Waters sums up the controversy neatly in his "H. H. Richardson and Photography" (2008), pp. 31ff.

28 Quoted in O'Gorman, *The Makers of Trinity Church* (2004), p. 75.

29 Van Rensselaer, *HHR and His Works* (1888), p. 63.

CHAPTER 10

1 Downing, *A Treatise on the Theory and Practice of Landscape Gardening* (1841), p. 40.

2 Norcross quoted in O'Gorman, *Selected Drawings* (1974), p. 27.

3 Brown, *1860–1930, Memories* (1931), p. 28.

4 Stanford White to Alexina Black Mease White, February 22, 1873.

5 Wight, "H. H. Richardson" (1886), p. 59.

6 See period photos in O'Gorman, *The Makers of Trinity Church* (2004), p. 114.

7 For miscellaneous construction dates, see O'Gorman, *Selected Drawings* (1974), pp. 42ff.

8 Ernest Bowditch, cited in O'Gorman, *The Makers of Trinity Church* (2004), p. 115.

9 A. J. Felter and John Banter, quoted in Susan R. Stein, "The New York State Capitol Controversy and the Rise of Architecture as a Profession," in *Proceedings of the New York State Capitol Symposium* (1983), p. 72.

10 *AABN*, March 11, 1876.

11 Richard Morris Hunt and A. J. Bloor, "Remonstrance of the New York Chapter of the American Institute of Architects, against the proposed changes in the plan for the building of the New Capitol," March 29, 1876, published in *Documents of the Assembly of the State of New York, One Hundredth Session, 1877* (Albany, NY: Jerome B. Parmenter, 1877), vol. 3, no. 28, pp. 3–4.

12 FLO to Charles Eliot Norton, June 7, 1876.

13 HHR to FLO, March 10, 1877.

14 Schuyler, *American Architecture and Other Writings* (1961), vol. 1, p. 177.

15 FLO quoted in Van Rensselaer, *HHR and His Works* (1888), pp. 118–19.

16 Stanford White to Augustus Saint-Gaudens, May 1878.

17 Stevenson, *Park Maker* (1977), p. 308.

18 HHR to FLO August 23, 1876.

19 Story recounted by a Richardson descendent to John I Mesick of Mesick, Cohen, Wilson, Baker.

20 Van Rensselaer, *HHR and His Works* (1888), p. 61.

21 Richardson, "A Description of the Church," in *Consecration Services* (1877), p. 63.

22 Cortissoz, *John La Farge: A Memoir and Study* (1911), p. 152.

23 Adams, "The Mind of John La Farge," in Adams et al., *John La Farge* (1987), p. 13, 17.

24 La Farge talk delivered to a society of young architects in 1892; reprinted in Waern, *John La Farge: Artist and Writer* (1896), p. 33.

25 La Farge talk, in Waern, *John La Farge* (1896), p. 33.

26 Cortissoz, *John La Farge: A Memoir and A Study* (1911), p. 154.

27 Richardson, "A Description of the Church," in *Consecration Services* (1877), p. 65.

28 Building committee minutes, quoted in Weinberg, "John La Farge and the Decoration of Trinity Church, Boston" (1974), p. 328.

29 La Farge to Trinity Church Building Committee, September 15, 1876.

30 Here and after, see Weinberg, "John La Farge and the Decoration of Trinity Church, Boston" (1974), pp. 329ff.

31 Quoted in ibid., p. 331.

32 La Farge, quoted in Weinberg, *The Decorative Work of John La Farge* (1977), p. 80.

33 Robert Treat Paine, Diary, November 2, 1876.

34 "Extracts from the Report of the Building Committee," in *Consecration Services* (1877), p. 75.

35 La Farge quoted in Weinberg, "John La Farge and the Decoration of Trinity Church, Boston" (1974), p. 334.

36 La Farge to Henry Parker, December 19, 1876.

37 HHR to FLO, November 26 and December 15, 1876.

38 Cortissoz, *John La Farge: A Memoir and Study* (1911), p. 32.

39 *Boston Transcript*, February 5, 1877.

40 Several researchers have examined the history of Norcross Brothers, including James O'Gorman (most recently in *The Makers of Trinity Church* [2004], pp. 105–17); Christopher F. Girr ("Mastery in Masonry: Norcross Brothers, Contractors and Builders," 1996); and Sara E. Wermiel ("Norcross, Fuller, and the Rise of the General Contractor in the United States in the Nineteenth Century," 2006). O'Gorman formulated the case for regarding the shared labors of Richardson and Norcross as akin to a partnership.

41 Brown would later become a noted Washington, DC, architect, architectural historian, and president of the AIA. Brown, *1860–1930, Memories* (1931), pp. 24–25.

42 Ernest Bowditch, quoted in O'Gorman, *The Makers of Trinity Church* (2004), p. 112.

43 *Consecration Services* (1877), p. 3.

44 *Boston Traveler*, February 9, 1877.

45 Henry-Russell Hitchcock favored the San Marco comparison (see his *The Architecture of H. H. Richardson and His Times*, 1936); see also Edgar Romig's *The Story of Trinity Church* (1952).

46 Irene Sargent, "Trinity Church, Boston, as a Monument of American Art," *Craftsman* 3 (March 1903), p. 337.

47 Richardson, "A Description of the Church," in *Consecration Services* (1877), p. 68.

48 *Century Magazine*, January 1885, pp. 323–38.

CHAPTER 11

1 See Sutton, *Charles Sprague Sargent and the Arnold Arboretum* (1970); and Morgan et al., *Community by Design* (2013), pp. 95–135.

2 Charles Sprague Sargent to FLO, June 26, 1874.

3 "Public Parks and the Enlargement of Town," deliverered to the American Social Science Association, February 25, 1870.

4 FLO to Charles G. Loring, January 21, 1871.

5 HHR to FLO, November 26, 1876, and May 13, 1877.

6 *AABN*, June 8, 1878.

7 FLO to Charles Sprague Sargent, July 8, 1874.

8 Sargent, "Arnold Arboretum: What It Is and Does," *Garden Magazine*, November 1917, p. 3.

9 Charles Sprague Sargent to FLO, February 5, 1885.

10 Quoted in Sutton, *Charles Sprague Sargent* (1970), p. 78.

11 HHR to FLO, November 26, 1876, and December 15, 1876.

12 Mumford, *The Brown Decades* (1931), p. 55.

13 "Education in Colonial Virginia," *William and Mary College Quarterly* 6, no. 2 (October 1897), p. 74, n1.

14 Report No. 12, Massachusetts School Board (1848).

15 *City Document No. 37. Report of the Trustees of the Public Library of the City of Boston, July 1852*; quoted in Whitehill, *Boston Public Library* (1956), p. 32.

16 Edward Everett to Boston City Council, June 7, 1851; quoted in Whitehill, *Boston Public Library* (1956), p. 23.

17 Ibid., pp. 620–21.

18 Initially $140,000, the gift eventually totaled $227,000. William R. Cutter, "A Model Village Library," in *New England Magazine* 1, no. 6 (February 1890), p. 618. The author knew whereof he spoke: Cutter was Woburn's second librarian.

19 Rufus Choate, October 9, 1856, quoted in Breisch, *Henry Hobson Richardson and the Small Public Library in America* (1997), p. 36.

20 Charles Bowers Winn, quoted in *Woburn Journal,* December 25, 1875.

21 Champney, Diary, August 7, 1876, cited in Breisch, *Henry Hobson Richardson and the Small Public Library in America* (1997), p. 110.

22 Kenneth Breisch develops this theme in greater detail in *Henry Hobson Richardson and the Small Public Library in America* (1997), p. 127.

23 *Woburn Journal,* November 8, 1881.

24 Quoted in O'Gorman, *Living Architecture* (1997), p. 162.

25 FLO to Bronson Case Rumsey, November 1884.

26 FLO to Joseph Phineas Davis, January 24, 1880.

27 FLO to Charles Henry Dalton, January 24, 1880.

28 FLO to Dalton and Davis, January 24, 1880.

29 F. A. Ames, quoted in "A Few Annotations," reprinted in Zaitzevsky, "The Olmsted Firm and the Structures of the Boston Park Systems" (1973), p. 170.

30 Van Rensselaer, *HHR and His Works* (1888), p. 68.

31 See Floyd, *Architecture after Richardson* (1994).

32 A. D. F. Hamlin, "The Ten Most Beautiful Buildings," *Brochure Series* 6 (January 1900), p. 13.

CHAPTER 12

1 Francis Kowsky draws attention to this connection in his biography of Vaux, *Country, Park, and City* (1998), p. 194.

2 Robert F. Brown reconstructed much of this story for his "The Aesthetic Transformation of an Industrial Community" (1977), pp. 12ff.

3 Here and after, quotations come from Ames's written account of the Gate Lodge conception and construction. F. L. Ames to W. M. Swain, November 20, 1881.

4 F. L. Ames to W. M. Swain, November 20, 1881.

5 F. L. Ames to W. M. Swain, November 20, 1881.

6 FLO, "A Few Annotations," reprinted in Zaitzevsky, "The Olmsted Firm and the Structures of the Boston Park Systems" (1973), p. 171.

7 Ibid.

8 Henry Van Brunt, "Henry Hobson Richardson, Architect," *Atlantic Monthly* 58 (November 1886), p. 692.

9 FLO to Oakes Angier Ames, [April 1882].

10 Ibid.

11 Interview with FLO Jr., quoted in Roper, *FLO* (1973), p. 383; *Brookline Chronicle,* March 2, 1889.

12 FLO to Frederick Newman Knapp, April 20, 1871.

13 M. G. Van Rensselaer, "Landscape Gardening—III," *AABN,* January 7, 1888.

CHAPTER 13

1   See Sam B. Warner's *Streetcar Suburbs* (1962) for a book-length analysis of this transformation.

2   "A Study in Railroad Gardening," *Donahoe's Magazine* 53, no. 6 (May 1905), p. 650; and Robinson, "A Railroad Beautiful" (1902), p. 564.

3   Robinson, "A Railroad Beautiful" (1902), p. 564; and FLO to Mariana Griswold Van Rensselaer, September 23, 1893. See also William Trelease, "A Biographical Memoir of Charles Sprague Sargent," quoted in Sutton, *Charles Sprague Sargent* (1970), p. 343.

4   Ochsner, "Architecture for the Boston and Albany Railroad" (1988), p. 113.

5   Ibid., p. 114, n28.

6   Salisbury, *The State, the Investor, and the Railroad* (1967), p. 294.

7   Kirkland, *Men Cities and Transportation* (1948), vol. 1, p. 118.

8   Robinson, "A Railroad Beautiful" (1902), pp. 564–65.

9   Van Rensselaer, *HHR and His Works* (1888), p. 102.

10 For a more detailed analysis of Richardson's railroad sketches, see chap. 6, "Commuterism," in O'Gorman, *H. H. Richardson: Architectural Forms for an American Society* (1987), pp. 112–25.

11 FLO to Bronson Case Rumsey, November 1884.

12 [Sargent], "The Railroad Station at Auburndale, Massachusetts" (1889), p. 125.

13 Van Rensselaer, *HHR and His Works* (1888), p. 100.

14 Phillips, "The Evolution of the Suburban Station" (1914), p. 124.

15 Bradford Lee Gilbert, "Picturesque Suburban Railroad Stations," *Engineering Magazine*, quoted in Ochsner, "Architecture for the Boston and Albany Railroad" (1988), p. 116.

16 [Sargent], "The Railroad Station at Auburndale, Massachusetts" (1889), pp. 124–25.

17 Robinson, "A Railroad Beautiful" (1902), p. 567.

18 Phillips, "The Evolution of the Suburban Station" (1914), pp. 124; and Sargent, "The Railroad Station at Auburndale, Massachusetts" (1889), p. 125.

19 Leo Marx, "The Railroad in the Landscape: An Iconological Reading of a Theme in American Art," in Danly and Marx, *The Railroad in American Art* (1988), p. 183.

20 Mark Twain, *A Tramp Abroad* (Hartford, CT: American Publishing Company; London: Chatto & Windus, 1880).

21 O'Gorman, "On Vacation with H. H. Richardson" (1979), p. 2.

22 HHR to Julia Richardson, July 9, 1882.

23 HHR to Julia Richardson, July 12, 1882.

24 HHR to Julia Richardson, July 10, 1882.

25 HHR to Julia Richardson, July 12, 1882.

26 Herbert Jacques, quoted in Van Rensselaer, *HHR and His Works* (1888), p. 28.

27 HHR to Julia Richardson, August 25, 1882.

28 HHR to Julia Richardson, June 22, 1882.

29 "Too Good Not to Tell," *Old Farmer's Almanac* (1912), p. 12. Note that Brooks's biographer observed that the trip became "the occasion of humorous anecdotes, in which the humor ran beyond the actual fact." Allen, *Life and Letters of Phillips Brooks*, vol. 2 (1900), p. 335.

30 Herbert Jacques, quoted in Van Rensselaer, *HHR and His Works* (1888), pp. 28, 29, 32.

31 Phillips Brooks to Robert Treat Paine, August 29, 1882, in Allen, *Life and Letters of Phillips Brooks*, vol. 2 (1900), p. 336.

32 HHR to Julia Richardson, August 12, 1882.

33 HHR to Julia Richardson, August 27, 1882.

34 Van Rensselaer, *HHR and His Works* (1888), p. 27.

35 Phillips Brooks to Robert Treat Paine, August 29, 1882, in Allen, *Life and Letters of Phillips Brooks*, vol. 2 (1900), p. 336.

36 Herbert Jacques, quoted in Van Rensselaer, *HHR and His Works* (1888), p. 32.

CHAPTER 14

1 HHR to FLO, April 6, 1883.

2 Zaitzevsky and Griswold, *Fairsted: A Cultural Landscape Report* (1997), p. 10.

3 HHR to FLO, April 6, 1883.

4 FLO Jr. to Laura Wood Roper, September 16, 1951.

5 FLO to Charles Eliot Norton, November 9, 1879.

6 Shepley, "Reminiscences," p. 2.

7 Hale, "H. H. Richardson and His Work" (1894), p. 515.

8 Coolidge, "Henry Hobson Richardson, 1838–1886" (1927).

9 Glessner, *The Story of a House* (1923, 1963), p. 12.

10 Hale, "H. H. Richardson and His Work" (1894), pp. 527–28.

11 Here and after, quotations regarding the workings of the Richardson office are in Van Rensselaer, *HHR and His Works* (1888), pp. 127–31.

12 Coolidge, "H. H. Richardson and His Works" (n.d.), pp. 5–6.

13 HHR to Henry Adams, April 7, 1884.

14 [Warren], "Mourned by Lovers of Art" (1886).

15 Elzner, "A Reminiscence of Richardson" (1892), p. 15.

16 FLO to John Charles Olmsted, September 12, 1884.

17 Waverly Keeling, "Home of Frederick L. Olmsted," *Chicago Inter-Ocean*, 1896.

18 Journal and Account Book, 1877–1890, cited in Zaitzevsky and Griswold, *Fairsted: A Cultural Landscape Report* (1997), p. 12, n21.

19 "Random Notes about F.L.O's Brookline Office, 1883," FLO Jr. to Laura Wood Roper, June 1952. Laura Wood Roper Papers, Library of Congress.

20 FLO Jr. to Laura Wood Roper, June 16, 1952, p. 2.

21 FLO to FLO Jr., September 5, 1890.

22 FLO to FLO Jr., January 7, 1895.

23 Eliot, *Charles Eliot, Landscape Architect* (1901), p. 35.

24 FLO to Mrs. William Dwight Whitney, December 16, 1890.

25 FLO Jr. to Laura Wood Roper, June 7, 1952.

26 FLO to Ariel Lathorp, July 7, 1890.

27 Waverly Keeling, "Home of Frederick L. Olmsted," *Chicago Inter-Ocean*, 1896.

28 Italics added. FLO Jr. to Laura Wood Roper, June 1, 1952.

29 *Newport Journal*, April 29, 1876. This quotation is found in Ochsner and Hubka, "H. H. Richardson: The Design of the William Watts Sherman House" (1992), a valuable essay on the Newport mansion.

30 See Mark Wright's excellent article, "H. H. Richardson's House for Reverend Browne, Rediscovered" (2009), p. 83.

31 HHR to Mrs. E. W. Stoughton, August 1, 1833.

32 C. H. Blackall, "Boston Sketches—Suburban Work," *Inland Architect and News Record* 13 (April 1889), pp. 53–54.

33 Sheldon, *Artistic Country Seats*, vol. 1 (1886), p. 157.

34 Lydia Lyman Paine, Diary, August 27, 1883, Massachusetts Historical Society.

35 Floyd, "H. H. Richardson, Frederick Law Olmsted, and the House for Robert Treat Paine" (1983), pp. 230, 256.

36 Robert Treat Paine to FLO, January 12, 1884.

37 Lydia Lyman Paine, Diary, October 28, 1883, Massachusetts Historical Society.

38 Ibid., July 19, 1884.

39 George Lyman Paine, quoted in Clifford, "Stonehurst Chronology, 1882–1893."

40 Paine and Pope, *Paine Ancestry* (1912), p. 287.

41 Walter Clark to Robert Treat Paine, September 1, 1885.

42 Lydia Paine, Diary, September 24, 1885, Massachusetts Historical Society.

43 FLO to Robert Treat Paine, November 5, 1885.

44 Ibid.

45 Brooks, "Henry Hobson Richardson" (1886), p. 6.

46 Richardson, "Specifications for Dwelling House for Mrs. Robert T. Paine, Jr. at Waltham, Massachusetts" (1885), p. 19. Robert Treat Paine Trust, Stonehurst Archives.

47   Emily Lyman Storer to Edith Storer, August 10, 1910. Clifford and Paine, *Stonehurst* (2007), p. 27, n50.

48   Sheldon, *Artistic Country Seats*, vol. 1 (1886), p. 157.

49   Brooks, "Henry Hobson Richardson" (1886), p. 5.

50   O'Gorman, *Living Architecture* (1997), p. 172.

CHAPTER 15

1   Dykstra, *Clover Adams* (2012), p. 87.

2   Henry James to Elizabeth Boott, January 7, 1886. "City of Conversation" was also a James coinage describing the nation's capital. See Henry James, *The American Scene* (New York: Harper & Brothers, 1907), p. 329.

3   Marian Adams to Robert William Hooper, January 15, 1882. Given subsequent events, Elizabeth Davis Bancroft's words seem sadly prescient.

4   Marian Adams to Robert William Hooper, November 5, 1882.

5   Ibid.

6   FLO in Clark, *Annual Report of the Architect of the United States Capitol* (1882), p. 15.

7   Here and after, FLO to Senator Justin S. Morrill, June 9, 1874.

8   FLO to Whitelaw Reid, November 26, 1874.

9   FLO in Clark, *Annual Report* (1882), p. 14.

10   FLO to Edward Clark, October 1, 1881.

11   FLO to Edward Clark, July 20, 1886.

12   *New York Tribune*, October 17, 1871. In fact, Mrs. O'Leary was in bed when the fire started in her barn.

13   Whitelaw Reid to John Hay, January 30, 1883.

14   Marian Adams to Robert William Hooper, May 13, 1883. The Hays inherited half of Amasa Stone's estate, estimated at $6 million.

15   Marian Adams to Robert William Hooper, March 3, 1878.

16   Marian Adams to Mrs. Donald Cameron, quoted in Friedlaender, *Henry Hobson Richardson, Henry Adams, and John Hay* (1970), p. 235.

17   Marian Adams to Robert William Hooper, March 3, 1878.

18   Henry Adams to John Hay, August 10, 1883.

19   Cater, *Henry Adams and His Friends* (1947), p. xlix.

20   Marian Adams to Robert William Hooper, quoted in Friedlaender, *Henry Hobson Richardson, Henry Adams, and John Hay* (1970), 235.

21   Marian Adams to Clara Hay, December 6, 1883.

22   Henry Adams to Marian Adams, March 15, 1885.

23   Charles Francis Adams, "The Sifted Grain and the Grain Sifters," *American Historical Review* 6, no. 2 (January 1901), p. 199.

24 Henry Adams to John Hay, June 25, 1882.

25 Marian Adams to Robert William Hooper, May 20, 1883.

26 Henry Adams to Charles Milnes Gaskell, March 26, 1872.

27 Mrs. Ward Thornton to L. Bancel La Farge, n.d.; quoted in Weinberg, *The Decorative Work of John La Farge* (1977), p. 128, n1.

28 Adams, *Esther* (1884), p. 73.

29 Ibid., pp. 116–17.

30 Henry Adams to John Hay, January 18, 1884.

31 HHR to Henry Adams, February 28, 1884.

32 Henry Adams to John Field, September 20, 1884.

33 HHR to John Hay, December 3, 1884.

34 Henry Adams to John Hay, March 7, 1885.

35 Henry Adams to Marian Adams, April 10, 1884.

36 Henry Adams to Marian Adams, April 12, 1885.

37 Henry Adams to John Hay, April 20, 1885.

38 Henry Adams to John Hay, October 26, 1884.

39 Henry Adams to John Hay, September 1885.

40 Henry Adams to John Hay, July 17, 1885.

41 HHR to Henry Adams, September 28, 1885.

42 HHR to John Hay, December 8, 1885.

43 Quoted in Chalfant, *Better in Darkness* (1994), p. 450.

44 Quoted in O'Gorman, *Living Architecture* (1997), p. 171.

45 John Hay to Henry Adams, December 9, 1885.

46 Henry Adams to John Hay, December 31, 1885.

47 HHR to John Hay, December 10, 1885.

48 Henry Adams to Brooks Adams, March 3, 1872.

49 Henry Adams to Elizabeth Cameron, September 18, 1899.

CHAPTER 16

1 The sources for this and subsequent meetings with Richardson are the Glessners themselves, namely Frances Glessner's contemporaneous notes in her "Journals (1879–1921)"; John Glessner's jottings in "For Contemplated Paper on Richardson, House Building, Etc. 1890–1914" (1914); and his published essay, *The Story of a House* (1923). The words spoken by the principals all come verbatim from these documents.

2 Wight, "H. H. Richardson" (1886), p. 59.

3 HHR to John J. Glessner, April 21, 1885.

4 John J. Glessner, Journal, September 17, 1884.

5 Impressions of Richardson's office offered by his contemporaries were numerous; those drawn upon here include Welles Bosworth's "I Knew H. H. Richardson" (1951); A. O. Elzner's "A Reminiscence of Richardson" (1892); Peter Wight's "H. H. Richardson" (1886); and those of Richardson's eldest child, Julia Shepley, in her "Reminiscences" (n.d.).

6 Glessner, "For Contemplated Paper on Richardson" (1914), pp. 1, 2.

7 Van Rensselaer, *HHR and His Works* (1888), p. 12.

8 Ibid., p. 125.

9 Coolidge, "H. H. Richardson and His Works" (n.d.), p. 5.

10 Glessner, "For Contemplated Paper on Richardson" (1914), p. 38.

11 William Bross, editor of the *Chicago Tribune*, quoted in Beveridge and Rocheleau, *Frederick Law Olmsted: Designing the American Landscape* (1998), p. 71.

12 FLO and Calvert Vaux, "Preliminary Report upon the Proposed Suburban Village at Riverside, near Chicago," September 1, 1868, in *FLO Papers*, vol. 8 (2013), p. 280.

13 Over the ensuing decades, further development would shrink the common land by several hundred acres.

14 Here and after, Olmsted and Vaux, "Report" (March 1871), in *FLO Papers*, supplementary series, vol. 1 (1997), pp. 206–38.

15 [Warren], "Mourned by Lovers of Art" (1886).

16 Glessner, "For Contemplated Paper on Richardson" (1914), pp. 29, 19.

17 *Chicago Tribune*, September 30, 1885, and October 1, 1885.

18 *Chicago Tribune*, October 25, 1885.

19 Schuyler, *American Architecture and Other Writings* (1961), vol. 1, p. 264.

20 *Chicago Tribune*, October 25, 1885.

21 Here and after, HHR to Hayden Richardson, December 27 and 28, 1885.

22 HHR to John Hay, December 31, 1885.

23 HHR to George F. Shepley, December 31, 1885.

24 HHR to Julia Richardson, February 6 and 7, 1886.

25 HHR to Julia Richardson, February 8, 1886.

26 Van Rensselaer, *HHR and His Works* (1888), p. 26.

27 Richardson, *Description of Drawings* (1884), p. 4.

28 Ibid., p. 29.

29 HHR to George F. Shepley, March 21, 1886.

30 Shepley, "Reminiscences," p. 6.

31 Glessner, *The Story of a House* (1923), p. 10.

32 Ibid., p. 10.

33 Olmsted, quoted in Van Rensselaer, *HHR and His Works* (1888), p. 118–19.

34 FLO and HHR, quoted in Van Rensselaer, *Richardson and His Works* (1888), pp. 118–19.

35 FLO to Mariana Griswold Van Rensselaer, May 2, 1886.

36 Olmsted recounted the Washington evening for Mrs. Van Rensselaer in the May 2 letter and added further details subsequently after she agreed to write the book that became *Henry Hobson Richardson and His Works* (1888).

CHAPTER 17

1 Van Rensselaer, *HHR and His Works* (1888), p. 36.

2 Brooks, "Henry Hobson Richardson" (1886), pp. 4, 7.

3 O'Gorman, "Documentation: An 1886 Inventory of H. H. Richardson's Library, and Other Gleanings from Probate" (1982), p. 150.

4 E. W. Hooper to F. L. Ames, May 3, 1886; reprinted in Wickersham and Milford, "Richardson's Death, Ames's Money, and the Birth of the Modern Architectural Firm" (2014), pp. 123–24.

5 For a more detailed account of the birth of Shepley, Rutan and Coolidge, see Wickersham and Milford, "Richardson's Death, Ames's Money, and the Birth of the Modern Architectural Firm" (2014).

6 All commentary on the house from Mrs. Glessner's diary, as assembled in Glessner, "*The Story of a House* (1923), pp. 70–75.

7 The buildings included the Allegheny Courthouse, the Cincinnati Chamber of Commerce, and the unbuilt Hoyt library in Michigan. See O'Gorman, *Selected Drawings* (1974), p. 35, n78.

8 Quoted in Lynes, *The Tastemakers* (1954), p. 148.

9 Van Rensselaer, *HHR and His Works* (1888), p. 36.

10 Van Rensselaer, *HHR and His Works* (1888), p. 24.

11 Van Rensselaer, "Public Buildings (1)," *Century Magazine* 27, no. 6 (May 1884); reprinted in Van Rensselaer, *Accents as Well as Broad Effects* (1996), p. 139.

12 "Churches," *Century Magazine* 29, no. 7 (January 1885); reprinted in Van Rensselaer, *Accents as Well as Broad Effects* (1996), p. 192.

13 Van Rensselaer, "Public Buildings (1)," *Century Magazine* 27, no. 6 (May 1884); reprinted in Van Rensselaer, *Accents as Well as Broad Effects* (1996), p. 139.

14 FLO to Mariana Griswold Van Rensselaer, first letter of May 6, 1886.

15 FLO to Mariana Griswold Van Rensselaer, second letter of May 6, 1886.

16 FLO to Mariana Griswold Van Rensselaer, August 11, 1886.

17 Mariana Griswold Van Rensselaer to Richard Watson Gilder, October 25, 1886.

18 Major, *Mariana Griswold Van Rensselaer* (2013), p. 8.

19 The contract for *Henry Hobson Richardson and His Works*, together with a mix of correspondence, ledgers, a reader's report, and other documents, are in

the Houghton Mifflin Company records at Houghton Library, Harvard University, MS Am 2105. See also Yanni, "'The Richardson Memorial'" (2007), pp. 27–36. The final sales total is cited as 484 books sold; a few additional copies would have been provided gratis to the author, Sargent, Olmsted, and Mrs. Richardson, among others.

20   "Henry H. Richardson," *Nation* 47 (August 2, 1888), p. 94.

21   "The Architect Richardson," *Literary World* 19 (June 9, 1888), p. 180.

22   FLO to Mariana Griswold Van Rensselaer, June 14, 1888.

23   See Woods, "The Photograph as Tastemaker (1990); and Waters, "H. H. Richardson and Photography" (2008).

24   Charles A. Coolidge, "Random Jottings" (n.d.), Olmsted file, Architecture of Stanford University Collection, Stanford UniversityArchives.

25   For a fuller discussion, see Morgan et al., *Community by Design* (2013), chap. 4.

26   Larson and Brown, *The Spirit of H. H. Richardson on the Midland Prairies* (1988), p. 27

27   See Floyd, *Architecture after Richardson* (1994).

28   For a fuller discussion, see Thomas J. Schlereth, "H. H. Richardson's Influence in Chicago's Midwest, 1872–1914," in Larson and Brown, *The Spirit of H. H. Richardson on the Midland Prairies* (1988), pp. 44ff.

29   See Tselos, "Richardson's Influence on European Architecture" (1970); and Hitchcock, *The Architecture of H. H. Richardson and His Times* (1966), pp. 333–34.

30   FLO to Mrs. William Dwight Whitney, December 16, 1890.

31   FLO to Charles Eliot, October 28, 1886.

32   FLO to Mariana Griswold Van Rensselaer, June 1, 1893.

33   FLO to Mariana Griswold Van Rensselaer, December 21, 1887.

34   FLO to Mariana Griswold Van Rensselaer, August 11, 1886.

35   Van Rensselaer, "Landscape Gardening: A Definition," *Garden and Forest* 1 (February 29, 1888), p. 2.

36   Van Rensselaer, "Landscape Gardening, II," *AABN* 22 (December 3, 1887), pp. 263–64.

37   FLO to Mariana Griswold Van Rensselaer, April 9, 1888.

38   Van Rensselaer, *Art Out-of-Doors* (1893), pp. xi–xii.

39   FLO to Mariana Griswold Van Rensselaer, June 1893.

CHAPTER 18

1   Here and after, the primary source regarding FLO's initial August 1888 meeting with G. W. Vanderbilt is Olmsted himself, in his letter to Frederick John Kingsbury, January 20, 1891.

2   FLO to Frederick John Kingsbury, January 20, 1891.

3 Roper, *FLO* (1973), p. 347.

4 FLO to Richard Pindell Hammond Jr., October 5, 1886.

5 FLO to George W. Vanderbilt, July 12, 1889.

6 FLO to William A. Thompson, November 6, 1889.

7 FLO to William Stiles, March 10, 1895.

8 Story recounted by Olmsted apprentice Warren Manning, cited in Bryan, *Biltmore Estate* (1994), p. 88.

9 FLO to Charles McNamee, May 17, 1889.

10 FLO to George Washington Vanderbilt, July 12, 1889.

11 FLO to William A. Thompson, November 6, 1889.

12 FLO to Elizabeth Baldwin Whitney, December 16, 1890.

13 FLO to FLO Jr., June 28, 1891.

14 Daniel Burnham speech of March 25, 1893.

15 FLO to John Charles Olmsted, November 9, 1882.

16 FLO to FLO Jr., September 5, 1890.

17 FLO to John Charles Olmsted, October 27, 1890. The italics are Olmsted's.

18 Schuyler, "'The Most Critical & the Most Difficult' Project" (2015), p. 381.

19 Quoted in Baker, *Richard Morris Hunt* (1980), p. 428.

20 Catherine Clinton Howland Hunt, Diary, August 1, 1895, quoted in Baker, *Richard Morris Hunt* (1980), p. 431.

21 FLO to John Charles Olmsted, May 10, 1895.

22 John Olmsted to FLO Jr., May 17, 1895.

23 FLO Jr. to Charles Eliot, April 26, 1895.

24 FLO Jr. to Laura Wood Roper, September 29, 1951.

25 FLO to FLO Jr., July 23, 1895.

26 FLO to "Folks at Home," January 20, 1900, quoted in Roper, *FLO* (1973), p. 474.

27 Kinnard, "The Life and Works of Mariana Griswold Van Rensselaer, American Art Critic" (1977), p. 269.

EPILOGUE

1 "Recollections of Arthur A. Shurcliff, 1952," Frederick Law Olmsted Papers, Library of Congress.

2 Elizabeth Hope Cushing, "Shurcliff, Arthur Asahel (Shurtleff)," in Charles A. Birnbaum and Robin Karson, *Pioneers of American Landscape Design* (New York: McGraw Hill, 2000), p. 351.

3 Sullivan, *Kindergarten Chats and Other Writings* (1947), p. 30. Note that one phrase in Sullivan's original text—"who has somewhat to say"—has been altered for clarity.

4   O'Gorman, *Three American Architects: Richardson, Sullivan, and Wright* (1991), p. 3. Wright was speaking of Sullivan's attitude, but he clearly shared the sentiment, given what O'Gorman calls Wright's "characteristic dissemblance."

5   Ralph Adams Cram, *My Life in Architecture* (1936), pp. 31–32.

6   Charles Eliot Norton to FLO Jr., September 3, 1903.

7   FLO to Ignaz Anton Pilat, September 26, 1863.

8   The description "long-headed" was applied to FLO by Henry Whitney Bellows in a letter to James Miller McKim, August 18, 1865.

Sources

The most essential sources are the papers. The primary repository of Richardson's drawings is Harvard University's Houghton Library, along with Harvard's Graduate School of Design, where there are other miscellaneous holdings, including an autograph sketchbook (1869–75). The immense resource that is the archive of the Olmsted firm's drawings and documents, "Photos of Olmsted Archives, Frederick Law Olmsted NHS, NPS," is available on Flickr: https://www.flickr.com/photos/olmsted_archives/sets/.

The bulk of Richardson's surviving correspondences is on deposit at the Archives of American Art in Washington, D.C. Among the correspondence is a significant trove of family letters. These include a number from Richardson's stepfather and brother during the Civil War era; numerous Hayden family letters between Richardson's wife, Julia Hayden Richardson, and her mother and father, in particular during the early days of Julia and Hal's marriage.

Richardson wrote relatively little; Olmsted, on contrast, wrote a great deal. The bulk of his letters, reports, and papers are at the Library of Congress. While a large selection has been edited and published by the Johns Hopkins University Press papers project (see below), scans of the originals can be viewed online at https://www.loc.gov/collections/frederick-law-olmsted-papers/. The Olmsted collection at the Library of Congress also includes some invaluable research conducted by biographer Laura Wood Roper in preparing *FLO: A Biography of Frederick Law Olmsted* (1973), including a trove of

correspondence with her subject's son, Rick, regarding his childhood memories of his father.

Colleagues, friends, and collaborators of both men are survived by
papers and other materials. In researching this book, I consulted the
following collections: Henry Adams, Massachusetts Historical Society;
A[lred]. J[anson]. Bloor, New-York Historical Society; Phillips Brooks,
Houghton Library, Harvard University; Century Association; Theodore
F[relinghuysen]. Dwight, Massachusetts Historical Society; Richard
Watson Gilder, New York Public Library; John and Frances Glessner,
Glessner House; John Hay, John Hay Library, Brown University; Hough-
ton Mifflin Company records, Houghton Library, Harvard University;
John Charles Olmsted, Frances Loeb Library, Special Collections, Har-
vard University; Lydia Lyman Paine, Massachusetts Historical Society;
Laura Wood Roper Papers, Library of Congress; Augustus Saint-
Gaudens, Rauner Library, Dartmouth College; Trinity Church Archives,
Massachusetts Historical Society; Richard Grant White (father) and
Stanford White (son), New-York Historical Society.

The books and periodicals consulted are listed hereafter:

Adams, Ann Jensen. "The Birth of a Style: Henry Hobson Richardson and the Com-
    petition Drawings for Trinity Church, Boston." *Art Bulletin* 62, no. 3 (Septem-
    ber 1980), pp. 409–33.
Adams, Henry. *The Education of Henry Adams.* Boston: Houghton Mifflin Co., 1918.
———. *The Letters of Henry Adams, 1868–1885.* Vol. 2. Cambridge, MA: Harvard
    University Press, 1982.
[Adams, Henry.] *Esther: A Novel.* New York: Henry Holt and Company, 1884. Pub-
    lished bearing the pen name Frances Snow Compton.
Adams, Henry. "John La Farge, 1830–1870: From Amateur to Artist." PhD diss., Yale
    University, 1980.
Adams, Henry, James L. Yarnall, Kathleen A. Foster, Linnea H. Wren, H. Barbara
    Weinberg, and Henry A. La Farge. *John La Farge.* New York: Abbeville Press, 1987.
Adams, Marian. *The Letters of Mrs. Henry Adams, 1865–1883.* Edited by Ward Tho-
    ron. Little, Brown, and Company, 1936.
Allaback, Sarah. *The First American Women Architects.* Urbana: University of Illinois
    Press, 2008.
The Allegheny County Courthouse and Jail. Pittsburgh, PA: Courthouse Gallery/Forum,
    Allegheny County Courthouse, 1977.
Allen, Alexander V. G. *Life and Letters of Phillips Brooks.* 3 vols. New York: E. P. Dutton
    & Company, 1900–1901.

The Ames Memorial Building. Monographs of American Architecture, no. 3. Boston: Tichnor, 1886.

Anderson, Isabel, ed. *Larz Anderson: Letters and Journals of a Diplomat.* New York: Fleming H. Revell Co., 1940.

———. *The Letters and Journals of General Nicholas Longworth Anderson.* New York: Fleming H. Revell Co., 1942.

Architecture of H. H. Richardson and His Contemporaries in Boston and Vicinity. Boston: Society of Architectural Historians, 1972.

Around the Station: The Town and the Train. Framingham, MA: Danforth Museum, 1977.

Atkinson, Edward. "Slow-Burning Construction." *Century Magazine* 37, no. 4 (February 1889), pp. 566–79.

Austin Hall, Harvard Law School, Cambridge, Mass.: H. H. Richardson, Architect. Boston: James R. Osgood & Company, 1885.

Baker, Paul R. *Richard Morris Hunt.* Cambridge, MA: MIT Press, 1980.

Baldwin, Charles C[rittenton]. *Stanford White.* New York: Dodd, Mead & Co., 1931.

Beale, Margaret E. "H. H. Richardson's Brattle Square Church: Drawings and Development." Typescript, 1976. Fine Arts Department, Harvard University.

Beveridge, Charles E., ed. *Frederick Law Olmsted: Plans and Views of Pubic Parks.* Baltimore, MD: Johns Hopkins University Press, 2015.

Beveridge, Charles E., and Susan L. Klaus. *The Olmsteds at Biltmore.* Bethesda, MD: National Association for Olmsted Parks, 1995.

Beveridge, Charles E., and Paul Rocheleau. *Frederick Law Olmsted: Designing the American Landscape.* New York: Rizzoli, 1995. A slightly revised edition in a smaller format was published by Universe Books, 1998.

Bosworth, Welles. "I Knew H. H. Richardson." *Journal of the American Institute of Architects* 16 (September 1951), pp. 115–27.

Bowles, Samuel. *Across the Continent: A Summer's Journey to the Rocky Mountains, the Mormons, and the Pacific States, with Speak Colfax.* Springfield, MA: Samuel Bowles & Company, 1866.

———. *Our New West.* Hartford, CT: Hartford Publishing Company, 1869.

Breisch, Kenneth A. *Henry Hobson Richardson and the Small Public Library in America: A Study in Typology.* Cambridge, MA: MIT Press, 1997.

Brooks, Phillips. "Henry Hobson Richardson." *Harvard Monthly* 3, no. 1 (October 1886), pp. 1–7.

Brown, Glenn. *1860–1930, Memories: A Winning Crusade to Revive George Washington's Vision of a Capital City.* Washington, DC, 1931.

———. "Stanford White." *Quarterly Bulletin of American Institute of Architects,* July 1906, pp. 107–8.

Brown, Robert F. "The Aesthetic Transformation of an Industrial Community." *Winterthur Portfolio* 12 (1977), pp. 35–64.

[Brown, Robert F.] *The Architecture of Henry Hobson Richardson in North Easton, Massachusetts*. North Easton, MA: Oakes Ames Memorial Hall Association and Easton Historical Society, 1969.

Bryan, John M. *Biltmore Estate: The Most Distinguished Private Place*. New York: Rizzoli International Publications, 1994.

Bubenzer, Brian Peter. "The Arthurian Architecture of H. H. Richardson." PhD diss., University of Wisconsin-Madison, 2002.

Buffalo Architecture: A Guide. Cambridge, MA: MIT Press, 1981.

Bunnell, L. H. "How the Yo-Semite Valley Was Discovered and Named." *Hutching's California Magazine* 35 (May 16, 1859), pp. 498–505. http://www.yosemite.ca.us /library/hutchings_california_magazine/35.pdf.

Bunnell, Lafayette H. *Discovery of the Yosemite and the Indian War Which Led to That Event*. Chicago: Fleming H. Revell, 1880.

Caldwell, Wilber W. *The Courthouse and the Depot: The Architect of Hope in an Age of Despair; A Narrative Guide to Railroad Expansion and Its Impact on Public Architecture in Georgia, 1833–1910*. Macon, GA: Mercer University Press, 2001.

Callahan, Helen C. "Upstairs-Downstairs in Chicago." *Chicago History* 6, no. 4 (Winter 1977–78), pp. 194–209.

Carlhian, Jean Paul, and Margot M. Ellis. *Americans in Paris: Foundations of America's Architectural Gilded Age; Architecture Students at the École des Beaux-Arts, 1846–1946*. New York: Rizzoli, 2014.

Carr, Ethan. "Eastern Design in a Western Landscape: Olmsted, Richardson, and the Ames Monument." Library of American Landscape History, news blog, April 3, 2015. lalh.org.

Cater, Harold Dean, ed. *Henry Adams and His Friends: A Collection of His Unpublished Letters*. Boston: Houghton Mifflin Co., 1947.

Century Association. *The Century 1847–1946*. New York: Century Association, 1947.

Chafee, Richard. "Richardson's Record at the Ecole des Beaux-Arts." *Journal of the Society of Architectural Historians* 36 (1977), pp. 175–88.

———. "The Teaching of Architecture at the Ecole des Beaux-Arts." In *The Architecture of the Ecole des Beaux-Arts*, ed. Arthur Drexler, pp. 60–109. London: Secker & Warburg, 1977.

Chalfant, Edward. *Better in Darkness: A Biography of Henry Adams; His Second Life, 1862–1891*. Hamden, CT: Archon Books, 1994.

Cincinnati Astronomical Society. *Richardson, the Architect and the Cincinnati Chamber of Commerce Building*. Cincinnati, OH: Cincinnati Astronomical Society, 1914.

Clark, Edward. *Annual Report of the Architect of the United States Capitol for the Fiscal Year Ending June 30, 1882*. Washington, DC: Government Printing Office, 1882.

Clark, T. M. "H. H. Richardson." *Nation* 151 (August 23, 1888), p. 151.

Clifford, Ann. "John Evans (1847–1923) and Architectural Sculpture in Boston." MA thesis, Tufts University, 1992.

———, compiler. "Stonehurst Chronology, 1882–1893." n.p.

Clifford, Ann, and Thomas M. Paine. *Stonehurst: The Robert Treat Paine Estate; An American Masterwork by H. H. Richardson and F. L. Olmsted.* Waltham, MA: Robert Treat Paine Historical Trust, 2007.

Codman, Richard. *Reminiscences of Richard Codman.* Boston: North Bennet Street Industrial School, 1923.

Coffin, Sarah D. "The Furniture of Henry Hobson Richardson: Its Form and Setting in Time and Place." BA thesis, Yale University, 1973.

Consecration Services of Trinity Church, Boston, February 9, 1877. Boston: Trinity Church Vestry, 1877.

Cook, Clarence. *A Description of the New York Central Park.* New York: F. J. Huntington, 1869.

Coolidge, Charles A. "Henry Hobson Richardson, 1838–1886." In *Later Years of the Saturday Club, 1870–1920,* ed. M. A. DeWolfe Howe. Boston: Houghton Mifflin Co., 1927.

———. "H. H. Richardson and His Works." Speech given before Boston Society of Architects. Typescript, 6 pp., n.d. Richardson Papers, Archives of American Art.

Coolidge, John. "H. H. Richardson: Architect of the American Suburb." Film. 26 minutes. Cambridge, MA: Fogg Fine Arts with John Coolidge, 1977.

———. "H. H. Richardson's Youth: Some Unpublished Documents." In *In Search of Modern Architecture,* ed. Helen Searing, pp. 165–71. Cambridge, MA: MIT Press, 1982.

Cortissoz, Royal. *John La Farge: A Memoir and a Study.* Boston: Houghton Mifflin Co., 1911.

Cram, Ralph Adams. *My Life in Architecture.* Boston: Little, Brown and Co., 1936.

Crowninshield, Benjamin. *A Private Journal: 1856–1858.* Cambridge, MA: Riverside Press, 1941.

Curran, Kathleen. "The Romanesque Revival, Mural Painting, and Protestant Patronage." *Art Bulletin* 81, no. 4 (December 1999), pp. 693–722.

Danly, Susan [Walther]. "The Landscape Photographs of Alexander Gardner and Andrew Joseph Russell." PhD diss., Brown University, 1983.

Danly, Susan, and Leo Marx, eds. *The Railroad in American Art: Representations of Technological Change.* Cambridge, MA: MIT Press, 1988.

De Long, David G., Helen Searing, and Robert A. M. Stern. *American Architecture: Innovation and Tradition.* New York: Rizzoli, 1986.

Dieterich, H. R., Jr. "The Architecture of H. H. Richardson in Wyoming: A New Look at the Ames Monument." *Annals of Wyoming* 28 (April 1966), pp. 49–53.

Dilsaver, Lary M., ed. *America's National Park System: The Critical Documents.* Lanham, MD: Rowman & Littlefield, 1994.

Dinnerstein, Lois. "Opulence and Ocular Delight, Splendor and Squalor: Critical Writings in Art and Architecture by Mariana Griswold Van Rensselaer." PhD diss., City University of New York, 1979.

Dorsheimer, William. *The Life and Public Service of the Honorable Grover Cleveland*. Philadelphia, PA: Hubbard Brothers, 1884.

Dow, Charles Mason. *Anthology and Bibliography of Niagara Falls*. 2 vols. Albany: State of New York, 1921.

———. *The State Reservation at Niagara: A History*. Albany, NY: J. B. Lyon Co., 1914.

Downing, Andrew Jackson. *The Architecture of Country Houses*. Philadelphia, PA: D. Appleton & Co., 1850.

———. *Cottage Residences*. New York: Wiley and Putnam, 1842.

———. *A Treatise on the Theory and Practice of Landscape Gardening, Adapted to North America*. New York: Wiley and Putnam, 1841.

Drawings and Plans by Ambroise-Alfred Baudry, Julien Guadet and Gustave-Adolphe Gerhardt. Presentation volume gifted to H. H. Richardson, 1865. Avery Library, Columbia University.

Drexler, Arthur, ed. *The Architecture of the Ecole des Beaux-Arts*. London: Secker & Warburg, 1977.

Dryfhout, John H. *The Work of Augustus Saint-Gaudens*. Hanover, NH: University Press of New England, 1982.

Dykstra, Natalie. *Clover Adams: A Gilded and Heartbreaking Life*. Boston: Houghton Mifflin Harcourt, 2012.

Eaton, Leonard K. *American Architecture Comes of Age: European Reaction to H. H. Richardson and Louis Sullivan*. Cambridge, MA: MIT Press, 1972.

Edwards, Lee M. "Hubert Herkomer in America." *American Art Journal* 21, no. 3 (1989), pp. 48–73.

Eliot, Charles W. *Charles Eliot, Landscape Architect, a Lover of Nature and of His Kind, Who Trained Himself for a New Profession, Practiced It, and through It Wrought Much Good*. Boston: Houghton Mifflin Co., 1901.

Elzner, A[lfred]. O[scar]. "A Reminiscence of Richardson." *Inland Architect and News Record* 20 (September 1892), p. 15.

Embury, Aymar, II. "A Great Man in Eclipse." *Saturday Review*, March 7, 1936, pp. 20–21.

Fabos, Julius Gy, Gordon T. Milde, and V. Michael Weinmayr. *Frederick Law Olmsted, Sr.: Founder of Landscape Architecture in America*. Amherst: University of Massachusetts Press, 1968.

Farnham, Anne. "H. H. Richardson and A. H. Davenport: Architecture and Furniture as Big Business in America's Gilded Age." In *Tools and Technologies: America's Wooden Age*, ed. Paul B. Kebabian and William C. Lipke, pp. 80–91. Burlington: University of Vermont, 1979.

Fein, Albert. *Frederick Law Olmsted and the American Environmental Tradition*. New York: George Braziller, 1972.

Fitch, James Marston. *American Building: The Forces That Shape It*. Boston: Houghton Mifflin Co., 1948.

Fletcher, Banister. *Sir Banister Fletcher's A History of Architecture*. 19th ed. London: Butterworths, 1987.

Floyd, Margaret Henderson. *Architecture after Richardson: Regionalism before Modernism—Longfellow, Alden, and Harlow in Boston and Pittsburgh.* Chicago: University of Chicago Press, 1994.

———. *Henry Hobson Richardson: A Genius for Architecture.* New York: Monacelli, 1997.

———. "H. H. Richardson, Frederick Law Olmsted, and the House for Robert Treat Paine." *Winterthur Portfolio* 18, no. 4 (1983), pp. 227–48.

Forbes, J. D. "Shepley, Bulfinch, Richardson and Abbott: An Introduction." *Journal of the Society of Architectural Historians* 17 (Fall 1958), pp. 19–31.

French, H. W. *Art and Artists in Connecticut.* Boston: Lee and Shepherd, 1879.

Friedlaender, Marc. "Henry Hobson Richardson, Henry Adams, and John Hay. *Journal of the Society of Architectural Historians* 29, no. 3 (October 1970), pp. 231–46.

Friedrich, Otto. *Clover.* New York: Simon and Schuster, 1979.

Gass, John B. "American Architecture and Architects, with Special Reference to the Works of the Late Richard Morris Hunt and Henry Hobson Richardson." Paper read to the Manchester Society. *Journal of the Royal Institute of British Architects,* February 4, 1896, pp. 229–33.

Gilder, Richard Watson. *Letters of Richard Watson Gilder.* Edited by Rosamond Gilder. Boston: Houghton Mifflin Co., 1916.

Girr, Christopher F. "Mastery in Masonry: Norcross Brothers, Contractors and Builders, 1964–1924." MS thesis, Columbia University, 1996.

Glessner, J[ohn]. J[acob]. "For Contemplated Paper on Richardson, House Building, Etc. 1890–1914." Typescript. n.d.. Glessner House Museum.

———. "[Recollections]. 1800 Prairie Avenue, Chicago." Typescript, 4 pp., n.d. Richardson Papers, Archives of American Art.

———. *The Story of a House: H. H. Richardson's Glessner House.* Chicago: Glessner House Museum, 2011. Glessner's memory piece was prepared for his children in 1923.

Gowans, Alan. *Images of American Living.* Philadelphia, PA: J. B. Lippincott Company, 1964.

Greeley, Horace. *An Overland Visit from New York to San Francisco in the Summer of 1859.* New York: C. M. Saxton, Barker, 1860.

Grenbeaux, Pauline. "Before Yosemite Art Gallery: Watkins' Early Career." *California History* 57, no. 3 (Fall 1978), pp. 220–41.

Grob, Gerald N. *Mental Institutions in America: Social Policy to 1875.* New York: Free Press, 1973.

Grossman, Elizabeth Greenwell. "H. H. Richardson: Lessons from Paris." *Journal of the Society of Architectural Historians* 67, no. 3 (September 2008), pp. 388–411.

Guiffre, Samuel Leonard. "A Documentation of Grace Episcopal Church, Medford, Massachusetts, by Henry Hobson Richardson: A Study of His Gothic Revival Period." MA thesis, Tufts University, 1975.

Hale, Edward. "H. H. Richardson and His Work." *New England Magazine* 17, no. 4 (December 1894), pp. 513–32.

Hall, Lee. *Olmsted's America: An "Unpractical Man" and His Vision of Civilization.* Boston: Little, Brown, 1995.

Heckscher, Morrison H. "Creating Central Park." *Metropolitan Museum of Art Bulletin* 65, no. 3 (Winter 2008), pp. 1–3, 5–74.

Heskel, Julia. *Shepley, Bulfinch, Richardson and Abbott: Past to Present.* Boston: Shepley, Bulfinch, Richardson and Abbott, 1999.

"H. H. Richardson's Men." Typescript, 6 pp., n.d. Richardson Papers, Archives of American Art.

Hill, L. Draper, Jr. *The Crane Library.* Quincy, MA: Trustees of the Thomas Crane Public Library, 1962.

Hitchcock, Henry-Russell. *The Architecture of H. H. Richardson and His Times.* New York: Museum of Modern Art, 1936. Reprint: Cambridge, MA: MIT Press, 1966.

———. *Richardson as a Victorian Architect.* Northampton, MA: Smith College, 1966.

Homolka, Larry Joseph. "Henry Hobson Richardson and the 'Ames Memorial Buildings.'" PhD diss., Harvard University, 1976.

———. "H. H. Richardson at North Easton: A Study of Three Commissions from the Ames Family; The Ames Free Library (1877–83), the Oakes Ames Memorial Town Hall (1879–81) and the F. L. Ames Gate Lodge (1880–81)." MA thesis, Harvard University, 1965.

Howat, John K. *Frederic Church.* New Haven, CT: Yale University Press, 2005.

Howe, M. A. DeWolfe. *Later Years of the Saturday Club, 1870–1920.* Boston: Houghton Mifflin Co., 1927.

Hubka, Thomas C. "H. H. Richardson's Glessner House: A Garden in the Machine." *Winterthur Portfolio* 24, no. 4 (Winter 1989), pp. 209–30.

Huntington, David C. "Church's Niagara: Nature and the Nation's Type." *Texas Studies in Literature and Language* 25, no. 1 (Spring 1983), pp. 100–138.

———. *The Landscapes of Frederic Edwin Church: Vision of an American Era.* New York: George Braziller, 1966.

Huntley, Jen A. *The Making of Yosemite: James Mason Hutchings and the Origin of America's Most Popular National Park.* Lawrence: University Press of Kansas, 2011.

Huth, Hans. "Yosemite: The Story of an Idea." *Sierra Club Bulletin* 33, no. 3 (March 1948), pp. 47–78. http://www.yosemite.ca.us/library/yosemite_story _of_an_idea.html.

Javert, Carl. "James Platt White: A Pioneer in American Obstetrics and Gynecology." *Journal of the History of Medicine and Allied Sciences,* Fall 1948, pp. 488–506.

Kalfus, Melvin. *Frederick Law Olmsted: The Passion of a Public Artist.* New York: New York University Press, 1990.

Karson, Robin. *A Genius for Place: American Landscapes of the Country Place Era.* Amherst: University of Massachusetts Press, 2007.

Kebabian, Paul B., and William C. Lipke, eds. *Tools and Technologies: America's Wooden Age.* Burlington: University of Vermont, 1979.

Kelly, Bruce, Gail Travis Guillet, and Mary Ellen W. Hern. *Art of the Olmsted Landscape*. New York: New York City Landmarks Preservation Commission, 1981.

Kelly, Franklin, and Gerald L. Carr. *The Early Landscapes of Frederic Edwin Church, 1845–1854*. Fort Worth, TX: Amon Carter Museum, 1987.

Kilmurray, Elaine, and Richard Ormond, eds. *John Singer Sargent*. Princeton, NJ: Princeton University Press, 1998.

Kinnard, Cynthia Doering. "The Life and Works of Mariana Griswold Van Rensselaer, American Art Critic." PhD diss., Johns Hopkins University, 1977.

Kirkland, Edward Chase. *Men Cities and Transportation*. 2 vols. Cambridge, MA: Harvard University Press, 1948.

Klare, Michael T. "The Architecture of Imperial America." *Science and Society* 33, no. 3 (Summer–Fall, 1969), pp. 257–84.

Koch, Robert. "American Influence Abroad, 1886 and Later." *Journal of the Society of Architectural Historians* 18, no. 2 (May 1959), pp. 66–69.

Koehler, Sue A., and Jeffrey R. Carson. *Sixteenth Street Architecture*. Vol. 1. Washington, DC: Commission of Fine Arts, 1978.

Koenigsburg, Lisa. "Marina Van Rensselaer: An Architecture Critic in Context." In *Architecture: A Place for Women*, ed. Ellen Perry Berkeley, pp. 41–54. Washington, DC: Smithsonian Institution Press, 1989.

Kowsky, Francis R. *The Architecture of Frederick Clarke Withers and the Progress of the Gothic Revival in America after 1850*. Middletown, CT: Wesleyan University Press, 1980.

———. *The Best Planned City in the World: Olmsted, Vaux, and the Buffalo Park System*. Amherst: University of Massachusetts Press, 2013.

———. *Buffalo Projects: H. H. Richardson*. Buffalo, NY: Burchfield Center, 1980.

———. *Country, Park, and City: The Architecture and Life of Calvert Vaux*. New York: Oxford University Press, 1998.

———. "H. H. Richardson's Ames Gate Lodge and the Romantic Landscape Tradition." *Journal of the Society of Architectural Historians* 50, no. 2 (June 1991), pp. 181–88.

———. "Municipal Parks and City Planning: Frederick Law Olmsted's Buffalo Park and Parkway System." *Journal of the Society of Architectural Historians* 46, no. 1 (March 1987), pp. 49–64.

———. "The William Dorsheimer House: A Reflection of French Suburban Architecture in the Early Work of H. H. Richardson." *Art Bulletin* 762, no. 1 (March 1980), pp. 134–47.

Kowsky, Francis R., and Charles E. Beveridge. *The Distinctive Charms of Niagara Scenery: Frederick Law Olmsted and the Niagara Reservation*. Niagara Falls, NY: Buscaglia-Castellani Art Gallery of Niagara University, 1985.

La Farge, John. *An Artist's Letters from Japan*. New York: Century Co., 1897.

Lange, Alexandra. "Founding Mother: Mariana Griswold Van Rensselaer and the Rise of Architecture Criticism." *Places Journal*, February 2013.

Langton, W. A. "The Method of H. H. Richardson. *The Architect and Contract Reporter* 53 (March 9, 1900), pp. 156–58.

Larkin, Oliver W. *Art and Life in America.* New York: Holt, Rinehart and Winston, 1949, 1960.

Larson, Paul Clifford, and Susan M. Brown. *The Spirit of H. H. Richardson on the Midland Prairies: Regional Transformations of an Architectural Style.* Ames: Iowa State University Press, 1988.

Lewis, Arnold. "Hinckeldeyn, Vogel, and American Architecture." *Journal of the Society of Architectural Historians* 31, no. 4 (December 1972), pp. 276–90.

Ludlow, Fitz-Hugh. "Seven Weeks in the Great Yo-Semite." *Atlantic Monthly* 23, no. 10 (June 1864), pp. 739–54.

Luedtke, Luther S. *Making America: The Society and Culture of the United States.* Chapel Hill: University of North Carolina Press, 1992.

Lynes, Russell. *The Art-Makers of Nineteenth-Century America.* New York: Athenaeum, 1970.

———. *The Tastemakers.* New York: Harper & Brothers, 1954.

MacDougal, Elisabeth Blair. *The Architectural Historian in America.* Washington, DC: National Gallery of Art, 1990.

Major, Judith K. *Mariana Griswold Van Rensselaer: A Landscape Critic in the Gilded Age.* Charlottesville: University of Virginia Press, 2013.

Martin, Edwin Winslow, ed. *The Life and Public Services of Schuyler Colfax, Together with his Most Important Speeches.* San Francisco, CA: H. H. Bancroft & Co., 1868.

Martin, Justin. *Genius of Place: The Life of Frederick Law Olmsted.* New York: Da Capo Press, 2011.

Marx, Leo. *The Machine in the Garden: Technology and the Pastoral Ideal in America.* New York: Oxford University Press, 1964.

Matherly, Polly A. "Quincy Granite Railroad." National Register of Historic Places Inventory. Boston, 1973.

Mauro, Lisa J. "A Sense of Place: Branding the Richardson Olmsted Complex through Architectural Motif." MFA thesis, Rochester Institute of Technology, 2011.

McGreevy, Patrick V. *Imagining Niagara: The Meaning and Making of Niagara Falls.* Amherst: University of Massachusetts Press, 1994.

McKibbin, David. *Sargent's Boston.* Boston: Museum of Fine Arts, 1956.

McKinsey, Elizabeth. *Niagara Falls: Icon of the American Sublime.* Cambridge: Cambridge University Press, 1985.

Meeks, Carroll L. V. *The Railroad Station: An Architectural History.* New Haven, CT: Yale University Press, 1956.

Meister, Maureen, ed. *H. H. Richardson: The Architect, His Peers, and Their Era.* Cambridge, MA: MIT Press, 1999.

Mendel, Mesick Cohen, Architects. *The New York State Senate Chamber and Related Spaces: A Historic Structure Report.* Albany, NY, 1978.

Mills, J. Saxon. *Life and Letters of Sir Hubert Herkomer, C.V.O., R.A.: A Study in Struggle and Success.* London: Hutchinson & Co., 1923.

Miner, Edward F. "Memoir of Orlando Whitney Norcross." *Transactions of the American Society of Civil Engineers* 84 (1921), pp. 896–98.

Molloy, Mary Alice. "Richardson's Web: A Client's Assessment of the Architect's Home and Studio." *Journal of the Society of Architectural Historians* 54, no. 1 (March 1995), pp. 8–23.

Moore, Charles. *Daniel Hudson Burnham, Architect, Planner of Cities.* Vol. 1. Boston: Houghton Mifflin Co., 1921.

———. *The Life and Times of Charles Follen McKim.* Boston: Houghton Mifflin Co., 1929.

Morgan, Keith, Roger G. Reid, and Elizabeth Hope Cushing. *Community by Design: The Olmsted Firm and the Development of Brookline, Massachusetts.* Amherst: University of Massachusetts Press, 2013.

Mortice, Zach. "When Henry Met Frederick." *Landscape Architecture Magazine* 105, no. 4 (April 2015), pp. 40, 42.

Mumford, Lewis. *Architecture.* Chicago: American Library Association, 1926.

———. *The Brown Decades.* New York: Dover Publications, 1931, 1971.

———. *The South in Architecture.* New York: Da Capo Press, 1967.

Naef, Weston. *Carleton Watkins in Yosemite.* Los Angeles, CA: J. Paul Getty Museum, 2008.

Nash, Roderick. *Wilderness and the American Mind.* Rev. ed. New Haven, CT: Yale University Press, 1967, 1973.

Nolen, John. "Frederick Law Olmsted and His Work. II. The Terraces and Landscape Work of the United States Capitol at Washington." *House and Garden* (March 1906), pp. 117–28.

Ochsner, Jeffrey Karl. "Architecture for the Boston and Albany Railroad, 1881–1894." *Journal of the Society of Architectural Historians* 47, no. 2 (June 1988), pp. 109–31.

———. *H. H. Richardson: Complete Architectural Works.* Cambridge, MA: MIT Press, 1982; updated softcover ed., 1984.

———. "H. H. Richardson's Frank William Andrews House." *Journal of the Society of Architectural Historians* 43, no. 1 (March 1984), pp. 20–32.

Ochsner, Jeffrey Karl, and Dennis Alan Andersen. *Distant Corner: Seattle Architects and the Legacy of H. H. Richardson.* Seattle: University of Washington Press, 2003.

Ochsner, Jeffrey Karl, and Thomas C. Hubka. "H. H. Richardson: The Design of the William Watts Sherman House." *Journal of the Society of Architectural Historians* 51, no. 2 (June 1992), pp. 121–45.

O'Gorman, James F. "America and H. H. Richardson," in *American Architecture: Innovation and Tradition,* ed. David G. De Long, Helen Searing, and Robert A. M. Stern. New York: Rizzoli, 1986.

————. "Documentation: An 1886 Inventory of H. H. Richardson's Library, and Other Gleanings from Probate." *Journal of the Society of Architectural Historians* 41, no. 2 (May 1982), pp. 150–55.

————. "Henry Hobson Richardson and Frank Lloyd Wright." *Art Quarterly* 32, no. 3, pp. 292–315.

————. *H. H. Richardson: Architectural Forms for an American Society.* Chicago: University of Chicago Press, 1987.

————. *Living Architecture: A Biography of H. H. Richardson.* New York: Simon and Schuster, 1997.

————, ed. *The Makers of Trinity Church in the City of Boston.* Amherst: University of Massachusetts Press, 2004.

————. "Man-Made Mountain: 'Gathering and Governing' in H. H. Richardson's Design for the James Monument in Wyoming." In *The Railroad in American Art: Representations of Technological Change,* ed. Susan Danly and Leo Marx. Cambridge, MA: MIT Press, 1988.

————. "The Marshall Field Wholesale Store: Materials toward a Monograph." *Journal of the Society of Architectural Historians* 37, no. 3 (October 1978), pp. 175–94.

————, ed. "On Vacation with H. H. Richardson: Ten Letters from Europe. *Archives of American Art Journal* 19, no. 1 (1979), pp. 2–14.

————. "O. W. Norcross, Richardson's 'Master Builder': A Preliminary Report." *Journal of the Society of Architectural Historians* 32, no. 2 (May 1973), pp. 104–13.

————. *Selected Drawings: H. H. Richardson and His Office; A Centennial of His Move to Boston, 1874.* Boston: David R. Godine, 1974.

————. "Some Architects' Portraits in Nineteenth-Century America: Personifying the Evolving Profession." *Transactions of the American Philosophical Society* 103, no. 4, pp. i–xxi, 1–94.

————. *Three American Architects: Richardson, Sullivan, and Wright, 1865–1915.* Chicago: University of Chicago Press, 1991.

————. "A Tragic Circle." *Nineteenth Century* 2 (Autumn 1976), pp. 46–49.

Olmsted, Frederick Law. *The Papers of Frederick Law Olmsted.* Baltimore, MD: Johns Hopkins University Press, 1977–2015. This multivolume collection consists of the following: Vol. 1, *The Formative Years, 1822–1852,* 1977. Vol. 2, *Slavery and the South, 1852–1857,* 1981. Vol. 3, *Creating Central Park, 1857–1861,* 1983. Vol. 4, *Defending the Union: The Civil War and the U.S. Sanitary Commission, 1861–1865,* 1986. Vol. 5, *The California Frontier, 1863–1865,* 1990. Vol. 6, *The Years of Olmsted, Vaux & Company, 1865–1874,* 1992. Vol. 7, *Parks, Politics, and Patronage, 1874–1882,* 2007. Vol. 8, *The Early Boston Years, 1882–1890,* 2013. Vol. 9, *The Last Great Projects, 1890–1895,* 2015. Supplementary series, vol. 1, *Writing on Public Parks, Parkways, and Park Systems,* 1997. Supplementary series, vol. 2, *Plans and Views of Public Parks,* 2015.

————. *Walks and Talks of an American Farmer in England.* Vol. 1. New York: G. P. Putnam, 1852

————. "The Yosemite Valley and the Mariposa Big Trees, A Preliminary Report." First published in *Landscape Architecture,* vol. 43 (October 1952), 1952; available online at https://www.yosemite.ca.us.

Olmsted, Frederick Law, Elisha Harris, J. M. Trowbridge, and H. H. Richardson. *A Letter Introductory.* Staten Island, NY: Staten Island Improvement, 1871.

Olmsted, Frederick Law, Jr., and Theodora Kimball, eds. *Forty Years of Landscape Architecture.* 2 vols. Vol. 1: *Frederick Law Olmsted, Landscape Architect, 1822–1903: Early Years and Experiences.* New York: G. P. Putnam's Sons, 1922. Vol. 2: *Frederick Law Olmsted, Landscape Architect, 1822–1903: Central Park as a Work of Art and as a Great Municipal Enterprise, 1853–1895.* New York: G. P. Putnam's Sons, 1928.

Olmsted, John Charles. *[Mariposa] Journal of John C. Olmsted.* N.p., 1864–65. John Charles Olmsted Papers, Harvard University.

"The Organization of an Architect's Office, No. II." *Engineering and Building Record* 21, January 11, 1890, p. 165.

O'Toole, Patricia. *The Five of Hearts: An Intimate Portrait of Henry Adams and His Friends, 1880–1918.* New York: Clarkson Potter, 1990.

Paine, Robert Treat. "Report on the Activities of the Trinity Church Building Committee, 1872–1877." Handwritten manuscript, unpaged. n.d. Trinity Church Archive.

Paine, Sarah Cushing, and Charles Henry Pope. *Paine Ancestry: The Family of Robert Treat Paine, Signer of the Declaration of Independence.* Boston: David Clapp & Son, 1912.

Pevsner, Nikolaus, ed. *The Picturesque Garden and Its Influence outside the British Isles.* Washington, DC: Dumbarton Oaks, 1974.

Phillips, J. H. "The Evolution of the Suburban Station." *Architectural Record* 36 (August 1914), pp. 122–27.

Pierson, William H., Jr. "Richardson, H. H." In *The Macmillan Encyclopedia of Architects,* ed. Adolph Placzek. New York: Free Press, 1982.

————. "Richardson's Trinity Church and the New England Meetinghouse." In *American Public Architecture: European Roots and Native Expressions,* ed. Craig Zabel and Susan Scott Munshower, pp. 12–56. University Park: Pennsylvania State University, 1989.

Pinchot, Gifford. *Biltmore Forest, the Property of Mr. George W. Vanderbilt: An Account of Its Treatment, and the Results of the First Year's Work.* Chicago: Lakeside Press, 1893.

————. *Breaking New Ground.* New York: Harcourt, Brace, 1947.

Price, Charles. "Henry Hobson Richardson: Some Unpublished Drawings." *Perspecta* 9/10 (January 1, 1965), pp. 199–210.

Proceedings of the New York State Capitol Symposium. Albany, NY: Temporary State Commission on the Restoration of the Capitol, 1983.

Randall, Richard H., Jr. *The Furniture of H. H. Richardson*. Boston: Museum of Fine Arts, 1962.

Ranney, Victoria Post. *Olmsted in Chicago*. Chicago: Open Lands Project, 1972.

Report of the Boston Landmarks Commission on the Potential Designation of the Hayden Building as Landmark under Chapter 772 of the Acts of 1975. Boston: Boston Landmarks Commission, 1977.

Richardson, Albert D. *Beyond the Mississippi: From the Great River to the Great Ocean*. Hartford, CT: American Publishing Co., 1867.

Richardson, H. H. *Austin Hall, Harvard Law School, Cambridge, Massachusetts*. Boston: J. R. Osgood & Co., 1885.

———. *Description of Drawings for the Proposed New County Buildings for Allegheny County, PA*. Boston: privately printed, 1884.

———. "A Description of the Church." Published as part of the *Consecrations Services of Trinity Church, Boston, February 9, 1877*, and reprinted since.

———. "Henry Hobson Richardson Sketchbook, 1869–[1875]." Harvard Fine Arts Library, Special Collections. Transcription appears as appendix 44 in James F. O'Gorman, *Selected Drawings: H. H. Richardson and His Office; A Centennial of His Move to Boston, 1874*, pp. 211–16. Boston: David R. Godine, 1974.

Robinson, Charles Mulford. "A Railroad Beautiful." *House and Garden* 2, no. 11 (November 1902), pp. 564–70.

———. "Suburban Station Grounds." *House and Garden* 5, no. 4 (April 1904), pp. 182–87.

Romig, Edgar D. *The Story of Trinity Church*. Boston: Wardens and Vestry, Trinity Church, 1952.

Roper, Laura Wood. *FLO: A Biography of Frederick Law Olmsted*. Baltimore, MD: Johns Hopkins University Press, 1973

Rosbe, Judith Westlund. *Marion in the Golden Age*. Charleston, SC: History Press, 2009.

Rosenzweig, Roy, and Elizabeth Blackmar. *The Park and the People: A History of Central Park*. Ithaca, NY: Cornell University Press, 1992.

Runte, Alfred. "Beyond the Spectacular: The Niagara Falls Preservation Campaign." *New-York Historical Society Quarterly* 57 (January 1973), pp. 30–50.

———. *Yosemite: The Embattled Wilderness*. Lincoln: University of Nebraska Press, 1990.

Russell, Carl Parcher. *One Hundred Years in Yosemite: The Story of a Great Park and Its Friends*. Yosemite National Park, CA: Yosemite Association, 1992.

Rutan, Charles H. *A specification, Which, with the accompanying Drawings, describe the work to be performed, and the materials to be used, in the erection of a City Hall Building on Eagle street extending between Maiden Lane and Pine street, in the City of Albany, County of Albany, State of New York: from the Drawings and under the superintendence of H. H. Richardson, Architect*. Brookline, MA, n.d. Avery Library, Columbia University.

Rybycznski, Withold. *Clearing in the Distance: Frederick Law Olmsted and America in the Nineteenth Century.* New York, Scribner's, 1999.

Saint-Gaudens, Homer. *The Reminiscences of Augustus Saint-Gaudens.* 2 vols. New York: Century, 1913.

Salisbury, Stephen. *The State, the Investor, and the Railroad: The Boston and Albany.* Cambridge, MA: Harvard University Press, 1967.

Samuels, Ernest. *Henry Adams.* Cambridge, MA: Harvard University Press, 1989.

[Sargent, Charles Sprague.] "The Railroad Station at Auburndale, Massachusetts." *Garden and Forest* 2 (March 13, 1889), pp. 124–25.

———. "The Railroad Station at Chestnut Hill." *Garden and Forest* 2 (April 3, 1889), pp. 159–60.

Scheyer, Ernst. "Henry Adams and Henry Hobson Richardson," in *Journal of the Society of Architectural Historians* 12, no. 1 (March 1953), pp. 7–12.

Schlesinger, Arthur M. *The Rise of the City, 1878–1898.* New York: Macmillan, 1933.

Schneekloth, Lynda H., Marcia F. Feuerstein, and Barbara A. Campagna, eds. *Changing Places: Remaking Institutional Buildings.* Fredonia, NY: White Pine Press, 1992.

Schulman, Vanessa Meikle. *Work Sights: The Visual Culture of Industry in Nineteenth-Century America.* Amherst: University of Massachusetts Press, 2015.

Schuyler, David. "'The Most Critical & the Most Difficult' Project: Frederick Law Olmsted's Biltmore." *North Carolina Historical Review* 42, no. 4 (October 2015), pp. 361–86.

Schuyler, Montgomery. *American Architecture and Other Writings.* Edited by William H. Jordy and Ralph Coe. 2 vols. Cambridge, MA: Harvard University Press, 1961.

Scully, Vincent. *The Shingle Style and the Stick Style: Architectural Theory and Design from Downing to the Origins of Wright.* New Haven, CT: Yale University Press, 1955, 1971.

Seale, William. "Glowing Revival for 'Most Beautiful Room in America." *Smithsonian* 12, no. 8 (November 1981), pp. 146–50, 152–53.

Searing, Helen, ed. *In Search of Modern Architecture: A Tribute to Henry-Russell Hitchcock.* Cambridge, MA: MIT, 1982.

Sears, John F. *Sacred Places: American Tourist Attractions in the Nineteenth Century.* New York: Oxford University Press, 1989.

Sexton, Nanette. "Watkins Style and Technique in the Early Photographs." *California History* 57, no. 3 (Fall 1978), pp. 242–51.

Sheldon, George [William]. *Artistic Country Seats.* 2 vols. New York: D. Appleton and Co., 1886–87.

Shepley, Mrs. George F. [Julia Richardson]. "Reminiscences." 7 pp., n.d. Richardson Papers, Archives of American Art.

Simpson, Jeffrey. *Art of the Olmsted Landscape: His Works in New York City.* New York: New York City Landmarks Preservation Commission, 1981.

Smith, Herbert F. *Richard Watson Gilder.* New York: Twayne Publishers, 1970.

"Some Incidents in the Life of H. H. Richardson," *American Architect and Building News* 20, no. 565 (October 23, 1886), pp. 198–99.

Special Report of New York State Survey on the Preservation of the Scenery of Niagara Falls. Albany: C. Benthuysen & Sons, 1880.

Stamp, Gavin. "Lost Lululaund." *Apollo* 168 (December 2008), pp. 72–73.

Stebbins, Theodore E., Jr. "Richardson and Trinity Church: The Evolution of a Building." *Journal of the Society of Architectural Historians* 27, no. 4 (December 1968), pp. 281–98.

Stevenson, Elizabeth. *Park Maker: A Life of Frederick Law Olmsted.* New York: Macmillan Publishing Co., 1977.

Stillgoe, John R. "The Railroad Beautiful Movement: Landscape Architecture and the Railroad Gardening Movement, 1982." *Landscape Journal* 1, no. 2 (Fall 1982), pp. 57–66.

Strong, George Templeton. *The Diary of George Templeton Strong.* Edited by Allan Nevins and Milton Halsey Thomas. 4 vols. New York: Macmillan Co., 1952.

Strong, Janet Adams. "The Cathedral of Saint John the Divine in New York: Design Competitions in the Shadow of H. H. Richardson, 1889–1891." PhD diss., Brown University, 1990.

"Studio and Office of H. H. Richardson," *American Architect and Building News* (December 1884), p. 304.

Sullivan, Louis H. *Autobiography of an Idea.* New York: Press of the American Institute of Architects, 1924.

———. *Kindergarten Chats and Other Writings.* New York: Wittenborn, Schultz, 1947.

Sutton, S. B. *Charles Sprague Sargent and the Arnold Arboretum.* Cambridge, MA: Harvard University Press, 1970.

Thoron, Ward, ed. *The Letters of Mrs. Henry Adams, 1865–1883.* Boston: Little, Brown, and Company, 1936.

Townsend, Horace. "H. H. Richardson, Architect." *Magazine of Art* 17 (1894), pp. 133–38.

Truettner, William H. "The Genesis of Frederic Edwin Church's *Aurora Borealis*." *Art Quarterly* 31, no. 3 (Fall 1968), pp. 266–83.

———, ed. *The West as America: Reinterpreting Images of the Frontier, 1820–1920.* Washington, DC: National Museum of American Art, 1991.

Tselos, Dimitri. "Richardson's Influence on European Architecture." *Journal of the Society of Architectural Historians* 29, no. 2 (May 1970), pp. 156–62.

Twombly, Robert, and Narciso G. Menocal. *Louis Sullivan: The Poetry of Architecture.* New York: W. W. Norton & Company, 2000.

Upton, Dell. *Architecture in the United States.* New York: Oxford University Press, 1998.

Van Brunt, Henry. *Architecture and Society: Selected Essays of Henry Van Brunt.* Edited by William A. Coles. Cambridge, MA: Harvard University Press, 1969.

Van Rensselaer, M[ariana]. G[riswold]. "Frederick Law Olmsted." *Century* 46, no. 6 (October 1893), pp. 860–67. Reprinted in Van Rensselaer, *Accents as Well as Broad Effects* (1996), pp. 284–99.

Van Rensselaer, Mariana Griswold. *Accents as Well as Broad Effects: Writings on Architecture, Landscape, and the Environment, 1876–1925.* Edited by David Gebhard. Berkeley: University of California Press, 1996.

Van Rensselaer, Mrs. Schuyler [Mariana Griswold]. *Art Out-of-Doors: Hints on Good Taste in Gardening.* New York: Charles Scribner's Sons, 1893.

———. *Henry Hobson Richardson and His Works.* Boston: Houghton Mifflin Co., 1888.

Van Zanten, David T. "H. H. Richardson's Glessner House, Chicago, 1886–1887." *Journal of the Society of Architectural Historians* 23, no. 2 (May 1964), pp. 106–11.

Vogel, Susan Maycock. "Hartwell and Richardson: An Introduction to Their Work." *Journal of the Society of Architectural Historians* 32, no. 2 (May 1973), pp. 132–46.

Waern, Cecelia. *John La Farge: Artist and Writer.* London: Seely & Co., 1896.

Warner, Sam B. *Streetcar Suburbs: The Process of Growth in Boston, 1870–1900.* Cambridge, MA: Harvard University Press and MIT Press, 1962.

[Warren, Herbert Langford.] "Mourned by Lovers of Art: The Career of the Famous Architect, H. H. Richardson." *New York Star,* May 2, 1886.

Warren, H. Langford. *Picturesque and Architectural New England: Architectural Features.* 2 vols. Boston: D. H. Hurd & Co., 1899.

Waters, Michael J. "H. H. Richardson and Photography." Typescript, 55 pp., 2008. Frances Loeb Library, Special Collections, Harvard University.

Watkins, Carleton. *In Focus: Carleton Watkins.* Los Angeles, CA: J. Paul Getty Museum, 1997.

Webster, J. Carson. "Richardson's American Express Building." *Journal of the Society of Architectural Historians* 9, nos. 1–2 (March 1950), pp. 21–24.

Weinberg, Helene Barbara. *The Decorative Work of John La Farge.* New York: Garland Publishing, 1977.

———. "John La Farge and the Decoration of Trinity Church, Boston." *Journal of the Society of Architectural Historians* 33, no. 4 (December 1974), pp. 323–53.

Weingarten, Lauren S. "Naturalized Nationalism: A Ruskinian Discourse on the Search for an American Style of Architecture." *Winterthur Portfolio* 24, no. 1 (Spring 1989), pp. 43–68.

Wermiel, Sara E. "Norcross, Fuller, and the Rise of the General Contractor in the United States in the Nineteenth Century." *Proceedings of the Second International Congress on Construction History* 3 (2006), pp. 3297–313.

White, Stanford. *Stanford White: Letters to His Family.* Edited by Claire Nicolas White. New York: Rizzoli, 1997.

Whitehill, Walter Muir. *Boston Public Library: A Centennial History.* Cambridge, MA: Harvard University Press, 1956.

Wickersham, Jay, and Christopher Milford. "Richardson's Death, Ames's Money, and the Birth of the Modern Architectural Firm." *Perspecta* 47 (August 2014), pp. 113–27.

Wight, Peter B. "H. H. Richardson." *Inland Architect and Builder* 7 (May 1886), pp. 59–61.

Wilkinson, Burke. *Uncommon Clay: The Life and Works of Augustus Saint-Gaudens.* San Diego, CA: Harcourt Brace Jovanovich, 1985.

Wilson, Richard Guy. "The Early Work of Charles F. McKim: Country House Commissions." *Winterthur* 14, no. 3 (Autumn 1979), pp. 235–67.

Wodehouse, Lawrence. "William Appleton Potter, Principal 'Pasticheur' of Henry Hobson Richardson. *Journal of the Society of Architectural Historians* 32, no. 2 (May 1973), pp. 175–92.

Woods, Mary N. *From Craft to Profession: The Practice of Architecture in Nineteenth-Century America.* Berkeley: University of California Press, 1999.

———. "The Photograph as Tastemaker: The *American Architect* and H. H. Richardson." *History of Photography* 14, no. 2 (April–June 1990), pp. 155–63.

Wormeley, Katharine Prescott. *The Other Side of War; with the Army of the Potomac: Letters from the Headquarters of the United States Sanitary Commission during the Peninsular Campaign in Virginia in 1862.* Boston: Ticknor and Company, 1889.

Wright, Mark. "H. H. Richardson's House for Reverend Browne, Rediscovered." *Journal of the Society of Architectural Historians* 68, no. 1 (March 2009), pp. 74–99.

Yanni, Carla. *The Architecture of Madness: Insane Asylums in the United States.* Minneapolis: University of Minnesota Press, 2007.

———. "'The Richardson Memorial': Mariana Griswold Van Rensselaer's *Henry Hobson Richardson and His Works.*" *Nineteenth Century* 27, no. 2 (Fall 2007), pp. 27–36.

Zabel, Craig, and Susan Scott Munshower, eds. *American Public Architecture: European Roots and Native Expressions.* University Park: Pennsylvania State University, 1989.

Zaitzevsky, Cynthia. *Frederick Law Olmsted and the Boston Park System.* Cambridge, MA: Harvard University Press, 1982.

———. "A New Richardson Building." *Journal of the Society of Architectural Historians* 32, no. 2 (May 1973), pp. 164–66.

———. "The Olmsted Firm and the Structures of the Boston Park Systems," *Journal of the Society of Architectural Historians* 32, no. 2 (May 1973), pp. 167–74.

Zaitzevsky, Cynthia, and Mac Griswold. *Fairsted: A Cultural Landscape Report for the Frederick Law Olmsted National Historic Site.* Vol. 1. Boston: NPS/Arnold Arboretum, 1997.

ILLUSTRATION CREDITS

Page 2: University of Wyoming/American Heritage Center. 20: *Olmsted and Kimball, Forty Years of Landscape Architecture*, vol. 1 (1922), frontispiece. 36: Harvard College Album, Class of 1859. 44: *The New-York Times*, May 1, 1858. 46: New York Public Library. 47: Victor Prevost, photographer/New York Public Library. 50: Historic New England. 52: National Park Service/Frederick Law Olmsted National Historic Site. 62: *Henry Hobson Richardson and His Works* (1888), by Mariana Griswold Van Rensselaer. 66: National Park Service, Adams National Historic Park. 83: Library of Congress/Prints and Photographs. 89: Yosemite National Park Archives, Museum, and Library. 107: National Park Service/Frederick Law Olmsted National Historic Site. 119: Archives of American Art. 130 and 135: Courtesy of Francis Kowsky. 142-143: National Gallery of Art/Corcoran Collection. 152: *American Architect and Building News*. 155: Houghton Library, Harvard University (MS Typ 1096). 160: *Henry Hobson Richardson and His Works*. 166: Houghton Library, Harvard University (MS Typ 1096). 173: *Henry Hobson Richardson and His Works*. 185: *American Architect and Building News*/Boston Public Library. 194: Historic New England. 201: Library of Congress/Prints and Photographs. 202: *Henry Hobson Richardson and His Works*. 204: Houghton Library, Harvard University (MS Typ 1096). 205: Archives of American Art. 206: Houghton Library, Harvard University (MS Typ 1096). 210, 213, and 215: National Park Service/Frederick Law Olmsted National Historic Site. 217: Easton Historical Society and Museum. 218: National Park Service/Frederick Law Olmsted National Historic Site.

225: Houghton Library/Harvard University (MS Typ 1096). 228: Cervin Robinson, Photographer/Historic American Buildings Survey. 237: Library of Congress/Frederick Law Olmsted Papers. 239 and 240: *Henry Hobson Richardson and His Works*. 243 and 247: National Park Service/Frederick Law Olmsted National Historic Site. 251: Historic American Buildings Survey. 258: Robert Treat Paine Trust/Stonehurst Archives. 259, 265, and 266: National Park Service/Frederick Law Olmsted National Historic Site. 271, 274, and 277: Massachusetts Historical Society. 285: Glessner House. 287 and 288: Historic New England. 293: Photographs by George Glessner/Glessner House. 303: *Henry Hobson Richardson and His Works*. 311: Glessner House. 316: Museum of the City of New York. 332: The Biltmore Company. 335: National Portrait Gallery/Smithsonian Institution. 337: National Park Service/Frederick Law Olmsted National Historic Site.

Index